Early Language
and Teacher Edu

G000089388

EARLY LANGUAGE LEARNING IN SCHOOL CONTEXTS

Series Editor: Janet Enever, *Umeå University, Sweden*

The early learning of languages in instructed contexts has become an increasingly common global phenomenon during the past 30 years, yet there remains much work to be done to establish the field as a distinctive area for interdisciplinary investigation. This international research series covers children learning second, foreign and additional languages in educational contexts between the ages of approximately 3 and 12 years. The series will take a global perspective and encourage the sharing of theoretical discussion and empirical evidence on transnational issues. It will provide a platform to address questions raised by teachers, teacher educators, and policy makers who are seeking understanding of theoretical issues and empirical evidence with which to underpin policy development, implementation and classroom procedures for this young age group. Themes of particular interest for the series include: teacher models and teacher development, models of early language learning, policy implementation, motivation, approaches to teaching and learning, language progress and outcomes, assessment, intercultural learning, sustainability in provision, comparative and transnational perspectives, cross-phase transfer issues, curriculum integration – additional suggestions for themes are also most welcome.

All books in this series are externally peer-reviewed.

Full details of all the books in this series and of all our other publications can be found on http://www.multilingual-matters.com, or by writing to Multilingual Matters, St Nicholas House, 31–34 High Street, Bristol BS1 2AW, UK.

EARLY LANGUAGE LEARNING IN SCHOOL CONTEXTS: 3

Early Language Learning and Teacher Education

International Research and Practice

Edited by
Subhan Zein and Sue Garton

MULTILINGUAL MATTERS
Bristol • Blue Ridge Summit

DOI https://doi.org/10.21832/ZEIN2654
Library of Congress Cataloging in Publication Data
A catalog record for this book is available from the Library of Congress.

Library of Congress Control Number: 2018046140

British Library Cataloguing in Publication Data
A catalogue entry for this book is available from the British Library.

ISBN-13: 978-1-78892-265-4 (hbk)
ISBN-13: 978-1-78892-264-7 (pbk)

Multilingual Matters
UK: St Nicholas House, 31–34 High Street, Bristol BS1 2AW, UK.
USA: NBN, Blue Ridge Summit, PA, USA.

Website: www.multilingual-matters.com
Twitter: Multi_Ling_Mat
Facebook: https://www.facebook.com/multilingualmatters
Blog: www.channelviewpublications.wordpress.com

The policy of Multilingual Matters/Channel View Publications is to use papers that are natural, renewable and recyclable products, made from wood grown in sustainable forests. In the manufacturing process of our books, and to further support our policy, preference is given to printers that have FSC and PEFC Chain of Custody certification. The FSC and/or PEFC logos will appear on those books where full certification has been granted to the printer concerned.

Typeset by Nova Techset Private Limited, Bengaluru and Chennai, India.
Printed and bound in the UK by Short Run Press Ltd.
Printed and bound in the US by Thomson-Shore, Inc.

Contents

Contributors

Alison L. Bailey is professor of human development and psychology at the University of California, Los Angeles, USA. A graduate of Harvard University, Bailey is a developmental psycholinguist working on issues germane to children's linguistic, cognitive and social development, as well as teachers' academic English instructional and assessment pedagogies. She is a member of the National Assessment of Educational Progress Standing Committee on Reading and the National Council on Measurement in Education President's Classroom Assessment Task Force.

Nettie Boivin is an associate professor at Jyvaskyla University, Finland. Previously, she was an assistant professor at the Graduate School of Education, Nazarbayev University in Kazakhstan. She researches in various multilingual contexts (Kazakhstan, Malaysia, Qatar, Nepal, UK, Canada and Japan). Her research interests are migrant language, culture and identity multimodal knowledge construction.

Yuko Goto Butler is a professor of educational linguistics in the Graduate School of Education at the University of Pennsylvania, USA. She is also the director of the Teaching English to Speakers of Other Languages (TESOL) program at Penn. Her research interests include language assessment and second and bilingual language learning among children.

Valentina Carbonara is an Italian language teacher and a Post-Doc fellow in Applied Linguistics at the University for Foreigners in Siena, Italy. Her research interests include bilingualism, teaching language to young learners and translanguaging.

Junko Matsuzaki Carreira is an associate professor at Tokyo Keizai University, Japan. She completed her doctoral course in the Department of English and Literature at Tsuda College, and received her PhD in education from Tokyo Gakugei University United Graduate School of Education.

Chiou-hui Chou is an associate professor in the Department of English Instruction at National Tsing Hua University, Taiwan. Her research interests are in TESOL methods, English reading, lesson study and teachers' professional development.

Elisabeth Duursma is a senior lecturer in early childhood literacy at the University of Wollongong, Australia. She received her doctorate from the Harvard University Graduate School of Education. Her research focuses on language and literacy in the early years and father involvement.

Sue Garton is a reader in English language (TESOL) at the School of Languages and Social Sciences, Aston University, UK. She taught English in Italy for almost 20 years before joining Aston University in 2000. She has taught on both undergraduate and postgraduate courses in TESOL, as well as supervising PhDs in the field. She is series editor of the 15-volume Palgrave series *International Perspectives on English Language Teaching* and is currently editing *The Routledge Handbook of Teaching English to Young Learners* (both with Fiona Copland).

Katherine M. Griffin is a doctoral candidate in education (Human Development and Psychology Division) at the University of California, Los Angeles, USA. Her research interests center on children's beliefs and attitudes about wealth, poverty and economic inequality; how families and schools shape children's understanding of social class; and how school contexts help shape children's socioemotional and linguistic development.

Larissa Jenkins graduated from the University of Wollongong, Australia, with a BEd – The Early Years (Honours). She was a recipient of the university medal for her outstanding academic performance across the entire undergraduate degree. She is now teaching at an early childhood service in Melbourne. Within her current position, Larissa is able to ensure all children, particularly those from culturally and linguistically diverse backgrounds, receive the best possible education and care.

Yasemin Kırkgöz is a professor at the English Language Teacher Education Department, Çukurova University, Turkey. Her key areas of research are foreign language education policy, teaching English to young learners, teacher education and curriculum design. She has published articles on these topics in international journals and has written several book chapters.

Le Van Canh is an associate professor in the College of Linguistic and International Studies, Vietnam National University, Hanoi, Vietnam, where he has been involved in teaching English as a foreign language teacher and teacher educator for more than 30 years. He earned his doctoral degree in applied linguistics from the University of Waikato (New Zealand) and has published numerous articles and book chapters in the area of English language teacher education.

Gee Macrory is Associate Head of the Department of Primary Education at Manchester Metropolitan University (MMU), UK. Before joining MMU in 1990, she taught foreign languages (primarily French) in schools and colleges and spent two years as a local authority English as an Additional Language (EAL) advisory teacher, mostly in primary schools. At MMU, she has had extensive experience of pre- and in-service training for primary and secondary languages teachers.

Rashmita S. Mistry is a professor of human development and psychology at the University of California, Los Angeles, USA. Her program of research examines the consequences of family socioeconomic resources and disadvantage (i.e. poverty) for children's academic and social development, children's reasoning about social status and social identity development (i.e. social class, race/ethnicity, nationality) and the implications of school-level socioeconomic diversity on teaching, learning and children's development.

Catherine Neilsen-Hewett is a senior lecturer in education at the University of Wollongong (UOW), Australia. She is the academic director of the early years program at UOW. Her research expertise includes development in early childhood, importance of positive peer relationships, early childhood pedagogy and practice.

Tomoko Shigyo received her MA in English language and literature and completed her doctoral course in the Department of English and Literature at Tsuda College, Japan. She is an assistant professor of English education in elementary schools in Tokyo Future University, Japan. She is currently researching in-service and pre-service teacher education.

Subhan Zein (PhD, Australian National University) has trained teachers in Australia and Indonesia and teaches at the University of Queensland, Australia. He has published in *Applied Linguistics Review, Professional Development in Education, Journal of Education for Teaching, English Today,* among others. He is the lead editor of *English Language Teacher Preparation in Asia: Policy, Research and Practice* (Routledge) and editor of *Teacher Education for English as a Lingua Franca: Perspectives from Indonesia* (Routledge).

Yuefeng Ellen Zhang is an assistant professor at the Department of Curriculum and Instruction in the Education University of Hong Kong, Hong Kong. She is a council member of the World Association of Lesson Study. Her research and publications focus on effective teaching and learning, lesson study, teacher professional development and school leadership.

1 Introduction to Early Language Learning and Teacher Education: International Research and Practice

Subhan Zein

The past two decades have witnessed profound changes in the social, economic and political contextualisation of language. In the rapidly changing political, social and globalised economic landscapes of the 21st century, language has become cultural capital – mastery of two or more languages has been closely linked with business prospects, state diplomacy, intellectual pursuits and employment opportunities (Grenfell, 2014; Rhodes, 2014; Woolhouse *et al.*, 2013). A significant educational policy change characterising this tendency is early language learning: the teaching of a foreign or second language to children. Early language learning policies have become a worldwide phenomenon where the second or foreign language is taught as a subject or is used as a medium of instruction (Baldauf *et al.*, 2011; Garton *et al.*, 2011; Rhodes, 2014; Williams *et al.*, 2013). Early language learning policy has even been dubbed as 'possibly the world's biggest policy development in education' (Johnstone, 2009: 33).

This present volume focuses on one major issue resulting from the introduction of early language learning policies worldwide: teacher education. The edited volume specifically deals with the teacher education of early language learning teachers occurring in various forms of teacher professional learning, including, but not limited to teacher collaboration, mentoring and supervision, teacher classroom discourse and pedagogical content knowledge. This introductory chapter provides the background of the volume, identifying its rationale and aim. The chapter also discusses a few themes of the volume, outlines its structure and provides a final word.

Rationale and Aim of the Volume

The implementation of policies on early language learning has posed worldwide concerns over the shortage of adequately trained teachers (Butler, 2015; Copland *et al.*, 2014; Emery, 2012; Enever, 2014; Richards *et al.*, 2013; Rowe *et al.*, 2012; Williams *et al.*, 2013) and the inadequacy of teacher education programmes (Le & Do, 2012; Zein, 2016a). The rapid development in policies do not always work in a parallel manner with the provision of pre-service and in-service teacher education courses for early language learning teachers (Enever & Lindgren, 2016). As Rixon (2017: 82) argued,

> even the most carefully planned, widely welcomed and feasibly scoped of policy innovations may still be a complex matter, usually needing substantial material and financial support, but above all requiring fundamental shifts in attitudes, teacher knowledge and teacher skills which are not easily brought about.

This is most evident in the case of early introduction of English. All over the world, primary English education policies have actually created unprecedented challenges for teacher education (e.g. Butler, 2015; Emery, 2012; Enever *et al.*, 2009; Enever, 2014; Zein, 2016a). Wilden and Porsch (2017a) reviewed major studies on primary English as a Foreign Language (EFL) education in Europe, and they concluded that despite the clarity as to what constitutes 'good FL teaching', teachers struggle to appropriately implement their methodological knowledge and that 'the evidence on primary FL teachers' target proficiency is sketchy at best' (Wilden & Porsch, 2017a: 13). In countries such as Germany, the introduction of English in primary schools and its transition to secondary schools pose challenges to teacher educators in terms of the provision of knowledge about teaching and learning in primary and secondary education (Porsch & Wilden, 2017a: 68). A similar situation is also found in the context of primary EFL in East Asian countries: China, Japan, South Korea and Taiwan (Butler, 2015). In her review of the East Asian countries, for example, Butler (2015: 309) stated that 'part of the challenge is that we don't fully understand what qualifications teachers need to successfully teach FLs to young learners', highlighting the various issues relating to teachers' limited language proficiency and limited pedagogical content knowledge. In China in particular, the task to provide instruction to more than 130 million primary school children (Hu & McKay, 2012) means that intensive programmes such as the ITDEQC (Improving Teacher Development and Educational Quality in China) Project will have to be massively expanded (Thomas *et al.*, 2018). In the Southeast Asian context, the issue of designing professional development programmes that can cater for the specific needs of primary school English teachers is a shared concern in Indonesia (Zein, 2017) and Malaysia (Kabilan & Veratharaju, 2013), two countries that are confronted with the urgent task to provide instruction to approximately 26 million and 3 million children, respectively. In Argentina, the shortage of qualified and proficient teachers is one major factor affecting the teaching of English in the country. Focus is now placed on developing training programmes that can help teachers understand about child language acquisition, play-based learning and motivating tasks and activities to foster learning (Education Intelligence, 2015).

Despite its worldwide prominence, English is not the only language that early language learners are studying. There are also languages such as French, Hindi, Italian, Mandarin, Spanish, etc. whose introduction in early language learning settings has posed challenges for teacher education. In the context of children learning other languages such as Spanish, Korean and Mandarin in the USA, provision of assistance and bilingual programmes may be available through either government-funded local education agencies or state and locally-funded programmes. Nonetheless, concerns about teacher preparation have been articulated, as the need to produce teachers to meet the enormous growth of multilingual language learners has become more pressing (Bailey & Osipova, 2016: 175–189). In fact, focus on good teachers and quality instruction is a major theme in the review of early language learning in the USA in the past three decades (Rhodes, 2014). In Australia, new policy directions to engage with Asia through its 'Asia literacy' and 'Asia capability' have been recently set out in *Australia in the Asian Century White Paper*. However, the shortage of adequately trained teachers of Asian languages such as Hindi, Indonesian, Japanese and Mandarin in primary schools has been voiced, highlighting the urgent need for systematic teacher professional learning to meet the increasing demand for early language learning (Midgley, 2017). In Austria, most primary teachers who teach French and Italian alongside English are not trained as foreign language specialists, so they do not demonstrate good proficiencies in these languages (Jantscher & Landsiedler, 2000). In New Zealand, the requirement for learning languages including French, Hindi and Chinese, has resulted in the increasing demand for the teacher education of new language teachers in primary schools (Kerr *et al.*, 2014).

This background gives the impetus to this edited volume. The volume grew from the editors' shared concern that teachers in many school contexts worldwide still struggle to meet the demands of early language pedagogy (see, for example, Emery, 2012; Copland *et al.*, 2014; Rowe *et al.*, 2012; Williams *et al.*, 2013; Zein, 2016a, 2017). Even the implementation of various initiatives including the employment of non-specialist classroom teachers to teach languages (Emery, 2012; Rowe *et al.*, 2012), the establishment of teacher preparation programmes for early language learning (Williams *et al.*, 2013) and the reassignment of secondary teachers to teach languages at the primary level (Stelma & Onat-Stelma, 2010), does little to tackle the difficulties associated with teaching languages to early learners. Overall, the common pattern is that teacher education globally now finds itself confronted by multiple, complex challenges and the need to prepare early language teachers and assist them in their professional development has become more apparent.

Moreover, there is a distinct lack of publications delivering insights into this focal area of interest. Research into teacher education of modern foreign languages has been limited and lacking in focus (Grenfell, 2014). According to Grenfell (2014), most research has been small-scale, formative and explorative, leaving an apparently significant gap on theories of language teacher professionalisation. Consequently, progress on the knowledge base of language teacher education remains minimal (Evans & Esch, 2013; Wright, 2010), much less the knowledge base of *early* language teacher education. This volume responds to this gap – it compiles studies with diverse methodological tenets including case study (Chapter 3), mixed methods (Chapter 11), multivocal ethnography (Chapter 4) and quasi-experimental longitudinal study (Chapter 13) to enhance understanding of teacher education for early language teachers.

The collection is part of the Multilingual Matters' *Early Language Learning in the School Context Series* and following the scope of the series, the volume aims to cover early language learning for children aged between 3 and 12 years old who learn second, foreign and additional languages. This means the school contexts covered in the volume comprise of pre-schooling (3 to 5 years old) and primary schooling (6 to 12 years old). These include the school contexts of, for example, French–English immersion classes in the USA (Chapter 13), primary English as a foreign language (EFL) education in Indonesia (Chapter 4), bilingual English as an additional language (EAL) childhood education in Australia (Chapter 12) and bilingual Italian kindergarten in Turkey (Chapter 10). The diverse scope of school contexts represented in this volume reflects the proliferation of early language learning that has reached educational contexts in many countries around the world.

Overall, the chapters aim to highlight examples of research into current practice in the professional enhancement of early language learning teachers from around the world, but with an emphasis on the implications for practitioners. In other words, this volume is a publication that describes current research and identifies examples of good practice, following the direction taken in recent publications that underscore the importance of supporting early language learning teachers through research-informed teacher education (Enever & Lindgren, 2017; Wilden & Porsch, 2017b). Such an endeavour is essential in order to better support teachers (Enever & Lindgren, 2016) and inform policy decisions, especially given the central role of policy in pre-service teacher education (Zein, 2016a) and government-based training institutions in the professional development of teachers (Zein, 2016b).

In the following two sections of this chapter, I will identify how globalisation and the inseparable relationship between theory and practice underlie the writing of this edited collection.

From Global to Local, and Local to Global

Globalisation in its most simplistic sense refers to the expansion, acceleration and intensification of global interconnection. While it is not the purpose of this volume to consider globalisation per se, many of the chapters are grounded in the context of globalisation and how it has affected teacher education in early language learning. This is shown by Butler (Chapter 2), Le (Chapter 3), Zein (Chapter 4), Zhang (Chapter 5), Chou (Chapter 7), Kirkgöz (Chapter 8), Boivin (Chapter 9) and Carreira and Shigyo (Chapter 11). In Chapters 2, 5, 9 and 11, respectively, it is shown that the global popularity of English as an international language has become the precursor for introducing the language to young learners. In Chapters 3, 4, 7 and 8, increased proficiency in English for the global world means curricular alterations in primary education, inevitably leading to changes in teacher education. The policy-driven initiatives on early language learning teacher education occurring in the regional or national contexts identified in this volume are more than an economic imperative – they also reveal the impact of globalisation. In other words, they demonstrate the deeply embedded and substantial impact of globalisation on the teacher education of early language learning teachers, highlighting its profound, and arguably positive, effect on worldwide education processes.

The problem with the discourse of teacher education in the context of globalisation is, according to Angus (2007), its sole emphasis on the strong, totalising versions of globalisation theory that merely associates globalisation with neo-liberal features such as managerialism, competition and market arrangements. Such a discourse fails to consider the continuum occurring simultaneously at the local, national and regional levels, and can best describe teacher education practices. The stance taken in this volume, on the other hand, is one that does not see global cultures as fusing into one cultural identity. Following the local variability approach, this volume views teacher education as an international concern with complexities across countries and continents (Spring, 2015). It is also context bound. This context-bound nature of teacher education is reflected in the fact that the volume brings together an international group of scholars based in the four continents of Asia, Australia, Europe and North America to provide international perspectives on research and issues in early language learning teacher education that results from globalisation, drawing from their particular contexts. Thus, the contributions of these researchers constitute a series of extended research-based chapters in a wide range of geographical contexts; for example, Australia, Indonesia, Japan,

Taiwan, Turkey, UK, Vietnam and USA. The inclusion of chapters on teacher education for early language learning in Kazakhstan and Hong Kong in particular is an attempt to promote studies from less documented contexts, as opposed to European contexts (e.g. Enever, 2014; Wilden & Porsch, 2017a) such as Germany (see Deters-Phillip, 2017; Porsch & Wilden, 2017) that have received significant attention in recent years.

Thus, while being framed within globalisation, the chapters in this volume also reflect early language learning teacher education that considers unique localities in their diverse schooling contexts. These include the teaching of modern foreign languages (e.g. French, German and Spanish) at mainstream primary education (Chapter 6), English–Russian primary classrooms in Kazakhstan (Chapter 9), bilingual kindergarten education for Turkish children learning Italian (Chapter 10) and a longitudinal study from kindergarten to Year 3 dual language (French–English) immersion classes (Chapter 13). Even in the context of English language teaching, there are diverse contexts such as EAL and EFL. The former is represented in the focus of bilingual EAL childhood education involving monolingual and bilingual educators in Australia (Chapter 12), while the latter is elucidated by the processes of teacher learning in Japan (Chapter 11) and Vietnam (Chapter 4).

The diverse contexts foreground the notion that quality teaching is unique to the locality where the teaching is carried out. As suggested by Goodwin (2010: 30), learning to teach

> does not rest on techno-rational skills or proceed in a linear, predictable fashion. Rather, we know that learning to teach is complex, contextually specific, autobiographically grounded, and informed by sociopolitical realities. This is why quality teaching often looks different in different settings.

The fundamental task of teacher education across the countries represented in this volume may be the same: to prepare early language teachers in knowledge of and skills for teaching, and to orient them to develop certain dispositions to be effective teachers. However, what is needed within individual contexts, the requirements for qualifications in different locales and the cultural and normative practices of teaching will always be locally specific. Clearly, teacher education practices may have similarities with labels such as classroom action research, reflection, practicum and mentoring. Nonetheless, the instantiation of these practices is shaped by the context, settings and politics of countries and communities in which the pedagogy is formulated, developed and implemented (Hamilton & Loughran, 2016). Early language learning teacher education is of no exception.

Overall, it is our commitment in this volume to offer contents that are diverse and insightful while also contextually fitting to the specific countries where the studies were carried out. This makes the volume relevant to early language learning teachers in various local contexts as well as teacher educators and academics within the broader teacher education field.

The Inseparable Relationship between Theory and Practice

Another stance taken in the presentation of this volume is one that views the inseparable relationships between research and practice. We believe in the high value of empirical research to inform practice on the teacher education of early language learning teachers in the global world, and vice versa. Recent publications on early language learning have highlighted this position (e.g. Enever & Lindgren, 2016, 2017; Wilden & Porsch, 2017b) and the breadth of the volume reflects this paradigm.

First, the intention of the chapters is to demonstrate that the work of early language learning teacher education in the global world goes well beyond the transmission of teaching techniques or strategies of teaching (Korthagen, 2016; Loughran *et al.*, 2016). Loughran *et al.*, (2016: 416) stated that teacher education should be 'an educative process that develops thoughtful, informed and highly able professionals' who demonstrate 'willingness to reframe, reconsider, contextualise and problematise their practice rather than seek to mimic or replicate the practices of those they observed through their experiences in teacher education'.

This intention is reflected in the way chapters in this volume attempt to contextualise research to cater for the specific needs of early language learning teachers in teacher education through a redirection towards the early learner domain. This is evident because Jenkins, Duursma and Neilsen-Hewett (Chapter 12), Le (Chapter 3), Zein (Chapter 4) and Griffin, Bailey and Mistry (Chapter 13) all argue for the centrality of teachers to understand young learners and design their pedagogy accordingly. Jenkins, Duursma and Neilsen-Hewett argue that adequate support for children from diverse cultural and linguistic backgrounds requires strong understanding 'of the unique need of bilingual children in the early education context.' Similarly, Griffin, Bailey and Mistry postulate that increasing awareness of learners' bilingual identity requires teachers' ways of discussing and cultivating the development of bilingual identity with dual-language immersion students. Le shows that teachers' lack of awareness of the needs and characteristics of young learners adds weight to the complexity of the meaning-making of lived experiences of teachers, especially those novice teachers who are more than likely to find rising tensions between expectations and reality during their first years of teaching. In Zein's chapter, the central tenet of pedagogy lies in teachers' ability to develop speech modification strategies following a series of realised process of imagining themselves as a child.

Secondly, the chapters in this volume all point to the pedagogy of teacher education that develops alignment between practice and theory, emphasises reflection and focuses on depth rather than breadth of curriculum (Kitchen & Petrarca, 2016; Korthagen, 2016). In this volume, the development of such a pedagogy for early language learning teacher education is made manifest through the provision of a variety of learning experiences that stimulate introspection, collaboration, awareness-raising and learning from experiences. In other words, the shared principle underpinning these chapters is to encourage teachers to find the linkage between the intangible concepts and principles examined in the literature and the context of their classroom through cooperative participation (Kitchen & Petrarca, 2016; Korthagen, 2016). A rigorous collective participation in which teachers are encouraged to engage in activities that foster reflective enquiry through discussions, collaborative planning and individual and/or group practice is most evident in Chapter 4 (Zein) that analyses teachers' way of imagining themselves as a child to promote scaffolded instruction and Chapter 5 (Zhang), which discusses learning study. In the cases of Chou (Chapter 7), Kirkgöz (Chapter 8) and Boivin (Chapter 9), this process is built upon the paradigm of enquiry that allows input from experts when appropriate and to provide support as required (through coaching or mentoring). Furthermore, clinical experiences where teachers observe learning situations and witness how effective teacher educators and teachers assist them in the process of student learning are at the core of a number of chapters.

Various authors highlight the practical orientation in relation to the need to prepare prospective teachers to develop abilities to imagine themselves as young leaners (Chapter 4), to develop understanding of new orthographies in teaching foreign languages (Chapter 6), to work collaboratively in action research projects (Chapter 8) and to develop and evaluate syllabus in cross-curricular projects (Chapter 11). Chapters 7 to 9 all highlight the integral role of mentoring and supervision in teacher education. They show how teacher professional learning can be made manifest through professional learning communities that create a continuum from the voices of teachers and teacher educators and the collaborative work between them. Furthermore, problem-based learning that stems from the everyday reality of teacher professional learning forms the core tenet of teacher preparation to resolve the theory–practice divide through critical reflection. In Chapter 4, this appears through reflection on teachers' discourse and how activities in speech modification can help improve teacher pedagogy. Similarly, collaborative learning that promotes critical reflection has been suggested by Macrory in Chapter 6 in order to overcome the challenges occurring due to the introduction of new orthographies in primary classroom.

The inseparable relationship between research and practice demonstrated in all the chapters in this volume sets the tone for congruency between teacher education content and teachers' needs. Content congruency is the single determining factor in the transformation of teachers' professional knowledge and skills, increased understanding of their professional roles and improved teaching efficacy (Flores, 2016; Kitchen & Petrarca, 2016; Korthagen, 2010, 2016; Rollnick & Mavhunga, 2016). This is the underpinning principle upon which specific pedagogical approaches for effective teacher education must be built (Flores, 2016; Korthagen, 2010, 2016) amid the complexity of early language learning. This assertion is fitting, given the little emphasis on the learner domain in the research context of language teacher education. Ellis (2010: 95) argued that the overall goal of a language teacher education that utilises second language acquisition (SLA) research is 'to contribute to teacher-learning by assisting teachers to develop/modify their own theory of how learners learn an L2 in an instructional setting.' This assertion is further supported by the occurrence of waves of criticisms against current teacher education programmes worldwide that provide no references to the specific needs of early language learning teachers (e.g. Le & Do, 2012; Emery, 2012; Enever, 2014; Rhodes, 2014; Rowe *et al.*, 2012; Zein, 2016a, 2016b, 2017).

Thus, all chapters in this volume underscore the inseparable relationship between research and practice by aiming to produce reflective teachers through the provision of a variety of learning experiences that stimulate introspection, collaboration, awareness-raising and learning from experiences. While on the one hand this is indicative of the eagerness of the authors to capture the demanding and challenging process of teacher learning, on the other hand, it is also parallel to their overarching aim to conceive teacher education as beyond the process of training to deliver. This would prove useful as a point of departure for the development of more dynamic and integrative approach to thinking and implementing teacher education (Gray, 2010).

The Structure of the Volume

The volume is divided into four parts. Part 1 deals with the complexity of teacher learning, encompassing Chapters 3 to 6. Part 2 focuses on innovations in mentoring and teacher supervision. It consists of Chapters 7 to 9. Part 3 discusses strategies in programme development. This part consists of Chapters 10 and 11. Part 4 consists of two chapters: Chapters 12 and 13. These chapters emphasise perceptions, knowledge and assessment in early language learning teacher education.

Prior to embarking on the four parts of the book, it is necessary to gain an overview of teacher education and early language learning. A systematic synthesis of recent research on the education of teachers of English for young learners (EYL) in Southeast and East Asian contexts is provided by Butler in Chapter 2, focusing on countries, namely China, Japan, Indonesia, South Korea, Taiwan, Thailand and Vietnam. Butler thoroughly reviews empirical studies on the teacher education of EYL teachers, particularly: (1) teachers' qualifications; (2) native-English speaking (NS) teachers and non-native-English speaking (NNS) teachers; (3) teacher mentoring and professional development; and (4) classroom research. Given its focus on Southeast and East Asian context, generalisations cannot be drawn from this chapter; however, many aspects discussed in the chapter are relevant to other contexts.

Part 1 focuses on the complexity of teacher learning. This issue of complexity in consideration of how children learn languages and what teachers do in the classroom has been recently acknowledged in teacher education (see Enever & Lindgren, 2017). In this volume, the complexity of building a thorough understanding of young learners means that having relevant training qualifications does not suffice. As one of Carbonara's participants in Chapter 10 stated:

> I studied Applied Linguistics and I used to teach to adult learners, thus I was focusing on language learning process. But working with children, I feel that my teaching method should be more child-centred. (T8)

The complexity of early language learning teacher education builds upon teacher knowledge, draws on local context and experience, is grounded in enquiry and encourages the ability to solve problems. The four chapters in this part attempt to capture such complexity while increasing sensitivity to context. This is first started by Le Van Canh in Chapter 3. Using narrative enquiry, Le explores the professional learning of a teacher who had graduated from a pre-service teacher education and taught at a primary school in Hanoi, Vietnam. Le shows that teacher learning is dynamic and complex, affected by multiple factors that are directly to the individual teacher such as cognitions and emotions, as well as professional ecology including salaries, teaching workload and availability of professional development activities. Similarly, I write Chapter 4 to explain the complexity of classroom discourse in primary English classroom. In the chapter, I am interested in analysing teachers' speech modification features. The findings of the study suggest that imagining one's self as a child could help teachers develop flexibility in modifying their speech. Suggestions for teacher education are drawn from the study that employed multivocal ethnography to collect data, cultivating the critical discussions of teachers and teacher educators. In Chapter 5, Yuefeng Zhang writes about the complex experiences of six pre-service English language teachers in Hong Kong in implementing learning study as a means of professional enhancement. Utilising qualitative research methods including focus groups discussions, classroom observations and analysis of documents, Zhang explores the potential of learning study in empowering teachers to transform their teacher-dominated approach into a learner-centred one while allowing them to develop continuous reflection of their practice. Similar complex considerations are also found in Chapter 6 where approaches to foreign language orthographies for young learners become the concern of its author, Gee Macrory. Against the backdrop of the recent nationwide introduction of modern foreign languages such as French and German in the UK, Macrory reports on a project involving 55 student teachers within an Initial Teacher Education system at a UK-based university. She investigates the literacy approaches used by teachers and the training offered to student teachers, pointing to the need for 'a model of teacher education that promotes collaborative learning, one that can serve to promote a more effective pedagogy irrespective of the writing system or orthography involved.' The complexity of teacher learning works against the simplistic views that prospective teachers should receive all the training that prepares them for teaching and that they can carry for the remaining of their career (Loughran *et al.*, 2016). In the various topics that they covered, the four chapters in Part 1 demonstrate such a complexity, highlighting a cohesive whole of understanding of the pedagogy of teacher education that makes teaching more effective to influence student learning (Korthagen, 2016).

Part 2 focuses on innovations on mentoring and supervision for early language learning teachers. The three chapters in this part (Chapters 7 to 9) demonstrate a focus on the descriptions and interpretations of mentors' or supervisors' thinking processes and identity formation, and how these are juxtaposed with evidence on prospective teachers' performance and teaching behaviour. This reiterates the interconnections between the internal processes of reasoning and the contextual factors affecting the pedagogy of teachers and teacher educators (Orland-Barak, 2014, 2016) as well as the alignment between technical aspects of the practice and the social environment in which the practice is understood and enacted (Glazer, 2008). In Chapter 7, this is accomplished through a clinical model of supervision, as Chiou-Hui Chou is motivated to provide authentic opportunities for primary EFL teacher candidates to gain understanding of the professional practice of teaching in today's diverse classrooms. Gathering data from a wide range of data collection methods involving prospective primary EFL teachers in Taiwan, Chou explores some guiding TESOL principles to assist teachers develop the 21st century classroom practices for young learners. The clinical model of supervision that is utilised in her study could serve as a tool to open our understanding of prospective primary EFL teachers' development. Supporting teachers to deal with the daily issues emerging in the first critical years of their profession is the focus of Yasemin Kirkgöz's work in Chapter 8. The study was part of a collaborative action research (CAR) where Kirkgöz supervised the teachers to evaluate their teaching practice and identify a research focus. While highlighting the importance of CAR under the mentorship of teacher educator(s), in the chapter Kirkgöz also emphasises the vital need for a collaborative process between teacher educators/researchers and teachers. The promotion of action-oriented practice in the chapter adds an entirely new dimension to the scheme of mentoring for young learner English teachers. Though not stated explicitly, a collaborative mentoring process is also integral in Nettie Boivin's work in Chapter 9, which focuses on multiliteracies involving four Kazakh and Russian-medium primary schools whose students learn English in post-Soviet Kazakhstan. Boivin investigates the practice of the teachers who utilised ethnic Kazakh and or Russian oral stories in English as a narrative learning framework to embed multiliteracies for early language learning. The intensive interactions between course lecturer and prospective teachers is what makes the mentoring process evident in the chapter. Boivin also argues for new approaches being developed for teachers in multilingual settings to prepare students for the 21st century through professional development that places its core at the co-constructed, multimodal and collaborative nature of teacher education.

Part 3 consists of two chapters that focus on strategies on programme development for two languages (Italian and English) in two entirely different contexts: Turkey and Japan. In response to the increasing demand of teaching Italian in Turkey, Valentina Carbonara's work (Chapter 10) is in the context of teaching Italian language in a bilingual kindergarten. Carbonara utilises the already successfully implemented framework in an Italian–Turkish kindergarten in Istanbul, Turkey. As she outlines the framework, which consists of three main indicators: language proficiency, personal qualities and professional competences, Carbonara demonstrates how the framework could be used as a guideline to inform professional development of Italian bilingual teachers working at kindergarten level. Programme development is also the central tenet of Chapter 11, written by Junko Matsuzaki Carreira and Tomoko Shigyo. The data for their study were collected from 34 pre-service teachers attending a primary teacher-training programme at a university in Japan where English instruction, called foreign language activities, has been made available to children since 2011. With English being taught using a cross-curricular approach, Carreira and Shigyo's study investigated its implementation and how it could be incorporated into a pre-service syllabus. The central role of theory, practice and reflection as the fundamentals of teacher education (Kitchen & Petrarca, 2016) is what underpins the programme development component in the two chapters. In doing so, the authors have demonstrated the need 'to move beyond the surface structural features of teacher education programmes in order to understand the key elements of programme effectiveness' (Zeichner & Conklin, 2008: 271). The programme development in the two chapters also shows parallelism with recent tendency in the pedagogy of teacher education that identifies more integral focus on skills, knowledge, attitudes and experience of teachers (Korthagen, 2016).

The final part of the volume (Part 4) emphasises perceptions, knowledge and assessment in teacher professional learning in bilingual early language learning contexts in Australia and the USA. In Chapter 12, Larissa Jenkins, Elisabeth Duursma and Catherine Neilsen-Hewett write about perceptions and knowledge of bilingualism and relationships with children among early childhood educators (or teachers) in Australia. Employing a mixed-methods approach, Jenkins *et al.* explore whether mono- and bilingual educators differed in their understanding of bilingualism and in their perceptions of their relationships with bilingual children. The findings of their study point to the need to place greater emphasis on the training of educators in supporting the language development of both mono- and bilingual children that is contextually appropriate to the early childhood centres where they operate. In Chapter 13, Katherine M. Griffin, Alison L. Bailey and Rashmita S. Mistry write about what educators of young dual language immersion students learn from a bilingual approach to assessing development. Griffin *et al.* describe how their quasi-experimental, longitudinal study documented the educational experiences of early years schooling through the third grade of primary school students and teachers. They discuss how progress can be measured bilingually and identify the classroom practices for which teachers can support early language learners. The development of early language learning around the world has made the issue of perceptions, knowledge and assessment become more central. Rixon (2016), for example, highlighted the importance of parallelism between age-appropriate assessment with the development of policy implementation in early language learning. The development of teachers' perceptions and knowledge has also gained increasing prominence with the need for increasing teachers' knowledge about teaching and learning (Porsch & Wilden, 2017; Zein, 2017). The importance of the chapters in this final part therefore cannot be underestimated.

To conclude the volume, Chapter 14 is presented. It is written by Sue Garton to highlight emerging themes that have not been covered in this introductory chapter, including long-standing issues in policies on teacher education, shifting pedagogies and the role of collaboration. Garton also identifies future research directions.

Final Word

All in all, early language learning teacher education is broad in scope and wide in implementation, but it is still under-theorised. There is certainly much to address and a volume such as this can only hope to capture a fraction of the significant issues in our understanding of the theory and practice of early language learning teacher education. Nonetheless, the timeliness of the volume means it is probably a good start. The time has come for teacher educators and early language teachers to walk together on this journey of teacher education as we enter a new era of early language learning.

References

Angus, L. (2007) Globalisation and the reshaping of teacher professional culture: Do we train competent technicians or informed players in the policy process? In T. Townsend and R. Bates (eds) *Handbook of Teacher Education* (pp. 141–156). Dordrecht: Springer.

Bailey, A.L. and Osipova, A.V. (2016) *Children's Multilingual Development and Education: Fostering Linguistic Resources in Home and School Contexts.* Cambridge: Cambridge University Press.

Baldauf, Jr., R.B., Kaplan, R.B., Kamwangamalu, N. and Bryant, P. (2011) Success or failure of primary second/foreign language programmes in Asia: What do the data tell us? *Current Issues in Language Planning* 12 (2), 309–323. doi:10.1080/14664208.2011.609715

Butler, Y.G. (2015) English language education among young learners in East Asia: A review of current research (2004–2014). *Language Teaching* 48, 303–342. doi:10.1017/S0261444815000105

Education Intelligence (2015) *English in Argentina.* London: Education Intelligence, British Council.

Copland, F., Garton, S. and Burns, A. (2014) Challenges in teaching English to young learners: Global perspectives and local realities. *TESOL Quarterly* 48 (4), 738–762. doi:10.1002/tesq.148

Deters-Phillip, A.-C. (2017) Teacher language in German EFL classrooms at primary EFL: An interview study. In E. Wilden and R. Porsch (eds) *The Professional Development of Primary EFL Teachers: National and International Research* (pp. 209–223). Münster: Waxmann.

Ellis, R. (2010) Second language acquisition, teacher education and language pedagogy. *Language Teaching* 43 (2), 182–201. doi:10.1017/S0261444809990139

Emery, H. (2012) *A Global Study of Primary English Teachers' Qualifications, Training and Career Development. ELT Research Papers 12-08.* London: British Council.

Enever, J. (2014) Primary English teacher education in Europe. *ELT Journal* 68 (3), 231–242. doi:10.1093/elt/cct079

Enever, J. and Lindgren, E. (2016) Early language learning in instructed contexts – Editorial introduction. *Education Inquiry* 7 (1), 1–8. doi:10.3402/edui.v7.30954

Enever, J. and Lindgren, E. (2017) *Early Language Learning: Complexity and Mixed Methods.* Bristol: Multilingual Matters.

Enever, J., Moon, J. and Raman, U. (eds) (2009) *Young Learner English Language Policy and Implementation: International Perspectives.* Reading: Garnet Education.

Evans, M. and Esch, E. (2013) The elusive boundaries of second language teacher professional development. *The Language Learning Journal* 41 (2), 137–141. doi:10.1080/09571736.2013.790129

Flores, M.A. (2016) Teacher education curriculum. In J. Loughran and M.L. Hamilton (eds) *International Handbook of Teacher Education* (pp. 187–230). Singapore: Springer. doi:10.1007/978-981-10-0366-0_5

Glazer, J.L. (2008) Educational professionalism: An inside-out view. *American Journal of Education* 114 (2), 168–189.

Garton, S., Copland, F. and Burns, A. (2011) *Investigating Global Practices in Teaching English to Young Learners. ELT Research Papers 11-01.* London: British Council.

Gray, D.S. (2010) International perspectives on research in initial teacher education and some emerging issues. *Journal of Education for Teaching: International Research and Pedagogy* 36 (4), 345–351. doi:10.1080/02607476.2010.513839

Grenfell, M. (2014) Modern language teacher education. *The Language Learning Journal* 42 (3), 239–241. doi:10.1080/09571736.2014.950015

Goodwin, A.L. (2010) Globalization and the preparation of quality teachers: Rethinking knowledge domains for teaching. *Teaching Education* 21 (1), 19–32. doi:10.1080/10476210903466901

Hamilton, M.L. and Loughran, J. (2016) Looking beyond borders: Scholarship of teacher education. In J. Loughran and M.L. Hamilton (eds) *International Handbook of Teacher Education* (pp. 503–517). Singapore: Springer. doi:10.1007/978-981-10-0369-1_15

Hu, G. and S.L. McKay (2012) English language education in East Asia: Some recent developments. *Journal of Multilingual and Multicultural Development* 33 (4), 345–362. doi:10.1080/01434632.2012.661434

Jantscher, E. and Landsiedler, I. (2000) Foreign language education at Austrian primary schools: An overview. In M. Nikolov and H. Curtain (eds) *An Early Start: Young Learners and Modern Languages in Europe and Beyond* (pp. 13–28). Brussels: Council of Europe.

Johnstone, R. (2009) An early start: What are the key conditions for generalized success? In J. Enever, J. Moon and U. Raman (eds) *Young Learner English Language Policy and Implementation: International Perspectives* (pp. 31–42). Reading: Garnet Education Publishing.

Kabilan, M.K. and Veratharaju, K. (2013) Professional development needs of primary school English language teachers in Malaysia. *Professional Development in Education* 39 (3), 330–351. doi:10.1080/19415257.2012.762418

Kerr, A., Adams, R. and Skyrme, G. (2014) Research in applied linguistics and language teaching and learning in New Zealand (2006–2010). *Language Teaching*, 46 (2), 225–255. doi: 10.1017/S0261444812000535

Kitchen, J. and Petrarca, D. (2016) Approaches to teacher education. In J. Loughran and M.L. Hamilton (eds) *International Handbook of Teacher Education* (pp. 137–186). Singapore: Springer. doi:10.1007/978-981-10-0366-0_4

Korthagen, F.A.D. (2010) How teacher education can make a difference. *Journal of Education for Teaching: International Research and Pedagogy* 36 (4), 407–423. doi: 10.1080/02607476.2010.513854

Korthagen, F.A.D. (2016) The pedagogy of teacher education. In J. Loughran and M.L. Hamilton (eds) *International Handbook of Teacher Education* (pp. 311–346). Singapore: Springer. doi:10.1007/978-981-10-0366-0_8

Le, V.C. and Do, C.T.M. (2012) Teacher preparation for primary school English education: A case of Vietnam. In B. Spolsky and Y.-I. Moon (eds) *Primary School English-Language Education in Asia: From Policy to Practice* (pp. 106–121). New York: Routledge.

Loughran, J., Keast, S. and Cooper, R. (2016) Pedagogical reasoning in teacher education. In J. Loughran and M.L. Hamilton (eds) *International Handbook of Teacher Education* (pp. 387–421). Singapore: Springer. doi:10.1007/978-981-10-0366-0_10

Midgley, W. (2017) Which languages should Australian children be learning to get ahead. *The Conversation.* See http://www.abc.net.au/news/2017-03-24/which-languages-should-australian-children-be-learning/8383146 (accessed 18 April 2018).

Orland-Barak, L. (2014) Mediation in mentoring: A synthesis of studies in teaching and teacher education. *Teaching and Teacher Education* 44, 180–188. doi:10.1016/j.tate.2014.07.011

Orland-Barak (2016) Mentoring. In J. Loughran and M.L. Hamilton (eds) *International Handbook of Teacher Education* (pp. 105–140). Singapore: Springer. doi:10.1007/978-981-10-0369-1_4

Porsch, R. and Wilden, E. (2017) The introduction of EFL in primary education in Germany: A view from implementation research. In E. Wilden and R. Porsch (eds) *The Professional Development of Primary EFL Teachers: National and International Research* (pp. 53–72). Münster: Waxmann.

Richards, H., Conway, C., Roskvist, A. and Harvey, S. (2013) Foreign language teachers' language proficiency and their language teaching practice. *The Language Learning Journal* 41 (2), 231–246. doi:10.1080/09571736.2012.707676

Rixon, S. (2016) Do developments in assessment represent the 'coming of age' of young learners English language teaching initiatives? In M. Nikolov (ed.) *The International*

Picture. In *Assessing Young Learners of English: Global and Local Perspectives* (pp. 19–41). New York: Springer.

Rixon, S. (2017) The role of early language learning teacher education in turning policy into practice. In E. Wilden and R. Porsch (eds) *The Professional Development of Primary EFL Teachers: National and International Research* (pp. 79–94). Münster: Waxmann.

Rhodes, N. (2014) Elementary school foreign language teaching: Lessons learned over three decades (1980–2010). *Foreign Language Annals* 47 (1), 115–133. doi:10.1111/flan.12073

Rollnick, M. and Mavhunga, E. (2016) The place of subject matter knowledge in teacher education. In J. Loughran and M.L. Hamilton (eds) *International Handbook of Teacher Education* (pp. 423–452). Singapore: Springer. doi:10.1007/978-981-10-0366-0_11

Rowe, J., Herrera, M., Hughes, B. and Cawley, M. (2012) Capacity building for primary languages through initial teacher education: Could specialist and nonspecialist student teachers' complementary skills provide a winning combination? *The Language Learning Journal* 40 (2), 143–156. doi:10.1080/09571736.2011.605904

Spring, J. (2015) *Globalization of Education: An Introduction* (2nd edn). London: Routledge.

Stelma, J. and Onat-Stelma, Z. (2010) Foreign language teachers organising learning during their first year of teaching young learners. *The Language Learning Journal* 38 (2), 193–207. doi:10.1080/09571731003790490

Thomas, S., Zhang, L. and Jiang, D. (2018) English teachers professional development and the role of professional learning communities to enhance teachers practice and student outcomes in China. In S. Zein and R. Stroupe (eds) *English Language Teacher Preparation in Asia: Research, Practice and Policy* (pp. 201–222). New York: Routledge.

Williams, G., Strubell, M. and Williams, G.O. (2013) Trends in European language education. *The Language Learning Journal* 41 (1), 5–36. doi:10.1080/09571736.2011.567355

Wilden, E., and Porsch, R. (2017a) Researching the professional development of primary EFL teachers: An introduction. In E. Wilden and R. Porsch (eds) *The Professional Development of Primary EFL Teachers: National and International Research* (pp. 7–26). Münster: Waxmann.

Wilden, E. and R. Porsch (eds) (2017b) *The Professional Development of Primary EFL Teachers: National and International Research.* Münster: Waxmann.

Woolhouse, C., Bartle, P., Hunt, E. and Balmer, D. (2013) Language learning, cultural capital and teacher identity: Teachers negotiating the introduction of French into the primary curriculum. *The Language Learning Journal* 41 (1), 55–67.

Wright, T. (2010) Second language teacher education: Review of recent research on practice. *Language Teaching*, 43 (3), 259–296. doi:10.1017/S0261444810000030

Zeichner, K. and Conklin, H.G. (2008) Teacher education programs as sites for teacher preparation. In M. Cochran-Smith, S. Feiman-Nemser, D. McIntyre and K.E. Demers (eds) *Handbook of Research on Teacher Education* (3rd edn, pp. 269–289). New York: Routledge.

Zein, M.S. (2016a) Pre-service education for primary school English teachers in Indonesia: Policy implications. *Asia Pacific Journal of Education* 36 (S1), 119–134. doi:10.1080/02188791.2014.961899

Zein, M.S. (2016b) Government-based training agencies and the professional development of Indonesian English for Young Learners teachers: Perspectives from complexity theory. *Journal of Education for Teaching: International Research and Pedagogy* 42 (2), 205–223. doi:10.1080/02607476.2016.1143145

Zein, M.S. (2017) Professional development needs of primary EFL teachers: Perspectives of teachers and teacher educators. *Professional Development in Education* 43 (2), 293–313. doi:10.1080/19415257.2016.1156013

2 How Teachers of Young Learners of English are Educated in East and Southeast Asia: Research-based Lessons

Yuko Goto Butler

Introduction

It has become increasingly popular worldwide to teach English as an international language to young learners (conventionally defined as children between the ages of 5 and 12 years old). While it has been suggested that teacher education is key for successful early English education (e.g. Enever, 2015), both pre- and in-service teacher training in many countries are carried out by trial and error, and teachers of young learners of English often struggle to meet policy requirements and expectations. In East and Southeast Asia, which have rapidly growing numbers of young learners of English, teacher training is often a high-pressure and challenging task (Butler, 2015; Spolsky & Moon, 2012). Some challenges are regionally specific, while others are common across countries and regions. This chapter aims to synthesize relevant major studies on teacher education for teaching young English learners in East and Southeast Asian contexts in order to develop a state-of-the-art understanding of this topic as well as to better inform teacher education policies in Asia and beyond. Reflecting the body of research on this topic, this review focuses on China (including Hong Kong), Japan, Indonesia, South Korea, Taiwan, Thailand and Vietnam. These countries are traditionally considered English-as-a-foreign-language (EFL) contexts (Choi & Lee, 2008), although the boundary between English-as-a-second language (ESL) and EFL is not always clear. For example, Hong Kong is recognized as an ESL/EFL context rather than an ESL context according to Choi and Lee's (2008) survey conducted among English language education specialists in Asia.

This chapter begins with an overview of primary school-level English language education polices in the focus regions while paying special attention to *personnel policies* – policies related to teachers and teacher training (Kaplan & Baldauf, 1997). After identifying major issues related to personnel policies in the regions, the chapter reviews studies that have the potential to inform policy decisions and implementations in the areas of (a) teachers' qualifications and (b) professional development for teachers of English at the primary school level. The chapter concludes with suggestions for future research and policy making and implementation in Asia.

This review primarily depends on published policy documents, policy analysis papers and empirical studies published in major international and regional journals and books in English from 2002 to 2017. Some widely cited major publications in local languages are included as well. Opinion papers and unpublished documents, including dissertations and masters' theses, are excluded. This is by no means an exhaustive review of the relevant issues and research in Asia; instead, it identifies specific problems and challenges related to the education of teachers of young learners of English in various societal and policy contexts in Asia and highlights the importance of negotiating with local agents and contexts when policies are developed and implemented.

Overview of Personnel Policies Concerning Primary School English Education

Most of the countries examined in this chapter offered some form of English education at the primary school level, as an elective or as a required subject in select geographic areas, before making it compulsory. (Note, however, that, as of 2017, English is not compulsory at primary school in Indonesia.) The implementation of English at primary school (EPS) as a compulsory subject has been carried out in a top-down manner throughout Asia (Li, 2011; Spolsky & Moon, 2012). In deciding to make the subject compulsory, governments uniformly addressed the importance of developing their citizens' command of English as a lingua franca for the nation's competitiveness in the global world. A widely held belief that 'the younger the better' for language learning also fed into support for EPS, especially among parents. It is important to note, however, that the extent to which the assumptions driving this decision – the critical role of English as a lingua franca and 'the younger the better' for English learning in Asia – reflect reality remains unclear (e.g. Kubota, 2015 for critical discussions for English as a lingua franca in Asia; Ojima *et al.*, 2011 for an example providing evidence against the assumption of younger learners' advantage in an Asian context). In practice, policy decisions for EPS in Asia were often made as a result of complicated interplays among various political, social and educational factors in the given country (e.g. Butler, 2007a, 2015), and sometimes at the expense of devaluing local languages (Kirkpatrick, 2011a).

Policy documents and policy analyses on EPS in the focus countries (Butler, 2007a, 2015; Chen, 2012; Choi & Lee, 2007, 2008; Jeon & Lee, 2006; Kang, 2012; Le & Do, 2012; Li, 2016; Moodie & Nam, 2015; Nguyen, 2011, 2017; Phuong & Nhu, 2015; Wang & Lin, 2013; Wu, 2012; Zein, 2015, 2016a) revealed that there are two major personnel policy issues: (a) who should teach and (b) how to secure 'qualified' teachers.

First is the policy decision concerning whether specialists (specialized English teachers) or generalists (homeroom teachers) should be the main agent teaching EPS. The focus countries made different decisions. Broadly speaking, China, Taiwan and Vietnam opted for specialists, while Indonesia, Japan, Korea and Thailand went with generalists. (In reality, however, nonspecialists in China, Taiwan and Vietnam sometimes teach English, particularly in rural areas, and specialists do sometimes teach English in Indonesia, Japan, Korea and Thailand.) Local specialists may be further categorized into different subtypes (e.g. Indonesia). Nonlocal teachers are also recruited and teach in various capacities, including native English speakers in Japan, Korea and Taiwan, as well as Filipinos in Vietnam. (Note that defining 'native speakers' is a complicated and controversial matter and it will be discussed later in the chapter.) Major personal policies in each group are summarized in Tables 2.1 and 2.2. The specialist approach (Table 2.1) requires recruiting large numbers of specialists, whereas the generalist approach (Table 2.2) requires training existing generalists on a massive scale. As described below, both approaches have distinct pros and cons, which in turn are deeply associated with qualifications for EPS teachers that are expected or prioritized in the given educational system and society.

The second major policy decision concerns strategies to secure qualified EPS teachers, how best to design and implement professional training, and how to allocate qualified human resources. A shortage of 'qualified' teachers and/or a regional gap in qualification among teachers is a serious problem in the focus countries. They have offered professional development (for both pre-service and in-service teachers) in various formats and lengths. Some training formats are more aligned with their traditional professional development models and others are newer models. Some training programs take direct, individual-based approaches, and others take a top-down, indirect, multilayered approach (so-called 'cascade models'). As is discussed below, overall results from studies that examined teacher training programs in Asia suggest the importance of considering social and educational factors where the training takes place.

In sum, personnel policies for EPS in Asia tend to address two major issues: namely, deciding (a) who should teach and (b) how to secure qualified teachers. Both issues are deeply associated with understanding the qualifications for EPS teachers and searching for contextually appropriate teacher-training models – topics that are discussed next.

Table 2.1 Primary English language education policies in China, Hong Kong, Taiwan and Vietnam (policies as of 2017)

Policies	China	Hong Kong	Taiwan	Vietnam
Official implementation	1978: mandated but not fully implemented 2001: as a compulsory academic subject (still allowing some flexibility)	1978: compulsory in all schools	1998: as an elective 2001: as a compulsory academic subject	1996: as an elective 2010: as a compulsory academic subject
Target grade levels	From Grade 3 (allowing flexibility depending on resource availability)	From Grade 1	From Grade 3 (allowing to start from Grade 1)	From Grade 3
Instructional hours	Three 40 min. lessons/week	17–21% of all instructional hours	Grades 3 & 4: one 40 min. lesson/week Grades 5 & 6: two 40 min. lessons/week	Four 40 min. lessons/week
Teacher types	Specialist	Specialist	Specialist	Specialist (schools hire English teachers on contract)
Suggested or required methods	Communicative in principle; Task-Based Language Teaching (TBLT) is recommended; aim to reach Level 2 in the National English Curriculum Standards (NECS)	Communicative; TBLT as part of Target-Oriented Curriculum Reform; e-learning	Communicative; teaching English through English (TETE) is required (but not in rural areas)	Communicative; aims to reach A1 in CEFR; content and language integrated learning (CLIL) introduced; specific emphasis on teaching mathematics and sciences

Required qualifications	Junior college diploma or BA (English at normal colleges)	BA in English-related major with a diploma in Education; passing level LPATE; four-months practicum; native or near- native proficiency	BA in English-related majors with credits in Education; passing Ministry of Education (MOE) exam; one-year training program and a six-months practicum; passing High Intermediate level in General English Proficiency Test (GEPT)	BA with Primary English Foreign Language Teachers (PEFLT) training (including practicum); CEFR B2 is required (but substantial gaps in reality)
In-service training	School- or self-funded; content and length vary; cascade models are often used, particularly in rural areas	School- or self-funded; 30 credit hours	Government-, school- and publisher-funded; minimum of 18 hours per year	Government-funded; local-government-funded; a cascade model; international aid for teacher training
NS teachers	No central policy; local policies	Aims to have one NS per school; each NS works with an experienced local NNS; native English-speaking teacher (NET) scheme; categorized into five levels	No central policy; hired by licensed recruitment agencies; Foreign English Teacher Recruitment Project (FETRP)	No central policy; locally decided through private agencies; many Filipinos
Other notes	Shortage of qualified teachers in rural areas; micro-teaching is rare in teacher training programs		Competitive to become English teachers in urban areas; shortage of qualified teachers in rural areas	Shortage of qualified teachers; primary education goes up to Grade 5

Table 2.2 Primary English language education policies in Indonesia, Japan, South Korea, and Thailand (policies as of 2017)

Policies	Indonesia	Japan	South Korea	Thailand
Official implementation	1993: as an elective (a local choice); some backdrops in 2013; uncertainness in policy directions	2001: as compulsory exploratory program 2020: as a compulsory academic subject	1997: as a compulsory academic subject	1996: as a compulsory academic subject
Targeted grade levels (as of 2016)	From Grade 4 (allowing to teach from an earlier grade)	(Starting in 2020) Grades 3 & 4 (exploratory program) Grades 5 & 6 (academic subjects)	From Grade 3 (2018: banned from teaching English at Grades 1–2)	From Grade 1
Instructional hours	Two 35 min. lessons/week	(Starting in 2020) Grades 3 & 4: one 45 min. lesson/week Grades 5 & 6: two 45 min. lessons/week (modules are allowed)	Grades 3 & 4: two hours/week Grades 5 & 6: three hours/week	Grades 1–3: one hour/week Grades 4–6: two hours/week Additional class hours are allowed (but the total instructional hours should not exceed 1,000 hours).
Teacher types	Generalists and specialists	Generalists and others (community volunteers, NSs, uncertified specialists, etc.)	Generalists and specialists (some of the specialists are English conversation instructors who are hired on contract)	Generalists
Suggested or required methods	Communicative but often difficult to implement in a test-oriented context	Communicative	Communicative; TETE is highly recommended (but not fully implemented)	Communicative; aims to reach A1 in CEFR

Required qualifications	BA (primary education for generalist and English language or ELT for specialist); no proficiency requirement; six-months practicum	BA in primary education (for generalists); no proficiency requirement; some BA holders in secondary education (specializing in English)	BA in primary education from 11 national universities of Education or one private university (Ewha); 'teacher recruitment examination for primary schools'; practicum (varies in length)	BA in education; TESOL certificate (preferred); passing MOEs teacher license exam and English proficiency test; three-months practicum
In-service training	Government-, school- and publisher-funded; content and length vary	Government-funded training for select teachers; a cascade model	Local government-funded or university-run trainings; content and length vary	Government-funded, universities and foreign organizations; content and length vary; a cascade model
NS teachers		As assistant language teachers with various capacities; Japan Exchange and Teaching (JET) program; private agencies	As English language instructors; categorized into five levels; Korean Ministry of Education's English Program in Korea (EPIK) and others; plans to have one NS at each school as assistant language teachers	
Other notes	Low salary and an unstable status of specialists; low proficiency; not sufficient training for PEFLT; no centralized curriculum		Competitive to become English teachers in urban areas	Enrichment classes are promoted to students with high abilities and motivation

Note: To create Tables 2.1 and 2.2, the following sources were consulted: Butler (2007a, 2015); Chen (2012); Choi & Lee (2007, 2008); Jeon & Lee (2006); Kang (2012); Le & Do (2012); Li (2016); Manh et al. (2017); Moodie & Nam (2015); Nguyen (2011, 2017); Phuong & Nhu, 2015; Qi (2016); Sze & Wong (1999); Wang & Lin (2013); Wu (2012); Zein (2015, 2016a).

Qualifications for Teaching EPS

Researchers have identified and listed qualifications for teachers in various ways, but the qualifications that are discussed in studies on EPS in Asia are largely (a) English language proficiency; (b) professional knowledge/skills for teaching English to young learners (YLs); and (c) classroom management and other general educational knowledge/skills for YLs. How each element is defined and valued greatly depends on specific cultural and educational contexts where EPS is conducted. Each of these elements is discussed in detail below.

English language proficiency

While policy analyses in Asia generally acknowledge that primary school teachers' English language proficiency is one of the most pressing concerns, there has been little empirical investigation of these teachers' English proficiency. Due to policies' strong promotion of communicative-based language teaching, EPS teachers' pronunciation skills and oral fluency are often problematized across the focus countries (e.g. Chou, 2008; Kusumoto, 2008; Le & Do, 2012; Phuong & Nhu, 2015; Zein, 2015, 2016a, 2017). It is important to note, however, that there is little evidence documenting the impact of teachers' pronunciation skills and oral fluency on young learners' pronunciation skills and oral fluency.

Policies usually indicate that an 'adequate level' of proficiency is necessary for EPS teachers (e.g. Choi & Lee, 2007), but what constitutes an 'adequate level' is often unspecified. Some countries/regions expect their EPS teachers to have 'a high intermediate level' but without stating the rationale for such decisions. In Vietnam, for example, the National Foreign Language 2020 Project asks primary school English teachers to obtain the Common European Framework of Reference for Languages (CEFR) B2 level of English. In reality, only half of the Vietnamese primary school teachers reached this level in 2014/15, although they have substantially improvement in the last few years (Manh et al., 2017). In Hong Kong, the government developed an English proficiency test for English teachers (Language Proficiency Assessment for Teachers of English, LPATE) and requires all English teachers (at both primary and secondary levels) to reach Level 3, which is estimated to roughly correspond to 6.5 in the International English Language Testing System (IELTS). Coniam and Falvey (2013: 153) described this as 'indicative of a level needed to operate at tertiary level' and 'a defensible standard for a non-native speaking teacher of English'. Notably, Hong Kong does not set separate standards for primary and secondary school English teachers. Whether or not the same standards should apply to both types of teachers is an empirical issue. After all, we do not yet have sufficient and reliable empirical data in Asia to inform policies to decide EPS teachers' proficiency levels.

In most Asian countries, EPS teachers' lack of confidence in their English proficiency has been a serious concern. Butler (2004) conducted a study at a relatively early stage of EPS implementation in Japan, Korea and Taiwan using the Stanford Foreign Language Oral Skills Evaluation Matrix (FLOSEM) and found that an overwhelming majority of local teachers (85.3% in Japan, 91.1% in Korea and 80.1% in Taiwan) evaluated their English proficiency as falling short of the perceived minimum level necessary for teaching English under the respective policy requirements. Judging from more recent investigations, EPS teachers – generalists in particular – continue to lack confidence in their English proficiency (e.g. Choi, 2014 in Korea; Le & Do, 2012 in Vietnam; Machida & Walsh, 2015 in Japan; Asriyanti et al., 2013; Zein, 2016a in Indonesia).

One can also assume that substantial regional gaps in resource availability and opportunities to use English, which are usually highly correlated with socioeconomic status (SES), contribute to gaps in teachers' confidence and preparation for teaching English. The regional gaps appear to be particularly serious in China, Indonesia, Thailand and Vietnam (e.g. Baker, 2016; Hamano, 2008; Husein, 2014; Vu & Pham, 2014; Wu, 2012; Zein, 2015). In addition, among upper- and middle-income families, a growing number of YLs receive private English lessons outside of school and such extra English learning seems to create added pressure for some EPS teachers. Song (2011) described a case in South Korea in which teachers' authority was threatened by students who participated in early study-abroad programs and obtained higher English proficiency and intercultural competency than their teachers.

A lack of confidence among teachers has the potential to influence their teaching. Butler (2007b) reported that Korean children were sensitive to local EPS teachers' lack of confidence in their use of English. In Japan, teachers with lower self-evaluated English proficiency tended to show more negative attitudes toward a variety of English (perhaps including their own) (Butler, 2007c). Although Best (2014) did not find a significant correlation between Thai EPS teachers' self-rated proficiency levels and their self-perceived teaching efficacy (perhaps partially due to her study's small sample size), her data suggest that such correlations may depend on the teachers' gender, age and teaching experience.

EPS teachers' English proficiency can also be discussed according to specific educational contexts and policy requirements. For example, Hong Kong's LPATE contains a classroom language assessment that examines candidates' ability to deliver a class in English (defined as grammatical/lexical accuracy, pronunciation, and use of language of interaction and instruction). There have been repeated reports of teachers getting high marks in the classroom language assessment section of the LPATE while performing poorly in the speaking and writing sections of the exam (Coniam & Falvey, 2013). Such discrepancies might indicate the shortcomings of using a proficiency test as a gatekeeper of teachers' English proficiency. Freeman *et al.* (2015), while not limiting their argument to Asian contexts, also proposed that teachers' language proficiency should be conceptualized uniquely, separately from a general proficiency model.

With the widespread promotion of communication-focused language teaching in Asia, primary school teachers are often encouraged to maximize their English use in their classrooms; in some contexts, teaching English through English only (TETE) is recommended by the policy (e.g. Korea and Taiwan). In referring to TETE contexts, Freeman *et al.* (2015) defined teachers' proficiency (English-for-teaching) in three functional areas: understanding and communicating lesson content; assessing students and giving feedback; and managing the classroom. Although nonverbal behaviors such as pointing and gestures can facilitate students' comprehension, researchers have found that YLs are not as good at detecting teachers' nonverbal behaviors as adult learners (Kamiya, 2016); teachers' linguistic abilities to give students clear verbal instructions and feedback appear to be particularly important for YLs. It is critical to note, however, that even in contexts where TETE is strongly promoted or required by the policy, it is not implemented well in practice at the primary school level (Kang, 2012; Rui & Chew, 2013). Studies found that when teachers do not implement TETE, the reason is not necessarily because they lack sufficient English proficiency to do so but often because they realize that TETE is not the best, or even a realistic, approach in their classroom contexts (e.g. Butler, 2015; Choi, 2014; Kang, 2008; Moodie & Nam, 2015). A blind implementation of TETE (or discouraging the use of nontarget languages) may devalue local teachers' bi- or multilinguistic resources that would facilitate YLs' awareness and their learning (e.g. Rui & Chew, 2013 for a case in China). With regards to the English proficiency of EPS teachers, previous studies have often overlooked how their multilingual competencies might in fact help them in their instruction. Some evidence also suggests that YLs are less comfortable with TETE than adults (e.g. Macaro & Lee, 2013 for a case in Korea).

Professional knowledge and skills, classroom management, and other qualifications

Using English in a professional context requires professional content knowledge and content-specific pedagogical strategies (e.g. knowledge about language acquisition, familiarity with communicative language teaching methods, various language assessment strategies, etc.). Insufficient professional knowledge often forces teachers to depend on their own 'traditional' English learning experience, which makes it difficult to apply communicative-based language teaching (CLT), as clearly exemplified in a case in Indonesia (e.g. Hawanti, 2014). It is critically important for EPS teachers to obtain professional knowledge and strategies *specifically meant for YLs*. Teachers, including those with degrees in English teaching, found it challenging to design and implement age-appropriate communicative tasks that can keep children's attention and motivation, particularly among children with diverse proficiency levels, while maintaining the socially expected level of order (Butler, 2015; Lee, 2014; Su, 2006). Implementing CLT among YLs often requires uniquely different pedagogical and classroom management skills from those for adult learners. Lee (2014) found that novice EPS teachers in Korea, despite having greater CLT knowledge than older generalists, felt more skeptical about the effectiveness of CLT, perhaps reflecting their lack of confidence in pedagogical and classroom management skills for YLs. It has also been reported that having secondary school English teachers teach primary school did not work well due to their lack of knowledge and experience working with children (e.g. Vu & Pham, 2014 in Vietnam).

The use of technology in primary classrooms is gaining in popularity, with teachers increasingly needing technology literacy; however, information regarding primary school teachers' technology literacy is limited. Observations indicate that even in contexts where teachers are relatively confident in their technology knowledge, they use technology primarily for maintaining children's attention in class and that technology is not used effectively for enhancing their English learning per se (e.g. Wu & Wang, 2015 in a case in Taiwan). It seems that teachers not only need technology knowledge, but also practical knowledge and experience of how best to use technology for learning in context. Regional gaps in access to technology in classrooms are also a serious challenge in China and some Southeast Asian countries (e.g. Phuong & Nhu, 2015 for a case in Vietnam).

One can argue that teachers' attitudes toward English teaching can be an important element of their qualification as teachers and would influence their pedagogy (Choi & Lee, 2007; Husein, 2014). Unlike other teaching professions, in which we can safely assume that teachers are genuinely motivated to teach the target subject, primary school teachers' motivation or commitment to teaching English seems to vary greatly in Asia. Studies reported that some teachers, generalists in particular, may not want to teach English or may not believe that teaching English should be their responsibility. For example, Le and Do (2012: 152) found that more than 60% of EPS teachers sampled in their survey in rural Vietnam believed that it was 'impossible' or 'almost impossible' to make YLs interested in English and that EPS would not be effective, particularly due to inadequate pedagogical support and grammar-focused exam requirements. Similarly, in Indonesia, the non-mandatory status of English in the school curriculum made primary school teachers (generalists) less enthusiastic about teaching English compared with other subjects (Hawanti, 2014; Zein, 2016a). Kusumoto's (2008) survey study in Japan showed that one third of the primary school teachers in her study did not think that English education was necessary at primary school.

Institutional or policy constraints may make it difficult for teachers to maintain a high degree of motivation to teach EPS. EPS specialists often have a lower or unstable status in their educational system or do not receive financial and other benefits that generalists may enjoy (e.g. Butler, 2007a for Japan; Kang, 2012 for Korea[1]; Hawanti, 2014; and Zein, 2016a for Indonesia; Nguyen, 2011 for Vietnam). In Korea, for example, EPS teachers are chosen by school principals out of the existing faculty; they may alternate between EPS and homeroom teaching regardless of whether they have an English-specialization credential as part of their primary education certificate. Moodie and Feryok's (2015) longitudinal case study of four Korean teachers described dynamic changes in the teachers' mind-sets in their commitment to English learning, English teaching and the interplay between them. Various factors – such as students' difficult behaviors, the school rotation system (public school teachers are required to rotate schools every once in a while in Korea) and extra administrative work imposed on English teachers – influenced their commitments. A teacher in their study with 12 years of experience as a generalist described having difficulties with classroom management after she became an English teacher due to the lower status of English teachers at her school. This example suggests a complex interplay among teachers' various qualifications (e.g. proficiency, professional knowledge and classroom management skills), commitments, affects and contextual factors in the given educational system.

Ambiguity of Expected Qualifications for NSs

As Kaplan and Baldauf (1997) discussed, when governments introduce a new language into the school curriculum, it is a common strategy for them to hire native speakers (NSs) of the target language. Indeed, recruitment of native English speakers is commonly exercised in Asia as well, more notably in East Asia. NSs are often hired to compensate for the lack of sufficient English proficiencies of local non-native speaking (NNS) teachers or a shortage of English teachers, particularly in rural areas. Hiring NSs can be promoted in part as a response to persistent requests from parents (Butler, 2015); however, the roles of NSs are not always clearly defined in policies in East Asia and teaching certificates are usually not required for NSs. Some countries, such as Korea and Hong Kong, categorize NSs into different levels based on their qualifications (e.g. a teaching certificate and experience teaching English) and adjust their salaries accordingly. Wang and Lin (2013) examined government-based NS policies in Japan, Korea, Taiwan and Hong Kong, and observed that, although precise expected duties of NSs in classrooms vary across these countries, they all have the following responsibilities: (a) NSs are required to co-teach the class with local NNS teachers and (b) they are expected to provide NNS teachers with professional development. These two responsibilities reveal ambiguous or even contradictory conceptualizations of NS teacher qualifications. On the one hand, inhibiting NSs from teaching independently in class, along with not requiring them to have a teaching certificate, downplays their pedagogical qualification as teaching specialists. On the other hand, their pedagogical expertise is assumed as a provider of teacher training for local teachers.

Such policy ambiguity makes collaboration between NS and NNS teachers difficult; both groups of teachers may have different expectations (Chen & Cheng, 2010; Luo, 2007; Machida & Walsh, 2015). According to Luo's (2007) study in Taiwan, for example, NNS teachers thought that NSs' lack of pedagogical knowledge and inflexibility in accommodating local educational practice were the major obstacles to co-teaching, whereas NS teachers believed that NNS teachers' poor English proficiency and unwillingness to try new English teaching methods posed the most significant challenges to co-teaching. Carless (2006), who focused on three 'good practices' of team teaching between NSs and NNSs (or what he called 'intercultural team teaching') from Japan, Korea and Hong Kong, identified a few common conditions for success. Such conditions included being sensitive to interpersonal relationships with local participants; developing relationships inside and outside of the classroom; being willing to compromise; letting go of minor obstacles; making a long-term commitment; and respecting local classroom practices even when holding different views (Carless, 2006: 350). Importantly, except for the last condition (which is specifically meant for NSs), all the other conditions apply to every teacher regardless of NS/NNS status.

Many applied linguists have criticized the concept of 'native speakers' and have questioned dichotomous conceptualizations of NSs and NNSs in the first place (e.g. Davies, 2003; Llurda, 2005). Accordingly, *the native-speaker norm for language teaching* – a hidden assumption underlying policies to hire NSs as English teachers – is arguably inappropriate. And yet Asian governments still seem to be largely committed to this idea. In particular, as we can see in descriptions of 'native speakers' in government-based NS recruitment programs, they defined very narrowly (i.e. as speakers of English from the *Inner Circle* regions such as the UK and USA (Kachru, 1982)). Such a narrow conceptualization of 'native speakers', along with setting 'native speakers' English' as the norm, may result in devaluing a variety of Englishes (including those of local NNS teachers) and, as Wang and Lin (2013: 5) warned, may potentially be 'jeopardizing the professional identity of local non-native English-speaking teachers'. Indeed, studies have shown that is it challenging to introduce a variety of Englishes in EPS classrooms in Asia. For example, Chen and Cheng (2010: 41) reported that 'native speakers' from South Africa faced difficulties teaching in Taiwan due to the locals' 'doubts on their accents'. Similarly, Kang (2012) addressed challenges in convincing parents in Korea that well-trained NNS teachers are highly capable of teaching English despite their 'non-native' accents. It is important to note that teachers' nonstandard accented English does not necessarily negatively influence YLs' actual comprehension (intelligibility) even when the children show a preference for 'standard native-speaker's' accents (Butler, 2007b).

Professional Development for Teachers of EPS

In order to make sure that EPS teachers develop the above-mentioned qualifications (i.e. English proficiency, professional knowledge/skills for teaching English to young learners, and classroom management and other general educational knowledge/skills for YLs), professional training is absolutely key. Governments in the focus countries, both at the central and local levels, offer various types of professional development opportunities to pre-service and in-service teaches. In recent years, researchers have conducted a growing number of case studies on ESP teacher trainings in Asia (e.g. Baker, 2016; Graham, 2009; Huong & Yeo, 2016; Lan & Wang, 2013; Moser *et al.*, 2012; Ping, 2013; Supriyanti, 2012; Vu & Pham, 2014; Zein, 2017). An overwhelmingly majority of these studies described the implementation processes of a particular training program and/or examined stakeholders' perceptions of their experiences with such trainings through surveys and interviews. A few of them also employed classroom observations. These studies revealed three major challenges in professional development of ESP teachers in Asia. First, since EPS is a recently implemented policy, governments need efficient means of training a massive number of EPS teachers. Second, given the emphasis on communicative-based language teaching (CLT), EPS teachers need to learn how to implement new pedagogical methods and strategies. And finally, as opposed to a traditional 'knowledge transmission' model of professional development, a new approach to teacher trainings is called for. These issues are elaborated on below.

Training a substantial number of new EPS teachers 'efficiently'

In order to meet the great demand for EPS teachers, as mentioned already, some Asian governments primarily ask generalists to teach English in addition to other subjects, whereas other countries train new specialists. When it comes to training generalists, South Korea initially took a direct approach, requiring all teachers to take a minimum of 120 hours of government-based training when EPS was first introduced. The majority of training hours were dedicated to improving teachers' English proficiency (e.g. Butler, 2015; Kang 2012). This approach requires substantial financial and labor commitments, but it is a way to ensure that all teachers access the minimum basic training to teach EPS. Other governments employed a top-down, multilayered approach – the so-called cascade model – to train teachers. In this model, a small group of teachers receive training initially and they in turn serve as trainers who transmit the information to other teachers. The advantage of the cascade model for the government is that it is much less expensive and less labor intensive than the direct model. Although empirical studies on cascade models in EPS in Asia are very limited, the handful of studies (e.g. Baker, 2016 for a case in Thailand; Ping, 2013 for a case in China; Hamano, 2008 and Vu & Pham, 2014 for cases in Vietnam) show a number of problems when the model was implemented. One of the major challenges appears to be that a fundamental premise of the cascade model – namely, to pass information down through the layers of teachers 'accurately' – does not meet the real needs of teachers. In the cascade model, in principle, there is no room for teachers to modify and adapt the information they receive to fit their own contexts or students' needs. A lack of follow-up support for teacher trainers (the teachers who received training initially) as well as for local teachers is a critical limitation in the cascade model. It may take some time for teacher trainers to learn how to lead in such a way that is considered appropriate in the given context (e.g. Baker, 2016). In Vietnam, a number of international agencies have used a cascade model of teacher training (Hamano, 2008), but the extent to which imported training models are effective in Vietnam needs to be systematically evaluated. In Indonesia, under the promotion of decentralized education policy, there is some bureaucratic tension between government-based training institutions and local administrators regarding how to implement the training and the role they should play in the process (Zein, 2016b). In essence, granting greater autonomy and allocating sufficient resources at the local levels are necessary in order for the participants to be satisfied with the training they receive.

Introducing new pedagogy for YLs

The second challenge is to train teachers to implement a communicative language teaching (CLT) pedagogy for young learners (Moser *et al.*, 2012). CLT differs from traditional grammar-translation methods that most teachers are familiar with, and in addition, what has proven to be effective in CLT for adult learners may not necessarily work well with YLs. As mentioned, while CLT is strongly advocated in language education, for it to be effective it must be adapted to the particular social and educational contexts as well as the learners' age (Butler, 2015; Thomas & Reinders, 2015). For creating workable adaptations, local and practical knowledge and experiences are indispensable. In both pre-service and in-service teacher trainings, however, one of the common problems reported is a lack of expertise in English teaching pedagogies *focusing on YLs among teacher trainers*. Although researchers have identified knowledge-based components necessary for EPS teachers (e.g. Chou, 2008; Zein, 2016c), we do not yet have comprehensive pedagogical methods and strategies for teaching a foreign language to YLs. This in turn relates to inadequate designing of the content of teacher training programs. Teacher trainers are often limited in their experience with using CLT with YLs and they may not have sufficient understanding of local teachers' practical needs (e.g. Nguyen, 2017; Supriyanti, 2012; Zein, 2015, 2016b). In some contexts, such as Indonesia, teacher trainers are constrained by various bureaucratic regulations that leave them with insufficient autonomy to better meet the needs of local teachers (Zein, 2016b). In many pre-service primary teacher training programs, the curriculum is already very crowded; securing enough course hours for English is a challenge in the first place, especially for generalists. And the curriculum tends to be theory-focused and often not targeted for YLs. Insufficient practicum hours in professional development (both pre-service and in-service trainings) also seem to be a common problem in Asia (Huong & Yeo, 2016; Wati, 2011; Zein, 2016b). Moreover, during the practicum, pre-service student teachers or novice teachers often find a substantial gap between what their mentors actually do in their classrooms and what they were taught to do in their pre-service training programs at college (e.g. Mann & Tang, 2012). The prevalence of hierarchical relations in Asian society often makes it difficult for student teachers or novice teachers to implement something new; it is not uncommon for them to simply follow their mentors' old-fashioned approaches (e.g. Nguyen, 2017). Sufficient follow-up during the practicum or the first year of teaching appears to be critical.

Introducing new approaches to professional development

The final major challenge is to implement a new approach to professional development. Nguyen (2017: 11) described Vietnam's teacher training as 'transmissive and prescriptive methods'. Judging from the available case studies (e.g. Huong & Yao, 2016; Supriyanti, 2012; Vu & Pham, 2014; Wati, 2011; Zein, 2016b, 2017), such methods still appear to be relatively common in many other parts of Asia as well. In the 'transmissive and prescriptive methods', student teachers and novice teachers observe experienced teachers' (or assigned mentors') lessons and learn from their practice. But this approach affords little opportunity for student teachers or novice teachers to converse about ideas, work with other teachers collaboratively or receive sufficient feedback on their own teaching. Mentors' understanding of their own roles appears to vary tremendously and mentors often fail to offer kinds of feedback that novice teachers want. For example, in a case study of four first-year novice teachers in Hong Kong, Mann and Tang (2012) found that mentoring did not work effectively, that mentors and mentees alike needed more support and that shared practice was not encouraged enough. They argued that experienced teachers may not necessarily be good mentors and that relatively inexperienced teachers may be more likely to play 'a collaborative and empathetic role' (Mann & Tang, 2012: 489).

In place of traditional 'transmissive and prescriptive methods', more mutual and reflective professional development methods have been promoted in Asia in recent years. In those methods, through a cycle of observation, demonstration, evaluation and modification of lessons, teachers have sufficient opportunities to reflect back on their own practice. Such reflective methods are perceived positively by participants (e.g. Lan & Wang, 2013; Ping, 2013; also see Kirkgöz, Chapter 8 in this volume). As a way to create a collaborative or collegial atmosphere in order to maximize teachers' opportunities for reflection in Asian contexts, peer or group mentoring/coaching has gained increasing attention. Although there are few empirical studies on peer-group mentoring/coaching among EPS teachers, judging from studies conducted among secondary school English teachers in Asia (e.g. Nguyen, 2017), the approach is promising. Providing a collegial and supporting environment is not enough, however. Butler and Yeum (2016), by examining teachers' mutual feedback and reflective comments during a semester-long online peer-coaching session among EPS in-service teachers in Korea, found that teachers need to develop a series of competencies – what they called 'dialogic competence' – in order to make valuable exchanges to facilitate self-reflection and mutual learning. It may take some time, as well as long-term support, for teachers to develop such competence.

Conclusions and Implications

This chapter identifies major issues and challenges regarding EPS language policies and teacher education in China, Indonesia, Japan, South Korea, Taiwan, Thailand and Vietnam. Although the focus has been on select Asian regions, many of the issues discussed apply to contexts beyond Asia.

First, the field needs a better understanding of EPS teachers' qualifications. EPS teachers' insufficient English proficiency is frequently articulated in both academic and public discourses. There is no question that EPS teachers' English proficiency is important; however, EPS teachers' proficiency should be defined in contexts. As Kirkpatrick (2011b) suggested in the context of the Association of Southeast Asian Nations (ASEAN), one can argue that both teachers' and learners' proficiency goals should be determined in relation to the local use of English as a lingua franca. In determining teachers' necessary proficiency level, therefore, it is important to avoid basing it on a native speaker's norm. In defining proficiency, closer attention to other qualifications is necessary as well. More empirical studies examining the relationship between teachers' qualifications and their actual teaching performance are needed. Such studies should be used to inform curriculum development for teacher training and certification guidelines (for both local and NS teachers).

Second, the language education profession needs a better understanding of communicative-based teaching pedagogy targeting young learners. Studies across regions repeatedly report a lack of expertise among teacher trainers – both at the university and local (mentor) levels. The field of instructed second language acquisition has largely developed around adult learners until relatively recently, and our knowledge and expertise targeting young learners remains limited. More basic and applied research, particularly EPS teachers' action research, should be encouraged.

Finally, we need to better understand the 'effectiveness' of different professional development approaches. Most studies are based on stakeholders' perceptions (through surveys and interviews). While stakeholder insights are critically important to better understand their needs, we need more ways of capturing the effectiveness of these professional development activities. As we have seen above, cascade models are still popular in Asia, but we know little about how information is 'transmitted' at local levels. We also know little about the effectiveness of newer professional development approaches for EPS teachers in Asia, such as peer/group mentoring and online professional courses. Importantly, we need a long-term perspective on such evaluations. From previous studies, it is apparent that short-term, one-shot trainings/workshops have limited effects. Past research also suggests that not only mentees, also but many mentors, need to have professional training. In essence, as Phung and Nhu (2015) suggested, long-term sustainable support for teachers are the key for successful implementatiocn of EPS.

Note

(1)   Lower status among English conversation teachers was discussed.

References

Asriyanti, E., Sikki, A., Rahman, A., Hamra, A. and Noni, N. (2013) The competence of primary school English teachers in Indonesia. *Journal of Education and Practice* 4 (11), 139–146.

Baker, L.L. (2016) Re-conceptualizing EFL professional development: Enhancing communicative language pedagogy for Thai teachers. *TEFLIN Journal* 27, 23–45.

Best, B. (2014) A study of elementary school Thai English teachers' perceived English proficiency and self-reported English teaching efficacy. *Language in India* 14 (7). See http://www.languageinindia.com/july2014/barbarathaieslteachersfinal.html (accessed 28 October 2018).

Butler, Y.G. (2004) What level of English proficiency do elementary school teachers need to attain in order to teach EFL?: Case studies from Korea, Taiwan, and Japan. *TESOL Quarterly* 38 (2), 245–278.

Butler, Y.G. (2007a) Foreign language education at elementary schools in Japan: Searching for solutions amidst growing diversification. *Current Issues in Language Planning* 8 (2), 129–147.

Butler, Y.G. (2007b) How are nonnative-English-speaking teachers perceived by young learners? *TESOL Quarterly* 41 (4), 731–755.

Butler, Y.G. (2007c) Factors associated with the notion that native speakers are the ideal language teachers: An examination of elementary school teachers in Japan. *JALT Journal* 29 (1), 7–40.

Butler, Y.G. (2015) English language education n among young learners in East Asia: A review of current research. *Language Teaching* 48 (3), 303–342.

Butler, Y.G. and Yeum, K. (2016) Dialogic competence of primary school English teachers in online peer coaching: A case study in South Korea. *The Journal of Asia TEFL* 13 (2), 72–89.

Carless, D.R. (2006) Good practices in team teaching in Japan, South Korea and Hong Kong. *System* 34, 341–351.

Chen, C. (2012) Framework and implementation of primary school English education in Taiwan. In B. Spolsky and Y.-I. Moon (eds) *Primary School English-Language Education in Asia: From Policy to Practice* (pp. 167–186). New York: Routledge.

Chen, C.W. and Cheng, Y. (2010) A case study on foreign English teachers' challenges in Taiwanese elementary schools. *System* 38, 41–49.

Choi, J.-H. (2014) Primary school novice teachers' perceptions of English education and development of English teaching skills. *Primary English Education* 20 (4), 349–373.

Choi, Y.-H. and Lee, H.-W. (2007) A model of English teacher development in Asia based on surveys on teacher qualifications and education programs. *The Journal of Asia TEFL* 4 (4), 1–34.

Choi, Y.-H. and Lee, H.-W. (2008) Current trends and issues in English language education in Asia. *The Journal of Asia TEFL* 5 (2), 1–34.

Chou, C. (2008) Exploring elementary English teachers' practical knowledge: A case study of EFL teachers in Taiwan. *Asia Pacific Education Review* 9 (4), 529–541.

Coniam, D. and Falvey, P. (2013) Ten years on: The Hong Kong language proficiency assessment for teachers of English (LPATE). *Language Testing* 30 (1), 147–155.

Davies, A. (2003) *The Native Speaker: Myth and Reality.* Clevedon: Multilingual Matters.

Enever, J. (2015) The advantages and disadvantages of English as a foreign language with young learners. In J. Bland (ed.) *Teaching English to Young Learners: Critical Issues in Language Teaching with 3–12 Year Olds* (pp. 13–29). London: Bloomsbury.

Freeman, D., Katz, A., Gomez, P.G. and Burns, A. (2015) English-for-teaching: Rethinking teacher proficiency in the classroom. *ELT Journal* 69 (2), 129–139.

Graham, S. (2009) From the bottom up: A case study of teacher training for primary school teachers of English in a Thai school in Northern Eastern Thailand. *ELTED* 12. See https://www.researchgate.net/publication/265002887_FROM_THE_BOTTOM_UP_A_CASE_STUDY_OF_TEACHER_TRAINING_FOR_PRIMARY_SCHOOL_TEACHERS_OF_ENGLISH_IN_A_THAI_SCHOOL_IN_NORTH_EASTERN_THAILAND (accessed 1 October 2017).

Hamano, T. (2008) Educational reform and teacher education in Vietnam. *Journal of Education for Teaching* 34 (4), 397–410.

Hawanti, S. (2014) Implementing Indonesia's English language policy in primary schools: The role of teachers' knowledge and beliefs. *International Journal of Pedagogies and Learning* 9 (2), 162–170.

Huong, L.P.H. and Yeo, M. (2016) Evaluating in-service training of primary English teachers: A case study in central Vietnam. *Asian EL Journal* 18 (1), 34–51.

Husein, R. (2014) A profile of exemplary teachers of English for young learners at the elementary school. *Jurnal Pedidikan Humaniora* 2 (4), 311–321.

Jeon, M. and Lee, J. (2006) Hiring native-speaking English teachers in East Asian countries. *English Today* 22 (4), 53–58.

Kachru, B.B. (1982) *The Other Tongue: English Across Cultures.* Urbana, IL: University of Illinois Press.

Kamiya, N. (2016) The effect of learner age on the interpretation of the nonverbal behaviors of teachers and other students in identifying questions in the L2 classroom. *Language Teaching Research.* doi:10.1177/1362168816658303

Kang, D.-M. (2008) The classroom language use of a Korean elementary school EFL teacher: Another look at TETE. *System* 36, 214–226.

Kang, H.-D. (2012) Primary school English education in Korea: From policy to practice. In B. Spolsky and Y. Moon (eds) *Primary School English – Language Education in Asia: From Policy to Practice* (pp. 79–108). New York: Routledge.

Kaplan, R.B. and Baldauf, R.B. (1997) Language planning: From practice to theory. Clevedon: Multilingual Matters.

Kirkpatrick, A. (2011a) English as a medium of instruction in Asian education (from primary to tertiary): Implications for local languages and local scholarship. *Applied Linguistics Review* 11, 99–119.

Kirkpatrick, A. (2011b) English as an Asian lingua franca and the multilingual model of ELT. *Language Teaching* 44 (2), 212–224.

Kubota, R. (2015) *Gurōbaruka syakai-to gengo kyoiku: kuritekaru-na shiten-kara [Language education in an era of globalization: critical perspectives]*. Tokyo: Kuroshio.

Kusumoto, Y. (2008) Needs analysis: Developing a teacher training program for elementary school homeroom teachers in Japan. *Second Language Studies* 26 (2), 1–44.

Lan, M.H. and Wang, K.-P. (2013) The effects of reflective teaching on an intensive teacher training program. *Indonesian Journal of Applied Linguistics* 3 (1), 81–102.

Le, V.C. and Do, C.T.M. (2012) Teacher preparation for primary school English education: A case of Vietnam. In B. Spolsky and Y. Moon (eds) *Primary School English-Language Education in Asia: From Policy to Practice* (pp. 139–166). New York: Routledge.

Lee, M.W. (2014) Will communicative language teaching work? Teachers' perceptions towards new educational reform in South Korea. *Indonesian Journal of Applied Linguistics* 3 (2), 1–17.

Li, J. (2016) *Quest for World-Class Teacher Education: A Multiperspectival Study on the Chinese Model of Policy Implementation*. Singapore: Springer.

Li, M. (2011) Shaping socialist ideology through language education policy for primary schools in the PRC. *Current Issues in Language Planning* 12 (2), 185–204.

Llurda, E. (ed.) (2005) *Non-Native Language Teachers: Perceptions, Challenges and Contributions to the Profession*. New York: Springer.

Luo, W.-H. (2007) A study of native English-speaking teacher programs in elementary schools in Taiwan. *Asia Pacific Education Review* 8 (2), 311–320.

Macaro, E. and Lee, J.H. (2013) Teacher language background, codeswitching, and English-only instruction: Does age make a difference to learners' attitudes? *TESOL Quarterly* 47 (4), 717–742.

Machida, T. and Walsh, D.J. (2015) Implementing EFL policy reform in elementary schools in Japan: A case study. *Current Issues in Language Planning* 16 (3), 221–237.

Manh, D.D., Nguyen H.T.M. and Burns, A. (2017) Teacher language proficiency and reform of English language education in Vietnam, 2008–2020. In D. Freeman and L.L. Dréan (eds) *Developing Classroom English Competence: Learning from the Vietnam Experience* (pp. 19–33). Phnom Penh: IDP Education.

Mann, S. and Tang, E.H.H. (2012) The role of mentoring in supporting novice English language teachers in Hong Kong. *TESOL Quarterly* 46 (3), 472–495.

Moodie, I. and Feryok, A. (2015) Beyond cognition to commitment: English language teaching in in South Korean primary schools. *The Modern Language Journal* 99 (3), 450–469.

Moodie, I. and Nam, H.-J. (2015) English language teaching research in South Korea: A review of recent studies (2009–2014). *Language Teaching* 49 (1), 63–98.

Moser, J., Harris, J. and Carle, J. (2012) Improving teacher talk through a task-based approach. *ELT Journal* 66 (1), 81–88.

Nguyen, H.T.M. (2011) Primary English language education policy in Vietnam: Insights from implementation. *Current Issues in Language Planning* 12 (2), 225–249.

Nguyen, H.T.M. (2017) *Models of Mentoring in Language Teacher Education.* Switzerland: Springer.

Ojima, S., Matsuba-Kurita, N., Nakamura, N., Hoshino, T. and Hagiwara, H. (2011) Age and amount of exposure to a foreign language during childhood: Behavioral and ERP data on the semantic comprehension of spoken English by Japanese children. *Neuroscience Research* 70 (2), 197–205.

Phuong, L.N.T. and Nhu, T.P. (2015) Innovation in English language education in Vietnam for ASEAN 2015 Integration: Current issues, challenges, opportunities, investments and solutions. In R. Stroupe and K. Kimura (eds) *ASEAN Integration and the Role of English Language Teaching* (pp. 104–120). Phnom Penh: IELTS.

Ping, W. (2013) Perspectives on English teacher development in rural primary schools in China. *Journal of Pedagogy* 4 (2), 208–219.

Qi, G.Y. (2016) The importance of English in primary school education in China: Perceptions of students. *Multilingual Education* 6 (1). doi: 10.1186/s13616-016-0026-0

Rui, T. and Chew, P.G.-L. (2013) Pedagogical use of two languages in a Chinese elementary school. *Language, Culture and Curriculum* 26 (3), 317–331.

Song, J. (2011) Globalization, children's study abroad, and transnationalism as an emerging context for language learning: A new task for language teacher education. *TESOL Quarterly* 45 (4), 749–758.

Spolsky, B. and Moon, Y. (eds) (2012) *Primary School English – Language Education in Asia: From Policy to Practice.* New York: Routledge.

Su, Y.-C. (2006) EFL teachers' perceptions of English language policy at the elementary level in Taiwan. *Educational Studies* 32 (3), 265–283.

Sze, P. and Wong, H. (1999) The Hong Kong English syllabus and its relevance for English learning in a context of compulsory schooling. *Hong Kong Educational Research Journal* 14 (2), 253–278.

Supriyanti, N. (2012) Challenges in providing trainings for English teachers of elementary schools. *Journal of Education and Learning* 6 (3), 161–166.

Thomas, M. and Reinders, H. (eds) (2015) *Contemporary Task-Based Language Teaching in Asia.* London: Bloomsbury.

Vu, M.T. and Pham, T.T.T. (2014) Training of trainers for primary English teachers in Viet Nam: Stakeholder evaluation. *The Journal of Asia TEFL* 11 (4), 89–108.

Wang, L.-Y. and Lin, T.-B. (2013) The representation of professionalism in native English-speaking teachers recruitment policies: A comparative study of Hong Kong, Japan, Korea, and Taiwan. *English Teaching: Practice and Critique* 12 (3), 5–22.

Wati, H. (2011) The effectiveness of Indonesian English teachers training programs in improving confidence and motivation. *International Journal of Instruction* 4 (1), 79–104.

Wu, X. (2012) *Primary English education in China: From policy to practice.* In B. Spolsky and Y.-I. Moon (eds) *Primary School English-Language Education in Asia: From Policy to Practice* (pp. 1–28). New York: Routledge.

Wu, Y.-T. and Wang, A.Y. (2015) Technological, pedagogical, and content knowledge in teaching English as a foreign language: Representation of primary teachers of English in Taiwan. *Asia-Pacific Education Review* 24 (3), 525–533.

Zein, M.S. (2015) Preparing elementary English teachers: Innovations at pre-service level. *Australian Journal of Teacher Education* 40 (6), 104–120. doi:10.14221/ajte.2015v40n6.6

Zein, M.S. (2016a) Elementary English education in Indonesia: Policy developments, current practices, and future prospects. *English Today.* doi:10.1017/S0266078416000407

Zein, M.S. (2016b) Factors affecting the professional development of elementary English teachers. *Professional Development Education* 42 (3), 423–440. doi:10.1080/19415257.2015.1005243

Zein, M.S. (2016c) Pre-service education for primary school English teachers in Indonesia: Policy implications. *Asia Pacific Journal of Education* 36 (S1), 119–134. doi:10.1080/02188791.2014.961899

Zein, M.S. (2017) Professional development needs of primary EFL teachers: Perspectives of teachers and teacher educators. *Professional Development in Education* 43 (2), 293–313. doi:10.1080/19415257.2016.1156013

Part 1

The Complexity of Teacher Learning

3 Unpacking the Complexity of Learning to Teach English to Young Learners: A Narrative Inquiry

Le Van Canh

Introduction

The widespread introduction of English as a foreign language in primary schools across the globe has been described by Johnstone (2009: 33) as 'possibly the world's biggest policy development in education'. Accordingly, there has been a considerable amount of research investigating multiple issues related to the teaching of English to primary school students. The most notable issues include language policy and planning (e.g. Baldauf *et al.*, 2012; Butler, 2015), contextual challenges (e.g. Copland *et al.*, 2014; Garton, 2014), teachers' research engagement (e.g. Barkhuizen, 2011), pre-service teacher education (e.g. Enever, 2014; Zein, 2015, 2016a), and teachers' target language proficiency and their needs for professional development (Butler, 2004; Kabilan & Veratharaju, 2013; Zein, 2017).

By contrast, empirical inquiries into how primary English teachers make sense of their experiences to develop their practical knowledge (Elbaz, 1983) remain scarce, particularly in Asian contexts, where few studies such as Chou's (2008) investigation into how three Taiwanese in-service teachers' conceptualized their practical knowledge, have been documented. As Johnson (2009: 2) has noted, 'The professional education of teachers is, at its core, about *teachers as learners of teaching*' (original emphasis). And if the learning of teaching constitutes the central mission of second language teacher education, then it is imperative to deepen our understanding of teacher learning. As a result, Copland and Garton (2014) calls for more research into teacher education in teaching English to young learners (EYLs).

The study reported in this chapter is an attempt to offer an insight into how practicing teachers create personal understanding and meaning regarding teaching English to young learners (TEYLs) by using their lived experiences. Empirical data will be used to inform teacher educators and policy makers of the complexity of teacher learning and necessary changes to support the natural emergence of teacher learning. The chapter begins with a literature review of teacher learning, followed by the description of the Vietnamese primary school English-language teacher education. Next, the methodological choice for data collection and analysis is outlined before the discussion of the results related to the process of teacher learning as well as the contextual influence on that process. The chapter concludes with suggestions on how to create a social ecology for teacher learning experiences to be powerful enough to transform teaching.

Teacher Learning

The field of second language teacher education has shifted from behaviourist to cognitive to situated, social and distributed views of human cognition to a complex, chaotic systems ontology (Burns *et al.*, 2015; Feryok, 2010; Golombek & Doran, 2014). Prior to the 1970s, second language teacher education was greatly influenced by the linear epistemology, according to which teachers were trained to master a set of skills and competences, assuming that they would apply those skills and competences to their classroom teaching. Teacher-training qualifications, which were offered by teacher training institutions, were believed to be adequate for good teaching. However, from the 1980s, the nature of teacher learning was reconceptualized (Bailey & Nunan, 1996; Burns & Richards, 2009; Freeman & Richards, 1996). As a result of this movement, teacher learning and thinking have become established as core concepts in educational research (Freeman, 1996), which has led to a re-examination of the stories and common assumptions by which teaching and teacher education are done. This emergent research agenda is based on the new epistemological stance that views teaching as a complex cognitive undertaking, and human cognition as being socially situated and distributed (Borg, 2003; Burns *et al.*, 2015; Lave & Wenger, 1991; Putnam & Borko, 2000). This sociocognitive approach views teachers as individuals who learn, shape and are shaped by the activity of teaching.

According to sociocognitive theorists, teacher learning 'is usefully understood as a process of increasing participation in the practice of teaching, and through this participation, a process of becoming knowledgeable in and about teaching' (Adler, 2000: 37). In a similar vein, Golombek and Johnson (2004: 309–310) see teacher learning as 'a dynamic, socially mediated process that occurs as a direct result of participation in social activities that are structured and gain meaning in historically and culturally situated ways.'

These theoretical perspectives are in line with ecologically informed approaches to research on learning and development, which are concerned with the quality of learning environments, and account for temporal and spatial dimensions of development (van Lier, 2004). Accordingly, teacher learning is contextually situated and constructed by individual teachers as they interact with the social and professional conditions of the environments in which they learn and teach. The learning context, be it the course classroom, the school classroom or the virtual environment, can either enhance or inhibit learning. This sociocognitive approach to teacher education and teacher learning recognizes that a bottom-up approach to research, which starts with teachers and what they do, will help to identify ecologies of practices and consider the pivotal role of context in teacher education research (Kubanyiova & Feryok, 2015). However, Zein (2016b: 218), in investigating the professional development of Indonesian teachers of English for young learners, has pointed out the inadequacy of this approach to teacher professional development in explaining the complexity of teacher professional learning as 'various factors and actors' are interrelated 'in a dynamic fashion'.

Very recently, recognizing the inherent complexity and situatedness of teacher learning, scholars (Burns *et al.*, 2015; Feryok, 2010; Golombek & Doran, 2014), called for the adoption of the complexity theory (Larsen-Freeman & Cameron, 2008) to second language teacher research in order to gain insights into how second language teachers make meaning of their experiences. The complexity theory places great emphasis on the initial conditions, since these 'form the system's landscape and influence the trajectory of the system as it changes' (Larsen-Freeman & Cameron, 2008: 230). Investigating teacher learning from a complexity theory perspective implies a thorough understanding and an appreciation of how initial conditions shaped by the teacher's past experiences, present circumstances and future images configure the varied directions and pathways of their professional development. This line of thinking has been adopted by Kiss (2012), who analyzed student teacher learning in an intensive postgraduate course, focusing specifically on how teachers made meaning by drawing on their past experiences. Kiss concluded from his study that teacher learning can be viewed as dynamic, non-linear, dependent on initial conditions (prior experiences), unpredictable and chaotic, and that this perspective has important implications for teacher education programmes. Zein (2016b) also used complexity theory to frame his study on the professional development of Indonesian primary school teachers of English. He noted the highly complex nature of professional development when it involves various actors in different layers of education, among which government-based training institutions are most prominent. Opfer and Pedder's (2011) literature review on teacher professional learning demonstrates that teacher learning emerges from the complex interaction among elements of three subsystems: the teacher, the school, and the learning activity. The literature review, however, reveals the need to have more in-depth qualitative studies that are to zoom out the lens of investigation in order to tease out the complexity of teacher learning. Such zooming out is further warranted by a lack of attention to how primary school teachers learn to teach EYLs. Those investigations are particularly necessary in Asian countries, where the lowering of the starting age of learning English has been phenomenal in recent years, despite the lack of both a pedagogy that is appropriate for young learners (Copland & Garton, 2014) and adequately trained teachers in these contexts (Nunan, 2003).

As Cameron (2001: 1) has noted, 'Knowledge about children learning is seen as central to effective teaching.' While the 'younger-is-better' assumption is a common motivation to the introduction of English to the primary school, policy makers tend to ignore the fact that in order to maximize learning and provide support and challenge in learning, it is crucial for the teacher to be well-informed about the learner. It is vital for EYL teachers, therefore, to have information about the physical, emotional, conceptual and educational characteristics of the young learner and consider certain issues and views on how children think and learn. This makes TEYLs is more complex than it is commonly assumed.

In this study, teacher learning covers both 'learning in pre-service courses and learning through in-service training on the job, which is non-formal, individual and social processes of learning in which [teachers] participate as they are becoming teachers and doing the work of classroom teaching' (Freeman, 2006: 241). Specifically, the study is aimed to unpack the complexity of the meaning-making of lived experiences by a practising EYL teacher within the context of a Vietnamese primary school. Therefore, the complexity theory is adopted for the study. There are three major reasons for the adoption of the complexity theory for the study. First, the theory recognizes 'the lived complexity of the work of language teaching, how that work is learned, and how it is carried out' (Burns et al., 2015: 597). It rejects simplistic cause and effect explanations of teacher learning, which is the legacy of behaviourism, and accepts the non-linear, dynamic nature of teacher learning (Larsen-Freeman & Cameron, 2008). Another reason is that the adoption of the complexity theory is aligned with the fourth ontology – the complex, chaotic systems ontology – recommended by Burns et al. (2015) for researching teacher learning.

Primary School English-Language Teacher Education in Vietnam

The standard path into the career of foreign language teaching in Vietnam is a three-year junior college (cao đẳng sư phạm) or four-year university (đại học sư phạm) degree of foreign language education. The training programme is composed of three domains: (1) foundational courses including Marxist philosophy, child psychology, educational psychology and Vietnamese culture; (2) English proficiency domain (or subject-matter knowledge domain) including communicative skills in English, phonology, grammar, semantics, pragmatics, discourse analysis, English literature and the target culture; and (3) pedagogical content knowledge including the practicum. While English was officially introduced into the primary school curriculum in 2010 with four instructional hours (35 minutes each) per week, starting from Grade 3, many primary schools in urban areas started the teaching of English as an optional subject as early as 1997 (Le & Do, 2012; Nguyen, 2011). However, teacher education institutions in Vietnam did not provide the training of primary school English-language teachers until 2010. The 14-credit Pedagogical Content Knowledge Domain for primary school English language teachers consists of six courses (see Table 3.1) although there may be minor variation from institution to institution.

According to Nguyen (2013: 48), pre-service teacher education in Vietnam could only help trainee teachers to have superficial pedagogical content knowledge while too little attention was given to 'contextual knowledge, pedagogical reasoning and decision making'. Put differently, the Vietnamese contemporary teacher education programme can, at best, help trainee teachers to pick up the 'tricks of the trade', to use Lortie's (1975) words, rather than understanding the underlying principles of teaching young learners and the relationship of teaching to learning.

In Vietnam, teacher continuing professional development is commonly called in-service teacher education (*bồi dưỡng giáo viên*), which tends to refer to one-shot in-service workshops that are organized top-down once a year during the summer vacation either nationally or locally. The cascade model is commonly used (Hamano, 2008) and lecturing by university professors the common mode of delivery. The duration of these courses or workshops varies from one day to a couple of weeks (Pham, 2001) with the number of participant teachers ranging from 50 to more than 100. It is not unusual if 200 participant teachers are seated in one large hall listening to lectures. Vietnamese educators and administrators tend to believe that teacher change is simply a linear process, which is rooted in teachers' accumulated subject-matter knowledge and pedagogical content knowledge (Le, 2011). The input of in-service courses is either commissioned by the central or provincial educational authorities or decided by the teacher educators

Table 3.1 The pedagogical content knowledge domain in the pre-service training for primary school English language teachers

Courses	No. of credits
(1) Introduction to primary English language teaching methodology	2
(2) The phonics	2
(3) Teaching vocabulary and grammar to primary school students	2
(4) Teaching listening and speaking to primary school students	2
(5) Teaching reading and writing to primary school students	2
(6) Teaching English through stories	2

(i.e. university lecturers) themselves, rather than based on thorough needs analysis and context analysis (Le, 2002). Although the courses introduce teachers to topics directly related to their daily classroom practice, such as how to use stories, poems and chants in their classes, teachers are never asked to report back on their experience, their successes and any issues they face. In addition, the follow-up support to teachers to assist them in coming to terms with what they have been exposed to on courses is completely unavailable. Understandably, this training approach fails to prepare teachers 'to tackle the unpredictable complexities' (Zein, 2017: 309) of TEYLs.

Within their school-based community of practice, Vietnamese teachers seem to be unaware of how to exchange their ideas in a democratic and dialogical manner with other community members (Le & Nguyen, 2012; Saito et al., 2008). Conferences, professional exchanges, and sharing of books and materials appear to be luxuries that the majority of teachers cannot afford. Teachers' salaries are low while the provision of funding for teachers to participate in local and international professional conferences is not regulated even at the tertiary level. In addition, the majority of Vietnamese primary English-as-a-foreign-language (EFL) teachers are female (approximately 95%), who, in addition to their heavy teaching load, have to fulfil their culturally defined family duties such as child-caring, cooking, doing housework, etc.

Given the fact that teachers were not trained adequately in teaching English to the primary school students, research on how practising teachers learn to teach and the complexities of that learning would be worthwhile. Insights into how teachers acquire their understanding of classroom practice through their lived experiences in addressing the multiple challenges such as inadequate resources and large class size (Copland et al., 2014) or inequality of access (Zein, 2016c) in TEYLs will inform teacher educators of how to support both trainee teachers and practising teachers more effectively. The present study was, thus, conducted in an attempt to make sense of the researched teacher's professional growth as a result of her everyday classroom practice, participation in teacher development programmes or professional conversations with colleagues. Thus, the main research questions in this narrative inquiry are the following:

(1) How does the practising teacher (re)construct her knowledge of teaching English to primary school students through her lived experience?
(2) To what extent is her (re)construction of knowledge of teaching shaped by social and institutional conditions under which her learning to teach takes place?

Research Methodology

Adopting the complexity theory for researching teacher learning requires that the system under investigation needs to be bounded in some way for research purposes, while consciously acknowledging its interconnectedness with a wider range of systems and further subsystems beyond the scope of the particular study (Larsen-Freeman & Cameron, 2008). Burns *et al*. (2015: 597) also call for the need to focus on 'the lived complexity of the work of language teaching, how that work is learned, and how it is carried out'.

In this study, the focus is on a single case study of a primary school EFL teacher concentrating on sociohistorical aspects of her learning to teach English to primary school students within the context of a Vietnamese state-run primary school. As a research method, case study research is especially useful for investigating complex and dynamic systems given its in-depth but holistic focus on a single bounded system (Stake, 2000; Yin, 2009).

The data were collected by means of the teacher's narratives (Barkhuizen *et al*., 2014), which aim at understanding how people make meaning of their lived experience by presenting it through a story (Clandinin & Connelly, 2000). The benefits of narrative inquiry fit well the purpose of the present study, which is aimed at exploring how the practising teacher's professional knowledge of teaching English to young learners grew out of her lived experiences within the social ecosystem in which her activity was embedded.

The teacher, whose pseudonym is Loan, was selected for this study because she appeared to be representative to the population of Vietnamese primary school teachers of English working in state-owned schools in many aspects. She was first trained at a Hanoi-based three-year junior college to teach English to junior secondary school students (Grades 6–9), and after graduation, she was selected to continue her study for the four-year university bachelor's degree in teaching English to primary school students. Up to the time when this study was conducted, she had been teaching English in a Hanoi-based state-owned primary school for six years. She was married and had one small child to look after. This is a typical case (Duff, 2008; Miles & Huberman, 1994; Savin-Baden & Major, 2013) as approximately 95% of Vietnamese primary school teachers of English are young, married females, aged 25–32 years and have a similar professional training background. Like the majority of Vietnamese state-owned primary schools, Loan's school had her as the only teacher of English due to the staffing policy that is regulated by the number of instructional hours. She had to teach all students from Grade 3 to Grade 5.

In a narrative inquiry, researchers 'elicit, co-construct, interpret, and, in their retelling, represent participants' accounts of lived and imagined personal experience' (Barkhuizen, 2011: 393). In this study, Loan's story of her lived experience as an English language learner and teacher throughout her six-year teaching career at a Vietnamese primary school was constructed and reconstructed over a period of three months. It started with a narrative of nearly 4000 words and was continued and reshaped through her email exchanges with me. In addition, I had a one-hour face-to-face talk with her about her learning and teaching experiences. Through these discursive activities, I established a narrative dialogue with the participant teacher in order to mediate her meaning-making of her teaching and learning experiences (Barkhuizen *et al.*, 2014). To help Loan better express herself comfortably and accurately, her story, the email exchanges and personal talk were conducted in Vietnamese. The English translation was sent back to Loan to verify the authenticity of her lived stories and give consent for my use of them.

A thematic and grounded theory approach (Barkhuizen *et al.*, 2014: 74) was adopted for the analysis of the data, and the process involved 'repeated reading of the data, coding and categorization of data extracts, and their reorganization under thematic headings' (Barkhuizen *et al.*, 2014: 75). In this way, categories are grounded in, or emerge from, the data, rather than be predetermined. Specifically, the data were first sorted chronologically from the time Loan entered the junior teacher college to the sixth year of her teaching career (the time when this study was undertaken). Second, the data were arranged into themes that were related to Loan's learning-to-teach experiences.

Loan's Storied Learning Experiences

Dream realized: Entry into the teacher junior college

As a little girl, Loan dreamt of becoming a teacher and she worked as a private tutor in mathematics, literature, physics and English with young learners while she was a junior secondary school girl. She thought she was born to be a teacher, but she wanted to become a teacher of literature. However, when she was in Grade 12 (the last grade of the senior secondary school), she was inspired by her English language teacher and a close friend of hers, and this made her change her mind. She passed the entrance examination and became a student majoring in business English at a Hanoi-based junior teacher college in 2007. She felt quite frustrated at the thought that she would never have the chance to work as a full-time teacher of English. Luckily, the college responded positively to the students' petition and decided to put all students of her cohort into the teacher training department. In the new department, she enormously enjoyed the courses on educational psychology and English language teaching methodology, and she realized that her dream had been revived. While at the teacher training college, she had the feeling that teaching was not as complex and challenging as she had thought it to be as it was simply the use of specific teaching techniques for different pedagogical purposes.

Vision versus reality tensions during the practicum

Loan wrote that she experienced terrible shocks during the practicum at a junior secondary school because what she experienced there conflicted with her vision of teaching. When she started teaching real students in a real classroom during the practicum, she found out that teaching was more challenging than she thought it was. Her lack of knowledge about the students made her unable to predict the problems that were likely to occur in the classroom while planning the lesson. For example, when she planned the lesson, she was only concerned about the textbook input without thinking about how the students learned. This made her 'nervous about the questions the students raised' and 'about how to adapt the activities in the textbook to the students with mixed linguistic abilities.' She then studied the whole curriculum, talked with her cooperating teacher and other teacher trainees, as well as had informal chats with the students to 'learn how to design activities that were more appropriate to the students' and 'how to use visual aids more effectively.' Through those talks, she 'became more confident in teaching' and was positively assessed at the end of the practicum.

First year's teaching: Negotiation of meaning with stakeholders

Upon graduation from the university, Loan was contractually hired to teach English to kindergarten children. As she was not trained to teach these very young children, she felt quite puzzled. After a short time, she came to realize that she could use the pedagogical content knowledge that she had been taught to these very young children. Her observed difference was that the lessons were 'focused on words, sentences rather than linguistic skills [listening, speaking, reading and writing]. Each lesson was a series of activities, and the greatest challenge was how to move the children from one activity to another so as to make them fully engaged.' She believed that for these young children, visual aids played an important role because 'without visual aids, the children became distracted very quickly.' However, she was unable to deal with the problem of classroom discipline, that is, 'how to control children' inappropriate behaviors in the classroom'. To maintain classroom discipline, she had to 'talk too much' and frequently suffered from a 'serious sore throat'. This made her lose enthusiasm for teaching kindergarten children.

Having finished her first year teaching English to this group of kindergarten children, she secured a permanent teaching position at her current Hanoi-based primary school, where English is a compulsory subject from Grade 3 as in the majority of other state-owned primary schools. At the new school, the principal was at first unhappy with her teaching strategies as they thought that the teacher should allow the students to write down what they wanted to say first to make speaking easier for the students and that more emphasis should be placed on grammar. She was also expected to use Vietnamese frequently in the classroom; however, after she explained that 'communication, especially production and comprehension, is the key objective of teaching English to the primary school students' the principal did not seem to intervene any more. Loan said that she was lucky as in other primary schools, teachers were prescribed to follow exactly the procedures of teaching other school subjects and to use Vietnamese to teach English.

While she managed to negotiate with the school principal about the teaching strategies that she thought were appropriate to the students, Loan failed to achieve the same results with the parents who complained that their children's grammar and translation skills were not satisfactory. These parents wanted their children to get excellent scores in grammar- and translation-based tests so that they would be admitted to the best lower secondary schools in the future. For these parents, Loan tried to explain that 'grammar should be taught differently to the primary school students. Unlike students of the higher grades (i.e. lower and upper secondary schools), primary school students should be taught simple grammar without the teacher's much use of metalanguage such as tense, aspect, person, etc.' While Loan acknowledged that she was not yet capable of finding ways to cope with the parental pressures, her teaching focused more on the grammatical and lexical items that were commonly found in the tests or examinations. She explained in the follow-up interview that she did this as a compromise between the parental demands of preparing their children for the examinations and her perceived needs to develop the students' communicative ability in English. She explained further that she often used chants to teach grammar to make it easier for the students to memorize the taught grammatical items.

Experiencing physical and emotional fatigue

Loan described herself as an enthusiastic and dedicated teacher in her first years' teaching. She planned the lesson carefully, finding ways 'to engage the students in classroom activities' and to motivate herself. But as the amount of work increased, she became physically and emotionally fatigued. She described,

> As I am the only teacher of English in my school, I have to teach 13 classes [of grades 3–5] with each class having more or less 50 students totaling 26 class periods a week. In addition to the regular teaching load, I have to prepare the students for all kinds of tests, pen-and-paper tests, online tests to choose good students at the district level and the municipal level. In general, I have to shoulder all sorts of things that are related to English in the school. I feel quite stressful. Especially, I am completely burnt out with tests and examinations, particularly the oral test, and marking. I cannot invest as much time thinking of ways to make the lessons more creative as I wish. Sometimes I teach like a robot. Consequently, I don't see much improvement in the way I teach after six years in the career.

In the follow-up interview, Loan said honestly,

> The teaching schedule at the school plus private teaching [for extra income], housework, and child-caring all take up too much of my time. I cannot arrange regular time to plan the lesson as carefully as I wish except for when I am observed by inspectors [for evaluation]. I actually feel ashamed of this and I expect this will be changed in the future. Anyway, I do avail myself of any time available, during the interval between lessons, on the way to school, before bedtime, to think of new ideas that help my teaching more creative.

Loan was also concerned about her language attrition. She complained that her English proficiency was eroded gradually because 'there are no opportunities to use meaningful English except for some common classroom expressions' she used to communicate with the students.

Reconstructing and theorizing practical knowledge

In 2014, Loan was sent on a two-month intensive professional development course funded by the National Foreign Language Project 2020. She described this experience as follows:

> Although it is a two-month training course organized during the summer vacation, it helped me refresh my pedagogical knowledge. I had the opportunity to share, exchange my ideas with, and learn useful ideas from, other colleagues, which I tried experimenting in my school with my students after the course. This kind of socialization was impossible to me at the school because I am the only one teaching English in my school.

After the training course, she enrolled in a graduate course for a master's degree in teaching English as a foreign language offered by a domestic university. The course input stimulated her to self-reflect upon her teaching and she became aware that she needed to make some radical changes in her teaching. For example, she challenged many aspects of her teaching, such as overusing games without thinking of their educational value, using the communicative approach inappropriately, using undifferentiated activities in a mixed-level class and over-routinizing her teaching.

Her reflection in light of the input from the graduate course has helped her to become aware of the need to understand the students in order to design more student-centred activities, to emphasize the role of interaction, and to be dynamic and flexible in using Vietnamese. Regarding her future action, she expressed honestly,

> I wish to have less heavy teaching schedule so that I can have more time for self-study and to have colleagues to share my professional concerns. Especially I am eager to have the opportunities to attend professional development and English proficiency development courses regularly. The

courses can be online, not necessarily formal. The courses will help to sharpen my professional skills and competences or they will be worsened over time during my career life as a primary school teacher. Besides their professional values, these courses will reduce my stress and refresh my passion for professional development and for the teaching career.

Discussion

Unlike the Korean primary school English teachers in Moodie and Feryok's (2015) study, whose commitment to teaching was urged by their families, Loan, in this study, was affectively committed to teaching. She had the strong desire to become a teacher, and, as a result, she was happy when her dream came true. Unfortunately, her affective commitment to teaching led to well-intentioned but ineffective practice due to the lack of an appropriate knowledge base of teaching English to young children. Loan believed that teaching was simply the adoption of specific techniques of teaching grammar, vocabulary and language skills such as listening, speaking, reading and writing to any group of learners. Loan did not seem to be aware that some of the teaching approaches in which she had been trained were more appropriate to adult learners than young learners in large classes with very basic teaching and learning facilities and different educational traditions (Enever & Moon, 2009; McKay, 2003). For example, she acknowledged that she had been using the PPP (presentation-practice-production) model in her teaching since she started her teaching career. It is evident that her expertise is 'in language learning and teaching rather than in primary school pedagogy' (Copland et al., 2014: 757).

Unlike the teachers in the study by Copland et al. (2014), Loan was really concerned about tests and examinations. Although she wished to develop the children's basic skills in using English for communication, she was under external pressure of preparing them for language-focused examinations. She acknowledged that parental pressures to prepare their children for high achievements in tests and examinations made her focus more on explicit grammar teaching. This is because of the competitive nature and the tradition of norm-referenced examinations in Vietnamese educational culture (Le, 2015, 2017). Given the children's target language proficiency, their age and the amount of formal teaching of three hours a week, the value of explicit grammar teaching, albeit through chants as reported by Loan, might be questioned (Copland et al., 2014).

An important issue, which has not been adequately researched and is revealed in this study, is teacher professional isolation. Being the only teacher of English in her school, which is not uncommon in a good number of Vietnamese primary schools, Loan had to function in a context more of isolation than of rich professional dialogue. Within the period of her six-year career, she had only one opportunity to attend a professional development workshop where she could share her teaching experience and to learn from her colleagues from other schools. In other words, the picture of professional development for Vietnamese EYL teachers is not one of 'colleagues who see themselves as sharing a viable, generalized body of knowledge and practice' (Lortie, 1975: 79). Although Loan's personal practical knowledge was largely shaped by her past learning experience, that knowledge did not seem to be critically examined or open to scrutiny due to the lack of social interaction, shared repertoire of actions, discourses and tools (Wenger, 1998) with others within their ecologies of practice. This professional isolation plus heavy teaching load, the need to teach in private classes to compensate for her low salary as well as family responsibilities, meant Loan was unable to reflect critically on her teaching for improvement, despite some of her self-reported changes resulting from her graduate study. All these contextual factors reduced Loan's interest in learning both through practice and through meaning (Lieberman & Pointer Mace, 2008), and her motivation towards conceptual change (i.e. the transformation of existing beliefs systems) became eroded. So, this might be indicative of one big issue concerning teaching English at Vietnamese primary schools: inadequate training, big class sizes, professional isolation, emotional fatigue, poor learning conditions and poor teaching.

As shown in Loan's story, her personal practical knowledge was largely shaped by her past learning experience, such as using undifferentiated activities as well as her experience teaching kindergarten children and the primary school students. This absence of a knowledge base of teaching English to young learners is evidently a matter of concern. As Loan was not adequately trained to understand how young children think and learn, her lack of understanding of the young learners is demonstrated in both the first time she attended the practicum and in her initial experience of teaching English to kindergarten children. In her story, Loan also acknowledged that her lack of knowledge of the children made her focus on the coursebook input, rather than on how the young students would learn while planning the lesson.

The findings of this study also lend further support to the view that teacher learning is complex and dynamic (Burns et al., 2015; Feryok, 2010; Golombek & Doran, 2014) situated in a web of emotions, motivations and future visions. All of these factors are in a dynamic relationship with the immediate microcontext of the classroom and school culture, the larger context of local and national educational policies, which are, in turn, embedded in the broader context of sociocultural and political values and norms (Zein, 2016b). Loan was affectively committed to teaching, but then she became burnt out because of many contextual factors such as the teaching schedule, parental pressures of preparing the children for high scores in examinations, family responsibilities, etc. Consequently, she experienced inertia in teaching. Then, the new knowledge she gained from her graduate study helped her to develop new future visions for her professional development.

Conclusions

Although the present study was limited to the teacher's accounts, which fails to build support for patterns as a means to go beyond the study itself to larger frameworks of understandings, it uncovers some fundamental issues related to teacher education for TEYLs.

EYL teachers need, among other knowledge and skills, to have adequate knowledge of children's psychology and how they learn at different ages (Cameron, 2001, 2003; Enever, 2014; Zein, 2015). In this regard, teacher education programmes in Vietnam, like the case of Indonesia (Zein, 2017), do not pay adequate attention to teachers' knowledge of child psychology, which helps to provide 'a frame of reference for teachers in recognising the kinds of children they deal with ... [so as to] help teachers develop appropriate strategies they need to build the positive teacher-student interpersonal relationship that is influential in sustaining student motivation' (Zein, 2017: 309). This highlights the need to revise the current EYL teacher education programmes in Vietnam towards a greater emphasis on knowledge about how young learners think and learn. In particular, teachers need to be aware that in the classroom context where children have a few English lessons a week like Vietnam, young learners tend to learn slowly but forget quickly. In such a context, teacher education programmes need to develop EYL teachers' observational skills so that they have 'eagle eyes' to watch how each child is attending, understanding and participating, and use that information to meet the learning needs of the child. Knowledge of the young learners and how they learn English is more critical to success in TEYLs than the codified knowledge about language and language teaching as reported in Loan's story. The overemphasis on teaching methods at the expense of knowledge of child psychology will mean teachers will fail to see young learners not just as learners but also daughters and sons, brothers and sisters with their own personalities and interests (Cameron, 2001).

Another concern is teacher policy. Teacher learning, as we understand it, draws on the teacher's own inner resource for change. It is centred on personal awareness of the possibilities for change and of what influences the change process. It builds on the past, because recognizing how past experiences have or have not been developmental helps identify opportunities for change in the present and future. It also draws on the present, in encouraging a fuller awareness of the kind of teacher one is now and of other people's responses to oneself. It is a self-reflective process, because it is through questioning old habits that alternative ways of being and doing are able to emerge. Among other challenges, such as low salaries, target language proficiency and a heavy teaching schedule (Copland *et al.*,

2014), teacher isolation is a great concern, which may be exclusive of Vietnamese state-owned primary schools because of the country's staffing policy. All these social and institutional conditions mean teachers become emotionally and physically fatigued, leading to the erosion of their ability to self-regulate professional development. This professional isolation is bound to discourage teachers from making significant conceptual changes in their teaching due to the lack of change catalysts. Therefore, the challenge is that a balance has to be found between teaching schedules, professional development and teachers' home life so that every teacher can access ongoing professional development opportunities for professional growth.

From a complexity thinking perspective, the central issue is, I believe, teacher education for TEYLs and elsewhere must confront how to foster teacher learning about, from, in and for practice. This issue cannot be addressed satisfactorily unless there are strategies that tie together the construction of teacher education as learning and teacher education as policy in sophisticated and intriguing ways.

References

Adler, J. (2000) Social practice theory and mathematics teacher education: A conversation between theory and practice. *Nordic Mathematics Educational Journal* 8 (3), 31–53.

Bailey, K.M. and Nunan, D. (eds) (1996) *Voices from the Language Classroom.* New York: Cambridge University Press.

Baldauf, R.B., Kaplan, R.B., Kamwangamalu, N. and Bryant, P. (eds) (2012) *Language Planning in Primary Schools in Asia.* London: Routledge.

Barkhuizen, G. (2011) Narrative knowledging in TESOL. *TESOL Quarterly* 45 (3), 391–414.

Barkhuizen, G., Benson, P. and Chik, A. (2014) *Narrative Inquiry in Language Teaching and Learning Research.* New York: Routledge.

Borg, S. (2003) Teacher cognition in language teaching: A review of research on what language teachers think, know, believe and do. *Language Teaching* 36 (2), 81–109.

Burns, A. and Richards, J.C. (eds) (2009) *The Cambridge Guide to Second Language Teacher Education.* Cambridge: Cambridge University Press.

Burns, A., Freeman, D. and Edwards, E. (2015) Theorizing and studying the language-teaching mind: Mapping research on language teacher cognition. *The Modern Language Journal* 99 (3), 585–601.

Butler, Y.G. (2004) What level of English proficiency do elementary school teachers need to attain in order to teach EFL? Case studies from Korea, Taiwan, and Japan. *TESOL Quarterly* 38 (2), 245–278.

Butler, Y.G. (2015) English language education among young learners in East Asia: A review of current research (2004–2014). *Language Teaching* 48 (3), 303–342.

Cameron, L. (2001) *Teaching Languages to Young Learners.* Cambridge: Cambridge University Press.

Cameron, L. (2003) Challenges for ELT from the expansion in teaching children. *ELT Journal* 57 (2), 105–112.

Chou, C.-H. (2008) Exploring elementary English teachers' practical knowledge: A case study of EFL teachers in Taiwan. *Asia Pacific Education Review* 9 (4), 529–541.

Clandinin, D.J. and Connelly, F.M. (2000) *Narrative Inquiry: Experience and Story in Qualitative Research.* San Francisco, CA: Jossey Bass.

Copland, F. and Garton, S. (2014) Key themes and future directions in teaching English to young learners: Introduction to the special issue. *ELT Journal* 68 (3), 223–230.

Copland, F., Garton, S. and Burns, A. (2014) Challenges in teaching English to young learners: Global perspectives and local realities. *TESOL Quarterly* 48 (4), 738–762.

Duff, P.A. (2008) *Case Study Research in Applied Linguistics*. New York: Lawrence Erlbaum Associates.

Enever, J. (2014) Primary English teacher education in Europe. *ELT Journal* 68 (3), 231–242.

Elbaz, F. (1983) *Teacher Thinking: A Study of Practical Knowledge*. New York: Nichols Publishing Company.

Enever, J. and Moon, J. (2009) New global contexts for teaching primary ELT: Change and challenge. In J. Enever, J. Moon and U. Raman (eds) *Young Learner English Language Policy and Implementation: International Perspectives* (pp. 5–21). Reading: Garnet Education.

Feryok, A. (2010) Language teacher cognition: Complex dynamic systems? *System* 38 (2), 272–279.

Freeman, D. (1996) The 'unstudied problem': Research on teacher learning in language teaching. In D. Freeman and J.C. Richards (eds) *Teacher Learning in Language Teaching* (pp. 351–378). Cambridge: Cambridge University Press.

Freeman, D. (2006) Teaching and learning in 'The age of reform': The problem of the verb. In S. Gieve and I.K. Miller (eds) *Understanding the Language Classroom* (pp. 239–262). New York: Palgrave Macmillan.

Freeman, D. and Richards, J.C. (eds) (1996) *Teacher Learning in Language Teaching*. Cambridge: Cambridge University Press.

Gao, X., Barkhuizen, G. and Chow, A.W.K. (2011) Research engagement and educational decentralisation: Problematising primary school English teachers' research experiences in China. *Educational Studies* 37 (2), 207–219.

Garton, S. (2014) Unresolved issues and new challenges in teaching English to young learners: The case of South Korea. *Current Issues in Language Planning* 15 (2), 201–219. doi:10.1080/14664208.2014.858657

Golombek, P.R. and Johnson, K.E. (2004) Narrative inquiry as a meditational space: Examining emotional and cognitive dissonance in second-language teachers' development. *Teachers and Teaching: Theory and Practice* 10 (3), 307–327.

Golombek, P. and Doran, M. (2014) Unifying cognition, emotion, and activity in language teacher professional development. *Teaching and Teacher Education* 39, 102–111.

Hamano, T. (2008) Educational reform and teacher education in Vietnam. *Journal of Education for Teaching: International Research and Pedagogy* 34 (4), 397–410.

Johnson, K.E. (2009) *Second Language Teacher Education: A Sociocultural Perspective*. New York: Routledge.

Johnstone, R. (2009) An early start: What are the key conditions for generalized success? In J. Enever, J. Moon and U. Raman (eds) *Young Learner English Language Policy and Implementation: International Perspectives* (pp. 31–41). Reading: Garnet Education.

Kabilan, M.K. and Veratharaju, K. (2013) Professional development needs of primary school English-language teachers in Malaysia. *Professional Development in Education* 39 (3), 330–351.

Kiss, T. (2012) The complexity of teacher learning: Reflection as a complex dynamic system. *Journal of Interdisciplinary Research in Education* 2 (1), 17–35.

Kubanyiova, M. and Feryok, A. (2015) Language teacher cognition in applied linguistics research: Revisiting the territory, redrawing the boundaries, reclaiming the relevance. *The Modern Language Journal* 99 (3), 435–449.

Larsen-Freeman, D. and Cameron, L. (2008) *Complex Systems and Applied Linguistics.* New York: Oxford University Press.

Lave, J. and Wenger, E. (1991) *Situated Learning: Legitimate Peripheral Participation.* Cambridge: Cambridge University Press.

Le, V.C. (2002) Sustainable professional development of EFL teachers in Vietnam. *Teacher Edition* 13, 36–42.

Le, V.C. (2011) Form-focused instruction: A case study of Vietnamese teachers' beliefs and practices. Unpublished doctoral thesis. Hamilton, New Zealand: University of Waikato.

Le, V.C. (2015) English language education innovation for the Vietnamese secondary school: The Project 2020. In B. Spolsky and K. Sung (eds) *Secondary School English Education in Asia: From Policy to Practice* (pp. 182–200). New York: Routledge.

Le, V.C. (2017) English language education in Vietnamese universities: National benchmarking in practice. In S. Park and B. Spolsky (eds) *English Education at the Tertiary Level in Asia: From Policy to Practice* (pp. 183–202). New York: Routledge.

Le, V.C. and Nguyen, T.T.M. (2012) Teacher learning within the school context: An ecological perspective. *Indonesian Journal of Applied Linguistics* 2 (1), 52–67.

Le, V.C. and Do, T.M.C. (2012) Teacher preparation for primary school English education: A case of Vietnam. In B. Spolsky and Y. Moon (eds) *Primary School English Language Education in Asia: From Policy to Practice* (pp. 106–128). New York: Routledge.

Liberman, A. and Pointer Mace, D.H. (2008) Teacher learning: The key to educational reform. *Journal of Teacher Education* 59 (3), 226–234.

Lortie, D. (1975) *School Teacher: A Sociological Study.* Chicago: University of Chicago Press.

McKay, S. (2003) Teaching English as an international language: The Chilean context. *ELT Journal* 57 (2), 139–148.

Miles, M. and Huberman, A.M. (1994) *Qualitative Data Analysis* (2nd edn). Thousand Oaks, CA: Sage.

Moodie, I. and Feryok, A. (2015) Beyond cognition to commitment: English language teaching in South Korean primary schools. *The Modern Language Journal* 99 (3), 450–469.

Nguyen, H.T.M. (2011) Primary English language education policy in Vietnam: Insights from implementation. *Current Issues in Language Planning* 12 (2), 225–249.

Nguyen, M.H. (2013) The curriculum for English language teacher education in Australian and Vietnamese universities. *Australian Journal of Teacher Education* 38 (11), 33–53.

Nunan, D. (2003) The impact of English as a global language on educational policies and practices in the Asia-Pacific region. *TESOL Quarterly* 37 (4), 589–613.

Opfer, V.D. and Pedder, D. (2011) Conceptualising teacher professional learning. *Review of Educational Research* 81 (3), 376–407.

Pham, H.H. (2001) Teacher development: A real need for English departments in Vietnam. *English Teaching Forum* 39 (4), 1–7.

Putnam, R. and Borko, H. (2000) What do new views of knowledge and thinking have to say about research on teacher learning? *Educational Researcher* 29 (1), 4–15.

Saito, E., Tsukui, A. and Tanaka, Y. (2008) Problems in primary school-based in-service training in Vietnam: A case study of Bac Giang province. *International Journal of Educational Development* 28 (6), 89–103.

Savin-Baden, M. and Major, C.H. (2013) *Qualitative Research: The Essential Guide to Theory and Practice.* New York: Routledge.

Stake, R.E. (2000) The case study method in social inquiry. In R. Gomm, M. Hammersley and P. Foster (eds) *Case Study Method* (pp. 19–26). London: Sage.

van Lier, L. (2004) *The Ecology and Semiotics of Language Learning.* Dordrecht: Kluwer Academic Publisher.

Wenger, E. (1998) *Communities of Practice: Learning, Meaning and Identity*. New York: Cambridge University Press.

Yin, R.K. (2009) *Case Study Research: Designs and Methods* (4th edn). Thousand Oaks, CA: Sage.

Zein, M.S. (2015) Preparing elementary English teachers: Innovations at pre-service level. *Australian Journal of Teacher Education* 40 (6), 104–120. doi:10.14221/ajte.2015v40n6.6

Zein, M.S. (2016a) Pre-service education for primary school English teachers in Indonesia: Policy implications. *Asia Pacific Journal of Education* 36 (S1), 119–134. doi:10.1080/02188791.2014.961899

Zein, M.S. (2016b) Government-based training agencies and the professional development of Indonesian English for Young Learners teachers: Perspectives from complexity theory. *Journal of Education for Teaching: International Research and Pedagogy* 42 (2), 205–223. doi:10.1080/02607476.2016.1143145

Zein, M.S. (2016c) Factors affecting the professional development of elementary English teachers. *Professional Development in Education* 42 (3), 423–440. doi:10.1080/19415257.2015.1005243

Zein, M.S. (2017) Professional development needs of primary EFL teachers: Perspectives of teachers and teacher educators. *Professional Development in Education* 43 (2), 293–313. doi:10.1080/19415257.2016.1156013

4 Imagining One's Self as a Child and Speech Modification: Implications for Teacher Education

Subhan Zein

Introduction

The progress and demands of globalisation have resulted in the teaching of English to learners at an even younger age. Many children at primary school level, usually between 7 and 12 years old, have started English instruction. Consequently, the young learner classroom has become a mainstream research interest over the past two decades (Copland *et al.*, 2014; Garton *et al.*, 2011). Previous studies, both at the global (e.g. Copland *et al.*, 2014; Emery, 2012) and local levels (e.g. Butler, 2005; Wu, 2012; Zein, 2015, 2017), have consistently indicated that adequate attention needs to be paid to English for young learners (EYL) teachers' communicative skills. Classroom discourse has been identified as one of teachers' communicative skill issues (Zein, 2017), suggesting that it warrants further investigation in teacher education.

The study reported in this chapter was conducted in the context of a teacher professional development programme. It aimed to investigate EYL teachers' speech modification as a means of classroom discourse. This chapter starts by looking at previous research on discourse in the primary classroom in relation to teachers' speech modification. It continues by describing the methodological tenets employed to gather data in this study. The chapter then presents the findings and discusses them in light of relevant literature. The findings of the study demonstrate that imagining one's self as a child contributes to speech modification efficacy. The chapter concludes with ideas for the incorporation of the findings into teacher education.

Speech Modification as Discourse in the EYL Classroom

Communication in the young learner classroom is very complex. There are multiple foci to the language being used; the teacher may use language in order to perform discourses such as seeking information, giving instructions, checking comprehension, offering advice, etc. (Walsh, 2011). In addition to the complex foci of language and its use, there is also rapid flow of classroom interaction. Young learners are expected to understand discourses, which more often than not are performed within a very short period of time, one immediately occurring after the other.

The complexity of language use often makes it difficult to comprehend what is happening, while the rapid flow of interaction may be confusing for young learners. They may find it difficult to understand the interactions occurring in the classroom, struggling in their ways to make sense of the world in which they live. But potential problems also occur in other areas of discourse. Young learners may also demonstrate discourse difficulties in keeping up with various tasks such as linking ideas, identifying the topic, recalling main ideas, keeping track of conversation, identifying and using pronouns, predicting ideas, providing examples or retelling events (James, 2007; Kyratzis & Cook-Gumperz, 2015). These discourse difficulties could have enormous ramifications – they could create communication misunderstanding as well as lack of confidence.

If teachers and learners are to work effectively together, they need to acquire what Walsh (2006) called, 'classroom interactional competence'. Teachers in particular must make use of a range of appropriate interactional and linguistic resources in order to promote dynamic, engaged learning (Walsh, 2011). Speech modification has been identified as one of the most important classroom discourse features that can be used to promote such dynamic and engaged learning (Walsh, 2006, 2011, 2013). Teachers' speech modification is a more restricted code of their spoken discourse whereby their pace of speech is slower, the volume louder and the intonation more deliberate. Teachers also make greater use of repetition, pausing, emphasis, gestures and facial expressions to help deliver meaning (Walsh, 2011). The importance of speech modification in language acquisition cannot be underestimated. Scholars unanimously agree that speech modification occurring during interaction promotes second language development (Gass, 2015; Gass & Mackey, 2007; Mackey & Goo, 2007; Walsh, 2006, 2011, 2013).

The first reason why speech modification is important for teachers is related to comprehension. Research from second language acquisition (SLA) demonstrates that speech modification allows for comprehensible input, which to a large extent determines a child's language acquisition (Gass, 2015; Gass & Mackey, 2007). When comprehension is facilitated, young learners are more likely to gain meaningful understanding within the classroom and further develop their language. When young learners understand the message, their learning is enhanced. They are able to engage in discussions about new topics and vocabulary, question things that they have not understood and develop new links of meaning to draw on (Kyratzis & Cook-Gumperz, 2015; Mahn, 2015).

Teachers therefore must utilise a wide range of linguistic resources through speech modification in order to facilitate comprehension. They must modify their speech because young learners need to understand the teacher's talk in order for them to be able to learn; it is unlikely for progress to occur if learners do not understand their teacher (Walsh, 2006, 2011, 2013). To facilitate comprehension, teachers can modify their speech by, for example, simplifying vocabulary and grammar. They can also omit the use of idiomatic or regional variations and employ more recognised forms of speech. Teachers can also make their pronunciation clearer as they slow down their articulation and use more standard forms. According to Walsh (2011: 7–9), there are also more subtle strategies of speech modification that teachers can use in order to clarify comprehension or to confirm meanings, including:

> confirmation checks, where teachers make sure they understand learners; comprehension checks, ensuring that learners understand the teacher; repetition; clarification requests, asking students for clarification; reformulation, rephrasing a learner's utterance; turn completion, finishing a learner's contribution; and backtracking, returning to an earlier part of a dialogue.

The second reason why speech modification is important has to do with language modelling. From the SLA perspective, the development of a child's language is not a process that occurs in a vacuum; rather, it is dependent on the quality, quantity and nature of the interactions that occur at home and in everyday settings through discourse. In other words, young learners' language develops through the opportunities to communicate with other language users, including parents, siblings, teachers and peers. They are the social environment models from which young learners learn to formulate language rules and conventions. In doing so, children begin a process of internalisation, that is, when they process verbal interactions, rationalise and organise them into thoughts through the internal language (Vygotsky, 1978). In the young learner schooling context, the teacher's speech in the target language (TL) may be the child's only exposure, because outside classroom exposure may be very limited. When young learners are exposed to experiences involving various language interactions in the classroom, they begin to analyse many aspects of communication and develop an understanding of how to use language effectively in different circumstances (James, 2007; Kyratzis & Cook-Gumperz, 2015). When they receive positive opportunities for exposure and experimentation with language, it is more likely that young learners experience optimal language exposure (Kyratzis & Cook-Gumperz, 2015). They learn about many aspects of language: vocabulary, discourse markers, topics, phonological conventions, grammatical conventions, genre conventions, purpose and audience (Rymes, 2016).

It is necessary that a teacher modify their speech in order to provide a model of appropriate TL (Walsh, 2006, 2011). First, the teacher needs to use appropriate pronunciation, intonation, sentence and word stress. While natural speech may not require modifications in terms of intonation or pacing, classroom discourse is different (Rymes, 2016). Classroom discourse requires considerable adjustment in the way it is presented in order to ensure young learners receive the TL appropriate to their level. That is the way the teacher models the language to provide learners with opportunities to hear the TL sounds and how the TL is pronounced. The teacher also needs to modify their speech in order to model how the TL is used in various contexts (Walsh, 2006, 2011). As young learners build arrays of experiences, their knowledge of language conventions begins to grow. Modifying the speech allows young learners to learn about how the teacher uses language in different situations, how the teacher adapts their language use between different audiences and how the teacher uses language to achieve a purpose.

Third, modifying the speech allows teachers to navigate the discourse in the classroom and ensure its flow. This is because the rapid flow and complexity of communication may result in young learners 'getting lost' from time to time. In this respect, the use of discourse markers to signal the beginnings and endings of various activities or stages in a lesson has been suggested (Walsh, 2011). Typical discourse markers such as 'right', 'OK', 'now', 'so', 'first and 'alright' indicate changes in the interaction or organisation of learning. They have the same function as punctuation on a printed page. Using discourse markers further enables teachers to guide learners through the discourse and maintain their attention (Walsh, 2011, 2013).

Fourth, speech modification is also important in the context of mediating learning. Education is a discursive process; it may be best explained by the quality of educational dialogue between the teacher and the learners (Mahn, 2015). In this respect, the dialogue enables young learners to interpret the verbal (or language) and symbolic (other ways in which meanings are communicated) behaviours that facilitate their learning. The dialogic process occurs through the joint construction of ZPD (zone proximal development), which is defined as 'the distance between a child's actual developmental level as determined by independent problem solving and the level of potential development as determined through problem solving under guidance or in collaboration with more capable peers' (Vygotsky, 1978: 86).

As the expert, the teacher is expected to be able to gauge the child's ZPD, for only after successfully gauging the zone can the teacher modify their speech as a means of scaffolding instruction, assisting children to perform a skill that they are unable to perform independently (Wood *et al.*, 1976). Thus, rather than using full, complex sentences, the teacher uses simplified sentences that allow for comprehension and further enable learners to acquire facility in L2 interaction (Walsh, 2011, 2013). This mediated interaction would increase learners' participation in the discourse and facilitate their learning (Mahn, 2015).

Despite its importance, studies consistently suggest how EYL teachers struggle to modify speech to cater for the needs of young learners, as found in various contexts including China (Wu, 2012), Indonesia (Zein, 2017) and Vietnam (Saito *et al.*, 2008). Mainstream research has not touched upon it, since most of the previous research on speech modification is in adult classrooms (Walsh, 2011, 2013) – it remains to be seen whether issues that are relevant to adult classrooms are also relevant to the EYL classroom. Furthermore, research into EYL teachers' classroom language by Copland and Yonetsugi (2016) focuses on the use of L1 and English as opposed to English only instruction, while Zein (2017: 302) only pointed to the importance of EYL teachers to 'grade their language', 'paraphrase' and 'chunk the language'. But it remains vague how EYL teachers deal with speech modification, which strategies they employ and to what extent. As a consequence, we have limited understanding as to what constitutes the appropriate qualifications and language level of young learner English teachers (Butler, 2015; Zein, 2017).

It is crucial to address this issue in teacher education. In order to improve their professional practice, EYL teachers need to gain a thorough understanding of the ways they modify their speech. Creating opportunities for teachers to examine their speech modification would enable them to construct realistic model of communication in the young learner classroom. Assisting teachers in understanding interactional processes and studying their own use of language and its effects on learning has the potential to enhance microscopic understanding of classroom processes and ways to improve their professionalism (Walsh, 2013). As Walsh (2011, 2013) argued, placing classroom discourse at the core of teacher education is an effective way to help their professional learning. Nonetheless, such a focus should not be exclusively on instructional strategies per se, but rather on the exploration of what teachers '*do* with students as they simultaneously reflect on how they *think about* students' (Molle, 2013: 119–120).

Research Methodology

The participants of the study were four EYL teachers and two teacher educators. The teachers who participated in this study were volunteers, as they undertook a teacher professional development programme developed by a university in Indonesia in association with a teachers' group and a government-based training agency. The teachers had between one month and more than five years of teaching experience behind them. They all graduated from an English language department. The teachers participating in this study were specialist teachers, teaching English to a wide range of classes from Grades 1 to 6 with approximately 90 minutes per week in each class. One of the teacher educators worked at the university, while the other was a trainer at the government-based training agency. They had more than 20 years of teaching and training experience behind them and a doctorate degree in either TESOL (teaching English to speakers of other languages) or applied linguistics. To maintain confidentiality, the teachers and teacher educators were referred to in this study by pseudonyms.

The research design took a multimodal, discursive and collaborative approach in terms of data collection and analysis (e.g. Molle, 2013; Schieble et al., 2015). To collect data for this study, multivocal ethnography (Tobin, 1988; Tobin et al., 1989) was employed using videotaped lessons of teachers and group discussions involving all the participants. For Tobin et al. (1989) there are three discrete perspectives in multivocal ethnography: (1) a series of videotaped or observed activities; (2) the perspective of 'insiders' who performed such activities; and (3) the perspective of 'outsiders' who were from the cultures in which the observed activities took place.

The present study took inspiration from Tobin et al.'s (1989) approach. In this study, the teachers' classes were videotaped as part of their professional development activity at the university. The employment of videotaped lessons of teachers allowed for the observation of natural discourses, in the same way that it has been used for recording and analysing interaction in educational contexts on teacher instructional strategies (Molle, 2013) and enactment of teacher identities (Schieble et al., 2015). Out of the videotaped lessons (360 minutes), five clips were selected. The clips were chosen in consultation with the teachers; they were selected because they represented speech modification situations. There were a few occasions where the same type of discourses occurred in different lessons, and in such a circumstance, the decision was made in consultation with the teachers, who provided opinions as to which clips best represented the type of discourse. The clips were merged into an approximately 25-minute video. Transcriptions of the video were created as subtitles for linguistic clarification (Cowan, 2014) where [ ] indicates overlapping utterances, ( ) means gestures and italicised words indicate they occurred in L1.

The subtitled video was then shown to the teachers and teacher educators. The teachers worked to analyse various aspects of the selected discourses in the video. By watching the video and reading the transcripts, the teachers could clarify the details of the setting and subtleties of facial expressions and gestures that were made during the interactions; they looked beyond the traditionally prioritised spoken and written linguistic modes (Cowan, 2014). The teachers examined speech modification(s) occurring in discourses such as how they responded to questions, how they gave explanation, how they gave instructions, etc. They evaluated whether the speech modification(s) were effective and identified factors contributing to their efficacy, or lack thereof. Overall, this multimodal approach allowed for the analytical and rhetorical interpretations of teachers' speech modifications. They further enabled exploration of insights into patterns when speech modifications were orchestrated in interactions (Kress, 2010; Molle, 2013).

Then the teachers reported the results of their discussion to the teacher educators. Both the teachers and teacher educators discussed the discourses shown in the video. They analysed 'a series of narratives, a series of interpretive and evaluative statements told in different voices' (Tobin, 1988: 176). In doing so, they reanalysed the discourses to challenge their beliefs and ideas, corroborate their positions or explore new insights into speech modification. The discussions between teachers and teacher educators allowed for analysis of the teachers' deep motives and general concerns about certain discourses in their classes. However, they also allowed for systematic analysis that provided in-depth exploration of scaffolding needed by the teacher educators to help teachers to reflect on and improve practice (Engin, 2015; Molle, 2013). In this respect, the voices are the voices of the insiders interpreting their own culture (i.e. the teachers) and the voices of the outsiders (i.e. the teacher educators). Thus, the video clips served as a stimulus for the production of a dialogically structured text, a process of analysing the same events from different perspectives and an ongoing dialogue between insiders and outsiders of different professional cultures.

Given the multi-party participatory nature of the study, the co-constructed views emerging from the interactions between teachers and teacher educators allowed for the development of an emic perspective that is 'more conducive to gaining a true understanding of interactional processes in the L2 classroom than the imposed perspective of the researcher' (Walsh, 2013: 13). This analytical approach aimed to increase the validity of data interpretation. The use of the multivocal ethnography as a research method in this study yielded data through the activities documented, the transcriptions and the comments emerging in the discussions between the teachers and teacher educators. Their comments are described and analysed in the following section.

Results and Discussion

The first two clips of the video showed the practices of Mr Mardi and Mr Adi in teaching two different groups of Grade 1 (aged 7 years old) students. In the first clip Mr Mardi assisted a pair of students. Upon completion he walked towards the front of the classroom. Suddenly one of the students asked him a question:

1	S1:	*'Jam' apa, Pak?* (inquisitive eyes)
		'Watch' what is it, Sir?
2	**Mr Mardi:**	Eh? (looking on her)
3	S1:	*'Jam', Pak. 'Jam' bahasa Inggrisnya?* (tilting her head)
		'Watch', Sir. 'Watch' what is it in English?
4	**Mr Mardi:**	*'Jam'? Oh, Jam.*
		Watch. Oh, 'Watch'.
5	S1:	*Apaan, Pak?*
		What is it, Sir?
6	**Mr Mardi:**	Eh?
7	S1:	*Apaan? Nggak kedengeran.*
		What? Can't hear you.
8	**Mr Mardi:**	Watch. WATCH (pronouncing woːtʒ)
9	S1:	A…
10	S2:	[woːtʒ…]
11	S1:	[woːtʒ…] … [woːtʒ…] *Nulisnya gimana?*
		How to write it? (tilting head)
12	**Mr Mardi:**	*Nulisnya? Ehm.. Begini.* (writing on S1's book)
		To write it? Ehm… This is how
13	S1:	*Oh, begit[uuu].* (nodding along)
14	S2:	*[Ohhh..]* w – a – t – c – h *(spelling out)*
15		*Kok nulisnya begitu ya, Pak?* (inquisitive eyes)
		Why the spelling looks like that, Sir?
16	**Mr Mardi:**	Namanya juga bahasa Inggris.
		Because it is English.
		(walking towards his desk, and then sat, watching over the students)

Then there was a clip of Mr Adi. The clip showed a scene where Mr Adi was monitoring students' work. At one point he stopped near a student and nodded along.

22	**Mr Adi:**	What is thaː…t?
23	S3:	*Apaan, Pak?*
		What is it, Sir? (smiling)
24	**Mr Adi:**	Whaaat…. is…. thaː..t?
		(translating: *'Apa…. itu…?,* raising eyebrows, pointing to a picture in the textbook)
25	S3:	*Oh, rumah, Pak.*

26	**Mr Adi:**	RUMAH?
		House? (looking at S5, S3's pair)
27		*Rumah?* (pointing at S5) What is *rumah?* In English? *Apa itu rumah?*
28	**S5:**	*House, Sir*
29	**Mr Adi:**	House... Very good! (smiling) Spelling? What is the spelling?
30	**S5:**	H-O-U-S-E.
31	**S3:**	E....U...
32	**Mr Adi:**	No, no (shaking head) H....O....U....S.....E...
33	**S3:**	*'E', Pak?* 'E', Sir? (tilting head)
34	**Mr Adi:**	No, 'H'. Robbie, writing. Can you write [sic] down? (tilting head)
35	**S5:**	(nodded, writing down on S3's book).
36	**S3:**	Oh, 'ha'! 'H' *sama dengan* 'ha'! 'H' is the same with 'ha'! (laughter)
37	**Mr Adi:**	(laughs) Yes. Now continue. H... [O.... U....S...E..]
38	**S3:**	[H....O....U....S]...E Oh, house!
39	**S4:**	(looking on S3's book, attempting to copy)
40	**Mr Adi:**	(pointing to S4). No (shaking head). Listen: H.... write. *Tulis...*
41	**S4:**	H...
42	**Mr Adi:**	O...U...S...E
43	**S4:**	(writing it down)
44	**Mr Adi:**	Good! (smiles). OK. Say it. HOuse.
45	**S3 and S4:**	Haus.
46	**Mr Adi:**	HOuse.
47	**S3 and S4:**	House (smiles).
48	**Mr Adi:**	HOuse. Yes, better. So, <u>HO</u>USE, what is it? (pointing to S6)
49	**S6:**	*Rumah, Pak.* House, Sir.
50	**Mr Adi:**	Very good (smiles). The spelling? (tilting his head)
51	**S6:**	H...O...O..
52	**Mr Adi:**	Ah, ah? (gesturing the third letter, raising his eyebrows)
53	**S6:**	H...O...U...[
54	**Mr Adi:**	[Y]e...s...
55	**S6:**	...S....E
56	**Mr Ardi:**	Excellent! (smile)
57	**Ss:**	(smiling, looking at one another in confidence)

In discussing the two clips above, the teachers found them in stark contrast, with Mr Mardi and Mr Adi showing different levels of engagement in terms of speech modification. Mrs Rosita and Mr Cecep thought there were several speech modification features that made the difference between Mr Mardi's and Mr Adi's instruction.

One contrast between the discourses of the two teachers is the volume of the voice. Mr Mardi used a normal voice when talking in the first place, until he was prompted to adjust his volume by S1 (lines 5–8), resulting in him uttering (wo:tʒ) loudly. However, he returned to speaking at his normal volume soon after (lines 12–16). Mr Adi, on the other hand, exhibited a range of volume modifications when talking to his students. He did not speak loudly in the beginning (line 22) but then spoke more loudly later on. He also appeared to have spoken louder than usual on different occasions (lines 26 and 44) to mark the lesson unit that was being discussed, 'House'. When asked why he did so, Mr Adi said that he wanted to facilitate comprehension. Many of his learners were unfamiliar with English words and how they were pronounced, so he increased the volume as necessary in order to help them better understand the lesson.

The second difference was in repetition. The teachers found that while Mr Mardi did not use repetition, Mr Adi did. He asked the learners to repeat after him, 'house', until they could pronounce it to the level that he deemed acceptable (lines 44–48). This then led Mr Adi to also check for comprehension that occurred twice in the extract (lines 27 and 48). First, he asked the learners what 'rumah' is in English (line 27); and second, he asked what 'house' is in Indonesian (line 48). In this respect, Mr Adi modified his speech, by alternating from the TL to L1 and the TL – he used the learners' L1, that is, Indonesian, in order to aid comprehension. By contrast, Mr Mardi did not check learners' comprehension. As soon as he wrote 'watch' for the learners, he only gave a brief comment on how English operates and walked towards his desk.

The next feature of speech modification that distinguished Mr Mardi's and Mr Adi's instruction was simplified syntax. Mrs Rosita stated that there was no evidence that Mr Mardi simplified his syntax, as he resorted to using Indonesian (lines 4, 12, 16) but this use of the L1 was not deemed valuable to aid instruction. Mr Adi, however, twice simplified his syntax. In line 29, he started with the word 'spelling' before continuing with a full, and yet simple, sentence 'What is the spelling?'. In line 34, he used the same strategy. He said, 'Robbie, writing,' before continuing with a request 'can you write [sic] down?'

Then, one of the teacher educators, Mr Handoko, asked Mrs Rosita and Mr Cecep to analyse the pronunciation of the two teachers. The teachers noticed that Mr Adi's pronunciation was more 'articulate' than Mr Mardi. They argued that Mr Adi's stressed words (lines 44, 46, 48) and clearly intoned sentences (e.g. line 46) were very noticeable. For them, Mr Adi demonstrated specific speech modifications in the domain of pronunciation. But the teachers could not see the same thing in Mr Mardi's clip, as his intonation, for example, did not vary. Mr Mardi acknowledged this lack of variety in pronunciation as a sign of his lack of proficiency. He highlighted this lack of variety as a weakness in his English language proficiency. He stated that,

> *Ya … emang atuh. Kelemahan saya emang di pronunciation. My weakness, I think. Susah, buat kalo ngomong sama anak-anak pokoknya. Tapi saya belajar.*

> Yes, it is true. My weakness is in pronunciation. My weakness. The bottom line is it is difficult for me to speak with children. But I am learning.

The teachers then pointed out that the case of speech modification was even clearer in Mr Adi, since he used facial expressions (e.g. smile) and gestures in order to help convey meaning. Mr Adi also tilted his head (line 34) in an attempt that appeared to have mimicked what S3 (line 33) did. Mr Adi did the same thing, tilting his head (line 48) and raising his eyebrows (line 50) later during the discourse.

Overall, it was apparent that Mr Adi employed various speech modification features including louder volume, more deliberate and articulate pronunciation (stress and intonation), repetition, simplified syntax and comprehension checks. Mr Adi also employed one speech modification feature that was not mentioned in the discussion: using discourse markers: 'OK' (line 44) and 'So' (line 48) to navigate the discourse (Walsh, 2011). All of these speech modification features helped Mr Adi to convey meaning as well as create meaning (Walsh, 2006, 2011). This was evident in line 47 when S3 and S4 were able to pronounce 'house', indicating their happiness with a smile. The most obvious result was seen in line 57 when the students were smiling and a few of them nodded, seemingly looking at one another in confidence. S3 in particular who looked a bit lost in line 23, gradually gained some confidence in line 35, and finally displayed her full confidence along with other students in line 57.

One thing that also helped Mr Adi's instruction was the use of facial expressions (smiling, raising eyebrows) and gestures (tilting head, pointing). The teachers agreed that these speech modification features, in addition to the multimodality of facial expressions and gestures (Kress, 2010), are very important when teaching young learners, given the saliency of comprehension for learning (Vygotsky, 1978, 1998). Mr Adi stated that these multimodal speech modification features are even more important when teaching lower level learners such as Grade 1.

Mr Doni made an overall evaluation of Mr Adi by saying:

> I think, in the clip Mr Mardi talked normal. Very normal. Like.. he was talking to teenagers. But in … Mr Adi is [sic] … he was very different. He … he modified his speech. He sounds [sic] like he was … he was talking to children, or maybe like … he was one of the children (laughter).

This was confirmed by Mr Adi. He stated that he had tried to modify his speech, including using facial expressions and gestures, as much as he could because he knew he was dealing with Grade 1 students. He philosophised that what helped him in his instruction was the way he imagined himself as part of the children, a strategy endorsed by Guz and Tetiurka (2013). He stated,

> When Mr Doni said that I was like one of the children ... (laughter), maybe .. maybe he was right. Because that's what I wanting [sic] to do. I want to imagine myself as being part of them, or being them, maybe, and talking like them. Then I can direct them to get what I want from them.

Mr Kartono, the other teacher educator, then brought the teachers' attention to Mrs Rosita's clip when she was teaching Grade 1 learners. In the clip a student asked her a question:

67	S6:	*Miss, kalo 'gede banget'?*
		Miss, if 'very big', what is it?
68	Mrs Rosita:	Besar sekali... maksudnyaaaa? (smiling)
69	S6:	Iya, Miss. 'Besar sekali'.
		Yes, Miss. 'Very big'.
70	Mrs Rosita:	OK... Fi:rst... what is 'besaaar'? (gesturing)
71	S6:	Ah?
72	Mrs Rosita:	In Engliiiish......What... is.... 'besa:r'? Be....sar?
73	S6:	Besar, Miss? E...
74	S7:	Big, Miss.
75	Mrs Rosita:	Yes, correct... Big. Biiiii......g.
		(gesturing, walking to the board, spelling) B.... (pointing to the board)
76	Ss:	Iii...
77	Mrs Rosita:	Iii...
78	Ss:	Gee...
79	Mrs Rosita:	Gee... B...I.....G. Big. Say... it...Everyone... Big.
80	Ss:	Big.
81	Mrs Rosita:	Big. Besar. What about 'Besar sekali'?
82	Ss:	(Silent)
83	Mrs Rosita:	Besar: Big. Besar sekali: Veeeee..... ry..... big.
		Very... big (writing on the board). Say it together... Ve....
84	Ss:	Ve..
85	Mrs Rosita:	Ry...
86	Ss:	Ry..

87	**Mrs Rosita:**	Ve…ry.
88	**Ss:**	Ve…ry.
89	**Mrs Rosita:**	Very.
90	**Ss:**	Very.
91	**Mrs Rosita:**	Very big.
92	**Ss:**	Very big.
93	**Mrs Rosita:**	Gooood!… Now.. what is… very big… again?
94	**Ss:**	Besar sekali, Miss. Besar sekali.
95	**Mrs Rosita:**	Very good!

Mr Kartono wanted the teachers to compare that clip with another one of Mrs Rosita when she was teaching Grade 5 learners as follows:

112	**Mrs Rosita:**	Does anyone know… the meaning of beautiful in … Indonesian?
113	**S1:**	Cantik.
114	**Mrs Rosita:**	Correct. The meaning of 'beautiful' is… 'cantik.' What can you say with
115		'beautiful'?… What word can go together with 'beautiful'?
116	**S1:**	Beautiful…. Beautiful woman!
117	**Mrs Rosita:**	Yes, correct. [thumbs up] Beautiful woman. What else?
118	**Students:**	(silent)
119	**Mrs Rosita:**	Oh look at this bird …[showing photo]. What can you say?

The teachers were a bit confused in distinguishing the difference between the two clips. Even Mrs Rosita herself was uncertain as to what it was that differed between them. They asked Mr Kartono to replay the clips. He did. After they watched it the second time, it was suggested that the difference was in pace. Mr Mardi thought that in both clips, Mrs Rosita appeared to have deliberately reduced her pace when talking to the different grade leaners. The other teachers concurred.

Mr Kartono stated that it is true that the slow pace of Mrs Rosita's speeches indicated her speech modification that helped her instruction (Walsh, 2006, 2011). However, the point he wanted to make was *pausing*. He highlighted how Mrs Rosita paused in between words when teaching the Grade 1 learners. This is evident, for example, when she said,

79	**Mrs Rosita:**	Gee… B…I…..G. Big. Say… it…Everyone… Big.

However, when she was teaching the Grade 5 learners, Mrs Rosita tended to pause in between longer constructions as in clauses or even sentences:

112   **Mrs Rosita:**   Does anyone know... the meaning of beautiful in ... Indonesian?
119   **Mrs Rosita:**   Oh look at this bird ...[showing photo]. What can you say?

This was the moment when Mr Handoko argued that this 'unrealised skill' of Mrs Rosita to pause in between words when dealing with lower level learners (Grade 1) and to pause in between phrases and sentences when dealing with higher level learners (Grade 5) could have been influenced by her ability to imagine herself as a young learner (Guz & Tetiurka, 2013). Mrs Rosita agreed. She thought that imagining herself to be one of the learners also helped to access their level of learning. Understanding that each age level has its own ZPD (Vygotsky, 1998), Mrs Rosita tried to gauge the ZPD of the specific age level of her Grade 1 students. She did it by first imagining herself as a young learner. She stated,

> If I can.. If I can imagine myself like them, or being them, I can access their level of learning. Then I can modify my speech. Then I won't talk like an adult. I would talk like a child, speaking to another child.

Thus, the two teachers, Mr Adi and Mrs Rosita imagined themselves as a young learner. If they were to teach adult beginner learners, both Mr Adi and Mrs Rosita stated that they still maintained their identity as adult teachers who could modify their speech at the level of the adult learners. But when they were teaching young learners, the two teachers found it more useful to imagine themselves as one of them. By imagining themselves to be one of the young learners, both Mrs Rosita and Mr Adi could place themselves at the same level with the learners, hence bringing them what they called 'an holistic understanding' of the learners. Vygotsky (1998: 200) maintained the importance of teachers to understand:

> the whole sequence of the course of child development, of all the features of each age, stage, and phase, of all the basic types of normal and anomalous development, of the whole structure and dynamics of child development in its many forms.

However, what made Mrs Rosita different from Mr Adi is the level of consciousness in modifying her speech. Mr Adi stated that his speech modification was deliberate; he still thought carefully about what to say and how to say it as a child – in his words, he had 'not been very natural about doing it.' Mrs Rosita's speech modification, on the other hand, was natural. It is true that her decision to imagine herself as a young learner was deliberate, but the pedagogical decision to modify her speech occurred at subconscious level. When asked whether she deliberately planned to speak like her Grade 1 students, Mrs Rosita said, 'No, I didn't.' She stated:

> I imagined myself accessing the zone, and being one of the learners. Once I was there, the speech modifications became natural. I was still a teacher, but not an adult teacher. I became like a young learner, being one of them. My speech modifications came naturally, I did not feel like I need to modify things deliberately. All natural.

When they re-examined the clips of Mrs Rosita, all the other teachers and teacher educators agreed how natural she was when modifying her speech. Her speech modification occurred effortlessly. This was done through the employment of more pronounced stressed words and intonation, pausing as she saw fit, reducing the pace of speeches, simplifying syntax and using repetition and comprehension checks. Scaffolding instruction in this respect does not come as a result of instruction being modified from the point of view of the teacher. Rather, it comes from the point of view of the learner because Mrs Rosita succeeded in imagining herself as a young learner, hence talking as if she was one, explaining as if she was one. Eventually this led to her success, as the learners were able to demonstrate their comprehension. Mrs Rosita employed this strategy while at the same time using the TL to check comprehension in the learners' L1. This is evident in the following lines:

93	**Mrs Rosita:**	Gooood!... Now.. what is... very... very big... again?
94	**Ss:**	Besar sekali, Miss. Besa::r sekali.
95	**Mrs Rosita:**	Ve:ry go:.....od!

Thus, Mrs Rosita's ways of guiding her learners in a slow, deliberate discursive process, even by looking for meaning in the learners' L1, were subconscious decisions. They occurred as a result of her success in imagining herself as one of the young learners.

Limitations of the Study

Methodologically speaking, the findings have some limitations because the study only reported on observations of teachers teaching in Grade 1 (representing lower level learners) and Grade 5 (representing higher level learners). Therefore, further research on how speech modification features may be used at different grades of primary schooling is warranted. Interpretation of the findings could have been more convincing had multivocal ethnographic statements had also been generated from teachers in, for example, Grades 3 and 4. Furthermore, the ethnographic nature of the study could have been strengthened had the study taken a longitudinal form. Clearly the multivocal ethnographic statements in this study are not the final word on teachers' practices of speech modification, but rather they are voices occurring in an ongoing dialogue. They are texts that require caution in terms of interpretation. Therefore, a study undertaken in a longer time span is needed in order to capture a more comprehensive portrait of teachers' and teachers educators' perspectives of speech modification in the EYL classroom.

Implications for Teacher Education

Despite the limitations, this study has demonstrated how the employment of speech modification features can lead to more effective instructional practices. Teachers' ability to modify their speech is an important discursive skill that fosters learning; however, speech modification features are not an end in themselves.

First, speech modification features best occur when teachers level themselves with young learners. The way Mrs Rosita and Mr Adi developed a specific pedagogy that imagines themselves as a young learner helped achieve this. Since they are in the early stage of language development, young learners' comprehension is limited. For this reason, it is vital for EYL teachers to access learners' ZPD. Accessing their ZPD would help teachers identify which might be the most effective speech modification features, such as reducing the pace of speech, using more pronounced stress and intonation, and employing clear articulate pronunciation. For the EYL teacher, this imagining procedure might not allow them to develop natural child-friendly discourse as in the case of Mrs Rosita, but it could at least prompt the EYL teacher to employ specific, deliberate modification features that are discourse appropriate the way Mr Ardi did it (Mahn, 2015; Vygotsky, 1998).

One challenge for teacher educators is to provide teachers with exposure to classroom discourses where they could learn to imagine themselves as a young learner. Teacher imagination in conceptualising the young learner as a second language learner could have a considerable role in bringing success to the learner's language acquisition (Guz & Tetiurka, 2013). What the EYL teacher needs is training that allows them to create predictions regarding young learners' possible responses to various classroom discourses by imagining what they might think and how they might behave. According to Guz and Tetiurka (2013: 419), it is necessary for teachers to 'create a mental image or a concept of a young learner by gathering knowledge about his or her developmental characteristics and fully grasping the pedagogical implications of this knowledge.' Teacher educators need to provide EYL teachers with opportunities for such mental image creation of the young learner. EYL teachers also need to be provided with tasks that require them to analyse their own language, or that of others, when imagining themselves as a young learner in a reflective, encouraging and engaging manner. In developing such mental image creation of the young learner, the employment of a series of speech modification features as a multimodal discursive practice is necessary (Kress, 2010). The fact that speech modification features were employed in combination with facial expressions, gestures, pictures and texts indicates that they are most effective when they are not done in isolation. Imagining oneself as a child could lead to successful implementation of reducing the pace of speech, gesturing, using pictures and texts and using clear articulate pronunciation; and their being implemented in combination would lead to greater success than, for example, reducing the pace of speech alone. Successful imagining of oneself as a young learner in a multimodal discursive practice could serve as comprehensible input and allow for the scaffolding of instruction that is well suited to the age and level of young learners. This is what makes it different from speech modification in teaching adult or teenage learners.

Support for teachers, especially the novice ones, to go through the process of developing a discursive pedagogy is vital. Teachers need time and encouragement to reflect critically upon their practice, which can block the possibility of considering discourse as a suitable pedagogical approach. With teacher education programmes exclusively focusing on two strands, language awareness and teaching methodology (Walsh, 2013), as in the case of those training EYL teachers (Zein, 2015, 2017), there is a demand for the development of a third strand where teachers' classroom discourse holds prominent importance. This chapter amplifies Walsh's (2011, 2013) advocacy for a strand on teacher education courses and programmes that deal specifically with interaction in the classroom; where EYL teachers receive assistance in observing, analysing, and developing awareness of their speech modification. Ongoing opportunities that model, guide and encourage the employment of speech modification features are crucial in order for teachers to be able to enhance their interactional competence (Walsh, 2013).

To plan for such professional development activities, teacher educators could benefit from the multivocal, collaborative and discursive methodology employed in this study. The elicitation of multiple perspectives of video clips through small-group discussions among teachers, guided by teacher educators, can be an invaluable tool for analysis of learning and teaching. Teachers in a given sociocultural context can reflect on what they do with and think about their learners, and then form dialogues that enable them to learn from and encourage one another (Molle, 2013). The methodology offers teachers opportunities to assess videos of their practice in reflective, structured ways. The process allows them to focus specifically on how their linguistic and non-verbal choices have an impact on their teaching, allowing them to build relationships with learners and scaffold instruction pertinent to their age and level (Schieble et al., 2015). The post-observatory nature of the methodology would also allow teacher educators to scaffold their instruction in ways that are reflective and encouraging for teachers (Engin, 2015).

References

Butler, Y.G. (2005) Comparative perspectives towards communicative activities among elementary school teachers in South Korea, Japan and Taiwan. *Language Teaching Research* 9 (4), 423–446.

Butler, Y.G. (2015) English language education among young learners in East Asia: A review of current research (2004–2014). *Language Teaching* 48, 303–342. doi:10.1017/S0261444815000105

Garton, S., Copland, F. and Burns, A. (2011) *Investigating Global Practices in Teaching English to Young Learners. ELT Research Papers 11-01.* London: British Council.

Copland, F. and Yonetsugi, E. (2016) Teaching English to young learners: Supporting the case for the bilingual native English speaker teacher. *Classroom Discourse* 7 (3), 221–238. doi:10.1080/19463014.2016.1192050

Copland, F., Garton, S. and Burns, A. (2014) Challenges in teaching English to young learners: Global perspectives and local realities. *TESOL Quarterly* 48 (4), 738–762. doi:10.1002/tesq.148

Cowan, K. (2014) Multimodal transcription of video: Examining interaction in early years classrooms. *Classroom Discourse* 5 (1), 6–21. doi:10.1080/19463014.2013.859846

Emery, H. (2012) *A Global Study of Primary English Teachers' Qualifications, Training and Career Development. ELT Research Papers 12-08.* London: British Council.

Engin, M. (2015) Trainer talk in post-observation feedback sessions: An exploration of scaffolding. *Classroom Discourse* 6 (1), 57–72. doi:10.1080/19463014.2014.919867

Gass, S.M. (2015) Comprehensible input and output in classroom interaction. In N. Markee (ed.) *The Handbook of Classroom Discourse and Interaction* (1st edn) (pp. 182–197). Malden, MA: Blackwell Publisher.

Gass, S.M. and Mackey, A. (2007) Input, interaction, and output in second language acquisition. In B. VanPatten and J. Williams (eds) *Theories in Second Language Acquisition: An Introduction* (pp. 175–199). Mahwah, NJ: Lawrence Erlbaum.

Guz, E. and Tetiurka, M. (2013) The role of teacher imagination in conceptualizing the child as a second language learner. *Studies in Second Language Learning and Teaching* 3 (3), 419–439.

James, A. (2007) Giving voice to children's voices: Practices and problems, pitfalls and potentials. *American Anthropologist* 109 (2), 261–272.

Kress, G. (2010) *Multimodality.* New York: Routledge.

Kyratzis, A. and Cook-Gumperz, J. (2015) Child discourse. In D. Schiffrin, D. Tannen and H.E. Hamilton (eds) *The Handbook of Discourse Analysis* (2nd edn) (pp. 681–704). Malden, MA: Blackwell Publisher.

Mackey, A. and Goo, J.M. (2007) Interaction research in SLA: A meta-analysis and research synthesis. In A. Mackey (ed.) *Input, Interaction and Corrective Feedback in L2 Learning* (pp. 379–452). Oxford: Oxford University Press.

Mahn, H. (2015) Classroom discourse and interaction in the Zone Proximal Development. In N. Markee (ed.) *The Handbook of Classroom Discourse and Interaction* (1st edn) (pp. 250–264). Malden, MA: Blackwell Publisher.

Molle, D. (2013) The pitfalls of focusing on instructional strategies in professional development for teachers of English learners. *Teacher Education Quarterly* 40 (1), 101–124.

Rymes, B. (2016) *Classroom Discourse Analysis: A Tool for Critical Reflection.* New York: Routledge.

Saito, E., Tsukui, A. and Tanaka, Y. (2008) Problems on primary school-based in-service training in Vietnam: A case study of Bac Giang province. *International Journal of Educational Development* 28, 89–103. doi: 10.1016/j.ijedudev.2007.08.001

Schieble, M., Vetter, A. and Meacham, M. (2015) A discourse analytic approach to video analysis of teaching: Aligning desired identities with practice. *Journal of Teacher Education* 66 (3), 245–260. doi:10.1177/0022487115573264

Tobin, J.J. (1988) Visual anthropology and multivocal ethnography: A dialogical approach to Japanese preschool class size. *Dialectical Anthropology* 13, 173–187.

Tobin, J.J., Wu, D.Y.H. and Davidson, D.H. (1989) *Preschool in Three Cultures: Japan, China, and the United States*. New Haven, CT: Yale University Press.

Vygotsky, L.S. (1978) *Mind in Society: The Development of Higher Psychological Processes*. Cambridge, MA: Harvard University Press.

Vygotsky, L.S. (1998) Child psychology. *The Collected Works of L.S. Vygotsky: Vol. 5. Problems of the Theory and History of Psychology*. New York: Plenum.

Walsh, S. (2006) *Investigating Classroom Discourse*. New York: Routledge.

Walsh, S. (2011) *Exploring Classroom Discourse: Language in Action*. New York: Routledge.

Walsh, S. (2013) *Classroom Discourse and Teacher Professional Development*. Edinburgh: Edinburgh University Press.

Wood, D., Bruner, J. and Ross, G. (1976) The role of tutoring in problem-solving. *Journal of Child Psychology and Psychiatry* 17, 89–100.

Wu, X. (2012) Primary English education in China: Review and reflection. In B. Spolsky and Y.-I. Moon (eds) *Primary School English-Language Education in Asia: From Policy to Practice* (pp. 1–22). New York: Routledge.

Zein, M.S. (2015) Preparing elementary English teachers: Innovations at pre-service level. *Australian Journal of Teacher Education* 40 (6), 104–120. doi:10.14221/ajte.2015v40n6.6

Zein, M.S. (2017) Professional development needs of primary EFL teachers: Perspectives of teachers and teacher educators. *Professional Development in Education* 43 (2), 293–313. doi:10.1080/19415257.2016.1156013

5 Learning to Teach: Pre-service English Language Teachers' Experience of Learning Study in Hong Kong

Yuefeng Zhang

Introduction

Driven by the force of globalization and the global rise of English, the past few decades have witnessed a rapid expansion of English language education to young learners (YL) all around the world (Emery, 2012). With the belief that it is better to begin language learning early to master the language well, many countries have started to teach English language from the beginning in primary schools (Copland *et al.*, 2014). For example, Hong Kong, with its history of being a British colony before 1997 and where the study reported in this chapter was conducted, adopted English as a compulsory subject from Primary 1 with the introduction of compulsory education in 1978 (Sze & Wong, 1999). English is so highly valued as a path to upward social mobility in the country that in recent years, English learning has even been spread to primary school and kindergarten children (Ng, 2011).

Along with the rapid expansion of English language education, one of the biggest challenges is to provide quality English language teachers with sufficient training to meet the huge demand in schools, especially to young learners (Emery, 2012). Teacher education for English for young learners (EYL) teachers is a complex process for teachers to interact with and with different stakeholders (Zein, 2016a) and is shaped by many contextual factors in schools (Zein, 2016c). The challenges encountered by in-service EYL teachers in classroom teaching include limited linguistic competence and pedagogical skills (Zein, 2016b, 2017), low motivation in students, classroom management, and difficulty in teaching speaking, writing and grammar (Copland *et al.*, 2014). Big class sizes with greater student diversity as a result of inclusive education has also made it difficult to use communicative approaches, maintain an orderly environment, and understand and cater for individual needs for many EYL teachers (Copland *et al.*, 2014). On top of the above challenges, pre-service EYL teachers may also encounter other challenges, such as getting acclimated to the complex working contexts by overcoming the dissonance between the ideal and reality (Golombek & Doran, 2014; Kaufman & Moss, 2010), and bridging the gap between the theory learned in tertiary pre-service teacher education and the reality of classroom practices in schools (Allen & Wright, 2014). To support EYL teachers to cope better with these challenges, one of the major solutions is to promote quality teacher education and continuous teacher professional development programmes (Emery, 2012; Copland *et al.*, 2014).

Previous studies have focused on different aspects of teacher education for EYL teachers. First of all, there have been studies providing a description of worldwide, continent-regional or country-specific development and challenges in teacher education (e.g. Emery, 2012; Enever, 2014; Zein, 2016a), with a call for more effective teacher education programmes to improve the quality of EYL teachers. Second, there have been studies in identifying teachers' needs in professional development, in terms of language proficiency, pedagogical skills, and knowledge about learners and contexts (Kabilan & Veratharaju, 2013; Zein, 2017) or challenges encountered by teachers (Copland *et al.*, 2014). These studies have argued that the teacher development activities should be designed to meet teachers' needs in professional development. Third, there have been studies investigating EYL teachers' development in certain areas, including the development of practical knowledge in teaching contexts (Chou, 2008), the complex interplay of teachers' cognition, emotions and commitment (Golombek, 2015; Golombek & Doran, 2014; Moodie & Feryok, 2015) at work and regarding their professional identity (Gu, 2011; Gu & Benson, 2015). The studies on teachers' development in emotions, commitment (Golombek, 2015; Golombek & Doran, 2014; Moodie & Feryok, 2015) and professional identity (Gu, 2011; Gu & Benson, 2015) have highlighted the importance of teachers' social-emotional development, which has often been neglected by the instruction-focused tradition of teacher education (Zhang, 2019, forthcoming). Last but not least, there have been studies discussing the roles of different stakeholders in supporting teacher development (Zein, 2016c); for example, the roles of government-based training agencies (e.g. Zein, 2016b).

The abovementioned efforts to explore effective approaches to promote professionalism of EYL teachers are far from conclusive. While most of the previous studies focused mainly on the professional development of individual EYL teachers, there is a need to investigate the application of teacher collaboration for combating challenges and promoting professional development of EYL teachers. As teacher collaboration is one of the key elements in enhancing student achievement (Goddard *et al.*, 2010), improving teaching professional learning (Amzat & Valdez, 2017) and sustaining innovative changes in schools (Poulos *et al.*, 2014), it may be an effective solution to help EYL teachers to tackle challenges encountered. This chapter reports a study on the professional development of a group of pre-service EYL teachers via a collaborative Learning Study project in Hong Kong.

Learning Study for Pre-Service Teacher Education in Hong Kong

While many countries (especially in the West) involve mainly generalist teachers in teaching English, schools in Hong Kong have begun to employ specialist language teachers to teach English from Primary 1 since 2005. Furthermore, all primary and secondary teachers are required to be trained graduates since 2004 (Lai & Grossman, 2008) and all English teachers are also required to pass mandatory benchmark examinations to prove they have met the language proficiency requirements. Learning study was first introduced to improve learning quality, promote pre-service teacher professionalism and enhance teacher collaboration in many countries or regions since 2000 (Zhang, 2015), including Hong Kong, Brunei, Singapore, Sweden and the UK. It is a type of collaborative action research with the following typical features of action research. The participating teacher adopts an enquiry-based approach and focuses on improving learning and teaching. It includes a process of diagnosing, action planning, action taking, evaluating and reflecting on learning (Susman & Evered, 1978). It is driven by the teacher who acts as a researcher and leads the process of solving the problems out of their interests (Stenhouse, 1975). It requires the teacher to examine their own practices via reflection in action (Richardson & Anders, 1994). And it helps bridge the gap between theory and practice (Schon, 1987).

Guided by variation theory (Marton, 2014), Learning Study follows a unique procedure, as illustrated in Figure 5.1.

The collaborative nature of Learning Study lies in its assembling a group of teachers who teach the same subject and year group (sometimes with university researchers or teacher trainers) into a team to explore collaboratively more effective ways of support student learning. The team first selects a topic, then identifies pupils' prior knowledge and difficulties in learning the topic through pre-test and pre-lesson interviews. Based on the evidence of these difficulties, the object of learning and critical aspects of the research lesson(s) are determined. Teachers then collaboratively design the lesson(s) (called research lesson(s)) and take turns to enact the lesson plan. While one teacher teaches a lesson, all the other team members observe the lesson. Immediately following each round of research lesson(s), the effectiveness of the teaching and learning is reviewed and

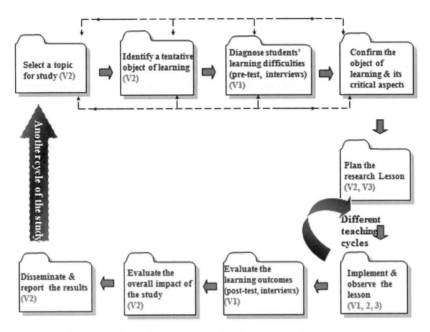

Figure 5.1 The procedure of Learning Study (Zhang, 2009: 5)

improvements to the plan are suggested. The revised plan is then implemented with the next class in the hope of achieving optimal teaching
results (Lo *et al.*, 2005). The number of lessons included depends on the
scale of the object of learning decided by the team. In the end, the team
will evaluate the whole project and reflect on their learning.

Learning Study bears three unique features. First, it includes teacher
collaboration in a cyclical process of experimenting with the pedagogical
design in at least two classes (or cycles). Through peer observation and
collaborative review of lessons, teachers can become more sensitive to
pupils' needs and the critical pedagogical designs contributing to effective learning (Lo *et al.*, 2005). Second, Learning Study adopts variation
theory as its guiding theory and focuses on students' learning of the
object of learning (concepts learned in order to achieve the objectives)
(Lo, 2012). Critical aspects are identified based on pupils' learning problems, difficulties and needs diagnosed by pre-tests and/or pre-lesson
interviews. Third, variation is used as a pedagogical tool for pupils to
experience differences and/or similarities of examples/inputs related to
the critical aspects purposefully and systematically, and to separate the
critical aspects effectively (Zhang, 2017).

Learning Study promote teachers' professional development by widen-
ing teachers' conceptions of teaching (Gao & Ko, 2009) and learning (Lee,
2008), improving their subject knowledge (Lo *et al.*, 2008), and enhancing
their ability to cater for individual differences (Lo *et al.*, 2008). During the

process, Learning Study transforms in-service teachers into learners (Pang, 2006), curriculum developers (Zhang, 2014) and researchers (Lo *et al.*, 2008). In the long run, it leads to the development of a community of teaching practice (Cheng, 2009). For pre-service teachers, Learning Study provides them with opportunities for reflecting on, designing and redesigning teaching in a collaborative atmosphere with peer support (Davies & Dunnill, 2008) and improves their lesson planning ability (Andrew, 2011). However, most of the above studies reported Learning Study projects by either in-service teachers or non-English pre-service teachers (Davies & Dunnill, 2008; Ko, 2012; Sims & Walsh, 2009), therefore the potential of using Learning Study in training pre-service EYL teachers is yet to be fully explored (Gierlinger *et al.*, 2016). Hence, this chapter fills in the knowledge gap by exploring the impact of Learning Study on a group of pre-service EYL teachers' professional learning in Hong Kong.

Research Design

Research questions

The study utilized qualitative research methods to address the following research questions:

(1) How was the Learning Study conducted by the six pre-service EYL teachers?
(2) What did the pre-service EYL teachers learn from the Learning Study?
(3) Did these pre-service EYL teachers encounter any challenges? If yes, what were the challenges?

Research context

Since 2007, Learning Study has been introduced as a 39-hour core course called 'Learning Study' in the training programmes for pre-service teachers in the Hong Kong Institute of Education (Ko, 2012) (see Appendix 1 for the arrangement of the 39-hour Learning Study course). Due to time limits, pre-lesson and post-lesson interviews were not included in the course. At the end, the pre-service EYL teachers did an oral presentation to report and evaluate their Learning Study project in the last lesson. Each pre-service teacher submitted a 1500-word individual essay to reflect on their own learning, describe the challenges they encountered and make recommendations for further improvement.

Research participants

All the 34 pre-service teachers who attended the Learning Study course in 2011–2012 were invited, with a group of six pre-service EYL teachers (Alice, Cindy, Fanny, Jade, Sarah and Tammy) agreeing to participate in the research. Among them, Sarah was 19 years old while the others were 20. At the time of the study, they were studying year 2 of a bachelor of English language education programme. They had little knowledge of the prospective pupils and limited pedagogical knowledge of English language teaching. None of them had experience of teaching a whole class in school, yet three of them (Fanny, Jade and Tammy) had experience of tutoring individual pupils after school. The author played the role of both teacher trainer and researcher in the study. As the teacher trainer, the author had the advantage of observing the EYL teachers throughout the whole project while also paying attention to reporting the EYL teachers' experiences and perspectives without adding her personal interpretation.

The six EYL teachers focused their Learning Study on enhancing pupils' English reading strategies in a primary school in Hong Kong, where Cantonese was the pupils' mother tongue while English was learned as a foreign language. Two primary four classes (aged 9–10, 24 pupils in class 1 and 25 pupils in class 2) were selected for the research lessons.

Data collection

Three qualitative research methods were employed in the study. First, nine 10-minute focus group interviews with all six pre-service EYL teachers were conducted at the end of each 3-hour lesson about the pre-service EYL teachers' experience in and learning from the Learning Study project. Second, observations were conducted throughout the whole Learning Study with field notes kept by the researcher about pre-service EYL teachers' participation in the Learning Study. Third, documents (e.g. teaching materials and individual reflective essays on learning and challenges) were analysed to triangulate with findings from interviews and observations.

Data analysis

Open coding and axial coding (Saldaña, 2009) was performed to analyse the data from interviews, observations and documents examined to create tentative codes for concepts and categories related to teachers' learning and challenges encountered in Learning Study. The data, concepts and categories were examined and constantly compared to identify linkages between concepts, to identify clusters and categories, and finally formulate answers to the three research questions.

Results

The findings in relation to the research questions are reported respectively in the following three sections.

Finding 1: Implementing the Learning Study project

The Learning Study project was conducted following the steps illustrated in Figure 5.1.

Choosing a topic for study

The Learning Study project was conducted in one of the author's partnership schools. The pre-service EYL teachers suggested the topic of English reading strategy, which was approved by the school teachers. Primary 4 pupils, who had studied English since Primary 1, were selected by the teacher trainer as the pupils were more mature than junior graders and therefore easier to manage in teaching. As it was the target pupils' first time to learn English reading strategies, the object of learning was specified by the team as 'guessing the meaning of difficult words with the help of contextual clues'. The pre-service EYL teachers also discussed and explored some prospective critical aspects of the object of learning, including different categories of contextual clues: pronouns, connectives, antonyms, synonyms, word structure, sentence structure and collocation.

Diagnosing pupils' learning needs with a pre-test

Then the pre-service EYL teachers designed a pre-test to diagnose whether the target pupils had mastered some English reading strategies. As they had no experience in designing a pre-test paper, the teacher trainer introduced the function, format, focus and structure of the pre- and post-tests, ways of analyzing the tests and provided some sample questions for the pre-service EYL teachers' references. The pre-service EYL teachers then picked the questions from the reference list for the pre-test and the post-test (for 15 minutes each with the same test paper) (see Appendix 1). Pupils were asked to read a passage and picked an answer from three choices about each difficult word: (A) if they have learned the word, they can explain the meaning; (B) if they do not know the word, they guess the meaning and explain the strategy; and (C) if they do not know the word and they do not want to guess the meaning. The pre-test was mailed to the target school, whose teachers helped to administer the test on the two target classes and sent the completed papers back within two weeks. The completed papers were then analyzed by the pre-service EYL teachers under guidance from the author.

Table 5.1 shows the result of the pre-test, which indicated that Class 1 had better prior knowledge than Class 2. Among the pupils who guessed the meaning (Choice B), only 44% of pupils in Class 1 and 29% in Class 2 used contextual clues to guess the meaning of difficult words. The remaining pupils either guessed the meaning based on their feelings or with a single-word strategy. For example, many pupils guessed the meaning 'foolish' as 'fish balls' thinking the two terms shared similar spelling,

Table 5.1 Pre-test results

Choice	A	B	C	Guessing with contextual clues	Guessing based on their feelings or single-word strategy
Class 1	13%	66%	21%	44%	56%
Class 2	8%	56%	36%	29%	71%

instead of looking for contextual clues. Based on the above observation, the following critical aspects were identified for the research lesson:

- The awareness that contextual clues are more effective than single-word strategy in guessing the meaning of difficult words.
- The strategy of guessing the meaning of difficult words by referring to different lengths of contextual clues (within the same sentence or in adjacent sentences).

Designing the research lesson

A 40-minute research lesson was designed collaboratively first by the pre-service EYL teachers and discussed with the teacher trainer. Seeing the pre-service EYL teachers did not use variation patterns purposefully in the lesson plan, the teacher trainer suggested the variation pattern in Table 5.2 should be added as Activity 1. Using the variation pattern, the teacher provided four different opportunities to guess the meaning of the same difficult word 'dumbbells' one after another: (1) a single-word strategy; (2) with contextual clues within the sentence; (3) with contextual clues in two sentences; and (4) with contextual clues in more sentences. By comparing the different guesses of meaning and discussing the strategies behind the guesses, pupils would be able to discern that using contextual clues is better than the single-word strategies (which was their existing strategy); and the more contextual clues they used, the more accurate their guesses would be.

In Activity 2, pupils would apply the strategy of using contextual clues to guess the meaning of different words. For such a purpose, the teacher trainer provided a list of examples for the pre-service EYL teachers to

Table 5.2 Variation patterns in the research lessons (Zhang, 2014)

Guessing the meaning of 'dumbbells'	Guess	Reading strategy used
(1) dumbbells		
(2) I bought a pair of dumbbells yesterday.		
(3) I bought a pair of dumbbells yesterday. I use them to keep fit.		
(4) I bought a pair of dumbbells yesterday. I use them to keep fit. They make the muscles of my arms stronger.		

select or adapt for the research lessons. Lastly, the pupils would do a worksheet on guessing difficult words to consolidate their understanding in Activity 3. The lesson would then be concluded with pupils summing up what they learned from the lesson.

The two cycles of research lesson

The research lesson was first taught in Class 1 by Alice, Cindy and Fanny while Jade, Sarah and Tammy and the teacher trainer observed the lesson. After the lesson, pre-service EYL teachers and the teacher trainer reflected on the effectiveness of the lesson based on the following list of questions:

- Were the critical features appropriate to pupils' learning?
- Was the variation pattern effective in enhancing pupils' learning of the critical aspects?
- Which activity went smoothly as planned and which one did not? Why/why not?
- How can the research lesson be improved?

After the reflection, a list of suggestions for further improvement was put forward for reference for the teachers teaching Class 2. Four days later, the revised lesson plan was enacted in Class 2 by Jade, Sarah and Tammy, while Alice, Cindy, Fanny and the teacher trainer observed the lesson. Table 5.3 summarizes the main differences between the two cycles of research lesson.

As shown by the pre-service EYL teachers in their oral presentation at the end of the project, Cycle 2 was more effective than Cycle 1 in four ways. First of all, time management was conducted in a better way to allow more time for detailed discussion and comparison of the use of strategies, the very critical aspects. This was achieved by cutting the number of examples and selecting examples appropriate for the pupils' level in Activities 2 and 3. Second, a focused question 'How did you come up with the guess?' was asked to engage pupils to reflect on their existing strategies, discern the new strategy of using contextual clues, applying the target strategy and evaluating the effectiveness of their application. Third, a clearer instruction was given to demonstrate how to do the worksheet. This provided scaffolding for pupils to develop from providing answers orally in Activity 2 to writing down guesses and explanations in the worksheet. Fourth, teachers utilized different strategies to engage pupils in discerning, discussion and sharing better by allowing more waiting time, asking more focused questions, encouraging pupils to speak louder and allowing more time to work on the worksheet. These revised practices had further enhanced pupils' experience of the variation patterns and consolidated pupils' grasp of the strategy, as shown in the post-test results reported below.

Still, room for improving Cycle 2 was identified by the team at the post-lesson reflection. The teachers needed to follow up with pupils' answers instead of always asking the same answers. For example, instead of asking

Table 5.3 Comparing the two cycles of research lesson (40 mins)

	Class 1	Class 2
Teachers	Alice, Cindy and Fanny	Jade, Sarah and Tammy
Observers	Jade, Sarah, Tammy and the author	Alice, Cindy Fanny and the author
Activity 1	• Guessing 'dumbbells' (10 mins) • Alice gave pupils less time for preparation before checking their answers • Alice forgot to ask pupils to discuss strategies	• Guessing 'dumbbells' (5 mins) • Jade gave pupils more time for preparation before checking their answers and invited more pupils to make a guess • Jade used key questions to engage pupils in discussing strategies: 'What's the meaning of ...?' 'How did you come up with the guess?'
Activity 2	• Applying the strategy in three examples (15 mins) • Cindy forgot to ask pupils to discuss strategies • Cindy walked to each pupil with a low voice and repeated their answers	• Applying the strategy in 3 examples (10 mins) • Sarah used key questions to engage pupils in discussing strategies • Sarah encouraged pupils to speak louder and encouraged more pupils to share opinions
Activity 3	• Doing a worksheet with six difficult words (10 mins) • Pupils began discussion while Fanny gave instruction • Many pupils did not know how to do the worksheet and left it blank • Fanny presented answers and explained strategies (5 mins)	• Tammy gave give instruction on how to do the worksheet (3 mins) • Doing a worksheet with three difficult words (10 mins) • Pupils finished the worksheet smoothly and presented answers and explain strategies (10 mins)
Conclusion	No	Pupils summed up learning (2 mins)

different pupils the same question 'What is the meaning of this word?', the teacher could ask follow-up questions such as 'Do you all agree?' or 'Do you have a different answer?' to develop the discussion better. Second, the pre-service EYL teachers needed to be more aware of and further check a greater variety of pupils' answers after they finished the worksheet. A few pupils had got wrong guesses due to careless inferring of meaning based on contextual clues. Asking them to share their process of working out the wrong guesses could help highlight other relevant critical aspects for further learning, that is, the skills of inferring meaning from contextual clues.

The post-tests

After the research lessons, the post-test (which was the same as the pre-test) was conducted in both classes to evaluate the effectiveness of the research lesson. The results of the post-test indicated that pupils in Class 2 had learned better than pupils in Class 1 (see Table 5.4). Among the pupils who chose B, 74% in Class 2 (45% more than the pre-test) used contextual clues to guess the meaning of difficult words, compared to 67% of pupils in Class 1 (23% more than the pre-test).

Table 5.4 Pre- and post-test results

Class test	A	C	B	Guessing with contextual clues	Guessing based on their feelings or single-word strategy
1_pre-test	13%	21%	66%	44%	56%
1_post-test	17%	8%	75%	67% (+23%)	33% (−23%)
2_pre-test	8%	36%	56%	29%	71%
2_post-test	12%	12%	76%	74% (+45%)	26% (−45%)

At the end of the project, the pre-service EYL teachers presented their case to 28 other pre-service EYL teachers in the tutorial class and each wrote an individual essay reflecting on their learning from different parts of the Learning Study project.

Finding 2: Learning to teach via Learning Study

The pre-service EYL teachers revealed that they had mainly benefited from the Learning Study project in five aspects. First, Learning Study enhanced the pre-service EYL teachers' sensitivity to pupil learning needs and changed their perceptions of teaching from teacher-dominated 'presentation' to 'genuine communication with pupils', thanks to the comparison between the teacher-controlled didactic teaching Cycle 1 and the improved teacher-pupil interaction in Cycle 2. As Alice said:

> The Learning Study has changed my view of being a primary teacher … now I realized that teaching is not only presentation. It is communication which takes an important role of education. Through effective communication, the teacher can get information of pupils' ability, need and the effectiveness of teaching.

And Tammy said:

> Through Learning Study, I have learned the importance of diagnosing pupils' difficulties. Many teachers in Hong Kong still use traditional methods to impart knowledge … they do not understand pupils' problems during or after a lesson, and thus the learning outcomes they set before usually cannot be achieved. The use of pre-test and post-test papers can solve this problem.

Second, Learning Study enhanced pre-service EYL teachers' knowledge of the selected object of learning. It started from a broad topic and narrowed down to an object of learning and its critical aspects for the research lesson. In Cycle 1, the use of strategies had not been highlighted sufficiently, which resulted in limited performances of pupils in both the worksheet and the post-test. In Cycle 2, teachers highlighted the use of strategies with key questions and spent more time on discussing strategies, which resulted in better test results. As Sarah said:

> Learning Study broadens my subject knowledge and pedagogical skills … it also focuses on the pupils' reasoning skills besides the ability to answer a question correctly … for example, even though some pupils guessed the meaning of the words correctly, we had to challenge them why they had such guesses so as to check if they really made use of the contextual clues.

Third, Learning Study enhanced the pre-service EYL teachers' pedagogical skills and classroom management skills, including questioning skills, giving clear instruction, time management and engaging pupils in activities. As Cindy said:

> I personally think the most difficult process should be the real teaching practice in Cycle 1. One possible reason was our inexperience in teaching. Another was the unpredictability of the classroom … while teaching, some pupils responded to the teachers actively by raising their hands but most of them shouted out their answers in their seats … the class was then out of control. Pupils kept chatting and paid little attention to the teachers.

And Fanny said:

> During my demonstration in Cycle 1, I distributed the worksheet and asked pupils to do it immediately. I didn't notice that I hadn't given enough instructions to them. When they were doing the worksheet, many pupils asked for clarification and explanation. After that, I discovered that it was my fault that I neglected the need of giving simple instructions.

The awareness of the lack of classroom management skills motivated the pre-service EYL teachers to ask the teacher trainer to share techniques and experience of engaging pupils, which led to the more effective classroom management in Cycle 2. The three first-time teachers, Alice, Cindy and Sarah, also benefited from observing more effective implementation of classroom management skills by more experienced teachers such as Fanny, Jade and Tammy.

Fourth, the pre-service EYL teachers found the collaboration with peer teachers very beneficial. Sharing the workload of teaching reduced the pressure and nervousness of the first-time teaching experience. Furthermore, peer observation of similar pedagogical designs implemented in different classes by peer teachers allowed them to learn from each other and better reflect on their own practices like 'looking into the mirror', as mentioned by Jade. It was the collaborative relay teaching that provided the opportunity of witnessing how the pedagogical design was refined and improved from Cycle 1 to Cycle 2 with a clearer systematic focus on English reading strategies.

Last, Learning Study aroused the pre-service EYL teachers of the importance of continuous reflection on and improvement of teaching practices. The teachers found the reflections after research lessons, at the end of the Learning Study, and even these at the nine post-lesson interviews with me very impactful for their professional learning. Collaborative reflections shared by the pre-service EYL teachers brought them multiple perspectives of analyzing learning and teaching of the same critical aspects and enhanced their professional thinking. Some teachers even said they would embrace continuous reflection for long-term professional development. As Tammy said:

> Through Learning Study, teachers can seek continuous improvement through reviewing problems, possible improvements and suggestions from peers, working collaboratively to create a better planning environment for pupils who are individual and unique in their needs and abilities.

Finding 3: Challenges for pre-service EYL teachers in Learning Study

Compared to in-service teachers, the pre-service EYL teachers needed much more guidance to complete a Learning Study project. First, the lack of subject knowledge slowed down some pre-service EYL teachers' grasp of the knowledge of the critical aspects. In this project, the pre-service EYL teachers were not aware that the reading strategy was the most critical and difficult aspect to pupils until the end of Cycle 1. Second, the lack of teaching experience and knowledge of target pupils prevented them from designing the lesson on their own. In this case, the teacher trainer had to provide the teaching materials from a previous Learning Study project by in-service teachers (see Zhang, 2014) for the pre-service EYL teachers' references. Even after in-service EYL teachers had picked examples from the materials for their teaching, they were not aware of the levels of difficulties until the teacher trainer raised the issues. Poor classroom management skills also reduced the effectiveness of Cycle 1 teaching when the first group of pre-service EYL teachers only engaged a few active pupils in learning. For example, Alice noted, 'I dare not ask the students who did not raise hands to answer my questions ... When students chatted noisily with each other, I didn't know how to stop them and draw their attention to the task.' Third, the lack of knowledge about tests also prolonged the process of designing and analysing pre- and post-tests. Starting from the scratch, the pre-service EYL teachers had to learn all the basic elements about diagnostic tests. As they were not able to design a test on their own, they adopted the test used by the in-service teachers.

Yet, as guided by variation theory, these learning problems, difficulties and needs of the pre-service EYL teachers actually created the focuses of and the opportunities of learning for the pre-service EYL teachers. Facilitating the Learning Study for the pre-service EYL teachers was also a Learning Study for the teacher trainer, who identified critical aspects of learning for the pre-service EYL teachers in the process of the Learning Study. Then the teacher trainer took the chance to design contrasts of different teaching practices for the pre-service EYL teachers' discernment of the target critical aspects. These included comparisons between the pre-service EYL teachers' own design and the in-service teachers' design, between Cycle 1 and Cycle 2, between pre- and post-tests as well as between the pre-service EYL teachers' performances at the beginning of Learning Study and at the end of the process. Therefore, the challenges encountered by the pre-service EYL teachers were transformed into learning opportunities by the teacher trainer.

Discussion and Conclusion

Learning Study was confirmed by the above findings to be effective in promoting EYL teachers' professionalism and developing their capability to tackle challenges in teaching with collaborative efforts. It develops pre-service EYL teachers in the four dimensions of professionalism as suggested in Menter *et al.* (2010): the effective teacher, the reflective teacher, the enquiring teacher and the transforming teacher. The EYL teachers as a team made deliberate efforts to maximize students learning effectiveness throughout the whole Learning Study. first, diagnosing pupils' learning needs with pre-tests reminded pre-service EYL teachers to plan their lessons to tackle pupils' learning difficulties. The clear identification of the object of learning and critical features based on pre-test data develops teachers' pedagogical knowledge about English language (Chou, 2008) and knowledge about student learning needs. Second, collaborative teaching, peer observation and collaborative reflections allowed pre-service EYL teachers to experience patterns of invariance and variance in terms of focuses of teaching, skills of presentation and strategies of engaging pupils in discussion, thus they were able to discern the critical aspects for their own professional learning and growth. The data-driven Learning Study practice transforms pre-service EYL teachers' teaching from a teacher-dominated approach to a pupil-oriented method (Wood, 2000), which is normally not easy for teachers to achieve (Enever, 2014).

Learning Study provided opportunities for the EYL teachers to examine continuously their own practices via reflection in action (Richardson & Anders, 1994). It developed their cognition and sensitivity about teaching and learning situated in a lived complex, chaotic context of language classrooms (Burns & Knox, 2011). The two cycles of teaching aroused their awareness of the relationship between teachers' pedagogical designs and student learning outcomes, and develop their pedagogical skills by observing and learning from each other. The findings seem to indicate that the pre-service EYL teachers benefited most when they were given the opportunities to contrast experiences and practices in different aspects of teaching, which were related to their professional learning needs and helped them cope with the difficulties they encountered in teaching. Meanwhile, collaborative planning and reviewing of lessons provided better technical, social and emotional support (Putnam & Borko, 2000) to facilitate the complex interplay of EYL teachers' cognition, emotions and commitment (Golombek, 2015; Golombek & Doran, 2014; Moodie & Feryok, 2015) in professional development.

Furthermore, Learning Study helped cultivate the EYL teachers' minds to explore learning and teaching using an enquiry-based approach. It is driven by teachers acting as researchers who lead the process of solving the problems out of their own interests (Stenhouse, 1975). Even though the teacher trainer provided substantial guidance and supporting materials, she mainly worked as a facilitator and supporter. The pre-service EYL teachers took charge of the decision making for designing, teaching, reviewing and revising the research lessons. They did not just learn variation theory, but also applied, tested and evaluated the feasibility of variation theory. In Learning Study, the pre-service EYL teachers are researchers (Stenhouse, 1975), project leaders (Fishman & Davis, 2006) and pedagogical knowledge producers. Learning Study prepares the pre-service EYL teachers to become independent practitioners via a collaborative and supportive experience from theory to practice. Such a bridging and transformative role between theory and practice is an essential feature for distinguishing Learning Study from teacher trainer-dominated approaches such as lectures or seminars for transmitting theories (Schon, 1987) and concepts to pre-service EYL teachers.

Remarkably, Learning Study is also an action research by the teacher trainer. It has actually transformed the author's way of seeing teacher training from a trainer-centred approach to a teacher-centred approach (Zhang, 2015). Learning Study provides a contextualized platform for the teacher trainer to conduct professional dialogues with pre-service EYL teachers. From the process of planning and teaching the research lesson, the teacher trainer can identify the pre-service EYL teachers' strengths and weaknesses and cater for the pre-service EYL teachers' professional learning needs for professional development through tailor-made pedagogical guidance and support in the pursuit of effective teaching and learning. Learning Study is actually appropriate for any teachers' professional learning at any stage.

In Hong Kong, where specialist teachers teach the key learning areas in primary schools (Chinese, mathematics and English), Learning Study has helped the specialist teachers develop more tailor-made teaching to cater for students' needs collaboratively in communities of practices (Cheng, 2009). The promotion of teacher collaboration is especially necessary and important when teachers encounter various challenges and pressures at work, ranging from learner diversity due to inclusive education (Copland *et al.*, 2014), increasing education reforms, heavy workload, accountability (Chan, 2011), change of teaching environments and/or levels of students

(Stelma & Onat-Stelma, 2010). Furthermore, Learning Study is a built-in professional development activity that can be integrated into their daily working practices and saves time. Therefore, in countries or regions where generalist teachers are assigned to teach English language to primary school children, Learning Study may also contribute to enhancing teacher collaboration, and developing EYL teachers' pedagogical knowledge and instructional skills. That is why Learning Study has also been adopted in a few countries in the West such as Sweden (Holmqvist, 2011), the UK (Davies & Dunnill, 2008) and Austria (Gierlinger *et al.*, 2016).

In conclusion, Learning Study provides the pre-service EYL teachers who do not have any teaching experience, with a platform to try every step of teaching a lesson and reduces the shock of facing a whole class of pupils for the first time. It also exposes pre-service EYL teachers to the complexity of classrooms (Burns & Knox, 2011) and arouses their awareness of some important pedagogical skills needed for effective teaching and learning. Teachers tend to learn best if their professional development activities are contextualized in real a classroom and are focused on improving pupils' learning of certain topics (Ball & Cohen, 1999; Stigler & Hibert, 1999). Learning Study builds up pre-service EYL teachers' sense of reflection on the effectiveness of teaching performances based on pupil learning outcomes and cultivates their mind as a reflective practitioner (Putnam & Borko, 2000; Richardson & Anders, 1994). It transforms teachers into autonomous learners by continuous pursuit of further improvement in their teaching practices. In the long run, it provides a mechanism for teachers to become life-long reflective practitioners. Learning Study is always a beginning of new learning, not an end.

References

Allen, J.M. and Wright, S.E. (2014) Integrating theory and practice in the pre-service teacher education practicum. *Teachers and Teaching: Theory and Practice* 20 (2), 136–151.

Amzat, I. and Valdez, N. (2017) *Teacher Empowerment toward Professional Development and Practices Perspectives across Borders.* Singapore: Springer.

Andrew, V.A. (2011) Using Learning Study to improve the teaching and learning of accounting in a school in Brunei Darussalam. *International Journal for Lesson and Learning Studies* 1 (1), 23–40.

Ball, D.L. and Cohen, D.K. (1999) Developing practice, developing practitioners: Toward a practice-based theory of professional education. In G. Sykes and L. Darling-Hammond (eds) *Teaching as the Learning Profession: Handbook of Policy and Practice* (pp. 3–32). San Francisco, CA: Jossey-Bass.

Burns, A. and Knox, J.S. (2011) Classrooms as complex adaptive systems: A relational model. *TESL–EJ* 15 (1), 1–25.

Chan, D.W. (2011) Burnout and life satisfaction: Does gratitude intervention make a difference among Chinese school teachers in Hong Kong? *Educational Psychology: An International Journal of Experimental Educational Psychology* 31 (7), 809–823.

Cheng, C.K. (2009) Cultivating communities of practice via learning study for enhancing teacher learning. *KEDI Journal of Educational Policy* 6 (1), 81–104.

Chou, C.-H. (2008) Exploring elementary English teachers' practical knowledge: A case study of EFL teachers in Taiwan. *Asia Pacific Education Review* 9 (4), 529–541.

Copland, F., Garton, S. and Burns, A. (2014) Challenges in teaching English to young learners: Global perspectives and local realities. *TESOL Quarterly* 48 (4), 738–762.

Davies, P. and Dunnill, R. (2008) 'Learning study' as a model of collaborative practice in initial teacher education. *Journal of Education for Teaching* 34 (1), 3–16.

Emery, H. (2012) A global study of primary English teachers' qualifications, training and career development. *ELT Research Papers*, 12-08. London: British Council.

Enever, J. (2014) Primary English teacher education in Europe. *ELT Journal* 68 (3), 231–242.

Fishman, B. and Davis, E.A. (2006) Teacher learning research and the learning sciences. In R.K. Sawyer (ed.) *The Cambridge Handbook of the Learning Sciences* (pp. 535–550). New York: Cambridge University Press.

Gao, X. and Ko, P. (2009) Learning study for primary school English teachers: A case story from Hong Kong. *Changing English* 16, 397–404.

Gierlinger, E.M., Spann, H. and Wagner, T. (2016) Variation theory in Austrian initial EFL teacher education: Potentials and challenges. *International Journal for Lesson and Learning Studies* 5 (2), 130–141.

Goddard, Y.L., Miller, R., Larson, R., Goddard, R., Madsen, J. and Schroeder, P. (2010) Connecting Principal Leadership, Teacher Collaboration, and Student Achievement. Paper presented at the Annual Meeting of the American Educational Research Association, May 3, 2010, Denver.

Golombek, P.R. (2015) Redrawing the boundaries of language teacher cognition: Language teacher educators' emotion, cognition, and activity. *The Modern Language Journal* 99 (3), 470–484.

Golombek, P. and Doran, M. (2014) Unifying cognition, emotion, and activity in language teacher professional development. *Teaching and Teacher Education* 39, 102–111.

Gu, M. (2011) Cross-border pre-service teachers in Hong Kong: 'to be or not to be integrated, that is the problem'. *Journal of Education for Teaching* 37 (2), 139–154.

Gu, M. and Benson, P. (2015) The formation of English teacher identities: A cross-cultural investigation. *Language Teaching Research* 19 (2), 187–206.

Holmqvist, M. (2011) Teachers' learning in a learning study. *Instructional Science* 39 (4), 497–511.

Kabilan, M.K. and Veratharaju, K. (2013) Professional development needs of primary school English language teachers in Malaysia. *Professional Development in Education* 39 (3), 330–351.

Kaufman, D. and Moss, D.M. (2010) A new look at preservice teachers' conceptions of classroom management and organization: Uncovering complexity and dissonance. *Teacher Educator* 45 (2), 118–136.

Ko, P.Y. (2012) Critical conditions for pre-service teachers' learning through inquiry: The Learning Study approach in Hong Kong. *The International Journal for Lesson and Learning Studies* 1, 49–66.

Lai, K.C. and Grossman, D. (2008) Alternate routes in initial teacher education: A critical review of the research and policy implications for Hong Kong. *Journal of Education for Teaching* 34 (4), 261–275.

Lee, J.F.K. (2008) A Hong Kong case of lesson study: Benefits and concerns. *Teaching and Teacher Education* 24 (5), 1115–1124.

Lo, M.L. (2012) *Variation Theory and the Improvement of Teaching and Learning.* Gothenburg, Sweden: Acta Universitatis Gothoburgensis.

Lo, M.L., Pong, W.Y. and Chik, P.M.P. (eds) (2005) *For Each and Everyone: Catering for Individual Differences through Learning Study.* Hong Kong: Hong Kong University Press.

Lo, M.L., Pong, W.Y., Kwok, W.Y. and Ko, P.Y. (eds) (2008) *Variation for the Improvement of Teaching and Learning Final Report*. Hong Kong: Centre for Learning-Study and School Partnership, The Hong Kong Institute of Education.

Marton, F. (2014) *Necessary Conditions of Learning*. New York: Routledge.

Menter, I., Hulme, M., Elliot, D. and Lewin, J. (2010) *Literature Review on Teacher Education in the 21st Century*. Edinburgh: Scottish Government Social Research.

Moodie, I. and Feryok, A. (2015) Beyond cognition to commitment: English language teaching in South Korean primary schools. *The Modern Language Journal* 99 (3), 450–469.

Ng, M. (2011) Teaching and learning of English in Hong Kong kindergartens: Patterns and practices. Unpublished PhD thesis, University of Hong Kong. See http://dx.doi.org/10.5353/th_b4723138 (accessed 22 May 2017).

Pang, M.F. (2006) The use of Learning Study to enhance teacher professional learning in Hong Kong. *Teaching Education* 17, 27–42.

Poulos, J., Culberston, N., Piazza, P. and D'Entremont, C. (2014) Making space: The value of teacher collaboration. *Education Digest* 80 (2), 28–31.

Putnam, R.T. and Borko, H. (2000) What do new views of knowledge and thinking have to say about research on teacher learning? *Educational Researcher* 29 (1), 4–15.

Richardson, V. and Anders, P.L. (1994) A theory of change. In V. Richardson (ed.) *Teacher Change and the Staff Development Process* (pp. 199–216). New York: Teachers College Press.

Saldaña, J. (2009) *The Coding Manual for Qualitative Researchers*. Thousand Oaks, CA: Sage.

Schon, D.A. (1987) *Educating the Reflective Practitioner: Toward a New Design for Teaching and Learning in the Professions*. San Francisco, CA: Jossey-Bass.

Sims, L. and Walsh, D. (2009) Lesson study with preservice teachers: Lessons from lessons. *Teaching and Teacher Education* 25 (5), 724–733.

Stelma, J. and Onat-Stelma, Z. (2010) Foreign language teachers organising learning during their first year of teaching young learners. *The Language Learning Journal* 38 (2), 193–207.

Stenhouse, L. (1975) *An Introduction to Curriculum Research and Development*. London: Heinemann.

Stigler, J. and Hiebert, J. (1999) *The Teaching Gap*. New York: Free Press.

Susman, G.I. and Evered, R.D. (1978) An assessment of the scientific merits of action research. *Administrative Science Quarterly* 23 (4), 582–603.

Sze, P. and Wong, H.(1999) The Hong Kong English syllabus and its relevance for English learning in a context of compulsory schooling. *Educational Research Journal* 14 (2), 253–278.

Wood, K. (2000) The experience of learning to teach: Changing student teachers' ways of understanding teaching. *Journal of Curriculum Studies* 32 (1), 75–93.

Zein, M.S. (2016a) Pre-service education for primary school English teachers in Indonesia: Policy implications. *Asia Pacific Journal of Education* 36 (S1), 119–134. doi:10.1080/02188791.2014.961899

Zein, M.S. (2016b) Government-based training agencies and the professional development of Indonesian English for young learners teachers: Perspectives from complexity theory. *Journal of Education for Teaching: International Research and Pedagogy* 42 (2), 205–223. doi:10.1080/02607476.2016.1143145

Zein, M.S. (2016c) Factors affecting the professional development of elementary English teachers. *Professional Development in Education* 42 (3), 423–440. doi:10.1080/19415257.2015.1005243

Zein, M.S. (2017) Professional development needs of primary EFL teachers: Perspectives of teachers and teacher educators. *Professional Development in Education* 43 (2), 293–313. doi:10.1080/19415257.2016.1156013

Zhang, Y. (2009) *Variation for the Improvement of Teaching and Learning Project: An English Case on Teaching Personal Pronouns of English Language.* Hong Kong: School Partnership and Field Experience Office, the Hong Kong Institute of Education.

Zhang, Y. (2014) How does Learning Study enhance school-based curriculum development? *Curriculum Perspectives* 34 (1), 1–10.

Zhang, Y. (2015) Sustaining Lesson Study in schools with positive peer leadership: A case study in Hong Kong. *The International Journal for Lesson and Learning Studies* 4 (2), 140–154.

Zhang, Y. (2017) How to teach English grammar to EFL learners: Insights from a learning study in Hong Kong. *Pedagogical Dialogue* 4 (22), 110–113. Center of Excellence, Nazarbayev Intellectual Schools, Astana, Kazakhstan.

Zhang, Y. (2019, forthcoming) Teacher education in Hong Kong. In M. Tatto and I. Menter (eds) *Knowledge, Policy and Practice in Teacher Education: A cross-national study.* London: Bloomsbury Publishing.

Appendix 1

Table 5.5 Schedule of the Learning Study course

Content/activity	Hours (3 hours per lesson)
(1) Learning Study and variation theory	6 (2 lessons)
(2) Case sharing and choosing a topic for study	3 (1 lesson)
(3) Diagnosing pupils' learning needs with a pre-test	9 (3 lessons)
(4) Planning the research lesson in Cycle 1	9 (3 lessons)
(5) Cycle 1: Teaching and reviewing research lesson in Class 1	3 (1 lesson)
(6) Preparing for the research lesson in Cycle 2	3 (1 lesson)
(7) Cycle 2: Teaching and reviewing research lesson in Class 2	3 (1 lesson)
(8) Report and reflection	3 (1 lesson)
Total	39 (13 lessons)

Appendix 2: The pre-test

Pre-test

Name: _____ (   ) Class: _____ Date: _____

Read the following passage and choose your own answer. (請細心閱讀以下文章, 然後選擇適當的答案。)

> A long time ago, there was a <u>foolish</u> farmer and everyone said he was stupid. He was called Sam. He lived in a <u>village</u> and it was far away from the city. One day someone gave Sam a bag of gold. Because he was afraid of losing the gold, he decided to <u>hide</u> the gold in his garden. He made a hole under a tree, put the gold inside and <u>covered</u> it with sand, so no one could see it. Suddenly, Sam came up with an idea. He wrote a note and put it on the tree. It said, 'There is no gold near the tree.' After that, he felt <u>relieved</u> and went to sleep happily.

The next day he wanted to get the gold. However, he found the bag of gold had <u>disappeared</u>. He looked everywhere, but could not see it.

1) <u>foolish</u>

A. 我知道這個字的意思, 它的意思是 _____ 。

B. 我不知道這個字的意思, 我猜它的意思是 _____ , 因為

_____ 。

C. 我不知道。

(Translation:

A. I know this word. It means _____ .

B. I do not know this word, but I guess it means _____ ,

because _____ .

C. I do not know this word.)

2) <u>village</u>

A. 我知道這個字的意思, 它的意思是 _____ 。

B. 我不知道這個字的意思, 我猜它的意思是 _____ , 因為

_____ 。

C. 我不知道。

3) <u>hide</u>

A. 我知道這個字的意思, 它的意思是 _____ 。

B. 我不知道這個字的意思, 我猜它的意思是 _____ , 因為

_____ 。

C. 我不知道。

4) <u>covered</u>

A. 我知道這個字的意思, 它的意思是 _____ 。

B. 我不知道這個字的意思, 我猜它的意思是 _____ , 因為

_____ 。

C. 我不知道。

5) <u>relieved</u>

A. 我知道這個字的意思, 它的意思是 _____ 。

B. 我不知道這個字的意思, 我猜它的意思是 _____ , 因為

_____ 。

C. 我不知道。

6) <u>disappeared</u>

A. 我知道這個字的意思, 它的意思是 _____ 。

B. 我不知道這個字的意思, 我猜它的意思是 _____ , 因為

_____ 。

C. 我不知道。

[End of paper 全卷完]

6 New Orthographies in the Primary Languages Classroom: A Challenge for Teacher Education

Gee Macrory

Introduction

At an international level, the introduction of primary languages teaching into school curricula in the past few decades has seen a substantial increase around the world. The global nature of this is underlined by the range of contexts (see, for example, Blondin *et al.*, 1998; Clyne *et al.*, 1995; Copland *et al.*, 2014; Enever *et al.*, 2009; Tinsley & Comfort, 2012; Rixon, 1992). At a European level, over the last 15 years or so, proposals from the European Commission (Commission of the European Communities, 2003) have raised the profile of early language learning considerably (Action Plan 2004–2006 for Language Learning and Linguistic Diversity, 2003; Barcelona: Bologna Declaration 1999; Lisbon Strategy, 2000; Education and Training, 2010). One of many pressing issues that face teachers and teacher educators in this context of change is that of literacy. In particular, when embarking upon the learning of another language, encountering a new orthography may be a challenge for early language learners who have only recently been introduced to the orthography of their first language. But this also represents a potential challenge to the teachers charged with introducing this, and by implication, to those of us in teacher education.

The challenges presented by these policy initiatives are considerable and have been documented by Enever (2011), reporting on the ELLiE Project which sought to provide a detailed insight into the policy and implementation processes for early foreign language learning (FLL) programmes in seven European countries. Although the diversity of provision across the countries involved was clear, the author notes the important relationship between policy features and outcomes. While key issues highlighted include the importance of subject knowledge, the role of the school, appropriate assessment and age-appropriate methodology, the report asserts the importance of teacher education, calling for greater investment in pre-service and in-service early primary FL teacher education in order for policies to be effectively implemented (Enever, 2011). Indeed, this reflects the emphasis that Enever places upon the importance of the FL teacher's role, and she comments that

> for the longer-term sustainability of early language learning in many contexts, the evidence suggests that it would be valuable for all early primary teachers to have adequate language skills and age-appropriate methodology skills to be able to include FL teaching as an integrated part of the broader school curriculum. (Enever, 2011: 147)

This is echoed by the findings of Tinsley and Comfort (2012: 8) who state that 'the quality of the teaching force is a key concern in research regarding the effectiveness of teaching new languages to young children [...] Teachers are central to the success of primary languages and serious investment needs to be set aside for their training and development.' They do, however, express concern that the introduction of languages in primary schools is frequently inadequately planned for in terms of teacher supply and training.

The English Context

It is clear that the issue of teacher supply and education is a worldwide concern. However, as Wright and Beaumont (2015) note, more local policy contexts shape the decisions that teacher educators have to make about, for example, the subject knowledge and pedagogic practices to include in a curriculum. The context of teacher training in any given situation necessarily shapes how teacher education is carried out, which brings us to the current situation in England, where primary languages only became a statutory part of the curriculum for upper primary (from age 7) in September 2014. The situation prior to this, however, was something of a chequered history: after an unsuccessful attempt in the 1970s (Burstall et al., 1974) to start up primary languages, the idea was given fresh impetus on publication of the National Languages Strategy in 2002, arising out of the Nuffield Foundation (2000). The proposal that primary languages become an entitlement at age 7 from 2010 onwards was described as the 'cornerstone' of the National Languages Strategy (DfES, 2002). Much progress in the few years following this was then achieved (see Cable et al., 2010; Driscoll et al., 2004; Wade et al., 2009). However, a change in government in May 2010 resulted in vastly reduced funding and an effective abandonment of the primary languages project until the decision was taken to make it a statutory part of the curriculum from September 2014. Nevertheless, Driscoll (2014: 259) strikes an optimistic note in suggesting that this decision 'marks a new and exciting era for a subject that has been hovering on the margins of acceptability for many years.'

The primary languages initiative is itself part of a bigger language learning picture, one where motivation and attainment in foreign languages in the UK are the subject of increasing concern (Coleman, 2009; Hagger-Vaughan, 2016; Ofsted, 2015; Tinsley, 2013; Tinsley & Board, 2015, 2016). It is worth reflecting on the hopes that were attached to the earlier – and abandoned – introduction of primary languages, expressed by Dearing (DfES, 2007: 37) in the assertion that

> languages in primary schools is the necessary foundation for a National Languages Strategy. The success of this element of the strategy is central to the future of languages post 14, and that turns very much on the quality of the teaching provided.

How much the decline in take-up of languages at age post-14 can be attributed to this is unclear, but the most recent survey notes that the percentage of pupils taking a GCSE (General Certificate of Secondary Education, the exam taken at age 16) has dropped from 76% in 2002 to 48% in 2015 (Tinsley & Board, 2016). This has serious implications for teacher supply, not only in terms of specialist teachers but for generalist primary school teachers. In all likelihood, a large percentage of students entering a course of teacher education have very limited knowledge of another language and many may have only studied one for the statutory three years between the ages of 11 and 14. The issue of who should teach primary languages has received much attention and studies show a preference for generalist primary class teachers (e.g. Driscoll *et al.*, 2004). There is clearly a potential tension between this and the issue of subject knowledge noted above, with a likely impact also on teachers' confidence in teaching it themselves. However, as Mitchell (2014: 207) observes, 'teaching and learning approaches must be appropriate for children's maturational level' and the generalist primary teacher is more likely to be in tune with this than a secondary trained specialist teacher.

Pedagogic Approaches: The Oracy–Literacy Debate

The confidence of the teacher is important as it may have implications for the pedagogic approach adopted, including the balance of oracy and literacy. Cable *et al.* (2010: 6) note that in primary languages generally, oracy has been given priority over literacy, commenting that

> literacy activities did not form a substantial part of most lessons, though there was evidence of increased attention to literacy over the three years of the study [...] the shortness of lessons and the relatively limited confidence and expertise among some staff appeared to constrain the amount of time spent on literacy activities.

The relative absence of literacy was despite the focus on this in government documentation: the Key Stage 2 [ages 7 to 11] Framework for Languages comments that

> The careful introduction of literacy skills as part of a rich learning environment, stimulating conversation and understanding in speech and writing can only be beneficial [...] from an early age children become familiar with the relationship between sounds and letters/characters in the new language. (DfES, 2005: 52)

More recently, National Curriculum requirements state that 'the teaching should provide an appropriate balance of spoken and written language and should lay the foundations for further foreign language teaching at key stage 3 [...] link the spelling, sound and meaning of words' (DfE, 2013).

The impact of including literacy activities in primary languages is an area lacking clear consensus, however. A recent project undertaken by Graham *et al.* (2014) to investigate linguistic and motivational outcomes across the primary–secondary transition examined whether oracy and literacy approaches for the teaching of French led to different outcomes for learners in Years 5, 6 and 7 of schooling. This found no definitive advantage for either approach, although the authors noted as a possible explanation the fact that the literacy activities in which learners were engaged remained largely at word and sentence level. They speculated that 'literacy activities that consist of word-level work are not sufficient to bring a clear advantage for a literacy-based approach', noting also that there was 'little evidence of instruction in grapheme-phoneme correspondences (GPCs)' (Graham *et al.*, 2014: 11–12). The doctoral study of Porter (2014: 338) 'recommends introducing Modern Foreign Languages (MFL) literacy as an integral part of an early start to language learning. However, it is essential that this is done sensitively as it is also evident that MFL literacy is challenging for all learners.'

The Challenge of a New Orthography

One aspect of literacy that may warrant closer attention is that of a new orthography, as some recent research indicates a possible need for a more systematic approach. The issue of transfer of reading skills from a first into a new language has received much attention in the literature (see, for example, Koda, 2005), but any discussion of transfer is necessarily a nuanced debate given the differences between writing systems and orthographies. For example, the move between a morphemic writing system such as Chinese and an alphabetic one presents different challenges from moving from one alphabetic system to another. Even within the same alphabetic system such as the Roman alphabet, different orthographies employ different grapheme–phoneme correspondences (GPCs). While some argue that prior literacy equips learners to grasp general mapping principles, there are also possible script-dependent issues. For example, Koda (2008) suggests that the distance between the first and second language affects the amount of print input and experience for learners. Furthermore, the younger the learner, the less prior experience can be brought to bear. Relevant also to this discussion is the concept of shallow and deep orthographies, in that some orthographies such as English and French are considered to be deep (Sampson, 1985) whereas others such as Spanish are seen as shallow on account of more regular GPCs. This is of course a continuum rather than a dichotomy, but there are implications for learning to read even in a first language (Perfetti & Dunlop, 2008) and an obvious need to consider this in second/subsequent language learning.

Various studies have thrown light upon the move from shallow to deep orthographies (and vice versa). Much research has focused on the learning of English as a foreign language; for example, Muñoz (2014) found that the move to English orthography posed difficulties for her first language Spanish speakers. When asked about the difficulties presented by learning English, for Grade 3 beginners 50% of their answers seemed to be triggered by problems with English spelling and its lack of transparency, prompting quotes such as 'words, how they are pronounced, you write them in one way and you pronounce them in another way'. Furthermore, these problems with English spelling remained at 32% for children in Grade 6 (Muñoz, 2014). However, this can also present problems in the opposite direction. Rafat (2016) found that the L2 speech of 40 novice English L1 learners of Spanish exhibited first language grapheme-to-phoneme orthographic effects, where phonological transfer led to non-target like productions in the early stages of language learning. He found that this was the case where there were the grapheme-to-phoneme correspondences considered to be different in Spanish and English – such as <v>-/b/, <d>-/ð/, <z>-/s/ – whereas the grapheme-to-phoneme correspondences considered to be the same in Spanish and English such as <m>-/m/, <n>-/n/ did not result in transfer. In the UK, some studies have pointed to the difficulties that learners experience with the written form of French. For example, Erler (2004) investigated pupils' knowledge of certain spelling-sound rules in French towards the end of their first year at secondary school. The results indicate that, with a few exceptions, pupils had little idea after one year of learning French about spelling-sound rules for principal vowel sounds in the language and for the general rule of silent final consonants. Erler's findings have been echoed in other research. Woore (2009), in a longitudinal study of 85 learners in their second year of learning French, found little discernible progress in decoding, and a further study in 2010, which investigated strategies used by a small group of 12 learners, noted the lack of secure underpinning in terms of knowledge of the GPCs of French (Woore, 2010). Marijanovic *et al.* (2009) found that their 9 to 11-year-old Croatian learners of French applied the GPC rules of their L1 Croatian when reading. In this case the learners were going from a shallower orthography to a more opaque one, that is, French. English learners of French are going from one opaque orthography to another, arguably rendering the task even more difficult, as the complex orthography of English means that learners possess multiple graphemic representations of phonemes. On the one hand, this means that learners might reasonably expect to encounter such complexity in a new language; on the other hand, it could be argued that this leads to greater confusion and that furthermore, those learners who are still establishing the GPCs of English may be at an even greater disadvantage. Alternatively, the L1 GPCs may be less entrenched, making the children more open to alternative sound-spelling links.

The implications for teaching are therefore not wholly clear-cut. Graham *et al.*'s (2014: 10) research, for example, was inconclusive. They reported that

> an effect of teaching approach was detected for learners with low levels of English literacy for whom a literacy approach seemed more beneficial by the time they got to Year 7, helping them to make more progress than learners who had received an oracy approach in primary school.

In another context, Johnson and Tweedie (2010) found a positive impact of phonemic awareness instruction in young EFL learners in Malaysia. A further possible advantage of introducing L2 literacy is suggested by Murphy *et al.* (2015), who found that second language literacy had a facilitative effect on first language (L1) literacy, a point made by the KS2 Framework (DfES, 2005: 52): 'the learning of the new language will be helped by children's previous understanding of their own language, and will in turn develop their general literacy skills.'

Since the Rose Report of 2006 (DfES, 2006), the approach to the teaching of first language reading in primary schools in England is increasingly in favour of systematic synthetic phonics. While this has not been without controversy (see Ellis & Moss, 2014), Ofsted (the inspection regime in England) (2012) noted that most schools were making explicit use of synthetic phonics programmes, suggesting that primary schools in England have an awareness of the role of GPCs in learning to read. This has had an impact upon initial teacher education programmes such that all student teachers are expected to be competent in this regard. This in turn, combined with awareness of the research findings outlined above, prompted some curiosity about possible implications for MFL literacy, with specific regard to orthography.

Aims of the Research

The research reported on here was carried out in order to investigate the implications of the issues outlined above for initial teacher education, through an exploration of the experiences of both undergraduate and postgraduate student teachers on school placements.

The research questions were:

- What are student teachers' opportunities to observe and teach MFL on placement in general?
- What are student teachers' opportunities to observe and teach MFL phonics?
- What are student teachers' views of the place of MFL phonics in the curriculum?
- What experience of literacy did student teachers have in the primary MFL classroom?
- What perceptions of schoolteachers' views did student teachers hold?

It was decided to target generalist student teachers who had chosen MFL as a specialist module as these were the most likely to have been offered opportunities to both observe and teach. I was aware of the possibility that the postgraduate and undergraduate student teachers were likely also to have had differing experiences, most notably because the former have a very intense one-year course spent largely in school and where all subjects have to be covered in a short space of time. This means that not only do they have less time at the university, they also have a great deal to learn while on placement, and their first placement in particular is heavily focused on what are known as the 'core' subjects: English, mathematics and science. This potentially limits the opportunities they get to teach beyond this. In contrast, the undergraduate students have a school placement in each of the academic years of the course, leaving more time for campus-based input as well a greater range of placements. At the time of the research being carried out, some of the undergraduates were in the last year of a four-year teacher training course which had been discontinued, so had experienced four school placements while the other final year undergraduates were in the final year of a new three-year teacher training course and so had only been on three school placements. The language most frequently taught is French, followed by Spanish and German (Tinsley & Board, 2016), all using the Roman alphabet.

Research Method

A total of 55 specialist primary trainees were involved in the research project. Of these, 23 were postgraduate who had two school placements, and 32 were undergraduates who had had three or four school placements. The data were collected in the spring and summer terms of 2015, and the spring term of 2016. This provided a total of 55 questionnaires with both Likert scale responses and some open text questions. Semi-structured interviews with a total of 10 student teachers (pairs and individual) were also conducted after they had completed their final placement in the summer and spring terms of 2015 and 2016. The questionnaire responses were a choice of: strongly disagree; disagree; neither agree nor disagree; agree; strongly agree, followed by a second section of open-text questions. For ease of reporting, agree and strongly agree are reported together as are the categories of disagree and strongly disagree.

Findings

The findings are reported below, focusing first upon the quantitative data with the undergraduate and postgraduate data presented side by side to enable comparison. This is followed by a consideration of the open-text comments and then finally by the themes emerging from the interview data. The implications of the overall findings are then discussed.

Opportunities to observe MFL teaching in school

Students were first asked about the opportunities they had to observe MFL classes. They were asked to respond to the statement: School-based training in my degree has provided sufficient opportunity to *observe* some MFL teaching.

In response to this, 50% of the postgraduate student teachers disagreed, compared to 33% who agreed that they had sufficient opportunities to observe primary languages teaching. Of the undergraduates, who had had more time spent on placement, the percentage who deemed their opportunities sufficient was only a little higher at 56%, whereas those who disagreed dropped to 16%. This leaves over a quarter who after three or four placements were still unable to agree or disagree.

Opportunities to practise MFL teaching in school

Student teachers were then asked about the opportunities they had to practise some MFL teaching. They were asked to respond to the statement: School-based training in my degree has provided sufficient opportunity to *practise* some MFL teaching.

In response to this statement, the opportunities to teach were reported as fewer. Of the postgraduate student teachers, only 17% agreed that they had had the opportunity to teach MFL with 75% disagreeing, suggesting that despite being specialists, very little opportunity was coming their way. As we might expect, the undergraduates fared somewhat better, with 37% agreeing they had had sufficient opportunity to teach, and 47% – nearly half – disagreeing. In both the postgraduate and undergraduate cases, the opportunities to observe were greater than those actually to teach. Given that observation suggests that there was some teaching taking place, it is interesting that this did not always seem to translate into an opportunity to practise.

Opportunities to observe MFL phonics in school

Student teachers were next asked about opportunities to observe the teaching of MFL phonics in school. They were asked to respond to the statement: I have had opportunities to *observe* the teaching of MFL phonics in the primary classroom.

Asked about this more specific aspect of pedagogy, only 9% of the postgraduates claimed to have had experience of observing the teaching of MFL phonics in the classroom, with 87% disagreeing, leaving very few 'on the fence'. These figures are not wholly dissimilar to the findings for the undergraduates, where only 19% agreed they had observed this in comparison to 78% saying they had not. Thus, in both cases, despite the fact that some observation in general of MFL teaching was reported, far fewer opportunities to observe this specific aspect of pedagogy were noted.

Opportunities to teach MFL phonics in school

Student teachers were then asked about opportunities to teach MFL phonics in the primary classroom. They were asked to respond to the statement: I have had opportunities to *teach* MFL phonics in the primary classroom.

Here, no postgraduate student teacher agreed with this statement, with 91% disagreeing. A slightly different response was found in the data from the undergraduates, where despite only 19% having previously stated they had not observed this, 25% had in fact apparently had the opportunity to teach MFL phonics, with only 63% disagreeing in comparison to the 78% who had not observed it. These figures suggest that a similar percentage were unable to agree or disagree. The fact that the undergraduates had more experience of teaching this than observing it is at first glance anomalous; however, it may reflect a certain willingness to put this into practice.

The importance of MFL phonics in developing MFL literacy

Finally, student teachers were asked about their views of the importance of phonics in the development of literacy in MFL. They were asked to respond to the statement: I think MFL phonics have an important role to play in developing literacy in MFL.

This item was designed to explore how much importance student teachers attached to the role of MFL phonics in developing MFL literacy. Here a clear majority of postgraduates agree, 87% with no-one disagreeing. On the other hand, of the undergraduates only one person disagreed but the percentage agreeing was noticeably lower than the post-graduates at 59%, meaning that roughly a third were undecided.

Open-text comments from questionnaires

The first three questions explored further the opportunities afforded to student teachers in the area of MFL phonics, including an invitation to describe further their experience, whether reading or spelling was impli-cated and whether an implicit or explicit approach was adopted. The answers bear out the findings reported above, with the vast majority reporting 'none' or 'nothing' when asked about experiences of MFL pho-nics, and thus unsurprisingly a large number of 'n/a' when asked about reading and spelling or implicit/explicit approaches. A rare offering from a year three undergraduate was:

> I had the opportunity to help the children pronounce the names of the planets based on phonics and what sounds go with the letters, eg. u = 'oo'.

Given the findings reported above, the lack of experience is not surprising, but is nevertheless a cause for concern as these placements are, after all, a *training* context.

When asked in the fourth question what they thought the place of MFL phonics was in the primary languages classroom, while some claimed not to be able to offer a view on account of their limited experi-ence, 37 of 55 (67%) offered a range of positive comments, including for example:

- PG ST: 'I think it is just as important as teaching phonics in English.'
- PG ST: 'As in English, I believe MFL phonics are vitally important to primary languages – particularly in relation to reading/decoding.'
- Year 4 UG: 'I think it enhances decoding of vocabulary, possibly increasing fluency and pronunciation.'
- Year 3 UG: 'I think it could help children learn MFL to make it slightly easier as they could use the phonics to help them read a variety of words as they do when learning to read and write in English.'

The next two questions explored their experiences of literacy in the pri-mary MFL classroom, as well as their perceptions of the views of primary practitioners. The responses suggest that in general, speaking and listen-ing activities predominate, with one Year 3 UG stating: 'all MFL teaching was done orally.' or another Year 3 UG stating: 'no experience of writing and reading MFL, purely speaking and listening.' There were a number of references to a focus on repetition, vocabulary teaching and occasional comments about teachers modelling pronunciation based on written words on a PowerPoint presentation. The student teachers also offered some insights into the possible underlying issues or explanations. Both undergraduates and postgraduates commented that MFL appeared to have a low priority in schools, 'low priority compared to other foundation subjects (PG); MFL not high in importance'. (Year 3), suggesting an inauspicious context for developing pedagogy. Their responses about what they thought might be the perceptions of primary practitioners regarding not only phonics, but reading and writing more generally, suggest a lack of confidence on the part of many. A Year 4 UG noted: 'I have experienced little MFL when in placement. I feel this is down to it not being of value to teachers. It is also due to confidence. Little writing in MFL as teacher subject knowledge is not strong.'

This is echoed in the comment from a Year 3 UG, 'I think that generally teachers are not confident in MFL phonics themselves so are wary of teaching this to the children in case it is not correct'. The use of the word 'fear' by several underscored the point.

Interview findings

The interview findings bore out the questionnaire data as well as allowing the student teachers to talk in more detail about the pedagogy observed and their training experiences. First, the low priority accorded to MFL was referred to several times. S, for example, commented that

> It was just thrown in at the end of the day. I don't think it was valued in the curriculum.

and

> E: I think that because of the attitude of the whole school they (the children) struggled to get into my enthusiasm.
>
> K: I've spoken to a few teachers and it doesn't really seem that it's at the forefront of their thinking.

This was not a universal picture, A noting that 'in school x, the kids and the head were really pro-Spanish'. This inconsistency is hardly surprising, as L observed 'the underlying problem is that MFL is not valued enough in this country.'

Student teachers' comments about subject knowledge and confidence were also echoed in the interview data – Y: 'I think MFL scares most teachers' or L: 'It's a case of having the confidence to go and do it yourself. I think a lot of teachers don't do that because they're afraid of their own subject knowledge.'

Comments such as the following hint at a link between confidence and pedagogy: Y stated that the teachers

> see languages as a very discrete topic because it is foreign and it is something that they're not that confident on so it's not in the same area, I think they just see it as something totally separate because maybe their experiences are, oh well we'll teach them the colours one week and the animals

next week or whatever, it's not seen as we're teaching them a language, like we're teaching them a few French words.

This suggests a less than systematic approach to planning and indeed some noted explicitly the lack of progression, with L commenting

One thing I did actually see, which was worrying, and highlights the need for progression and for planning in schools for progression what that the children in Reception were learning the same thing as the children in year 6.

When asked about the prevalence of literacy, responses were mixed with some reporting only oral skills observed. This seemed to depend on the school. As A noted, in one placement there was 'only speaking and listening' but in another placement: 'They start off learning the words from flash cards and then they write the list of words in their book, but by the end of each term they'll have written 2 or 3 sentences using the words'. However, S, in comparing two teachers, suggests that teachers' attention to written language may be linked to confidence:

I think it was a lot more oral with A because she was a specialist. With N it was more written – there's more of a safety net with the written word if you've got it up on the board and it's spelt correctly and you got it from a reputable resource so you focus more on reading and writing whereas with A it was about correct pronunciation.

E also commented that 'the teacher had put an emphasis on the writing because she wasn't confident speaking'.

Furthermore, many noted the extent to which work was often at word level and the prevalence of vocabulary teaching, often involving repetition. S commented:

I've seen mainly repetition, which is pronunciation, but not actually breaking it down, just repeating it lower or higher or in different voices [...] they just throw some words at you, but they wouldn't do that in English [...] it's easier just to say 'repeat after me' instead of breaking it down.

When asked more specifically about the role of phonics, there were further similar comments, such as M, who said,

I don't think they [the children] were necessarily aware of different sounds, they just knew how you say this word but had never explicitly broken it down into the sounds and then, like, decoding it and encoding it again. I don't think they were really aware of it … Their SK not being as strong, they think ok, vocabulary, words, let's go and just teach them all the words, just throw the words at them without thinking about how do they learn those words in the first place … I think it's quite difficult when you're introducing it in KS2 that you think of them being a long way away from the early years where they would do the phonics in English.

Several remarked on the difference in approach between L1 and L2 phonics. Y observed that

> Phonics is a priority to teach children to read in English but it's funny how that doesn't transfer to a second language [...] if you try to teach it (MFL) using phonics they'd be very surprised by that but obviously that's how they teach children to read English [...] and with an EAL child that's the first thing they do, right we'll put you in a phonics group.

Furthermore, A commented that

> Even the teachers who think that MFL could be important don't focus on phonics specifically but I guess it would help with decoding for reading and writing [...] if we need phonics to learn English surely you need phonics to learn another language.

Another, R, opined 'Funny, isn't it that in English we've had this big push for phonics, but not in MFL?'. Other comments such as this by E underlined the importance the student teachers attached to the role of written language: 'If the children have limited language skills, I find that they like having it written down because that's how they learn everything else ... with visual stimulus and often something written, but then we take it away in MFL'.

The observations made by these student teachers highlight the limited opportunities that they have to develop subject knowledge and pedagogy. Student teacher L, in discussing his university research project stated

> They were keen, that's what I found really interesting when I did my questionnaires, when I asked 'Would you change your pedagogical approach to teaching language if you had the subject knowledge?', every one of them gave a resounding 'yes', so, unfortunately, a lack of subject knowledge is forcing teachers down a path they don't want to go. They don't want to just stand there and repeat things over and over, but they don't feel capable of doing it any other way.

As C remarked, 'I don't think they're against it (MFL). I think they don't feel equipped to teach it. It's one of those subjects you don't really talk about.'

How did the schools respond to having MFL specialist student teachers? In a few cases, they capitalised on the presence of a specialist. For example, E, who is bilingual, reported that

> because I'm bilingual I was given all responsibility for teaching across the year, sometimes for teaching the years above and below [...] I felt like I was giving to the school, they saw me as being more able to teach it than they were. Another, C, said, when they heard that I was language specialist they said Oh you can do that so they threw me in and I took over.

Another student teacher (A) expressed gratitude that she had a chance to teach, saying that '... the teacher was kind enough to say if you want

20 minutes a week to do some German, have it.' Some had to seek out experiences for themselves. Y, for example, said that

> if there was a spare minute or a spare slot I would say like could I teach MFL please [...] but it was never suggested to me, it was never really given to me as an option, I just volunteered [...] I had to request to do it and they were like oh yeh you can do that but a bit surprised when I said it almost, because it's not a priority in the school.

R, however, despite having A level French reported that 'I was able to observe them, but they never gave any responsibility to me [...] In year 2 I taught a little bit, about families, words for mum, dad, sister.'

Discussion and Implications

What can we learn from these findings? First of all, this aspect of pedagogy – namely, the issue of phonics in the primary languages classroom – is one that our student teachers are largely positive about, if somewhat mystified by its apparent absence relative to the much higher profile that phonics has in the L1 English classroom. However, the findings suggest that school placements at present constitute an underdeveloped context for appropriate training in this area. That little attention seems to be currently paid to the role of phonics in MFL is perhaps unsurprising, given the generally low profile of MFL reported by the student teachers. The limited literacy activities reported and the nature of these reflect the earlier findings of Cable et al. (2010) and Graham et al. (2014).

In terms of their experiences, their apparent willingness to seek out opportunities where few were actually offered perhaps explains the finding that, at least for the undergraduates, there were more reported experiences of teaching MFL phonics than observing this. This is also consistent with the observations that teachers lacked confidence and subject knowledge, although on a more optimistic note we might suggest that, as some student teachers noted, there was some interest upon which to build. However, we have to conclude that the student teachers were more in a position of contributing to the schools, whether by what they themselves offered or by being given responsibility, rather than being in receipt of any actual training. Given the situation this is hardly surprising and in fact could be seen as an unreasonable expectation, particularly in an aspect of pedagogy that might be seen as requiring special expertise.

What might we consider as a way forward? First of all, we need to bear in mind that the evidence is inconclusive regarding the impact of a literacy focus in general (Graham et al., 2014), although, as noted above, Johnson and Tweedie (2010) found a positive impact of phonemic awareness instruction in an EFL context. More specifically, as already noted, we lack unequivocal evidence that a focus on MFL phonics is likely to be effective.

Nevertheless, a recent report on MFL pedagogy (Teaching Schools Council, 2016), albeit focused on secondary aged pupils, recommends explicit attention to MFL phonics in the early stages. This implies that this should also hold true for younger beginners, although we need research into the effect of this at different ages, there being considerable differences between children within the primary age range of 5 to 11 years. Whether children need an explicit understanding of how the writing system of the new language differs from their first language is thus debatable. However, less controversial is the idea that teachers should ideally have this subject knowledge to help them plan and sequence their input, and to draw upon at appropriate pedagogic moments in ways that can clarify in age-appropriate ways the differences and similarities between known and new languages. That in most primary schools in England there is understanding and knowledge of phonics in English, developing this across the age ranges taught and languages other than English should not be an insurmountable hurdle.

One way of addressing this is to adopt a collaborative approach whereby student teachers and mentors together develop both their subject knowledge and ways of working with children that explore the possibilities offered by interventions in this area. School-based tasks that require a joint approach can allow student teachers to share subject knowledge and pedagogic strategies with mentors who have the deeper understanding of how children learn than novice teachers. Such an approach would reflect what Wright (2010) sees as development in second language teacher education from a transmissive approach arising initially out of applied linguistics research to one that is much more sociocultural in orientation, and the Vygotskyian perspective argued for by Johnston (2015), who emphasises the importance of dialogic interactions between beginning teachers and teacher educators. For this, however, space is needed, defined by Barkhuizen and Borg (2010: 238) as 'space to reflect, to practise, to confer and to exercise autonomy'. If we are to consider the role of mentors in school-based teacher education, we need to think about their ability to act with agency and autonomy, arguably a challenge within the current audit culture (Thompson & Cook, 2013). Hammersley-Fletcher et al. (2017: 3) note that 'legitimised by discourses of standards and accountability and underpinned by political and media anxiety about educational quality and economic competitiveness, teachers and schools have lost much of their control over the what and how of teaching'. They go on to argue for the role of research in developing teachers' ability to 'think about education in ways that freed them as professionals to be more critical and creative in their approaches' (Hammersley-Fletcher et al., 2017: 13). Enabling the dialogic interactions advocated by Johnston may well in turn promote mentors' creativity and autonomy.

A further issue is what role the university-based experience consists of for our student teachers as this may indeed form the basis of the kind of school-based tasks described above. The findings in this small study point to MFL being seen as a discrete and separate entity in the curriculum, rather than the plurilingual approach advocated by, for example, Conteh *et al.* (2007), where children's repertoires are seen more holistically. Such an approach would have the additional benefit of including all the children's languages with their different writing systems. We need at university level then to consider our approach to the teaching of literacy, as we can so easily fall into the trap of modelling the opposite by separating the teaching of reading and writing from the teaching of MFL. It is all too easy to focus solely upon, in our context, English rather than adopting a more plurilingual approach to how children learn to read and write. This in turn would provide student teachers who do not specialise in MFL to have a broader understanding of what it means to be literate.

While this is a small study, the findings are strengthened by the fact that different students, at different time points, and in questionnaires and interviews provided very similar responses. The findings highlight the need to adopt a model of teacher education that promotes collaborative learning, one that can serve to promote a more effective pedagogy irrespective of the writing system or orthography involved.

References

Barkhuizen, G. and Borg, S. (2010) Editorial: Researching language teacher education. *Language Teaching Research* 14 (3), 237–240.

Blondin, C., Chandelier, M., Edelenbos, P., Johnstone, R., Kubanek-German, A. and Taeschner, T. (1998) *Foreign Languages in Primary and Pre-school Education: Context and Outcomes. A Review of Recent Research within the European Union.* London: CILT.

Burstall, C., Jamieson, M., Cohen, S. and Hargreaves, M. (1974) *Primary French in the Balance.* Windsor: NFER Publishers.

Cable, C., Driscoll, P., Mitchell, R., Sing, S., Cremin, T., Earl, J., Eyres, I., Holmes, B., Martin, C. and Heins, B. (2010) *Language Learning at Key Stage 2: A Longitudinal Study.* London: Department for Children, Schools and Families (DCSF Research Reports DCSF-RR198).

Coleman, J.A. (2009) Why the British do not learn languages: Myths and motivation in the United Kingdom. *The Language Learning Journal* 37 (1), 111–127.

Commission of the European Communities (2003) *Communication from the Commission to the Council, the European Parliament, the Economic and Social Committee and the Committee of the Regions, Promoting Language Learning and Linguistic Diversity: An Action Plan 2004–2006.* Brussels: CEC.

Conteh, J., Martin, P. and Robertson, L.H. (eds) (2007) *Multilingual Learning: Stories from Schools and Communities in Britain.* Bristol: Multilingual Matters.

Copland, F., Garton, S. and Burns, A. (2014) Challenges in teaching English to young learners: Global perspectives and local realities. *TESOL Quarterly* 48 (4), 738–762.

Clyne, M., Jenkins, C., Chen, I.Y., Tsokalidou, R. and Wallner, T. (1995) *Developing Second Language from Primary School: Models and Outcomes.* Canberra: National Languages and Literacy Institute of Australia Ltd.

Department for Education and Science (DfES) (2002) *Languages for All, Languages for Life: A Strategy for England.* London: HMSO.

Department for Education and Science (DfES) (2005) *Key Stage 2 Framework for Languages.* Nottingham: DfES Publications.

Department for Education and Science (DfES) (2006) *Independent Review of the Teaching of Early Reading* (Rose Report). London: HMSO.

Department for Education and Science (DfES) (2007) *Languages Review* (Dearing Report). London: HMSO.

Department for Education (DfE) (2013) *National Curriculum in England: Languages Programmes of Study*. See https://www.gov.uk/government/uploads/system/uploads/attachment_data/file/239042/PRIMARY_national_curriculum_Languages.pdf (accessed 29 October 2018).

Driscoll, P. (2014) A new era for primary languages. In P. Driscoll, E. Macaro and A. Swarbrick (eds) *Debates in Modern Languages Education*. London: Routledge.

Driscoll, P., Jones, J. and Macrory, G. (2004) *The Provision of Foreign Language Learning for Pupils at KS2*. London: DfES Report.

Ellis, S. and Moss, G. (2014) Ethics, education policy and research: The phonics question reconsidered. *British Educational Research Journal* 40 (2), 241–260.

Enever, J. (2011) *ELLiE, Early Language Learning in Europe*. London: British Council.

Enever, J., Moon, J. and Raman, U. (eds) (2009) *Young Learner English Language Policy and Implementation: International Perspectives*. Reading: Garnet Education.

Erler, L. (2004) Near-beginner learners of French are reading at a disability level. *Francophonie* 30, 9–15.

Graham, S., Courtney, L., Marinis, T. and Tonkyn, A. (2014) *Primary Modern Languages: The Impact of Teaching Approaches on Attainment and Preparedness for Secondary School Language Learning*. Final Report. Reading: Nuffield Foundation.

Hagger-Vaughan, L. (2016) Towards 'languages for all' in England: The state of the debate. *The Language Learning Journal* 44 (3), 358–375.

Hammersley-Fletcher, L., Clarke, M. and McManus, V. (2017) Agonistic democracy and passionate professional development in teacher-leaders. *Cambridge Journal of Education* 47 (4), 1–16.

Johnson, R.C. and Tweedie, M.G. (2010) Could phonemic awareness instruction be (part of) the answer for young EFL Learners? A report on the early literacy project in Malaysia. *TESOL Quarterly* 44 (4), 822–829.

Johnston, K. (2015) Reclaiming the relevance of L2 teacher education. *The Modern Language Journal* 99 (3), 515–528.

Koda, K. (2005) *Insights into Second Language Reading: A Cross-Linguistic Approach*. Cambridge: Cambridge University Press.

Koda, K. (2008) Impacts of prior literacy experience on second-language learning to read. In K. Koda and A.M. Zehler (eds) *Learning to Read Across Languages: Cross-Linguistic Relationships in First- and Second-Language Literacy Development* (pp. 68–96). Abingdon: Routledge.

Marijanovic, V., Panissal, N. and Billières, M. (2009) How do 9–11 year old Croatians perceive sounds and read aloud in French? In M. Nikolov (ed.) *Early Learning of Modern Foreign Languages: Processes and Outcomes* (pp. 149–165). Bristol: Multilingual Matters.

Mitchell, R. (2014) Making the case for the future of languages. In P. Driscoll, E. Macaro and A. Swarbrick (eds) *Debates in Modern Languages Education* (pp. 203–217). *London:* Routledge.

Muñoz, C. (2014) Exploring young learners' foreign language learning awareness. *Language Awareness* 23 (1–2), 24–40.

Murphy, V.A., Macaro, E., Alba, S. and Cipolla, C. (2015) The influence of learning a second language in primary school on developing first language literacy skills. *Applied Psycholinguistics* 36, 1133–1153.

Ofsted (2012) *Moving English Forward: Action to Raise Standards in English*. London: HMSO.

Ofsted (2015) *Key Stage 3: The Wasted Years?* London: HMSO.

Nuffield Foundation (2000) *Languages: The Next Generation*. London: Nuffield Foundation.

Perfetti, C.A. and Dunlap, S. (2008) Learning to read: General principles and writing system variations. In K. Koda and A.M. Zehler (eds) *Learning to Read Across Languages: Cross-Linguistic Relationships in First- and Second-Language Literacy Development* (pp. 13–38). Abingdon: Routledge.

Porter, A. (2014) An early start to French literacy: Learning the spoken and written word simultaneously in English primary schools. PhD thesis, University of Southampton.

Rafat, Y. (2016) Orthography-induced transfer in the production of English-speaking learners of Spanish. *The Language Learning Journal* 44 (2), 197–213.

Rixon, S. (1992) State of the art article: English and other languages for younger children: Practice and theory in a rapidly-changing world. *Language Teaching* 25 (2), 73–93.

Sampson, G. (1985) *Writing Systems*. London: Hutchinson Education.

Teaching Schools Council (2016) *Modern Foreign Languages Pedagogy Review: A Review of Modern Foreign Languages Teaching Practice in Key Stage 3 and Key Stage 4*. See https://www.tscouncil.org.uk/wp-content/uploads/2016/12/MFL-Pedagogy-Review-Report-2.pdf (accessed 13 October 2017).

Thompson, G. and Cook, I. (2013) The logics of good teaching in an audit culture: A Deleuzian analysis. *Educational Philosophy and Theory* 45 (3), 243–258.

Tinsley, T. (2013) *The State of the Nation: Demand and Supply of Language Skills in the UK*. London: British Academy.

Tinsley, T. and Board, K. (2015) *Languages for the Future: Which Languages the UK Needs Most and Why*. London: British Council.

Tinsley, T. and Board, K. (2016) *Language Trends 2015/16: The State of Language Learning in Primary and Secondary Schools in England*. Reading: Education Development Trust.

Tinsley, T. and Comfort, T. (2012) *Lessons from Abroad: International Review of Primary Languages. Research report*. London: CfBT Education Trust.

Wade, P., Marshall, H. and O'Donnell, S. (2009) *Primary Modern Foreign Languages Longitudinal Survey of Implementation of National Entitlement to Language Learning at Key Stage 2 Final Report*. London: National Foundation for Educational Research for DCFS.

Woore, R. (2009) Beginners' progress in decoding L2 French: Some longitudinal evidence from English modern foreign languages classrooms. *The Language Learning Journal* 37 (1), 3–18.

Woore, R. (2010) Thinking aloud about L2 decoding: An exploration of the strategies used by beginner learners when pronouncing unfamiliar French words. *The Language Learning Journal* 38 (1), 3–17.

Wright, T. (2010) Second language teacher education: Review of recent research on practice. *Language Teaching* 43 (3), 259–296.

Wright, T. and Beaumont, M. (eds) (2015) *Experiences of Second Language Teacher Education*. Basingstoke: Palgrave Macmillan.

Part 2

Innovations in Mentoring and Supervision

7 Prospective TEYL Teachers and Teacher Education: A Study of Teacher Supervision

Chiou-Hui Chou

Introduction

During the past few decades, Asian countries have started to strive to enhance students' communication ability in English (e.g. Littlewood, 2007). Teaching English to young learners (TEYL) has gained great attention in Asian contexts. As primary English education becomes more prevalent around the world (Rich, 2014), many Asian countries are making an effort to enact and improve mandatory English education in primary schools (Azman, 2016; Butler, 2014; Spolsky & Moon, 2012). However, research has shown that policy decisions have been generally unsuccessful due to inadequately trained and skilled teachers, mismatch between curriculum and pedagogical realities, and limited time dedicated to language teaching and learning (e.g. Baldauf *et al.*, 2011; Butler, 2015). As indicated, the quality of English outcomes depends largely on the quality of teaching and teachers, and the quality of the program (Murphy, 2014). Crucial factors such as teacher preparation as well as the teaching pedagogies and curricula appropriate to teaching young learners (e.g. Korkmaz, 2017; Zein, 2016a; Zhou & Ng, 2016) all raise some issues which deserve the attention of policy makers and language professionals. Therefore, for teacher education programs, how to prepare competent TEYL teachers to enter the workforce is imperative.

As university supervision of student teaching is a widely accepted practice to improve teaching quality (Sullivan & Glanz, 2013), this study responded to the call for preparing quality TEYL teachers as well as improving teaching quality and investigated prospective TEYL teachers' pedagogical content knowledge development. A number of researchers have pointed out that as TEYL continues to spread across the globe, it is inappropriate for TESOL (teachers of English to speakers of other languages) educators to just deliver theory in university classrooms (e.g. Copland *et al.*, 2014; Garton *et al.*, 2011; Rich, 2014). English teaching practice needs to be both context-specific (Bax, 1997) and developed by teachers at a local level to reflect their own teaching conditions and the particular needs of their young learners (Rich, 2014). Previous studies on TEYL teacher education have provided description of worldwide, continent-regional or country-specific practice (e.g. Emery, 2012; Enever, 2014; Zein, 2015), while others address issues such as professional development strategies to meet teachers' needs (e.g. Chou, 2011; Kabilan & Veratharaju, 2013; Zein, 2017), teacher education evaluation (e.g. Canh & Chi, 2012; Malakolunthu & Vasudevan, 2012) and the role of government-based training agencies (e.g. Zein, 2016b). Research on TEYL teacher supervision is in its infancy and this is how the present study could fill in the gap in the literature.

The study reported in this chapter was conducted in the context of a TEYL teacher education program in Taiwan. The researcher implemented a short-term field teaching activity into a TESOL methods course and explored the effects of supervised field teaching on prospective TEYL teachers' pedagogical knowledge development. It was on the premise that investigating the topic of supervision can open a window to an understanding of prospective TEYL preservice teachers' development, increase quality of TEYL teachers and improve TEYL teacher preparation programs (Gelfuso *et al.*, 2015). The research question is: To what extent is supervised field teaching experience successful in preparing TEYL teachers to apply TESOL principles to classroom teaching? The findings demonstrate that teacher-educator-supervised field teaching can make field teaching more authentic and practical for prospective TEYL teachers to learn and to meet the expectations of updated teaching methodologies (Rich, 2014). The chapter then concludes with ideas for the incorporation of the findings into teacher education to prepare quality teachers for quality teaching.

Background of the Study

Elementary English education in Taiwan

In Taiwan, *Grade 1–9 Curriculum Guidelines* was enacted in 2001. It was in this curriculum reform that two periods of English courses per week were officially mandated for fifth- and sixth-graders. Later, in 2005, one to two periods of English courses per week was mandated for third- and fourth-graders. In addition, one to two periods of English, not as a compulsory subject for first- and second-graders, could be implemented based on each school's curriculum design for their own needs.

In fact, in many parts of Taiwan, one or two periods of English classes for first- and second-graders are prevalent, since individual schools can

implement English courses as part of their international education programs, school-based specialty curriculum or as flexible extracurricular
activities. For example, in Taipei City and New Taipei City, three periods
are currently implemented for fifth- and sixth-graders and two periods for
first- to fourth-graders (e.g. Chen, 2012). Some cities in Taiwan, such as
Hsinchu City (the researcher's city) and Hsinchu County, also enforce
three periods per week for fifth- and sixth-graders, two periods for third-
and fourth-graders and one to two periods for first- and second-graders.
Increasing the number of English instruction hours for primary curricula
is on the rise.

English teacher credential programs in Taiwan

Today, eleven universities in Taiwan are authorized to operate primary teacher education programs and they are also the universities that
can offer primary English teacher education – courses mandated and
authorized by the Taiwan Ministry of Education (MOE), which are the
so-called 26-credit elementary English credential. University students
who intend to be English teachers need to be admitted by their university's
teacher education program first. After being accepted into the program,
they then choose to take the required 26 credits as their subject area.

Nowadays, the so-called 26-credit primary English credential can
only be obtained through a four-year teacher education curriculum organized with theoretical and practical components at a university. In addition to taking the necessary courses, before obtaining the English teacher
certificate, prospective teachers must possess an English competence
equivalent to the B2 level of the Common European Framework of
Reference for Languages: Learning, Teaching, Assessment (CEFR) in the
four areas of skill: speaking, reading, writing and listening.

After students complete the teacher preparation courses, they then
participate in a half-year practicum. The purpose of the practicum is to
situate them in a school (a) to get real classroom teaching and practice
teaching; (b) to get to know the subject they will be teaching and to learn
about classroom management; (c) to learn about school administrative
work on the job and the function of school administration; and (d) to
experience teacher responsibility and the role of the teacher as well as to
develop professional competence.

In Taiwan's educational practicum, primary teachers are invited to be
mentors by their schools. As primary English courses are taught by subject
teachers, they are generally not invited to be mentors. However, as previously indicated, practicum can offer prospective teachers an opportunity
to connect theory with practice under the guidance of their supervisors
(Gelfuso et al., 2015; Zeichner, 2010) and mentors are expected to provide
a place for student teachers to practice teaching. Examining the practicum
structure for primary English teachers in Taiwan, the researcher has

found teacher education programs need to arrange better practicum for student teachers to develop their pedagogical content knowledge. In order to strengthen the current practicum structure, the study set out to implement early field teaching experience for English student teachers during their university coursework to improve teaching performance and to nurture best practices.

Literature Review

Field experiences

Field experiences involve activities completed outside of the college classroom that correlate to and supplement the content being taught in that course. Prospective teachers can be engaged in activities in authentic situations in a teaching and learning setting through observation and participation. Teaching practice experience includes serial school experience, block school experience and internship (Wallace, 1991: 122). Carefully constructed field experiences coordinated with campus courses are more influential and effective in supporting student teacher learning than unguided and disconnected field experiences (Darling-Hammond, 2006). However, as Zeichner (2010) pointed out, a perennial problem in traditional university-sponsored teacher education programs has been the lack of connection between university-based teacher education courses and field experiences. There is a global consensus that teacher education must be improved and resources need to be elaborated. Furthermore, obstacles need to be eliminated to developing teacher education if it is to meet the challenges of the 21st century (Darling-Hammond, 2010; Gelfuso *et al.*, 2015; Hökkä & Eteläpelto, 2014; Hollins, 2011).

Teaching English to young learners all around the world has gained great attention (e.g. Bland, 2015; Butler, 2015; Rich, 2014) and the preparation of teachers has raised some issues. The issue that teacher education programs cannot prepare English teachers solely based on university courses has been discussed earlier (Korkmaz, 2017; Zein, 2016a). Recent studies also advocate for research in teacher education addressing the structures and activities that constitute quality field experiences (Campbell & Dunleavy, 2016). In response to the clinical teacher preparation model, Gelfuso *et al.* (2015) developed frameworks to enhance field experiences that can provide a critical context for prospective teachers to apply their theoretical and pedagogical university learning to practical K-12 settings with an emphasis of teacher supervision.

Teacher supervision

Earlier, Gebhard (1990: 107) stated 'language teacher supervision is an ongoing process of the teacher's education in which the supervisor observes what goes on in the teacher's classroom with an eye toward the goal of improved instruction.' Recently, Sullivan and Glanz (2013) wrote about the changing context of supervision and briefly state that supervision is viewed as central to the improvement of instruction. As indicated, 'supervision for the improvement of instruction will continue to the foremost concern of supervisors and other educational leaders well into the 21st century' (Sullivan & Glanz, 2013: 4). It is the process of engaging teachers in instructional dialogue for the purpose of improving teaching and increasing student achievement.

Research on teacher supervision in TESOL has generally been on the topics of models of teacher supervision (Bailey, 2006; Gebhard, 1984), the phases of clinical supervision (Gelfuso et al., 2015; Stoller, 1996; Sullivan & Glanz, 2013) and the role of supervisors and the effects of supervision (Chen & Cheng, 2013; Kayaoglu, 2012). Bailey (2006) discussed various models of teacher supervision. Freeman's (1982) and Gebhard's (1984, 1990) frameworks of supervision have informed much of the recent thinking about teacher supervision in English language teaching. Freeman (1982) identified three approaches that supervisors may choose when observing and giving feedback to language teachers: the supervisory approach, the alternatives approach and the nondirective approach. In the supervisory option, the teacher has little power to determine the issue under discussion. In the nondirective option, the teacher has extensive opportunities to direct the discussion and make decisions. In the alternatives option, the teacher and the supervisor jointly negotiate what actions to implement. As Bailey (2006) points out, a key factor to distinguish the above three approaches is power. Based on Freeman's model, Gebhard (1984) came up with five models of supervision: directive, alternative, collaborative, nondirective and creative. Gebhard (1984) indicates that teacher educators have a wide choice of supervisory behaviors they can use in the process of training second language teachers. In directive supervision, the teacher educator makes comments on student teachers' practice and gives them suggestions to be implemented in the classrooms. In alternative supervision, the teacher educator selects an issue from classroom teaching to be discussed with student teachers and gives them some alternatives to solve this problem in their teaching. In the collaborative model, the supervisor and the teacher work together to solve problems encountered in the classroom. In nondirective supervision, the teacher educator gives student teachers opportunities and allows them to come up with their own solution to classroom dilemmas. The creative supervision model is defined as the combination of the other four models (directive, nondirective, alternatives and collaborative) to approach teachers' specific needs in their educational context.

Given that teaching practice is a relevant context for observation, analysis and reflection, teacher supervision plays an important role in this process because it should be able to stimulate student teachers to reflect on their own practice if they take the leading role in problem solving and decision making (Burns & Richards, 2009). Models of supervision appear to be very much associated with supervisors' role in professional contexts in that 'supervisors' responsibilities have moved from being largely judgmental and evaluative to being more developmental in focus' (Bailey, 2006: 6). According to Wallace (1991), language teacher supervision can be divided into two broad categories – the prescriptive approach and the collaborative approach. Similarly, Young (2009) divided supervision into two categories. One is for developmental purposes, which is often seen as a collaborative model and one is for evaluative purposes, which is usually associated with prescriptive approaches. Recent research has emphasized a more collaborative approach to language teacher supervision (Bailey, 2009). Based on Weller's (1971) definition of clinical supervision, Sullivan and Glanz (2013) proposed reflective clinical supervision. There are three phases to the clinical supervision cycle: planning conference, observation and feedback conference. The newly added phase in reflective clinical supervision is professional development. According to Sullivan and Glanz (2013), in a collaborative model of supervision, a supervisor can focus on developing clear program goals and student performance goals, as well as nurturing best practices from teachers through a process of reflective questioning. In addition, as Kayaoglu (2012: 115) points out, an English-as-a-foreign-language (EFL) supervisor has to be able to 'diagnose problems specific to the field and recognize the complex characteristics of learning and teaching a foreign language.' In conclusion, a supervisor has to be able to motivate, guide and facilitate participants' learning, and observe classes and give constructive feedback to enable participants to grow by reflecting upon themselves and their classrooms. The above literature served as the framework for investigating this present study.

Methodology

Context of the study

The study was conducted in the researcher's three-hour TESOL methods course. In this project, during the first eight weeks of the semester, students received three hours of theory instruction and training per week and approximately one hour was allotted to them to apply the theories learned in the book to microteaching practice. For their midterm assessment, each student designed a lesson for their field teaching in December – to teach a Grade 2 or Grade 3 class based on the material and according to the syllabus of what the primary school students were learning. During the midterm week, each one demonstrated a microteaching lesson, practicing teaching major components in their lesson. Guidelines for evaluation were given and included the following elements: warm-up activities, teaching voice, techniques for teaching words and sentence structures, using teaching aids, design of teaching aids and worksheets, teacher-student interactions, student-student interactions, pair work or groupwork activities, wrap-up activities, teaching flow and posture (smile), as well as attire.

Before midterm, coordinating primary English teachers were contacted and asked to allow the student teachers to practice teaching individually in all their Grade 2 and Grade 3 classes for three consecutive weeks in December. The taught topics were: What color is it?, What can you do? and a Christmas-related topic. In November, participants conducted classroom observations, observing the specific class that each member was going to teach. The purpose of the observation was for them to get to know some basic background information about the students, such as how they interacted with the teacher and their English learning patterns, as well as their English teachers' teaching strategies. Then, starting in December, they practiced teaching in the primary school under the guidance of an English mentor teacher and the researcher.

The organization of the TESOL methods course aimed to carry pre-service teachers from theoretical methodological knowledge to a step-by-step practice in order to help them gain insight toward teaching English to young children. The rationale was that a TESOL educator should bring on effective teachers equipped not only with the theory of teaching, but also with the techniques for applying theory in practice. Rather than just developing pure knowledge of teaching theory and its practices, pre-service English teachers are supposed to develop effective teaching methods to teach young learners and explore their development.

Participants

In the context of this study, not every student was in the teacher education program. Thus, only the fourteen English pre-service teachers participated in this study, of whom twelve were female and two were male. All the names used in this chapter are pseudonyms to protect the anonymity of the participants.

Ethical consent forms were obtained and the purpose of this study was made clear to them. Each participant taught two lessons, which was one more than the rest of the class students taught, applying the TESOL theory they had learned. Their teaching practice was observed by at least one peer (sometimes by two to three based on their peers' schedule) and the researcher. At the end of teaching and observation, a conference was held with each participant to discuss their lesson. The primary teacher also gave them feedback written on an evaluation form provided by the researcher. Each participant's teaching performance and the problems they experienced in the classroom were also discussed. Generally, after class, they reflected on how successfully they were interacting with young learners and to what extent they implemented learned TESOL theories and conducted activities. They wrote their reflection and submitted them to an assignment platform to share with the researcher and their peers.

Data collection and analysis

A mixed methods approach was used for this research (Creswell, 2013). As Johnson *et al.* (2007: 123) state, mixed methods research 'combines elements of qualitative and quantitative research approaches (e.g. use of qualitative and quantitative viewpoints, data collection, analysis, inference techniques) for the broad purpose of breadth and depth of understanding and corroboration.' Moreover, as this study was conducted in a three-credit TESOL methods course in a semester, adopting a mixed method research design allowed the researcher to obtain all the data from the participants and explore their development from different perspectives. However, the researcher might encounter tasks in resolving discrepancies between different types of data.

Qualitative data were collected from lesson plans, semi-structured interviews, classroom observations, reflective journal writing and group discussions. Four open-ended interview questions were emailed to students for them to think about their learning in this project. All the audio recordings of the interviews were transcribed verbatim. Quantitative data were collected from a pre-questionnaire and a post-questionnaire. Two items were about the participants' knowledge about lesson planning and students' English ability. Six items were for participants to assess their teaching performance after each teaching practice. Participants self-indicated the degree to which they agreed to a statement based on a scale of 1 to 10.

The constant comparative method was used to guide the data analysis (Miles *et al.*, 2014); patterns and themes regrading participant's professional knowledge development were then identified. Data analysis went through several phases. In the first phase, the questionnaire results were analyzed. During the second phase, participants' lesson plans and reflective journal writing were examined to find the TESOL principles that the participants applied. In the third phase, reading participants' reflective journals, observation notes and the researcher's observation notes helped the researcher examine participants' rationales for applying the theories. In the fourth phase, looking at the oral data from interviews and discussion data, as well as all the written data, helped the researcher get the whole picture of the effects of this project. During the last phase of coding, pattern themes were created to further categorize and condense the data (Yin, 2014).

Findings and Discussion

A clinical reflective supervision stance of the four phases from Sullivan and Glanz (2013) was adopted to guide the research process and data analysis with an emphasis on improving student teachers' classroom performance. Next, Gebhard's (1990) models of supervision and the role of supervisors served as framework to guide the supervision direction. It was under the tenet of teacher supervision that TEYL student teachers' professional knowledge development was investigated.

In the following section, first, the researcher analyzed student teachers' teaching practice to explore their pedagogical content knowledge. Next, student teachers' teaching performance was examined to indicate their development. Exploring student teachers' demonstration of pedagogical content knowledge suggested the areas for the researcher to guide the student teachers to apply theory in practice. The researcher then wrapped up with the importance of teacher supervision in field teaching in TEYL teacher education.

Exploring pedagogical content knowledge

Based on Shulman (1986) and others, Konig *et al.* (2017: 122) proposed pedagogical content knowledge as 'knowledge of curriculum, teaching strategies, and students.' How did the participants apply theory in practice to teach young English learners? Figure 7.1 shows the activities embedded within the TESOL methodology and the principles most often used by the student teachers, which were: (a) using realia – such as bringing a basket of fruits to class, using stationery and using paints to teach colors; (b) board games – to integrate multiple skills in learning English, such as spelling words, saying words, answering questions and singing English songs; (c) bingo and tic-tac-toe games – to practice speaking and listening; (d) unscrambling the words – to increase phonemic awareness; (e) written production – expressing ideas using the learned words and structures; (f) total physical response method – listening, doing and

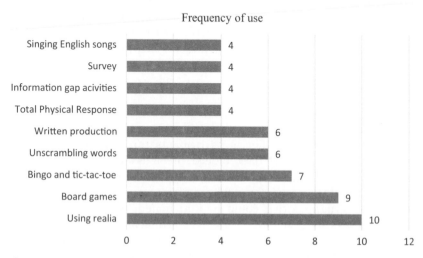

Figure 7.1 Activities used in this project

craft-making; (g) survey and information gap activities; and (h) singing English songs. Examining the above activities, the researcher found most were more oriented toward communicative language teaching (CLT) (Richards, 2006) – in which realia, meaningful communication and games for learners to motivate them to communicate were considered. As indicated, in the postmethod era (Kumaravadivelu, 2001), practitioners should be able to construct classroom-oriented theories of practice. These student teachers applied a variety of communicative activities to engage learners in English learning.

In designing activities, participants were very aware of using realia to show a context and to teach/review words or to review sentence structures for meaningful communication, such as 'What is it?' and 'What color is it?' They also paid attention to increasing students' phonemic awareness, phonics practice and syllable concept by applying unscrambling the words activities. As games are an essential, integral part of children's language learning (Read, 2007), they were used in each lesson. As the main activity in a lesson, board games were used most often for students to practice integrated skills; bingo or tic-tac-toe activities were also used as main activities to guide students to practice listening and speaking, as well as for group competition. These student teachers learned to make decisions and negotiate competing contextual demands to shape their language pedagogy toward student learning (Burns *et al.*, 2015).

How did the participants wrap up a class? If a teacher can decide how to teach, then there must be some cognitive capacity governing those decisions (Burns *et al.*, 2015). Each method carried with it a way of thinking. The CLT-oriented activities (Richards, 2006) that student teachers most often used to wrap up a lesson were for young learners to do independent writing – such as making a mini-book and writing down the learned words, using the focused sentence structures to write their ideas and writing a postcard to Santa. Evaluating students' learning results by doing listening and writing practice (or listen and color or listen and circle) was observed in four lessons. During the Christmas week, singing a song was observed in three lessons.

During observations, the researcher found some of the activities were implemented successfully while others did not run smoothly – which was also expressed and reported in the participants' teaching journals, observation notes and discussion data. Indeed, previous studies have indicated that language teaching is complex and problematic (Burns & Knox, 2011; Burns *et al.*, 2015). In spite of thoughtful planning, not every act of teaching created situations that could be anticipated, which usually arose during practice. For example, in Yu's first teaching in a second grade class, a survey activity was used. Before the class, she did not think it was necessary to put an enlarged worksheet on the board to tell students how to do it (Yu's first journal writing). While using this activity, she just drew a simplified version on the board and did not demonstrate the exact steps. She found students were confused and did not know how to do. As knowledge of teaching generally emerged directly from the activity of teaching (Cuenca, 2011), in this study, student teaching provided the participants with an opportunity to construct their own understandings of teaching based on the practical dilemmas they encountered in the field. According to Konig *et al.* (2017: 122), pedagogical content knowledge is 'conceptualized in a task-based way, that is, closer to the cognitive dimensions of interactive decision making in the classroom than to a conceptualization of teaching knowledge as disciplinary knowledge.'

Professional knowledge development

The participants' professional knowledge development was observed and depicted as follows: before moving to the realities of primary schools, through microteaching, the pre-service teachers planned lessons to help them put TESOL principles into practice; they took small steps forward by acquiring classroom skills within the critical yet safe environment of their peers. After the microteaching stage, the pre-service teachers further enhanced their planning and preparation skills while working with the supervisor and mentor teachers, as well as with their peers. After the first and the second field teaching and observation, they gradually and steadily moved toward more professional levels. The participants' professional knowledge development is presented and discussed in the quantitative and qualitative data in this section.

Quantitative data

The data indicate that the participants have different confidence levels with their pedagogical skills in relation to their field teaching experiences. This difference is depicted through graphs (see Figures 7.2 and 7.3). Data analysis highlights that they rated their teaching skills of showing confidence extremely high. Their ratings for classroom management skills and delivering activities, on the other hand, remained low.

Figures 7.2 and 7.3 demonstrate that participants have shown great improvements in the following areas: classroom management skills (+1.5), overall teaching performance (+1.2), knowledge about students (+1.6) and knowledge of lesson planning (+1.2). They indicated they had much more confidence in their teaching voice (7.5), interactions with students (7.6), their teaching performance (7.4), their knowledge of lesson planning (7.7) and knowledge about students (7.3), with an average above 7.3. The two areas where they have a lack of confidence are classroom management (6.8) and method of delivering groupwork or pair work (6.6), with an average of less than 7.

Examining the data, the researcher found the aspects for which participants increased their confidence levels most were their knowledge

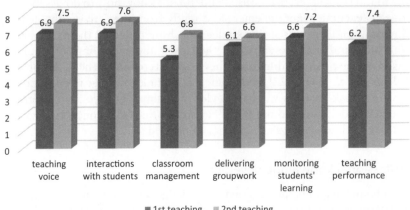

Figure 7.2 Teaching performance

about students and classroom management. Situating pre-service teachers in a primary classroom to practice teaching did contribute to their knowledge development about real teaching contexts – primary young learners and their learning styles.

It is understandable that as the participants were new to the students and had weak background knowledge about them, their performance during classroom teaching would not be perfect. In fact, the purpose of situating them in a real classroom to practice teaching young learners was to guide them to explore the aspects for which they were and were not well-prepared. The findings show that the aspects that student teachers

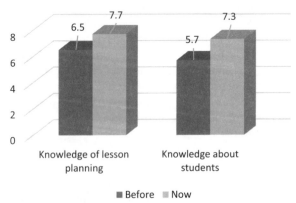

Figure 7.3 Knowledge about lesson planning and students

needed to strive for improvement on were classroom management strategies for lower graders, and delivering lessons and giving instructions more clearly. In the literature, novice teachers were more concerned with maintaining discipline and behavioral norms.

In addition, they found difficulty in explaining the rules for activities. Indeed, in teaching children English, even qualified teachers may find it a challenge to manage large classrooms (Chen & Cheng, 2013; Garton, 2014) and groups of children with mixed abilities (Garton, 2014; Garton et al., 2011). Moreover, using English only to deliver a lesson to students in lower grades was not an easy task, because of young learners' low levels of proficiency and non-native speaker teachers' disadvantage of lesser fluency (e.g. Butler, 2014). It did take practice for student teachers to use the simple words and sentence structures children had learned, as well as shorter sentences to accommodate children's short attention spans. As Pinter (2006) indicated, simplifications and modifications in their speech should be used in making the input comprehensible to children (Krashen, 1985). The problem of student teachers' lack of confidence in their English ability is almost universally identified in the literature (e.g. Garton et al., 2011). The perceived demands of CLT especially require teachers to teach in the target language. An inability to handle children's questions was also observed and reflected on by the participants. This study found failing to respond to or answer children's questions also led to a lack of confidence and an inability to manage students' behavior.

Qualitative data

Professional knowledge is seen as coming both from sources outside the teacher and from the teachers' own interpretations of their experiences. Although being a professional teacher implies that an individual possesses the appropriate pedagogical content knowledge, it is also important for a teacher be able to effectively cope with a certain range of situations and demonstrate teaching competence. An examination of all the reflective journals and observation notes yields qualitative data showing participants' professional knowledge development in the following summary:

- Using videos for teaching reflection is common (Kaneko-Marques, 2015). As Richards and Farrell (2005) indicated, a starting point in teacher development is an awareness of what the teacher's current knowledge, skills and attitudes are, and the use of such information as a basis for self-appraisal. Data from interviews showed that after viewing their own videos, participants knew they needed to walk toward students to engage them in activities and to invite their responses to their questions, not just stand in front of the blackboard to direct activities. In addition, walking toward students and inviting their responses would also help monitor students' learning and attention. Observing their pedagogical actions through videos, the participants became more reflective and self-evaluative, and they identified problems and searched for answers (Kaneko-Marques, 2015).

- In practicing meaningful communication, teachers' interactional practices can contribute to young learners' language development and to the success of language curricula (Chen & Wang, 2014). When the participants prepared real objects to create a context in which to teach words and to help the students feel comfortable to ask and answer questions, they walked toward the students to invite volunteers to pick an object to discuss (such as fruits in a basket, stationery in a box, or animal-shaped or flower-shaped balloons in a bag).

- Most of the participants prepared board games to integrate four-skill (speaking, reading, writing and listening) practice. Once they put up the board game poster for the whole class to play (divided into two groups), they found that only the student who was picked each turn was mostly involved in answering questions. The rest of the class were not given jobs to do and classroom management was weak. They found the activity was not the same as they practiced in microteaching. Thus, classroom management strategies were proposed for their second teaching to create more interactions between group members and with the teacher (Jane's second teaching reflection).

- To maximize opportunities for student interaction and to promote language use (Ellis, 1991), groupwork and pair work are important components of CLT. Information gap and survey activities were the major examples from the textbook during discussion on the topic of CLT (Larsen-Freeman & Anderson, 2011), thus when asked about applying TESOL principles in their lesson plans, some participants designed the two types for their first teaching plans. However, in teaching young learners, they found students did not completely understand the teacher's purpose and oral instruction as expressed in the interview data. Some learners just sat down and looked at each other's worksheets and copied the answers (Yu's first teaching reflection). Thus, after the first week teaching and observation, some participants modified their lesson plans and changed activities to be appropriate for the learners, such as using board games instead (Yu's second teaching).

- When presenting vocabulary to young learners, teachers can use things that they can see, feel, play with, touch and experience (Pinter, 2006). There were also some good examples where the participants related the content taught to the young learners' experience – to make the language real for them. For example, before the class ended, Wendy did a short practice review about color words. She approached students and randomly pointed to the students' shirts, jackets or stationery on their desk to ask, 'What color is it?'

Teacher supervision

Following Schön (1987), the researcher provoked and encouraged the participants to reflect on the aspects of their own teaching practice. In this study, following the four phases of a clinical reflective supervision proposed by Sullivan and Glanz (2013), the researcher found the field teaching project was an important stage for student teachers to explore their view of teaching in order to identify and solve issues that they felt relevant to their situation, rather than discuss issues identified by the university educator. The assignment of writing reflective journals then served as the platform for the participants to have an inner dialogue with themselves and for them to express their ideas to the educator. Participants' reflection often focused on a range of teaching ideas and classroom management strategies. For example, during Jane's second teaching, she used a score board to record the second graders' points based on each group's performance as the classroom management strategy. She wrote in her journal that in order to have good classroom management and to deliver her instruction smoothly, this method helped her to regulate student discipline. However, she reflected upon this aspect: instead of using this type of reward system, how could she manage students to follow her instructions for playing a game, just as the way students were in their English teacher's class.

A collaborative supervision model from Gebhard's (1990) seemed to work successfully during the project, where the student teachers and the supervisor worked together to solve problems encountered in the classroom. As supervision is considered to be a deliberate intervention into the instructional process with the aim of improving instruction (Sullivan & Glanz, 2013), in this project, the researcher found university coursework served the role of addressing up-to-date teaching principles in theory and textbooks, while field teaching experience supported student teachers' understanding of those principles as practiced in the real classroom. It was during the field teaching that participants and the university educator had valuable opportunities to modify, extend, hone and personalize their professional knowledge through teaching practice, reflection and observation. The student teachers and the university educator then became more proactive in their own teaching and professional lives. Conversations about children's learning effects, teaching performances and activity results provided concrete conditions for participants to reflect, share and construct their pedagogical content knowledge. It was found that supervision was a process of engaging student teachers 'in instructional dialogue for the purpose of improving teaching and increasing student achievement' (Sullivan & Glanz, 2013: 4). Then, the role of the supervisor was to support student teachers' pedagogical knowledge construction through collaborative discussions of their teaching practice (Kaneko-Marques, 2015). As they began to assume more instructional responsibility, they also needed active support and meaningful feedback from peers and the university supervisor.

The results of this study suggest that field experiences occur throughout teacher education programs and should be explicitly interrelated and intentionally organized so that each experience can build on and extend previous ones. Kayaoglu (2012: 115) indicates supervision is 'considered to be a deliberate intervention into the instructional process with the aim of improving instruction assuming a professional working relationship between teachers and supervisors.' In this study, the four phases of Sullivan and Glanz's (2013: 121) reflective clinical supervision model (planning, observation, feedback and professional development) were followed. The university instructor proposed different goals that she wanted the pre-service teachers to achieve during coursework and the field experiences – gaining theory from the coursework, planning lessons, microteaching, observing classes, practicing teaching, reflecting, learning with peers and receiving feedback for reflection. Then, in a second teaching practice context, the student teachers planned a second lesson, practiced teaching, reflected, received feedback and shared their learning results with the whole class. In this way, student teachers were provided with opportunities to make sense of their university coursework within the context of a real classroom and teaching under the university instructor's supervision. This study has shown that the above activities in the supervision cycle created structures and opportunities that positioned them to be able to bridge the gap between coursework and fieldwork through mediating theory and teaching practice (e.g. Darling-Hammond, 2010; Gelfuso et al., 2015; Zeichner, 2010).

Conclusion

This study investigated sending TEYL student teachers to practice what they had learned from a methods course in a short-term field teaching under the supervision of a university instructor. Following the trend for clinical reflective supervision (Sullivan & Glanz, 2013) and collaborative supervision (Gebhard, 1990), this study has shown successful results – the work in the field and the work on the courses should be fully integrated and relational, which echoed the advocacy of Darling-Hammond (2006), Zeichner (2010) as well as Gelfuso et al. (2015). In this well-supervised filed teaching experience, student teachers had opportunities to interact with the classroom context. This followed the premise that field experiences and university coursework informed one another. In this way, the university instructor also actively participated in field experience to support student teachers' knowledge development. Moreover, during this field-teaching project, the student teachers explored how to apply TESOL theories, how to examine their teaching results and developed their pedagogical content knowledge. This study demonstrated setting up a short-term field teaching project connected with a course in TEYL teacher education helped bridge the gap between curriculum and pedagogical realities.

In conclusion, to prepare quality TEYL teachers, this study asserts that pre-service teachers have to be given the opportunity to deliver instruction that addresses modern theory and to practice up-to-date English teaching methods. They should be advised to design appropriate activities to promote and enhance children's English learning. Following Gelfuso *et al.* (2015), the role of the university supervisor must shift from one of observation and immediate feedback to one of deep analysis and coaching within the framework of the content being taught. The results of this study hope to add to the growing body of literature in teaching TEYL around the world.

Implications and Suggestions

For TEYL teacher education, this study offers suggestions and implications for teacher educators locally and globally. Researchers in teacher education programs stress the essential need for a collaborative relationship in which school teachers and the faculty of educational institutes work together as partners to prepare student teachers for the teaching profession. In accordance with trends from all around the world, TEYL teacher education programs can also step into practice-based teacher education – partnerships with local primary schools so that preservice teachers will be offered field teaching during their study in university (Grossman, 2011; Zeichner, 2012). Then, a possible next step might be to research the role of primary English teachers as mentors in collaboration with teacher education programs.

Furthermore, supervisors should be able to develop strategies to improve prospective teachers' teaching practice and nurture reflective practice (Gelfuso *et al.*, 2015; Kaneko-Marques, 2015). They are also expected to support teachers' knowledge construction through collaborative reflections on their pedagogical practice. Because of these responsibilities, they should be highly qualified and experienced, as they need to be knowledgeable about teacher supervision, give constructive feedback and design collaborative projects in TEYL teacher education.

References

Azman, H. (2016) Implementation and challenges of English language education reform in Malaysian primary school. *3L: The Southeast Asian Journal of English Language Studies* 22 (3), 65–78.

Bailey, K.M. (2006) *Language Teacher Supervision: A Case-based Approach.* Cambridge: Cambridge University Press.

Bailey, K.M. (2009) Language teacher supervision. In A. Burns and J.C. Richards (eds) *Second Language Teacher Education* (pp. 269–278). New York: Cambridge University Press.

Baldauf, R.B., Kaplan, R.B., Kamwangamalu, N. and Bryant, P. (2011) Success or failure of primary second/foreign language programmes in Asia: What do the data tell us? *Current Issues in Language Planning* 12, 309–323. doi:10.1080/14664208.2011.609715

Bax, S. (1997) Roles for a teacher educator in context-sensitive language teacher education. *ELT Journal* 51 (3), 232–241. doi:10.1093/elt/51.3.232

Bland, J. (2015) *Teaching English to Young Learners: Critical Issues in Language Teaching with 3–12 Year Olds.* New York: Bloomsbury.

Burns, A. and Knox, J.S. (2011) Classrooms as complex adaptive systems: A relational model. *TESL-EJ* 15 (1), 1–25.

Burns, A. and Richards, J.C. (eds) (2009) *The Cambridge Guide to Second Language Teacher Education.* Cambridge: Cambridge University Press.

Burns, A., Freeman, D. and Edwards, E. (2015) Theorizing and studying the language-teaching mind: Mapping research on language teacher cognition. *The Modern Language Journal* 99 (3), 585–601. doi:10.1111/modl.12245

Butler, Y.G. (2014) Current issues in English education for young learners in East Asia. *English Teaching* 69 (4), 3–25. doi:10.15858/engtea.69.4.201412.3

Butler, Y.G. (2015) English language education among young learners in East Asia: A review of current research (2004–2014). *Language Teaching* 48 (3), 303–342. doi:10.1017/S0261444815000105

Campbell, S.S. and Dunleavy, T.K. (2016) Connecting university course work and practitioner knowledge through medicated field experiences. *Teacher Education Quarterly* 43 (3), 49–70.

Canh, L.V. and Chi, D.T.M. (2012) Teacher preparation for primary school English education: A case of Vietnam. In B. Spolsky and Y.-I. Moon (eds) *Primary School English-Language Education in Asia: From Policy to Practice* (pp. 106–128). New York: Routledge.

Chen, C. (2012) Planning and implementation of elementary school English education in Taiwan. In B. Spolsky and Y.-I. Moon (eds) *Primary School English-Language Education in Asia: From Policy to Practice* (pp. 129–144). New York: Routledge.

Chen, C.W. and Cheng, Y. (2013) The supervisory process of EFL teachers: A case study. *TESL-EJ* 17 (1), 1–21.

Chen, Z. and Wang, Q. (2014) Examining classroom interactional practices to promote learning in the young learner EFL classroom in China. In S. Rich (ed.) *International Perspectives on Teaching English to Young Learners* (pp. 45–65). New York: Palgrave Macmillan.

Chou, C. (2011) Teachers' professional development: Investigating teachers learning to do action research in a professional learning community. *The Asia-Pacific Education Researcher* 20 (3), 421–437.

Copland, F., Garton, S. and Burns, A. (2014) Challenges in teaching English to young learners: Global perspectives and local realities. *TESOL Quarterly* 48 (4), 738–762. doi:10.1002/tesq.148

Creswell, J.W. (2013) *Research Design: Qualitative, Quantitative, and Mixed Methods Approaches.* Thousand Oaks, CA: Sage Publications, Inc.

Cuenca, A. (2011) The role of legitimacy in student teaching: Learning to 'feel' like a teacher. *Teacher Education Quarterly* 38 (2), 117–130.

Darling-Hammond, L. (2006) *Powerful Teacher Education.* San Francisco, CA: Jossey-Bass.

Darling-Hammond, L. (2010) Teacher education and the American future. *Journal of Teacher Education* 61 (1–2) 35–47. doi:10.1177/0022487109348024

Ellis, R. (1991) *Second Language Acquisition and Language Pedagogy.* Clevedon: Multilingual Matters.

Emery, H. (2012) A global study of primary English teachers' qualifications, training and career development. *ELT Research Papers.* 12-08. London: The British Council.

See https://www.teachingenglish.org.uk/sites/teacheng/files/B487_ELTRP_Emery_ResearchPaper_FINAL_web_V2.pdf (accessed 28 October 2017).

Enever, J. (2014) Primary English teacher education in Europe. *ELT Journal* 68 (3), 231–242. doi:10.1093/elt/cct079

Freeman, D. (1982) Observing teachers: Three approaches to in-service training and development. *TESOL Quarterly* 16 (1), 21–27. doi:10.2307/3586560

Garton, S. (2014) Unresolved issues and new challenges in teaching English to young learners: The case of South Korea. *Current Issues in Language Planning* 15 (2), 201–219. doi:10.1080/14664208.2014.858657

Garton, S., Copland, F. and Burns, A. (2011) Investigating global practices in teaching English to young learners. *ELT Research Papers* 11-01. The British Council. See https://www.teachingenglish.org.uk/article/global-practices-teaching-english-young-learners (accessed 28 October 2018).

Gebhard, J.G. (1984) Models of supervision: Choices. *TESOL Quarterly* 18 (3), 501–514. doi:10.2307/3586717

Gebhard, J.G. (1990) The supervision of second and foreign language teachers. *ERIC Digest, ERIC Clearinghouse on Language and Linguistics (EDO-FL-90-06)*. Washington, DC: Center for Applied Linguistics.

Gelfuso, A., Parker, A. and Dennis, D.V. (2015) Turning teacher education upside down: Enacting the inversion of teacher preparation through the symbiotic relationship of theory and practice. *The Professional Educator* 39 (2). See http://wp.auburn.edu/educate/wp-content/uploads/2015/11/gelfuso-fall_15.pdf (accessed 28 October 2018).

Grossman, P. (2011) Framework for teaching practice: A brief history of an idea. *Teachers College Record* 113 (12), 2836–2843.

Hökkä, P. and Eteläpelto, A. (2014) Seeking new perspectives on the development of teacher education: A study of the Finnish context. *Journal of Teacher Education* 65 (1), 39–52. doi:10.1177/0022487113504220

Hollins, E. (2011) Teacher preparation for quality teaching. *Journal of Teacher Education* 62 (4), 395–407. doi:10.1177/0022487111409415

Johnson, R.B., Onwuegbuzie, A.J. and Turner, L.A. (2007) Toward a definition of mixed methods research. *Journal of Mixed Methods Research* 1 (2), 112–133. doi:10.1177/1558689806298224

Kabilan, M.K. and Veratharaju, K. (2013) Professional development needs of primary school English language teachers in Malaysia. *Professional Development in Education* 39 (3), 330–351. doi:10.1080/19415257.2012.762418

Kaneko-Marques, S.M. (2015) Reflective teacher supervision through videos of classroom teaching. *PROFILE Issues in Teachers' Professional Development* 17 (2), 63–79. doi:10.15446/profile.v17n2.44393

Kayaoglu, M.N. (2012) Dictating or facilitating: The supervisory process for language teachers. *Australian Journal of Teacher Education* 37 (10), 103–117. doi:10.14221/ajte.2012v37n10.4

Konig, J., Tachtsoglou, S., Lammerding, S., Straub, S., Nold, G. and Rohde, A. (2017) The role of opportunities to learn in teacher preparation for EFL teachers' pedagogical content knowledge. *The Modern Language Journal* 101 (1), 109–127. doi: 10.111/modl.12383

Korkmaz, S.C. (2017) Classroom research: What do ELT teacher trainees experience when performing collaborative group-work tasks? *Journal of Teacher Education and Educators* 6 (1), 31–52.

Krashen, S.D. (1985) *The Input Hypothesis: Issues and Implications*. New York, NY: Longman.

Kumaravadivelu, B. (2001) Toward a postmethod pedagogy. *TESOL Quarterly* 35 (4), 537–560. doi: 10.2307/3588427

Larsen-Freeman, D. and Anderson, M. (2011) *Techniques and Principles in Language Teaching* (3rd edn). Oxford: Oxford University Press.

Littlewood, W. (2007) Communicative and task-based language teaching in East Asian classrooms. *Language Teaching* 40, 243–249. doi:10.1017/S0261444807004363

Malakolunthu, S. and Vasudevan, V. (2012) Teacher evaluation practices in Malaysian primary schools: Issues and challenges. *Asia Pacific Education Review* 13, 449–456. doi:10.1007/s12564-012-9207-z

Miles, M., Huberman, A.M. and Saldana, J. (2014) *Fundamentals of Qualitative Data Analysis: A Methods Source Book*. Thousand Oaks, CA: Sage Publications.

Murphy, V.A. (2014) *Second Language Learning in the Early School Years: Trends and Contexts*. Oxford: Oxford University Press.

Pinter, A. (2006) *Teaching Young Language Learners*. Oxford: Oxford University Press.

Read, C. (2007) *500 Activities for the Primary Classroom*. Oxford: Macmillan Publishers.

Rich, S. (2014) The added value of international perspectives on teaching English to young learners. In S. Rich (ed.) *International Perspectives on Teaching English to Young Learners* (pp. 191–200). London: Palgrave Macmillan.

Richards, J.C. (2006) *Communicative Language Teaching Today*. New York, NY: Cambridge University Press.

Richards, J.C. and Farrell, T.S.C. (2005) *Professional Development for Language Teachers: Strategies for Teacher Learning*. Cambridge: Cambridge University Press.

Schön, D.A. (1987) *Educating the Reflective Practitioner*. San Francisco, CA: Jossey-Bass.

Shulman, L.S. (1986) Those who understand: Knowledge and growth in teaching. *Educational Researcher* 15 (2), 4–14.

Spolsky, B. and Moon, T. (eds) (2012) *Primary School English-Language Education in Asia: From Policy to Practice*. New York, NY: Routledge.

Stoller, F. (1996) Teacher Supervision: Moving Towards an Interactive Approach. *English Teaching Forum* 34 (2), 2–9.

Sullivan, S., and Glanz, J. (2013) *Supervision That Improves Teaching and Learning: Strategies and Techniques* (4th edn). Thousand Oaks, CA: Corwin Press.

Wallace, M. (1991) *Training Foreign Language Teachers: A Reflective Approach*. Cambridge: Cambridge University Press.

Weller, R. (1971) *Verbal Communication in Instructional Supervision*. New York, NY: Teachers College Press.

Yin, R.K. (2014) *Case Study Research: Design and Methods* (5th edn). Thousand Oaks, CA: Sage Publications.

Young, S. (2009) Supporting and supervising teachers working with adults learning English. *The CAELA Network*. Washington, DC: Center for Applied Linguistics. See http://www.cal.org/caelanetwork/resources/supporting.html (accessed 28 October 2018).

Zeichner, K. (2010) Rethinking the connections between campus courses and field experiences in college- and university-based teacher education. *Journal of Teacher Education* 61 (1–2), 89–99. doi:10.1177/0022487109347671

Zeichner, K. (2012) The turn once again toward practice-based teacher education. *Journal of Teacher Education* 63 (5), 376–382. doi:10.1177/0022487112445789

Zein, M.S. (2015) Preparing elementary English teachers: Innovations at pre-service level. *Australian Journal of Teacher Education* 40 (6), 104–120. doi:10.14221/ajte.2015v40n6.6

Zein, M.S. (2016a) Pre-service education for primary school English teachers in Indonesia: Policy implications. *Asia Pacific Journal of Education* 36 (S1), 119–134. doi:10.1080/02188791.2014.961899

Zein, M.S. (2016b) Government-based training agencies and the professional development of Indonesian English for young learners teachers: Perspectives from complexity theory. *Journal of Education for Teaching: International Research and Pedagogy* 42 (2), 205–223. doi:10.1080/02607476.2016.1143145

Zein, M.S. (2017) Professional development needs of primary EFL teachers: Perspectives of teachers and teacher educators. *Professional Development in Education* 43 (2), 293–313. doi:10.1080/19415257.2016.1156013

Zhou, Y. and Ng, M.L. (2016) English as a foreign language (EFL) and English medium instruction (EMI) for three- to seven-year-old children in East Asian contexts. In V.A. Murphy and M. Evangelou (eds) *Early Childhood Education in English for Speakers of Other Languages* (pp. 137–156). London: British Council.

8 Mentoring Young Learner English Teachers Working on Collaborative Action Research: Implications for Professional Development Programs

Yasemin Kırkgöz

Introduction

Since the 1990s, a number of curriculum innovations in English language teaching (ELT) have taken place in primary education in Turkey (Kırkgöz *et al.*, 2016), as in many other countries around the world including South Korea (Garton, 2014), Taiwan (Chou, 2008), Indonesia (Zein, 2016), Malaysia (Kabilan & Veratharaju, 2013) and Europe (Enever, 2014). After the first curriculum innovation in 1997, the English language started to be taught as a compulsory school subject for Grade 4 and Grade 5 students (aged nine years old) in Turkey. In 2005, the ELT curriculum was revised, and with the most recent curriculum change starting in the 2013–2014 teaching year, English is now being taught at a much younger age to primary Grade 2 students (aged around seven years old). Since teachers are a key factor in the successful implementation of the innovation (Fullan, 2007), there is a need to support teachers to cope with their daily emerging issues through teacher professional development opportunities, particularly during the first critical years following educational change (Kırkgöz, 2008).

The main objective of this chapter is to describe the mentoring provided to five young learner English teachers working in Grade 2 primary schools as part of a collaborative action research (CAR) teacher development project. Using exemplary cases from the teachers, the study illustrates how action research becomes a viable methodology when teachers have the opportunity to work collaboratively under the mentorship of a teacher educator, rather than working in isolation. Despite increasing evidence demonstrating the benefits that language teachers can gain from university–school collaborative action research, limited attention has been given to how university teachers/researchers collaborate with language teachers during this process.

The chapter starts with a discussion of the need to provide teachers with continuing professional development opportunities, particularly following the introduction of innovation into the English as a foreign language (EFL) curriculum. This is followed by a definition of mentoring, explaining the roles and responsibilities of a mentor. The next section offers a detailed outline of the mentoring process followed in the CAR professional development program. The impact of mentoring on enhancing teachers' professional development and helping them deal with classroom issues is presented in findings section of the chapter. Finally, the implications of this study in local and global contexts are given.

The Need for Continuing Professional Development

Teachers often find themselves confronted with a range of challenges and also feeling worried about using correct pedagogical techniques (Ingersoll & Strong, 2011). Such challenges become even more critical when teachers are required to implement changes in their teaching practice, particularly following curriculum innovation (Kırkgöz, 2008). Since primary EFL teachers are a key factor in the successful implementation of the innovation (Fullan, 2007), there is a need to support teachers to cope with their daily emerging issues through teacher professional development opportunities (Mann & Tang, 2012; Zein, 2017), particularly during the first critical years following educational change (Kırkgöz, 2008). This support can come from 'a significant other' (Carter & Francis, 2001: 256), in order to achieve teachers' pedagogical goals, redefine their instructional practices and teaching strategies, and reflect upon their teaching practices. Thus, being supported by more experienced colleagues through teacher professional development opportunities often emerges as an imperative need to expand teachers' classroom effectiveness regardless of the educational setting in which teachers work.

The review of the literature reveals that one of the most viable approaches to continuous professional development is through the collaborative action research (CAR) model (Kırkgöz, 2015; Mitchell et al., 2009). CAR has the benefit of offering an appropriate context and a framework for forming a community of practice or a community of inquiry (Bruce & Easley, 2000) within the classroom. A researcher and/or a teacher educator from a university can collaborate with practicing teachers to establish a partnership to enhance teachers' professional development through action research (Day & Hadfield, 2004; Kırkgöz, 2015;

Manesi & Betsi, 2013). Such a partnership enables teachers to receive constructive guidance and scaffolding, which can help enhance teachers' research knowledge and skills, and enable them to gain new ideas about language teaching and learning (Yuan & Lee, 2014; Wang & Zhang, 2014). Furthermore, close cooperation with a mentor can help teachers cope with the challenges emerging from their work contexts. Through communication between teacher educators (mentors) and practicing teachers (mentees), it is possible to establish shared beliefs, values and goals, and 'these shared things are the basis for our communities, which are, in turn, established, maintained and expanded through communication' (Carter & Francis, 2001: 248).

The present study attempts to highlight the way in which action research, mediated by a suitable mentoring program, may help teachers generate valuable insights into teaching and enhance their professional development. Through action-based inquiry, teachers are facilitated to better understand and extend their professional activity as well as reflecting on their teaching issues and problems. Action research is a 'cyclical or spiral process' of reflective teaching, involving a continuous evaluating and revising of one's own practice (Pollard *et al.*, 2008: 17). Besides, the act of reflecting, collecting information and observing classroom interaction to solve educational problems, is considered to be fundamental to any action research project (Punch, 2009). Through reflection, teachers enrich and construct professional knowledge and gradually acquire new insights for practice (Mena Marcos *et al.*, 2009). To investigate the nature of the mentoring experience for teachers, the following research question was framed: What is the impact of mentoring on young learner English teachers' professional development?

What is Mentoring?

Mentoring has been defined as an activity that is performed to support the transformative development of a mentee and to facilitate the mentee's deeper engagement with a professional community (Malderez, 2009). Nguyen (2017: 29–30) views mentoring as a 'process whereby teachers/ more capable teachers help each other to learn by providing each other with professional and emotional support.' Malderez and Bodóczky (1999, cited in Wyatt & Dikilitaş, 2015) identify five mentor roles: model, acculturator, support, sponsor and educator. These roles have been conceptualized by other researchers in other ways. Halai (2006) views the mentor as an expert-coach, a subject-specialist and a learner. As an expert-coach, the mentor draws upon educator skills in eliciting reflection, but they might also serve as a model. As a subject-specialist, they fulfil the educator role, focusing specifically on content knowledge. As a critical friend, they might offer psychological support while also helping as sponsor, engaging more fully in the community of practice (Lave & Wenger, 1991). Malderez

(2009: 259) notes that mentoring young learner teachers offers two kinds of help, that is, it is an 'organizational and educationally supportive process'. In addition, a mentor should give personal and professional support. While the former is intended to help particularly new teachers overcome feelings of insecurity, caused by things such as discipline problems and feeling unable to cope, the latter support is intended to contribute to the mentee's development as a teacher and to be responsive to the mentee's changing needs.

Methods

Multi-case study research design

In this mentoring program, a multi-case study research design was employed, in which each teacher (mentee) was conceptualized as a 'case'. Three reasons can be put forward for employing multi-case study as the methodological framework. First, to gain a deeper understanding of the impact of mentoring on teachers' professional development, case study presents 'in-depth portrayals of particular people or sites' (Casanave, 2010: 67). Second, to unify the findings presented rather than keeping the results of each case separate (Creswell, 2013: 97). Third, as noted by Baxter and Jack (2008), the evidence that is generated from a multi-case study is strong and reliable.

The study followed five young learner English teachers in Grade 2 primary education: Teacher 1, Teacher 2, Teacher 3, Teacher 4 and, Teacher 5, one male and four female, over seven months, looked at different sets of data they produced during CAR and recorded their experiences in their own words. The teachers were all Turkish native speaker teachers of English to young learners (aged around seven years old) teaching for an average of eight years. They were working in three different state primary schools. Teacher 3 was the only Grade 2 teacher in her school, but the remaining four teachers were working in two different primary schools. The rationale for having two teachers from the same school, where possible, was to encourage collaborative learning. Teachers came together with different experiences, background ideas, yet genuinely participated around an agenda of joint work forming a community of practice (Wenger, 1998).

The mentoring process

The mentoring process examined in this study was part of a CAR professional development program. As noted by Fowle (2000), in a mentoring program, the first meeting is crucial since it may set the tone for the whole relationship to gain the trust of the mentees. The mentoring process started with a 'general meeting' in which teachers were introduced to the principles of action research. The requirements for the Grade 2 ELT curriculum, which mainly focused on promoting young learners' oral–aural proficiency (see MNE, 2013 for details), were discussed. In addition, a collaborative partnership was established with the teachers and a sequence of activities was agreed upon. This was an initial opportunity to acculturate the teachers (Malderez & Bodóczky, 1999) into a community made up of individuals who had similar concerns with others in the group, feeling responsible and devoted to goals related to their action research in their classes and acting as active participants in this community of practice (Lave & Wenger, 1991).

In this mentoring program, lasting over the following seven months, the teachers, under the author's mentorship, completed four cycles of action research. For each cycle, teachers identified a problem and/or any aspect of teaching they wished to improve, designed an action plan, implemented this with their Grade 2 classes, reflected on their action and finally documented their action research projects (see Kırkgöz, 2016 for details). Each teacher was committed to designing detailed lesson planning and to talking that process through with the author in the discussion and interview sessions. The author then visited classrooms to observe lessons taught by the teachers (mentees) in the school and gathered observation data based on the mentees' implementation of action into practice in their lessons. Following on lesson observations, the author had discussions with the teachers, commented on their lesson and provided feedback.

In addition, each teacher (mentee) produced an action research project documenting their action research experiences and presented it in the focus group discussions, which were held after the completion of each action research cycle. Four focus group discussions were held after-school sessions of three to four hours' duration, which aimed to foster interactive talk around teachers' experience of action research projects, developed out of the practice of teachers' action research practices. This was also the platform to create 'a space for self-reflection' and to empower teachers to develop professionally. Also, the author individually interviewed each mentee to gain additional insight into their experiences. Teachers were also given a workshop on the drama techniques for young learners.

The mentoring process was concluded with a debriefing meeting in which the author would ask teachers to relate experiences during the process of their year's work, changes in their teaching practice or ideas about teaching English to young learners (TEYLs) resulting from participating CAR, as well as their perceptions of the value of the mentoring process. The ability of teachers to reflect on their teaching methods and interact with colleagues within communities of practice was further considered fundamental to every CAR project (Grossman et al., 2001). These conversations were intended to reveal 'well remembered events' (Carter & Gonzalez, 1993: 223) and important concerns. These meetings and discussions were audiotaped and the tapes were transcribed for analysis.

Reflecting on how the author supported the mentees in this situation, it is recognized that the author took on various mentor roles. The author provided support that is purposeful, constructive and proactive (Hobson, 2002) in accordance with the needs of the mentees. Teachers received individual support as they articulated concerns and problems about TEYLs in Grade 2 classes. In the problem identification stage, the author collaborated with teachers to investigate issues together, trying to find answers to the questions that emerged. To illustrate, the author read articles together with the teachers on how knowledge retention can be enhanced in young learner classrooms, how classroom management issues can be tackled and how cooperative learning can be promoted. This helped the author as the mentor and the mentees collaborate on specific research issues, where the author took on the role of a mentor as learner and an expert-coach (Halai, 2006) role by sharing my research expertise with the teachers. The author also guided the teachers to consult the relevant literature and do some research and commented on the teachers' developing plans and advising them. Giving advice was in the nature of 'facilitative', serving a catalytic function leading a teacher to self-reflection, self-discovery, self-monitoring and to 'create in the teacher the ability to be self-evaluative and autonomous' (Randall & Thornton, 2001: 120).

Data collection procedure

As the teachers' plans developed and were put into action in their classes, the author observed their lessons (approximately twice a month), held post-observation discussions/conferences with each of the five teachers after classroom observation to share reflective conversations with them on their implementation of action research and implications for further action research cycles. The author provided the teachers with support by guiding them to make connections between research ideas and teaching practices reflectively. In so doing, as the teachers' professional knowledge (Arnold, 2006) and knowledge of how to conduct action research increased, they were also supported through the workshops, during which the author provided support in the subject-specialist mentor role (Halai, 2006). Arnold (2006) suggests that feedback should not become a 'monologue' or simply a process of transmission by the mentor. He advises that mentors should encourage reflection in dialogue with their co-inquirers. Likewise, the author collaborated with the teachers to provide feedback that was in the nature of a dialogue based upon teachers' reflections.

Then, during one-to-one interviews and focus group discussions, the author asked the teachers stimulating questions to think deeply about their specific research issues, thereby creating learning opportunities (Orland-Barak & Rachamim, 2009) that would lead to knowledge growth (Wyatt & Arnold, 2012). Throughout these interviews and discussions, the author listened carefully to the teachers expressing their views, as new perspectives gradually emerged. After that, by elaborating on topics they were less aware of, the author engaged in nurturing their thought processes, which gave them an opportunity to deepen their understandings. In this way, the author took on the role of a critical friend (Child & Merrill, 2003) and educator (Malderez & Bodóczky, 1999). Besides providing workshops as a subject-specialist (Halai, 2006) on how to use drama in young learner classes, the author encouraged the teachers to present their ideas about action research to the whole group in focus group discussions held after completion of each action research cycle and engaged in discussion afterwards, thus providing opportunities for collaborative reflection (Malderez & Bodóczky, 1999) in the expert-coach role (Halai, 2006).

By encouraging the teachers to take an active part in sharing their action research experiences verbally through giving presentations at the focus group discussions and in written form (for written action research projects), the author helped them gain confidence in sharing action research findings with their colleagues and disseminating research findings with the wider community at the conference which was held after completion of the project. In this way, the author was acting as an acculturator of the teachers into the research community (Hobson & Sharp, 2005). Emotional and psychological support are also considered to be critical components of contemporary mentoring programs (He, 2009; Nguyen, 2017), leading to teachers' continuing professional development (Robson, 2006). Another aspect of my mentoring role was to provide the psychological support (Malderez & Bodóczky, 1999). Teachers felt the need to be motivated to continue, as part of community of practice. The author provided psychological support by means of meetings, numerous emails and phone calls.

Overall, the author's mentoring role to young learner teachers offered 'organizational and educationally supportive process' (Malderez, 2009: 259). The organizational role involved arranging meetings, observation of the teachers (the mentees), searching for articles, and 'the educationally supportive process' required scaffolding teachers during the action research process, working with the teachers as part of the action research process and giving feedback. Professional support should be responsive to the mentee's changing needs in different action research cycles. The author attempted to provide support that is purposeful, constructive and proactive (Hobson, 2002).

Data analysis

The procedures suggested by Stake (2006) were used as the framework for cross-case analysis. Accordingly, analysis of the qualitative data from the interviews and focus group discussions were performed in a recursive and iterative manner. The data were coded and analysed for patterns and themes corresponding to the research question. First, the interview data were examined in order to develop categories (Creswell, 2013), following a four-step process: read the transcribed interview data, identify themes, search for sentences that matched the themes and tally the instances for each theme. Then, similar themes were combined and they were ranked based on the percentage of instances of each theme. A similar procedure was attained to analyze the data from focus group discussions. Finally, data from these sources were compared and the participants' written reflections on their mentoring experience were used to validate and support the emerging themes found in the focus group discussions and interview data. The participants' action research projects and observation data were used for illustrative purposes. After analyzing the data for a single case (mentee), as suggested by Baxter and Jack (2008), cross-case comparison was carried out to understand the similarities and differences between the cases.

Findings

This section presents the results emerging from the impact of mentoring on five young learner teachers under four complementary headings obtained from the multiple data sources.

Impact of mentoring on young learner English teachers

Data was gathered from the teachers through interviews, focus group discussions, teachers' reflections and their action research projects. Analysis of the various kinds of data indicated that mentoring provided the teachers a number of benefits. First, it provided the teachers with the opportunity to increase their awareness of using new and innovative age-appropriate techniques. Another benefit of mentoring was to lead to a change in teachers' knowledge and understandings about the nature of TEYLs. It was also found that mentoring resulted in personal growth in self-confidence and improved their teachers' practice.

Increasing teachers' awareness of using new and innovative age-appropriate techniques

With the help of mentoring, teachers became aware of the new and innovative techniques that would be appropriate for young learners of this specific age (around 7 years old). This is illustrated by the teachers' reflections reported below.

Teacher 1 and Teacher 2 had been working in the same primary school. In the first action research project, they focused on resolving the issue of children becoming highly competitive during activities and not being cooperative enough. With the help of mentoring, they resolved this issue by applying a cooperative task called *the noun tree* project. As a result, reflecting on their action, teachers reported a noticeable increase in students' cooperation and interaction in completing the project cooperatively as opposed to perceiving the activity as a competition, as had happened previously. The teachers stated that they received positive feedback from the students and they also added that they were pleased they had the children perform the project with no competition but with cooperation. Teachers appreciated the value of the mentoring they had received during this process, stating that to receive support from an academic mentor made their lessons more productive and that they started to use new techniques and look at old methods and techniques with a critical eye (Kırkgöz, 2016).

Another teacher, Teacher 3, the only Grade 2 English teacher in her school, reflects upon her experience of how she has been able to resolve classroom management problems by working collaboratively with the support of her mentor, the author of this chapter, within a CAR paradigm. She stated that before she started this project she was uncertain about how to handle difficult pupils showing all sorts of misbehaviors. She desperately needed some guidance. She was happy that she had joined the project. By the end of four cycles of action research, she was able to find an ideal solution to classroom management problems, take control of the whole class, achieve a better management of activities, and handle noise and misbehavior. She continued reflecting that she was very thankful for getting support and collaboration as she learned new ideas. Of all the techniques, Six Thinking Hats helped her most in classroom management. She believed that she was now in full control of particularly this 2/D class whereas before she feared of losing control. Finally, she stated that there had been noticeable drop in the problematic behaviors.

The present study confirms Yuan and Lee's (2014) and Wang and Zhang's (2014) findings that constructive guidance and scaffolding received by the teachers through mentoring is helpful in enhancing teachers' knowledge and skills, and enabling them to gain new ideas about language teaching and learning.

Change in teachers' knowledge and understandings about the nature of TEYLs

The next impact of mentoring was that it helped extend teachers' knowledge and understandings of how to teach effectively this young age group. All the mentees in their interviews and focus group discussions reported that the professional development program provided them with information that enabled them to make changes in their own understanding of TEYLs. This change was related to a greater awareness of their perceptions of teaching at a younger age and how this influences their classroom actions. Specifically, Teacher 4 and Teacher 5 noted:

> Children in our grade two classes are young; they do not revise subjects at home. For these reasons, they quickly forget what they have learnt. Therefore, the problem we want to explore is: Why doesn't learning become permanent? How can we solve this problem?

Both teachers were supported to use real objects in their lessons. Observing the effect of real objects on enhancing young learner memory, both teachers developed confidence and enthusiasm for using various objects such as toy animals, masks, fruits and drama in successive action research cycles, rather than using the textbook as the sole teaching material.

The child-appropriate methodology that the teachers learned, such as the use activities, games and songs during the mentoring program, helped the teachers notice that they had not until then effectively delivered the new young learner curriculum, and encouraged them to use their new learning experiences to increase the quality of the education in their classes. The results indicated a change in the teachers' pedagogical understandings and teaching practices. The teachers developed and in some cases intensified their existing pedagogical beliefs that using a communicative- and activity-based approach would foster young learners' communicative competence, and increase their motivation and participation in lessons. To illustrate, reflecting on her classroom practice prior to and after the mentoring program, Teacher 1 stated that:

> I was focusing on textbook-bound teaching before this project. With the help of my mentor, I have understood that using real objects such as balloons, posters, masks and so on can enhance young learners' memory for learning new lexis. I started using real objects thanks to the support I received during this process. My self-confidence improved in using real materials, and I have realized that children can make associations between real objects and the concepts, and as a result their learning becomes more permanent in memory.

Teacher 2, similarly, stated that:

> Frankly speaking, I was not a person who would use real objects in the class. I used to believe that textbook activities would be sufficient. But now, I have started to use real objects and drama. I notice that children enjoy learning this way better. I also get positive response from the parents.

Teachers' written reflections on the impact of their action research engagement at the end of the four-cycle process indicated that their involvement in this project had been a very good opportunity for professional development. The male teacher explained that teaching through real objects had been a major change experienced by him in his profession. Another teacher, similarly, stated that while helping her students, she improved herself as a teacher. She felt happy that teaching a foreign language using real objects provided a permanent effect on remembering (Kırkgöz, 2017).

Personal growth in self-confidence and improved teaching practice

Teachers stated that focus group discussions offered the opportunity to engage in professional conversations with their colleagues and reflective activities developed knowledge they could apply in their own contexts. In the minds of the teacher participants, the meetings created a platform for learning and generated new understandings in each teacher reflecting on the ideas and their experiences. Concerning the mentoring they received during this process, all teachers acknowledged that they were able to explore new possibilities and perspectives on TEYLs, and that they gained useful insights from the support they received. This enabled them to form a better understanding of how to handle various classroom issues ranging from classroom management to how to deal with student forgetfulness and how to promote cooperation rather than competition among the students, and similar issues. The teachers also agreed that the support they received helped them to learn how to integrate theory into their practice.

The findings from the observational data, classroom documents and teacher interviews indicated that children developed positive attitudes towards the changes in classroom practice in English lessons and demonstrated a higher level of participation and motivation. They also seemed to have improved their spoken competence and vocabulary retention when their teachers introduced changes to their practice. Thus, the teachers reshaped their pedagogical beliefs about the applicability of new knowledge and skills, and they altered their teaching practice by using communicative activities, games, songs and drama. For example, elaborating on the impact of mentoring on her teaching practice, Teacher 5 said that:

> Student attention and interest increased. For example, the students were uninterested in lessons when I used textbooks. Many started to want to participate in the lesson when there is a game. When they're motivated, I become motivated as well, and it becomes easier to teach English children using activities.

These findings are consistent with the ideas of Wang and Zhang (2014) and Yuan and Lee (2014), that a university–school partnership can enable teachers to gain new ideas about language teaching and learning, and how to cope with the emerging challenges from their work contexts. The present findings also corroborate the findings of Bennetts (2002) who notes that quality mentoring should result in improved student learning and more effective teachers, as well as more and deeper mentee reflection. The author's experience of mentoring confirms that mentees have grown personally in self-confidence and improved their teaching practice after their participation in the CAR program. The findings of the study show that with the help of the scaffolding provided by the university facilitator, the teachers coped effectively with the reported classroom concerns in their action research, leading to professional learning and development.

Conclusion

The present study has investigated mentoring provided by an external facilitator – a university researcher – to five EFL young learner teachers, to overcome challenges emerging from teaching English in Grade 2 classes in a university–school collaborative project in Turkey. To observe the impact of the interventions in resolving the challenges, data were collected from observations, interviews, classroom artefacts, teachers' reflections and their action research reports. The study reveals that innovatory mentoring programs combined with CAR initiatives may help teachers' professional development in teaching young learners.

Holloway (2003: 88) maintains that 'only by providing support throughout teachers' careers can we ensure a sustainable pool of high-quality teachers for all students' and underlines ongoing mentoring as one type of support. This study suggests that CAR offers one promising avenue for supporting such learning. At the same time the present work contributes to a growing literature of school-based teacher education by providing action research oriented mentoring practice. The results of the present study also suggest that mentoring provided by the external facilitator, in this case, the university teacher educator, can support young learner teachers to overcome their classroom concerns and enhance their teaching practices.

This study was conducted in one specific context, yet the findings may offer insights for those teachers, teacher educators and in-service teacher education policy makers who are interested in conducting university–school action research partnerships. However, further studies concerning the implementation and impact of action research are needed to fully embrace this process in the field of language teacher education.

Implications for Professional Development Programs

Although it was conducted in a national context, the findings of the present study have a number of international implications for future practice in terms of design and implementations of teacher development programs.

Teachers who are required to implement changes in their teaching practice, particularly following curriculum innovation and those who have previously worked with adults or teenagers yet are now working with younger learners, need to be supported and guided with respect to managing children. Mentoring provides the teacher researchers with the opportunity to develop their personal and professional growth, and their teaching practices. Therefore, effective mentoring needs to be considered fundamental to a language teacher's development and it needs to be an integral part of in-service English language teacher professional development programs.

In addition, action research methodology through the university–school collaboration can be employed through the process of mentoring primary school young learner teachers. Action research has the potential to promote teacher effectiveness, professionalism and empowerment in language education (Burns, 2005, 2013; Edwards & Burns, 2016; Seider & Lemma, 2004). This study also suggests that a university facilitator can play an important role in this process by supporting teachers' improvement in classroom practice and professional growth by sharing their own knowledge and expertise, and that a university–school partnership can assist with this.

Several implications are also offered for the mentors, as emerged from the present study. First, mentors should possess versatile attributes. A mentor should have specific pedagogical knowledge and should serve as a collaborator by sharing their knowledge and expertise, bringing about change and improvement in teachers' teaching practices, modelling teaching practices and offering strategies on how to deal with emerging classroom problems through mentoring.

In addition, the mentoring relationship is crucial for the effectiveness of teacher professional development. A mentor should develop interpersonal relationships built on trust and openness to ensure that teacher's development and learning are taking place at deeper levels and teachers gradually build their confidence. As noted by Mitchell *et al.* (2009), by fostering a positive mentor–mentee relationship, CAR projects support teachers' professional development, help teachers increase their level of self-efficacy and also develop their intellectual capacities in order to cope with the demands of everyday classroom life. A mentor should provide guidance as a role model and advisor. As the facilitator, a mentor should encourage teachers to reflect upon their teaching practices and to take ownership in bringing about change and improvement. Finally, mentors should provide information and assistance, model appropriate teaching practice and provide feedback about the mentees' development and progress. Besides mentor–mentee training sessions, the mentor should also observe the classes of the mentees. The mentor should provide positive and sensitive feedback with suggestions for further improvement, where necessary.

This study makes a contribution to language teacher education research by illustrating how five young learner language teachers gained benefits in terms of their professional growth through CAR with scaffolding provided by a university researcher. While university-supported action research projects are quite limited for establishing professional development programs, the present study shows that action research supported by university–school collaboration and a suitable mentoring program may help teachers generate valuable insights into teaching and enhance their professional development. In this way, teachers systematically reflect on what they are doing and start questioning why and how they are doing it, which provides a strong impetus for their continuing professional development.

The present study focused on developing teachers' understanding about and practice of TEYLs through a mentoring program; yet, the study offers wider insights about and provides an example of the kind of professional learning needed to promote action-oriented practice more generally. In addition, it adds value to the literature on the professional development of English young learner teachers in several ways. First, collaborative action research through mentoring has not been done in the field of teacher education for young learner English teachers, particularly in the Turkish context. Hence, this is the first study to identify the issue and to come up with some solutions. Second, this is the first mentoring model to be developed in the Turkish context. It is therefore recommended that the model be adopted by teacher trainers and teacher educators on a national scale.

The present study differs from others in many ways. Previous research on university–school collaboration drew on data from limited sources. To illustrate, Yuan and Lee (2014) in their action research facilitated by university–school collaboration in China, used only interviews and teachers' action research reports. This study, by collecting different sets of data from such various sources such as interviews, lesson observations, focus group meeting discussions, teacher-created artifacts and teachers' action research projects, investigates in-depth portrayals of five young learner English teachers over seven months. As such, it makes an important contribution to the young learner teacher education literature.

Acknowledgments

The author acknowledges the funding provided by TÜBİTAK (The Scientific and Technological Research Council of Turkey) to conduct the present research with project no. 114K036 and extends her gratitude to the teachers who voluntarily participated in this project.

References

Arnold, E. (2006) Assessing the quality of mentoring: sinking or learning to swim? *ELT Journal* 60 (2), 117–124.

Baxter, P. and Jack, S. (2008) Qualitative case study methodology: Study design and implementation for novice researchers. *The Qualitative Report* 13 (4), 544–556.

Bennetts, C. (2002) Traditional mentor relationships, intimacy and emotional intelligence. *International Journal of Qualitative Studies in Education* 15 (1), 155–170.

Bruce, B. and Easley, J. (2000) Emerging communities of practice: Collaboration and communication in action research. *Educational Action Research* 8 (2), 243–259.

Burns, A. (2005) Action research: An evolving paradigm? *Language Teaching*, 38, 57–74.

Burns, A. (2013) Innovation through action research and teacher-initiated change. In K. Hyland and L.L.C. Wong (eds) *Innovation and Change in English Language Education* (pp. 90–105). Abingdon: Routledge.

Carter, K. and Gonzalez, L. (1993) Beginning teachers' knowledge of classroom events. *Journal of Teacher Education* 4 (3), 223–232.

Carter, M. and Francis, R. (2001) Mentoring and beginning teachers' work place learning. *Asia-Pacific Journal of Teacher Education* 29 (3), 249–262.

Casanave, C.P. (2010) Case studies. In B. Paltridge and A. Phakiti (eds) *Continuum Companion to Research Methods in Applied Linguistics* (pp. 66–79). New York: Continuum.

Child, A.J. and Merrill, S.J. (2003) Professional mentors' perceptions of the contribution of school/HEI partnerships to professional development and school improvement. *Journal of In-Service Education* 29 (2), 315–324.

Chou, C.-H. (2008) Exploring elementary English teachers' practical knowledge: A case study of EFL teachers in Taiwan. *Asia Pacific Education Review* 9 (4), 529–541.

Creswell, J.W. (2013) *Qualitative Inquiry and Research Design: Choosing among Five Approaches*. Thousand Oaks, CA: Sage.

Day, C. and Hadfield, M. (2004) Learning through networks: Trust, partnerships and the power of action research. *Educational Action Research* 12 (4), 575–586.

Edwards, E. and Burns, A. (2016) Language teacher action research: Achieving sustainability. *ELT Journal* 70 (1), 6–15.

Enever, J. (2014) Primary English teacher education in Europe. *ELT Journal* 68 (3), 231–242.

Fowle, C. (2000) Teacher training: A web of trust. *The Teacher Trainer* 14 (3), 6–8.

Fullan, M. (2007) *The New Meaning of Educational Change* (5th edn). London: Routledge.

Garton, S. (2014) Unresolved issues and new challenges in teaching English to young learners: The case of South Korea. *Current Issues in Language Planning* 15 (2), 201–219.

Grossman, P., Wineburg, S. and Woolworth, S. (2001) Toward a theory of teacher community. *The Teacher College Record* 103, 942–1012.

Halai, A. (2006) Mentoring in-service teachers: Issues of role diversity. *Teaching and Teacher Education* 22 (6), 700–710.

He, Y. (2009) Strength-based mentoring in pre-service teacher education: A literature review. *Mentoring and Tutoring: Partnership in Learning* 17 (3), 263–275.

Hobson, A.J. (2002) Student teachers' perceptions of school-based mentoring in initial teacher training (ITT). *Mentoring and Tutoring* 10 (1), 5–20.

Hobson, A.J. and Sharp, C. (2005) Head to head: A systematic review of the research evidence on mentoring new head teachers. *School Leadership and Management* 25 (1), 25–42.

Holloway, J.H. (2003) Sustaining experienced teachers. *Educational Leadership* 60 (8), 87–89.

Ingersoll, R. and Strong, M. (2011) The impact of induction and mentoring programmes for beginning teachers: A critical review of the research. *Review of Education Research* 81 (2), 201–233.

Lave, J. and Wenger, E. (1991) *Situated Learning. Legitimate Peripheral Participation (Learning in Doing: Social, Cognitive and Computational Perspectives)*. Cambridge: Cambridge University Press.

Kabilan, M.K. and Veratharaju, K. (2013) Professional development needs of primary school English language teachers in Malaysia. *Professional Development in Education* 39 (3), 330–351.

Kırkgöz, Y. (2008) A case study of teachers' implementation of curriculum innovation in English language teaching in Turkish primary education. *Teaching and Teacher Education* 24, 1859–1875.

Kırkgöz, Y. (2015) A collaborative action research teacher development programme. In K. Dikilitaş, R. Smith and W. Trotman (eds) *Teacher Researchers in Action* (pp. 387–398). Kent: The International Association of Teachers of English as a Foreign Language, Nos 2–3.

Kırkgöz, Y. (2016) Improving teaching practices through a university-school collaboration in young learner classrooms. In K. Dikilitaş, M. Wyatt, J. Hanks and D. Bullock (eds) *Teachers Engaging in Research* (pp. 89–99). Kent: The International Association of Teachers of English as a Foreign Language.

Kırkgöz, Y. (2017) Insights into the process of mentoring action research by teachers of young learners. In A. Burns, K. Dikilitaş, R. Smith and M. Wyatt (eds) *Developing Insights into Teacher-Research* (pp. 19–28). Kent: International Association of Teachers of English as a Foreign.

Kırkgöz, Y., Çelik, S. and Arıkan, A. (2016) Laying the theoretical and practical foundations for a new elementary English curriculum in Turkey: A procedural analysis. *Kastamonu Education Journal* 24 (3), 1199–1212.

Manesi, S. and Betsi, S. (2013) Collaborative action research projects: The role of communities of practice and mentoring in enhancing teachers' continuing professional development. *Action Researcher in Education* 4, 109–121.

Mann, S. and Tang, E.H.H. (2012) The role of mentoring in supporting novice English language teachers in Hong Kong. *TESOL Quarterly* 46 (3), 472–495.

Malderez, A. (2009) Mentoring. In A. Burns and J.C. Richards (eds) *Second Language Teacher Education* (pp. 259–268). Cambridge: Cambridge University Press.

Malderez, A. and Bodóczky, C. (1999) *Mentor Courses: A Resource Book for Trainer – Trainers.* Cambridge: Cambridge University Press.

Mena Marcos, J., Sanchez, M. and Tillema, H. (2009) Teacher reflection on action: What is said (in research) and what is done (in teaching). *Reflective Practice* 10 (2), 191–204.

Mitchell, S., Reilly, R. and Logue, M.E. (2009) Benefits of collaborative action research for the beginning teacher. *Teaching and Teacher Education* 25 (2), 344–349.

Nguyen, H.T.M. (2017) *Models of Mentoring in Language Teacher Education.* New York: Springer.

Orland-Barak, L. and Rachamim, M. (2009) Simultaneous reflections by video in a second order action research mentoring model: Lessons for the mentor and the mentee. *Reflective Practice* 10 (5), 601–613.

Pollard, A., Anderson, J., Maddock, M., Swaffield, S., Warin, J. and Warwick, P. (2008) *Reflective Teaching: Evidence-informed Professional Practice* (3rd edn). London: Continuum International Publishing Group.

Punch, K. (2009) *Introduction to Research Methods in Education.* London: SAGE Publications Limited.

Randall, M. and Thornton, B. (2001) *Advising and Supporting Teachers.* Cambridge: Cambridge University Press.

Robson, S. (2006) Supporting children's thinking in the foundation stage: Practitioners' views on the role of initial training and continuing professional development. *Journal of In-service Education* 32 (3), 341–357.

Seider S.N. and Lemma P. (2004) Perceived effects of action research on teachers' professional efficacy, inquiry mindsets and the support they received while conducting projects to intervene into student learning. *Educational Action Research* 12 (2), 219–238.

Stake, R.E. (2006) *Multiple Case Study Analysis.* New York: Guilford Press.

T.C. Millî Eğitim Bakanlığı Talim ve Terbiye Kurulu Başkanlığı [Republic of Turkey, Ministry of National Education (MNE)] (2013) İlköğretim Kurumları (İlkokullar ve Ortaokullar) İngilizce Dersi (2, 3, 4, 5, 6, 7 ve 8. Sınıflar) Öğretim Programı [Elementary (Primary and Lower Secondary) English Language Teaching Program (Grades 2–8)]. Ankara: T.C. Millî Eğitim Bakanlığı.

Wang, Q. and Zhang, H. (2014) Promoting teacher autonomy through university–school collaborative research. *Language Teaching Research* 18 (2), 222–241.

Wenger, E. (1998) *Communities of Practice. Learning, Meaning, and Identity.* New York: Cambridge University Press.

Wyatt, M. and Arnold, E. (2012) Video-stimulated recall for mentoring in Omani schools. *International Journal of Mentoring and Coaching in Education* 1 (3), 218–234.

Wyatt, M. and Dikilitaş, K. (2015) English language teachers becoming more efficacious through research engagement at their Turkish university. *Educational Action Research*, 1–21.

Yuan, R. and Lee, I. (2014) Action research facilitated by university-school collaboration. *ELT Journal* 69 (1), 1–10.

Zein, M.S. (2016) Pre-service education for primary school English teachers in Indonesia: Policy implications. *Asia Pacific Journal of Education* 36 (S1), 119–134. doi:10.1080/02188791.2014.961899

Zein, M.S. (2017) Professional development needs of primary EFL teachers: Perspectives of teachers and teacher educators. *Professional Development in Education* 43 (2), 293–313. doi:10.1080/19415257.2016.1156013

9 Collaboration, Construction, Reflection: 21st Century EYL Teacher Professional Development

Nettie Boivin

Introduction

Currently, through globalization, developing countries have embarked on a new language education policy of increasing the number of hours to learn English in early years (Butler, 2015; Enever, 2014; Hamid & Honan, 2012; Moodie & Feryok, 2015; Zhetpisbayeva & Shelestova, 2015). In many countries such as Malaysia and Kazakhstan, this occurs alongside the shift of learning from an English as a foreign language (EFL) context where the language is generally studied once or a few times a week, to English as an additional language (EAL) in a multilingual context (Pennycook, 2017). In this chapter, the term EAL is used to refer to primary children who are learning English in a context where they may use two or three other languages daily. It is noteworthy that in this context, English is not the national language nor the main language of schooling. However, a shift in the amount of English utilized in mainstream schools is evident in Kazakhstan's effort to implement daily lessons in English with the expectation that in secondary school, the language is to become the medium of instruction in subjects such as science and maths. This plan was made official by the President of Kazakhstan, who declared the expectation for Kazakhstani citizens to be trilingual and have English proficiency by 2020 (Nazarbaev State Address, 2007).

Despite this sudden shift in expected language learning outcomes, English for young learner (EYL) teachers lack adequate resources and in some cases appropriate training (Butler, 2015). This is unfortunate given the push for the newest pedagogical approaches, such as communicative competence, critical thinking and utilizing multimodality, have become increasingly stronger for 21st-century student learning. Language learning in the 21st century is a process where learning is co-constructed and occurs over time, not occurring instantaneously. Furthermore, EYL language learning requires a shift in perspective from what the new pedagogical methods and practices of language learning (e.g. student-centered and multiliteracies) to how these new learning methods are applied (Pinter, 2017). If in the 21st century language learning is co-constructed, socioculturally bound, while requiring social interaction and collaboration, then there is a gap between the product of learning best practices and the process involved in teaching English to young learners. This poses the question 'why does professional development (PD) not mirror a process of learning and one situated in an actual context?' Thus, there is certainly a gap between the need for retraining and the actually type of retraining that is provided (Moodie & Feryok, 2015). This is a gap that is not just specific to Kazakhstan but is also seen in South Korea (Moodie & Feryok, 2015) and Indonesia, where the production of quality EYL teachers 'is not contingent upon pre-service preparation alone' (Zein, 2016: 2).

The main aim of this chapter is to elucidate a new perspective to EYL teacher PD as it was embodied in a project that includes collaboration, construction and reflection (CCR) using Kazakhstan as the research context. The chapter starts with a discussion of the background educational context in Kazakhstan. The initial section addresses historical language policies, teacher practices, teachers' methods and present PD training. This is followed by a section reviewing the rationale of social collaborative interactional learning required at this age, how in the 21st century learning is co-constructed between teacher and learner, and the multimodality students negotiate to gain knowledge. The following section discusses the creation of the conceptual framework approach. The impact of the research and learning process will be presented. Finally, wider implications of the new research and the new EYL training approach will be discussed. Therefore, this study proposes a solution to the rapid implementation of English at the primary school level that is situated and researched over time in a real classroom learning process.

Background of the Study

Kazakhstan primary English language policies, practices and retraining

Initially, after gaining independence in 1991, the Kazakh government implemented a bilingual policy where Kazakh became the national language of government and Russian the functional language. Later, in 2007, this shifted to a trilingual policy with English as the global language of commerce (Dave, 2007). Kazakhstani primary schools have started to teach English earlier, in Grade 1 rather than in Grade 5, and increased the number of English lessons from weekly to daily (OECD, 2015). In 2016, research found that most schools have just started to transition in primary schools from an EFL to an EAL approach with early English learning occurring daily, but not as the medium of instruction (Zhetpisbayeva *et al.*, 2016). However, English language learning classes are still heavily grammar-based with textbook-bound individual learning. There is still little emphasis on speaking or communicative competence (Smagulova, 2008). Thus, many of the teachers at the lower primary school level have had very little experience in communicative approaches for teaching young learners. Teaching is teacher-centered, occurring individually rather than in groups and still centers on a traditional 1990s style text-book with drill activities. There are no communicative tasks. Historically, language teaching of both Kazakh and Russian was prescriptive, gram-mar-based and teacher centered, often concentrating on the practice of rote memorization (Burkhalter & Shegebayev, 2012; Suny, 1998). English taught as an EFL subject allowed for very little creativity or critical think-ing as it focused on language proficiency, pronunciation and skills (Zhetpisbayeva *et al.*, 2016). Moreover, teachers had little experience with the new type of expected classroom practices. There was little training done prior to implementing the policy (Davis, 2015).

In Kazakhstan, which is a multilingual learning context, the process of professional development houses several intersecting constraints hin-dering teachers' investment in innovative methods and approaches (Burkhalter, 2016). The primary teacher retraining that Kazakhstan employs utilizes a cascading model. This model has been adopted in a series of special private schools that train teachers working with interna-tional teachers, who model best practices. Afterwards, these teachers are expected to provide professional development (PD) to the mainstream teachers (Bridges, 2014); however, the pilot schools have a different cur-riculum, administrative duties and teaching resources. These are private schools with well-paid teachers whereas the mainstream teachers have multiple layers of constraints that do not exist in the private pilot schools (Bridges, 2014). Furthermore, the actual PD training has usually been heavily theoretical rather than practical. Another issue has been that the training occurs outside of an actual classroom, utilizing materials not always relevant to the local context (Shrum & Glisan, 2015). The peda-gogical methods taught in the PD sessions may be innovative, but they are shown outside the classroom, so teachers are unaware how to adjust for the needs of an actual classroom (Busch, 2010). Moreover, often these new practices take time to master effectively in class. Teachers perceive the new practices and methods to be too difficult to implement therefore they revert to prior practices (Hamid & Honan, 2012). Thus, while some PD workshops have attempted to move teachers away from Soviet-style teacher-centeredness and memorization towards critical thinking and a more student-centered approach, it occurs through presenting conceptual theories outside of a practical context (Burkhalter & Shegebayev, 2012; Zhetpisbayeva *et al.*, 2016).

Literature Review

EYL process

As international research indicates, children's language and literacy acquisition is a social practice that includes oral language, social interaction and community sociocultural interaction (Galindo & Sheldon, 2012). Researchers have argued that children should be active participants in the learning process and leaders of their own learning, as well as critical and independent (Johnson & Johnson, 2009). Children learn from a zone of proximal development, through scaffolding and through collaborative social interaction (Bruner, 1975; Johnson & Johnson, 2009; Vygotsky, 1978). Training teachers in EYL pedagogical methods and practices often overlook the fact that at this age learning is a process. Moreover, areas often not concretely highlighted in EYL PD are that there are sociocultural aspects inherent in language learning that are influenced by classroom dynamics, individual learning styles and mostly importantly, that each learning environment may produce differing learning outcomes (Cazden, 2001). This is particularly important for multilingual language learning contexts such as Malaysia, Canada or Kazakhstan. Moreover, at this age, learning does not occur immediately, but overtime.

Twenty-first century learning

In the 21st century, knowledge is rapidly shared via video, music, digital memes, social networks and symbolic representations such as emojis (Rowsell, 2013). Children are gathering meaning from a variety of sources and no longer require a simple skillset, but the intercultural competency to extract, digest and integrate meaning (Cope & Kalantzis, 2017). Therefore, learning is co-constructed and requires critical thinking. Twenty-first century language research views language learning as shared and co-constructed knowledge. At primary school age it is not predicated on skill-based language as proficiency. This term 21st century learning is a newer perspective to learning rather than being best practice. It is one that is being researched widely in multicultural language learning contexts such as Canada. Moreover, the term 21st century learning extends from the term multiliteracies (New London Group, 1996) which was coined in the 20th century, prior to social media and digital mobile devices. Present literacy educators such as Rowsell, and even Cope and Kalantzis (2017), consider language learning to occur in multiple spaces and as being co-constructed by students rather than teacher-centered (Cummins, 2009; Cope & Kalantzis, 2017; Rowsell, 2013). Rowsell (2013) argues students in the 21st century are mediating and negotiating meaning across multiple modalities. Moreover, they are co-constructing their own communication and knowledge. Therefore, the term 21st century learning includes not just pedagogical practices, but the overall learning context.

Many researchers argue that 20th century learning was individual, skill- and text-based, memorization-heavy and proficiency driven, and as such, is not needed in the 21st century (Abrams *et al.*, 2011; Ashton & Newman, 2006; Cope & Kalantzis, 2017). As research has shown, over the past 20 years this new type of learning extends past what the New London Group originally termed multiliteracies (Abrams *et al.*, 2011; Cope & Kalantzis, 2017; Cummins, 2009). Moreover, this term is best suited for researchers in multilingual rather than monolingual contexts. Furthermore, Ashton and Newman (2006: 829) stated that, 'today's teacher educators must develop students' capabilities, not just their skills and knowledge and in so doing they must relinquish power'. They argue for a shift, not in the tools teachers use, such as chalk, pen and laptop, but for how such tools are used for learning (Abrams *et al.*, 2011; Cope & Kalantzis, 2009). This shift in understanding of language and literacy learning is especially important in a multilingual language learning context such as Kazakhstan. However, this shift in how language students learn requires PD training that encapsulates these practices.

The gap mentioned above between policy expectations and in-service professional development was first noticed when the author taught MA students the concept of multiliteracies in several graduate courses at a Kazakhstan national university. Even with constant recycling of the concept in the various classes, the author came to realize that the MA students could define but not apply the multiliteracies approach. Consequently, the author designed a research project embedding transformative multiliteracies principles (Cummins, 2009) as they align to 21st century learning outcomes and formed the content the MA students had difficulty applying.

Conceptual framework

The conceptual framework used in this project incorporates a three-stage approach based on collaboration, construction and reflection (CCR). Each stage relies on multimodal, collaborative feedback occurring over time. This occurs from peer to peer, teacher to student and observer or in-service teacher to MA teacher. In addition, feedback is a collaborative component of assessment for learning (Black *et al.*, 2003) or learning by doing concepts (Carless, 2005).

Collaboration stage

The first part of the collaboration process is to understand the specific learning context in which the new approach is used. The author defines collaboration as sharing of knowledge and resources to work together overtime (Johnson & Johnson, 2009). In collaboration with primary English teachers, with their knowledge of the classroom students and the curriculum, the MA students designed special lessons that occurred over time. The special lessons were based on transformative multiliteracies pedagogy (TMP) (Cummins, 2009). This required students and teachers to understand the content topic as a framework in which the process of learning was enveloped.

Cummins' (2009) transformative multiliteracies pedagogy principles (TMP) contain components that reflect research on sociocultural aspects of primary school language learning, social interaction theories and the recent research perspectives of 21st century learning (collaboration, co-construction, critical thinking, relevance to prior knowledge and multi-modality) (Hoff, 2013). These five principles state that (1) students are viewed as inherently creative, therefore the teacher does not have to teach them how to be creative but just allow them to utilize creativity; (2) all students have prior knowledge and relevant linguistic and cultural capital; however, it is in a different language, so it is important to elicit the prior knowledge from the students; (3) lessons should be relevant to the age (generational), gender and ethnic/cultural identity of students; (4) students should collaborate and learn to think critically; and finally (5) all lessons should include multimodalities to support students' construction of meaning (Cummins, 2009).

In this project, the course lecturer and classmates gave feedback on the lessons based on the five TM principles. This allowed the MA students the opportunity to justify and adapt their choices. Then, based on feedback, the lessons were redesigned.

Construction stage

The word construction does not define the creation of the lessons. Rather it refers to the co-construction of the learning process. This is a layered and recursive process. MA students wrote critical reflections about both the lessons and the feedback (Gün, 2011). This provided opportunities to continue to learn collaboratively. Moreover, the process of videotaping lessons allowed for learning through observing, as the MA students were videotaping grades younger or older than their grade. Additionally, recursive feedback was provided from the course lecturer, peers and in-service teacher. The most important factor in the learning process was the recursive nature of the feedback.

Often, feedback is employed at the end as evidence of the quality of the training. In this framework, feedback is a crucial ongoing element and is considered 'feedback for learning rather than of learning' (Cope & Kalantzis, 2017), which is a component of 21st century learning. This collaborative 'assessment for learning' (Black et al., 2003) enabled students to co-construct knowledge together (Cope & Kalantzis, 2017). In the CCR framework, feedback was given orally, in written form, in online discussion and through video watching, which created a multimodal feedback process. This provided an interactive approach that occurred several times, providing recursive feedback (Okita & Schwartz, 2013).

Reflection stage

The final reflection stage consisted of a reflective forum for constructive discourse between MA multilingual students and the in-service EFL teachers. A forum with all the primary teachers, heads of English and all the MA students gave the rationale and showed the videos of how the activities connected to the transformative multiliteracies principles. A website was created for in-service teachers to access the special lessons. This enabled highlighting how the process of training changed over time and improved the learning of the concepts. The forum provided an opportunity for both MA students and primary teachers, after seeing multiliteracies applied in an actual context, to discuss their understanding of the concepts and the new PD approach.

The researcher investigated both the in-service teachers and MA students understanding and experience in the learning process of the conceptual framework to answer the following research questions:

(1) What are the primary school in-service English teachers' and MA students' beliefs about multiliteracies and do they shift over time?
(2) Can primary school in-service English teachers and MA students increase specific understanding of how to apply transformative multiliteracies principles?
(3) Does the CCR approach better facilitate investment and application of 21st century learning?

Methodology

Context of the study

The study was multisite and multiparticipant, conducted from the researcher's MA multiliteracies elective course. MA students were informed regarding the changes in the course syllabus prior to agreeing to participate. The project ran over a 15-week term. The special lessons discussed above were implemented in four mainstream primary schools. Due to the number of schools, participating lessons were videotaped for reflection, feedback and data analysis.

Participants

There were 16 participants. Eight were in-service English teachers from four mainstream primary schools (P1–8) and eight were MA students (P9–16). Most of the MA students had only a few years' teaching experience. Therefore, the study contained two sets of participants learning from each other. Final interviews with MA students occurred after course grades were submitted so as not to influence the responses. All participants (including parents, children and administrators) gave informed consent in Kazakh or Russian. The interviewer for the MA students was not the course lecturer. The MA students were informed that participation in the interviews was optional.

Procedures

The project began in the first two weeks of the MA course with an introduction to the project and the main principles (TMP) of the study. This included the students meeting with the primary English teachers, observing their assigned class and discussing the curriculum topics to be used as a theme for the four lessons (collaboration stage). Then, the MA students implemented their special lessons every third week. Two weeks were in class learning content, gathering peer and course instructors' feedback and redesigning the lessons. Then, in the third week, the MA student would implement the next lesson. This continued with the final MA elective class being the forum (reflection stage) with the in-service English teachers. Therefore, the process of the project was to take the eight MA students in a graduate multiliteracies elective course and create an opportunity for them to apply the transformative principles in an actual classroom over time. The project was constructed to mirror the learning process of primary school students (Pinter, 2017). Additionally, the project enabled the in-service English primary teachers to understand multiliteracies as a component of EYL best practices through observation and reflection.

Pre- and post-interviews with the in-service teachers were conducted before and after each special lesson. The interviews investigated in-service teachers pre- and post-lesson understanding of the five TMPs embedded in the lesson. The questions were open-ended and allowed the researcher to investigate shifts in their beliefs. The MA students wrote reflections after each lesson (Gün, 2011) while each lesson was videotaped by MA students' peers who were observing. Some lessons occurred in the morning while others were conducted in the afternoon. There were two MA students at each of the four schools. The rubric for grading the students' included not only the special lesson, but also changes in the lessons after feedback occurred. Videotaped lessons allowed for a more accurate assessment of the MA students' ability to apply multiliteracies in a classroom context. MA students were not graded on their teaching ability but on their application of the five transformative multiliteracies principles (TMPs).

The PD occurred over several months, so the in-service teachers were not observing experts implementing best practices but rather together, they were co-constructing learning of the new CCR approach. The multiliteracies lessons were conducted four times over three months with breaks for reflection and feedback between the lessons. Thus, MA students' observations, reflection and recursive feedback (Okita & Schwartz, 2013) was a learning process for MA students, their peers and the EYL in-service teachers. The rationale was that the in-service teachers, by being part of the process of observing and providing feedback, acted as 'students' co-constructing the PD knowledge with the MA students who were also learning. Thus, rather than expert novice interactional learning it became a trajectory of learning-through-doing process.

Data collection and analysis

The study utilized a mixed-method approach, which triangulated pre- and post-lesson semi-structured interview questions and feedback for the in-service teachers, peer feedback and self-reflective journals from the MA students, as well as data from the forum to answer the research questions. In addition, the videotaped lessons were utilized as data. There was an anonymous pre-research survey to assess background and attitudes to multiliteracies and prior PD experience. A final forum used the project website to host videos, lesson plans and a rationale for each activity in each lesson. The videos enabled the teachers to visualize both successes and failures in applying multiliteracies in the classroom. Finally, the in-service teachers and MA students were asked questions regarding the new CCR approach and whether it better enabled understanding of multiliteracies. All data and reflections were kept safe and confidential. The location and language of the interviews was the choice of the participants. Permission to videotape the classroom lessons was gathered through informed consent from the parents, students, teachers and school directors. The data collected from interviews, feedback, reflections and post-lesson forum were triangulated.

The data analysis utilized a grounded theory approach and the observations, feedback and interview data were coded (Charmaz, 2009). Using inductive and comparative analysis, the data were gauged for relationships between the data sets (Charmaz, 2009; Glaser & Strauss, 1967). The categories judged the degree of positivity and negativity of the response by using discourse assessment triangulated with direct responses to specific questions asked. First, the interview data assessed the degree of understanding of multiliteracies and views on the specific principles of TMP (creativity, collaboration and critical thinking, prior linguistic and cultural knowledge, relevancy to age, gender, culture and ethnic identity, and multimodality). The 16 participant data sets from the pre- and post-interviews were coded. Afterwards, each individual participant's interview data were compared to his or her feedback and reflections. Then, these were analyzed comparatively for the group of participants. Finally, ratings of the new type of professional development taken from the forum were triangulated with views in the feedback and self-reflections of the participants.

Findings and Discussion

In the following section, the findings will be analyzed and discussed. To discover what the initial beliefs of primary English in-teachers and MA students regarding multiliteracies were, the pre- and post-interviews were examined. Additionally, whether there were any shifts overtime in their beliefs will be discussed. Next, the lesson feedback and reflections were examined to assess for increases in understanding of how to apply transformative multiliteracies principles, by in-service and MA students. Finally, taking the data from the forum, the question of whether both cohorts of participants increased their investment in the new pedagogical practices for 21st century learning will be examined and if so, whether this was due to the CCR approach.

Beliefs about multiliteracies

The results from the pre- and post-interviews investigating what were the primary school in-service English teachers' and MA students' beliefs about multiliteracies showed that most participants stated they thought, 'Multiliteracies meant stories in three languages'. Moreover, after the initial lesson, in-service teacher participants still stated that multiliteracies are 'reading in multiple languages' or 'using text-based ethnic stories'. However, from the reflections and post-interview questions data it was revealed that over time their beliefs began to shift. Originally, in-service teachers believed language learning required daily assessment but not as a social interactive process. Their prior viewpoint to language and literacy learning is what Street (2000) refers to as autonomous literacy practices. Essentially, this is a viewpoint of language and literacy as not socioculturally interactive, but one that is independent skill-based learning. However, after the four lessons all the teachers stated they felt the students learnt more and were more engaged in communication through a variety of modalities. Also, data extracted from the MA students' reflections over the four lessons highlighted that they began 'noticing' when they had 'forgotten' to add multimodality/visuals to the activity to 'scaffold' the students understanding (P9, 10, 11, 14, 15). The data revealed overwhelmingly that they gained 'greater insight into how to apply this approach' when it occurred overtime (P9, 13, 14). The in-service teachers and the MA students stated the lessons facilitated an understanding of multiliteracies as a co-constructed, sociocultural interactional learning process (Rowsell, 2013; Pinter, 2017).

Understanding transformative multiliteracies principles

After examining videotaped lessons, feedback and reflections the data showed evidence to answer question two about specific understanding of and applying transformative multiliteracies principles. Additionally, the reflections and post-interview questions highlighted a shift in understanding how to allow co-construction, critical thinking and multimodality, which are all components of 21st century learning. Each participant was asked specific questions regarding the transformative multiliteracies principles. All the participants gave detailed examples from lessons observed.

Examples of better understanding of transformative multiliteracies principles will be grouped under the specific principles.

TMP # 1: Creativity

In the first lesson, it was illustrated that literacy can be fun and not solely text-based (Marsh, 2004). Initially, some of the teachers did not understand this concept because they viewed literacy as the outcome of using a textbook and memorization of grammar rules. In-service teacher feedback and reflections showed most teachers stated that the 'lessons were more creative than the traditional based lessons' (P 1, 2, 3, 4, 5, 8). Also, 'the students be more creative' and that they found 'this very interesting' (P 2, 3, 4, 6 and 7). When asked what they found particularly creative about the lessons, many highlighted that, 'students were making things' (P 1, 4, 5). In addition, some stated, 'I didn't expect them to be able to do it' (P2, 3, 8). Each lesson had to inspire student creativity.

TMP # 2: Collaborative and critical thinking

When asked about their understanding of collaboration and critical thinking they gave many specific examples. Regarding critical thinking, teachers stated that, 'the students learnt to understand different viewpoints' (P1, 4, 7). All teachers stated that every lesson had 'an activity that involved critical thinking' (P1, 2, 3, 4, 5, 6, 8). The data showed that when asked about collaboration they were 'surprised' that it could be done with the smaller children in Grades 1 and 2 (P 1, 3, 5, 7, 8). Moreover, they were interacting with the teacher in a more collaborative and applied manner. They gave the example of the little children who were not used to working collaboratively in groups. This was noted by some of the teachers who stated that, 'I was surprised that even the small children were able to work together. I never thought they could.' (P1, 3, 7). These opinions echoed the Soviet understanding that schooling occurs individually with students sitting in desks in rows. Therefore, the idea of collaboration and reflective feedback as part of a learning process was initially foreign to them.

TMP # 3: Prior knowledge as linguistic and cultural capital

Most teachers indicated in feedback, interviews or self-reflection that using prior knowledge regardless of language was beneficial for early language learners (P1–5, 6, 8). Several of the in-service teachers who had observed some of the other classes, not just their own, noticed how '(Students') answers were given in Kazakh … When the questions were in Russian, the answers came in Russian. This … benefit(s) the students' (P2, 5, 8). Moreover, many stated that 'I can see (students) tried to make a link with one story to Kazakh … It's good, kids can see how stories taken from each other' (P1, 3, 4, 5). They also stated that they were happy to see students 'support each other in group work' (P1, 2, 6). This led to the data highlighting prior cultural and linguistic capital when doing group work.

TMP # 4: Relevance to age, gender, cultural and ethnic identity

One of the things that teachers became aware of was how 'the students could create their stories, so they could connect the stories to themselves … The students could speak about themselves' (P1, 3, 7). Many of the other teachers 'liked how they connected local with international' and thought that 'this is good' (P1, 2, 3, 4, 6, 7). One of the best examples was how 'the grade 5 students drew, Kazakh version with traditional instruments. They connected our traditions with Harry Potter. There is a connection' (P1, 2). When all participants were asked about gender, culture, age or ethnic identity, they could give specific examples of this.

TMP # 5: Multimodalities

It was noticed by the in-service teachers that the special lessons incorporated videos, audio, online games, pictures and even emojis (P 1, 2, 3, 4, 5, 6, 7, 8). In discussing the special lessons, one of the best examples of multimodality was highlighted in a Grade 6 lesson. Teachers discussed how the MA students used 'the Snow Queen, she (MA teacher) did not just used the words of the story … but student used their own [words]' (P2, 3). Regarding multimodality, the teachers noted, 'They could show their different skills' (P2, 4, 6) and students could 'demonstrate drawing, another could show storytelling skills' (P1, 3, 5). Teachers also stated they realized that it was not just using multimodality or specifically technology, but how it was used that mattered the most. They stated that this understanding only occurred over the course of all the sessions.

Understanding and application through CCR

Regarding the study's effectiveness in shifting attitudes and understanding of the five principles of transformative pedagogical multiliteracies, the results from the forum were positive in illustrating a shift in all participants' perceptions and beliefs. Ninety-seven percent of in-service teachers and MA students stated they preferred the CCR approach and wished to have more training in the method. Additionally, many stated, 'practicing the theories' taught in class 'better facilitated' how to 'apply the different principles' (P9, 10, 12, 13, 14, 15). One reason was that they could see the actual application of the method over time. Based on the reflections and peer reviews, the CCR approach gave the students a stronger understanding of how to best adapt it to context. In addition, they gained a better understanding by watching classmates' special lessons. The teachers commented that one lesson did not change their minds but seeing their students gain confidence and ability to communicate, and their own process of giving reflective feedback, facilitated their understanding of the learning process.

Finally, in the forum discussion after viewing their lesson videos and those of their classmates they claimed a deeper understanding over time, of what each principle meant (P9–15). Many stated that 'I thought I had addressed culture, creativity or critical thinking in the activity but then observing other classmates I became more aware of how I could apply it better' (P9, 11, 13). 'The learning over several sessions helped me better understand how to actually apply these practices.' (P9, 11, 12, 15). The in-service teachers echoed these sentiments in the forum. Ninety-five per-cent of the MA students felt they learnt more from reflecting, feedback and observation. These results aligned with those from the in-service teachers' reflections and at the forum. Moreover, 95% of teachers thought the process of observation was good and 'wanted to get follow up train-ing' (P1, 2, 3, 8), 'Not just observation but overtime training was needed' (P5, 6, 7). It was noted that the results of the reflection and forum high-lighted how effective the 'CCR' framework was. Furthermore, when asked if professional development should change, 100% of the in-service teachers agreed with this statement. The MA students echoed this sentiment.

Overall, the CCR framework process occurred between the MA course professor, MA students and in-service teachers, culminating in a construction of the learning process that does not rely on an expert trans-mission of knowledge but on a newer model that employs a shared interac-tion and co-construction of knowledge in the 21st century (cf. Cope & Kalantzis, 2017). Therefore, the present study of PD teacher training pushes past the idea of 'best practices' to investigate if shifts in beliefs occur when teaching is observed as a co-constructed, sociocultural, multimodal learning over time.

From discussion on the forum, in-service teachers stated that they realized how the multiliteracies engage in more than just storybook read-ing and that students can co-construct the narrative in learning (Mui & Anderson, 2008). Additionally, MA students and in-service teachers better understood Cummins' (2009) TMP concepts after observing the children co-create from the story illustrations or relate character's experi-ences to their own lives. After having seen this in action, they compre-hended connecting the lesson to the relevancy of the students' gender, age or ethnic identity and allowing them to co-construct their knowledge (Gregory et al., 2004). These observations gave teachers a better under-standing over time of multiliteracies.

The study revealed to teachers what research showed, that each child has their own sociocultural capital that should be included in the learning process (Anderson et al., 2015). During the reflections of the lessons, it was highlighted that lessons were based on a sociocultural perspective (Cummins, 2009) and critical literacy concepts. This is an important find-ing not just for teachers working in a post-Soviet context, but also for language teachers from a monolingual context who may inadvertently omit the connection between students' home sociocultural identity and bridging that with classroom learning. For example, lessons utilizing tra-ditional stories, such as Balzac Boy, were usually from books published in

Russian, but our lessons utilized visual images from the Kazakh (Balzac Boy), Russian and English (Gingerbread Man) versions. The cards for the activities and pictures included Kazakh, Russian and English text, while the language of the lesson was English. This allowed the children to understand that stories are shared across cultures (Flewitt *et al.*, 2014). In addition, the lessons enabled the children to create their own version with their choice of characters for their story.

Today's EYL students live in a globalized multilingual context. One which views competencies and knowledge being extracted not just through text-based sources, but also from navigating across platforms and modalities (Abrams *et al.*, 2011; Cope & Kalantzis, 2017). The modality that ranged across the lessons observed by the teachers was a huge influencing factor in their stating they would use this approach. Participants stated it was not just the training, but also the observation of the applied multimodality that was the main factor in their understanding. They gave specific examples of how in one of the lessons the children liked the use of videos but were most engaged when they 'saw the international animation clip.' The pre-teens preferred 'cool' global transcultural multiliteracies (Boivin, 2016). The teachers stated they realized it was not just the technology, but also the connection to age- and gender-relevant content in the technology. Other similar studies in Bangladesh (Hamid & Honan, 2012) and South Korea (Moodie & Feryok, 2015) showed that more than just training is required for teachers' beliefs and practices to change. However, these studies did not address professional development as a learning process over time. This study revealed that observation and training, mirroring the EYL students' learning process over time, better enables teachers to apply concepts in 21st century learning.

Future Implications and Limitations

This study presents implications for future research approaches. It suggests that in-service English language teacher research must shift from testing a pedagogical method in early language learning to research that investigates PD as a learning process. The study revealed that it is not the content of in-service PD, but rather the way in which retraining and pre-service training is conducted, that is the most beneficial for developing countries trying to implement global English practices. Some researchers have begun call for such shifts (Gill *et al.*, 2004) but unfortunately, most are from the education field and not specifically the language learning research field. Early language learning, particularly in a multilingual context, requires a shift in PD perspective to one that views EYL teachers and language learning as co-constructing knowledge within a process. One of the limitations of the study is that it was conducted in a post-Soviet multilingual context not a traditional EFL context. Morever, Kazakhstan is a developing country and certain regions do not have access to the internet.

However, many lessons occurred without technology and this is a key point of multiliteracies; that is, modality can also be the use of puppets, drama or videos. The creativity of the students, not access to technology, is the most important aspect of this learning approach. This study argues that how we train future EYL teachers needs to change regardless of the type of language context (monolingual, bilingual or polylingual). We must create continuing professional development within an actual context, over time, that co-constructs and mediates practices *with* the students, not *at* the students. Future research is needed to compare, in several countries, the CCR approach as a possible solution to globalized implementation of early English language teaching in multilingual countries.

Conclusion

This chapter reports on a study that aims at a solution to overcome difficulties when shifts in language education policies are rapidly implemented. The study suggests that the implementation of a successful shift in educational policy requires a shift in EYL teacher professional development. Furthermore, it found that that the participants (MA students and in-service teachers) believed that training should be: (1) situated in a classroom; (2) observable, participatory and a shared interaction; and (3) over time, in a learning process – this was see as the best approach to EYL teacher professional development. It is argued here that learning is not knowledge that is memorized, but learning is knowledge that can be applied. Moreover, it is argued that how we perceive learning and training from a product to a process over time needs to be re-conceptualized, especially for EYL in a multilingual context. Thus, to achieve a shift in attitude to language learning, EYL professional development must shift from teaching the latest methods to collaborating with teachers on the acquisition of applied knowledge (Okita & Schwartz, 2013). There needs to be innovation not just in the practices, but also in a new approach to professional development, particularly for teachers training in a multilingual context. Furthermore, teachers who want students to be prepared for 21st century learning should demand continuing professional development that mirrors the co-constructed, multimodal and collaborative processes of teacher learning; one which does not separate the teacher from the context of the students' learning in the classroom and that occurs over time.

References

Anderson, A., Anderson, J. and Gear, A. (2015) Family literacy programs as intersubjective spaces: Insights from three decades of working in culturally, linguistically and socially diverse communities. *Language and Literacy* 17 (2), 41–58.

Abrams, S.S., Rowsell, J. and National Society for the Study of Education (2011) *Rethinking Identity and Literacy Education in the 21st Century*. New York: Teachers College, Columbia University.

Ashton, J. and Newman, L. (2006) An unfinished symphony: 21st century teacher education using knowledge creating heutagogies. *British Journal of Educational Technology* 37 (6), 825–840.

Black, P., Harrison, C., Lee, C., Marshall, B. and William, D. (2003) *Assessment for Learning: Putting It Into Practice*. Maidenhead: Open University Press.

Boivin, N. (2016) Multiliteracies of transnational and immigrant pre-teens: Meditating intercultural meaning. *Journal of Intercultural Communications Research* 45 (6), 470–486.

Bridges, D. (ed.) (2014) *Education Reform and Internationalisation: The Case of School Reform in Kazakhstan*. Cambridge: Cambridge University Press.

Burkhalter, N. (2016) *Critical Thinking Now: Practical Teaching Methods for Classrooms Around the World*. London: Rowman & Littlefield.

Burkhalter, N. and Shegebayev, M.R. (2012) Critical thinking as culture: Teaching post-Soviet teachers in Kazakhstan. *International Review of Education* 58 (1), 55–72.

Busch, D. (2010) Pre-service teacher beliefs about language learning: The second language acquisition course as an agent for change. *Language Teaching Research* 14 (3), 318–337.

Butler, Y. (2015) English language education among young learners in East Asia: A review of current research (2004–2014). *Language Teaching* 48 (3), 303–342.

Bruner, J.S. (1975) The ontogenesis of speech acts. *Journal of Child Language* 2, 1–19.

Carless, D. (2005) Prospects for the implementation of assessment for learning. *Assessment in Education* 12 (1), 39–54.

Cazden, C.B. (2001) *Classroom Discourse: The Language of Teaching and Learning* (2nd edn). Portsmouth: Heinemann.

Charmaz, K. (2009) Shifting the grounds: Constructivist grounded theory methods. In J.M. Morse, P.N. Stern, J. Corbin, B. Bowers, K. Charmaz and A.E. Clarke (eds) *Developing Grounded Theory: The Second Generation* (pp. 127–154). Walnut Creek: Left Coast Press.

Cope, B. and Kalantzis, M. (2009) 'Multiliteracies': New literacies, new learning. *Pedagogies: An International Journal* 4 (3), 164–195.

Cope, B. and Kalantzis, M. (eds) (2017) *e-Learning Ecologies: Principles for New Learning and Assessment*. London: Routledge.

Cummins, J. (2009) Transformative multiliteracies pedagogy: School-based strategies for closing the achievement gap. *Multiple Voices for Ethnically Diverse Exceptional Learners* 11 (2), 38–56.

Dave, B. (2007) *Kazakhstan-Ethnicity, Language and Power*. London: Routledge.

Davis, B.M. (2015) Comparison of the beliefs and values of two brothers: Edward and George Herbert. In N. Bakić-Mirić and D.E. Gaipov (eds) *Current Trends and Issues in Higher Education: An International Dialogue* (pp. 173–186). Newcastle Upon Tyne: Cambridge Scholars Publishing.

Enever, J. (2014) Primary English teacher education in Europe. *ELT Journal* 68 (3), 231–242.

Flewitt, R., Messer, D. and Kucirkova, N. (2014) New directions for early literacy in a digital age: The iPad. *Journal of Early Childhood Literacy* 15 (3), 289–310.

Galindo, C. and Sheldon, S.B. (2012) School and home connections and children's kindergarten achievement gains: The mediating role of family involvement. Early Childhood Research Quarterly, 27 (1), 90–103.

Gill, M.G., Ashton, P.T. and Algina, J. (2004) Changing preservice teachers' epistemological beliefs about teaching and learning in mathematics: An intervention study. *Contemporary Educational Psychology* 29 (2), 164–185.

Glaser, B.G. and Strauss, A.L. (1967) *The Discovery of Grounded Theory: Strategies for Qualitative Research*. Chicago: Aldine De Gruyter.

Gregory, E., Long, S. and Volk, D. (2004) *Many pathways to literacy: Young children learning with siblings, grandparents, peers and communities*. London: Routledge.

Gün, B. (2011) Quality self-reflection through reflection training. *ELT Journal* 65 (2), 126–135.

Hamid, M.O. and Honan, E. (2012) Communicative English in the primary classroom: Implications for English-in-education policy and practice in Bangladesh. *Language, Culture and Curriculum* 25 (2), 139–156.

Hoff, E. (2013) Interpreting the early language trajectories of children from low-SES and language minority homes: Implications for closing achievement gaps. *Developmental Psychology* 49 (1), 4–14.

Johnson, D.W. and Johnson, R.T. (2009) An educational psychology success story: Social interdependence theory and cooperative learning. *Educational Researcher* 38 (5), 365–379.

Marsh, J. (2004) The techno-literacy practices of young children. *Journal of Early Childhood* 2 (1), 51–66.

Moodie, I. and Feryok, A. (2015) Beyond cognition to commitment: English language teaching in South Korean primary schools. *The Modern Language Journal* 99, 450–469.

Mui, S. and Anderson, J. (2008) At home with the Johars: Another look at family literacy. *The Reading Teacher* 62 (3), 234–243.

Nazarbaev N.A. (2007) I'll share my thoughts with the people. Almaty: Mektep.

New London Group (1996) A pedagogy of multiliteracies: Designing social futures. *Harvard Educational Review* 66 (1), 60–93.

OECD (2015) Review of policies to improve the effectiveness of resource use in schools (school resources review). Country Background Report for Kazakhstan, JSC Ministry, Astana Kazakhstan.

Okita, S.Y. and Schwartz, D.L. (2013) Learning by teaching human pupils and teachable agents: The importance of recursive feedback. *Journal of the Learning Sciences* 22 (3), 375–412.

Pennycook, A. (2017) *The Cultural Politics of English as an International Language*. London: Taylor and Francis.

Pinter, A. (2017) Teaching young language learners. Oxford University Press.

Rowsell, J. (2013) Working with multimodality: Rethinking literacy in a digital age. Routledge.

Shrum, J.L. and Glisan, E.W. (2015) *Teacher's Handbook: Contextualized Language Instruction*. New York: Cengage Learning.

Smagulova, J. (2008) Language policies of Kazakhization and their influence on language attitudes and use. *International Journal of Bilingual Education and Bilingualism* 11 (3–4), 440–475.

Street, B. (2000) Literacy events and literacy practices. In M. Martin-Jones and K. Jones (eds) *Multilingual Literacies: Comparative Perspectives on Research and Practice* (pp. 17–29). Amsterdam: John Benjamins.

Suny, R.G. (1998) *The Soviet Experiment: Russia, the USSR, and the Successor States*. New York: Oxford University Press.

Vygotsky, L.S. (1978) *Mind in Society: The Development of Higher Psychological Processes*. Cambridge, MA: Harvard University Press.

Zein, M.S. (2016) Professional development needs of primary EFL teachers: Perspectives of teachers and teacher educators. *Professional Development in Education* 1–21.

Zhetpisbayeva, B.A. and Shelestova, T.Y. (2015) Difficulties of implementation of primary English education in the Republic of Kazakhstan: Language teachers' views. *Review of European Studies* 7 (12), 13.

Zhetpisbayeva, B., Shelestova, T.Y. and Abildina, S.K. (2016) Teachers' views on the implementation of English as L3. *International Electronic Journal of Elementary Education* 8 (4), 659–674.

Part 3

Strategies in Programme Development

10 Teaching Italian Language in a Bilingual Kindergarten in Turkey: A Framework for Teacher Training

Valentina Carbonara

Introduction

According to the latest research conducted by the Italian Minister of Foreign Affairs and International Cooperation (MAECI, 2016), Italian language is one of the most widely studied languages in the world. It is taught from university level to kindergarten, which implies a variety of teaching materials, methods and teachers' requirements.

However, this complexity is not always considered in Italian language policy abroad. This is especially evident at kindergarten level where the competences and skills required by teachers working in early bilingual education are concerned with both language teaching and childcare. Frameworks and guidelines for teacher professional development have been outlined for CLIL (Content and Language Integrated Learning) environments (Marsh *et al.*, 2010), for bilingual education (Mehisto, 2012: 81) and for young learners in primary school (Enever, 2017). However, most of the materials are related to English language and, even if they can be adapted in other contexts, there are still few indications for early language learning teachers' requirements in nursery and pre-school.

This study presents a framework of teachers' competences and skills, which can be useful for professional development training, addressing early language learning teachers working in Italian bilingual programmes at kindergarten level. The framework is the result of ethnographic observations (Blommaert & Dong, 2010) and of a process of micro-level language policy intervention conducted in an Italian–Turkish kindergarten in Istanbul (hereafter the school), in a time-span of three years. In this chapter, first the background to this study will be outlined, focusing on the main Italian and European frameworks of professional competences for teachers working in pre-primary schools and on the recruitment of teachers

of Italian as a foreign language (IFL) abroad. Afterwards, the research setting will be described and analysed across two different dimensions: the
context of the role of Italian language in Turkey and the school context.
The latter can be considered as a language policy starter at the micro-level,
since the school planned, tested and implemented a new language policy.
Then, the analysis and the findings of semi-structured interviews conducted with teachers and school board members regarding skills and competences required for IFL teachers working in bilingual kindergartens will
be illustrated. The data collected contributed to the design of the framework for professional development. Finally, the implications that this study
could offer for early language learning teacher education are presented.

Background to the Study

In the academic year 2014/2015, almost 2.5 million people were attending Italian language courses across different institutions and around 50%
of them were studying Italian at school level (MAECI, 2016). In addition
to 83 Italian cultural institutes and 110 Italian lectureships at the university
level, the Italian government directly supports eight Italian state schools,
43 Italian private schools officially recognised by MAECI and 86 Italian
departments in international, bilingual or European schools. However, the
international cultural and linguistic policy of the Italian government covers
only a small amount of the global offer of Italian outside of the country.
The discontinuity of the Italian language policy abroad during the 20th
century (Vedovelli, 2016) encouraged a huge number of local public and
private schools, universities, language centres and cultural centres to organise Italian language courses autonomously without the direct control or
economical support of MAECI (Diadori *et al.*, 2009: 15).

In the IFL teaching domain, one of the main reference points for the
definition of teacher's skills and competences is *DITALS*, *Certificazione di
Competenza in Didattica dell'Italiano a Stranieri* (Certification of
Competence in Teaching Italian to Foreigners), implemented since 1994 by
the University for Foreigners of Siena (Diadori, 2012). DITALS certification embeds the descriptors indicated in the 'European portfolio for student teachers of languages (EPOSTL)' (Newby *et al.*, 2007) and the
guidelines for teacher trainers and quality management in language education described in the 'TrainEd Kit' (Matei *et al.*, 2007) and in the
'QualiTraining Guide' (Muresan *et al.*, 2007), produced by the European
Centre for Modern Languages (ECML) of the Council of Europe. DITALS
certification is divided into three levels (DITALS basic, DITALS I and
DITALS II), with different access requirements. DITALS I is, in turn, differentiated according to learner profiles. The 'children's' profile of DITALS
certification addresses teachers working both in pre-primary and primary
schools, in Italy in multilingual classrooms with minority pupils and
abroad in foreign language (FL) contexts. However, there is no substantial

strand of research on the professional development of IFL teaching focusing on 3 to 6-year-old learners in bilingual settings. This partially reflects European documents: in 2015, the European Centre for Modern Languages (ECML) released the European portfolio for pre-primary educators, PEPELINO (Goullier *et al.*, 2015), which actually targets professional competences and attitudes of teachers of 3 to 6-year-old children, but without a sharp distinction between children learning a foreign language in bilingual settings and minority students acquiring the community language. The document seems more oriented towards the latter context, even if the professional competences described in PEPELINO are essential in both domains and can be adapted according to the settings.

Stepping back to Italian language abroad, at school level it is possible to identify two teacher recruitment methods, which reflect two very different teacher profiles and competences. Italian state schools, private schools recognised by the Italian government and Italian departments in international and European schools select teachers from a merit ranking managed by MAECI, which includes only Italian teachers who meet the requirements indicated by the Minister of Education, University and Research (MIUR) for teaching in Italy. To access the MAECI merit ranking, teachers must have tenure status in Italy which implies an official teaching qualification. For substitute teachers, they must have obtained the university credits corresponding to the subject category they would like to teach. Any specific training for teaching in a FL or bilingual context is provided, unless a teacher autonomously decides to undertake a specific university course or DITALS certification. The second recruitment channel is the one adopted by the huge number of local and private schools offering Italian language education without direct control by MAECI, and which are free to set their own teacher requirements. These rarely include an official Italian teaching qualification, but usually favour competences in IFL. Focusing on the pre-school level, the result of this dual-route selection is that in the first type of institution, teachers are usually well trained in early childhood care but are less skilled in FL education. On the other hand, in private schools, teachers might have very different backgrounds, usually not related to children's education, but they are more competent in teaching Italian as a foreign language. Considering this fragmentation in the domain of training and qualification, it is possible to affirm that the profile of pre-school IFL teacher does not officially exist; however, the professional development and training needs for this teaching context are concrete, as described in the following paragraphs.

Research Context: Italian Language in Turkey and the Study School

Italian has a long teaching tradition in Turkey and it is the fourth most studied language in the country after English, French and German

(Amadori & Campari, 2012). Its presence is related to both historical reasons and flourishing economic and political relations between Italy and Turkey. Most Italian courses have been introduced over the last 10 years, particularly those at university level. This is possibly due to the signing of the Bologna Accords in 2001, thanks to which Turkey became a member of the European Higher Education area. The growing interest in Italian at the level of higher education promoted the development of new Italian language schools and immersion programmes at earlier stages, such as kindergarten. This was the case of the study school.

The school is a Turkish private school that attempts to combine a more general pedagogical view with bilingual education in order to move beyond the mere language teaching, even if in compliance with the Turkish National Program. The school was founded in 1909 by the Salesian Society, a Roman Catholic religious organisation. The school went through several institutional changes over the years, but Italian language remained at the core of its educational curriculum. Today, one third of the lessons are taught in Italian at the primary school level, while at the middle school level, Italian is taught 8 hours per week as a second language, including CLIL teaching. Most of the students' parents are Turkish citizens who are attracted to the school because they work for Italian companies, or have studied Italian at high school or at university. Thus, they see an opportunity for their children to obtain professional advantages and cultural enrichment if they learn Italian as a foreign language.

From 2013, the school started to act as a language policy-starter (Chua & Baldauf, 2011), since the school board identified a specific 'language problem' and developed a related policy. The school's role as a policy initiator was fostered by two main elements. On the one hand, the general attractiveness of Italian culture abroad, especially in Turkey, is crucial. On the other hand, the lack of a systematic Italian language macro-policy planning abroad by the Italian government stimulates many institutions to autonomously project micro-policies, according to their needs (Vedovelli, 2016). Moreover, from 2011/2012, Turkish regulations allowed kindergartens and primary schools to re-introduce foreign languages as a medium of instruction in their programmes.

The 'language problem' of the school can be summarised as follows. In 2012, the school and the two Italian high schools in Istanbul agreed that the study school students achieving a B1 level certificate of proficiency will be allowed to access the high school directly, without attending the prep-year normally required for students who have never studied Italian before. Even if this agreement was considered a successful point for the school, at the end of middle school students are supposed to have developed a deeper cognitive academic language proficiency (CALP) in Italian, in order to deal with the more cognitively demanding Italian high schools programme. The possible solution identified by the school was the implementation of a new language policy, starting from kindergarten level, in order to promote higher linguistic competence. Until 2012, Italian was taught in kindergarten for a few hours per week, with the only goal of instilling a positive attitude in young learners towards the Italian language. The educational environment can provide opportunities for the development of bilingualism because children spend most of their time at school (Baker, 2007: 131). Thus, a bilingual education programme was identified as a possible solution to develop those linguistic and cognitive skills essential for the demanding context in which the students are supposed to continue their educational path after graduating from the school.

One of the steps of the policy implementation process included a preparatory in-depth study of bilingual education models. In contrast with the English language, which has ample academic literature regarding different types of bilingual programmes and several influential examples of good practices, there are only few references for the Italian language. For this reason, the school involved a team of specialists from the University for Foreigners of Siena in order to outline the programme; later, a trial version of the syllabus was designed and tested with 4- and 5-year-old children.

In the subsequent testing phase, the school board monitored several aspects and gathered a solid amount of data and information from multiple sources to get more reliable outcomes and consequently to support the decision-making process efficiently. Five elements to monitor were selected (school board, teachers, teaching, parents, students) and for each of them, the committee identified different types of assessment instruments to employ, according to the aim of the evaluation (Carbonara, 2016). This chapter draws on a wider three-year longitudinal study, focusing on the school board and teachers, and in particular, on the professional requirements considered to be crucial for the enactment of the programme.

Research Methodology

The aim of this study was to answer the following research questions:

(1) Which are the most required competences for an IFL teacher in a preschool bilingual context?
(2) What are the implications of IFL teacher competences for teacher education?

Participants

The participants involved in this study (Table 10.1) included three members of the school board and nine teachers who had been working in kindergarten for the last four years during the trial stage of the bilingual programme implementation. School board members will be referred to using the code 'SB' and teachers employing the code 'T'. Most of the teachers had a degree in applied linguistics or in the domain of language education. Only one teacher had a degree in childhood studies. The teachers coming from a different background were required to attained DITALS or another IFL qualification in order to fulfil the requirements described by Turkish law regarding employing foreign citizens. All the teachers and one member of the school board were Italians, while the other two members of the school board were Turkish, who had attained a C2 certificated level of competence in the Italian language. All the members of the school board had achieved a DITALS qualification, since they had a teaching role in the school: SB1 taught at primary school level, SB3 at middle school level, while SB2 had taught in kindergarten before the implementation of the bilingual programme.

Table 10.1 Teachers' background

	SB1	SB2	SB3	T1	T2	T3	T4	T5	T6	T7	T8	T9
Degree related to childhood studies (CS) or language education (LE)	/	CS	/	LE	CS	LE	/	LE	LE	/	LE	LE
DITALS or other IFL qualification	✓	✓	✓	✓	✓	✓	✓	/	✓	✓	✓	✓

Data collection and analysis

Semi-structured interviews were conducted across a time-span of three years with school board members and teachers in order to monitor the over-all orientation, obtain an insider perspective and understand the expectations towards the trial bilingual programme, in terms of needed competences, staff satisfaction and suggestions for programme improvement (Mehisto, 2012: 90). In this work, some extracts from the wider interviews corpus of about 18 hours will be illustrated, with regard to teachers' requirements, teaching challenges and professional development. The interviews, conducted at school in multiple sessions, after initial open-ended questions to elicit a general experience, gradually narrowed to focus on specific points of view (Charmaz & Belgrave, 2012). The participants were familiar to the author as the researcher, since she spent two years directly in the field with them.

The analysis of the data was based on the principles of grounded theory (Charmaz, 2006). The interviews were transcribed and analysed with NVivo 11 Pro (Bazeley & Jackson, 2013) following an iterative process of reading, open coding and refining of categories. In the first step, the transcript was explored and coded by trying to refer to the information in the text rather than to pre-existing categories, through researcher-denoted coding (Baralt, 2012: 230). Afterwards, free nodes were organised hierarchically in tree nodes, attempting to conceptualise the most significant and recurrent categories.

In order to pattern data conceptualisation, the weight and frequency of the nodes was measured (Table 10.2).

Table 10.2 Nodes, sources and references

Tree nodes		Free nodes	Sources	References
Linguistic competences needed		Italian native-like competence	12	15
		Good competence in Turkish	12	14
		Avoiding language compartmentalisation	11	19
		Being able to adapt speech to children	4	6
Theoretical competences needed	Childhood education area	Pedagogical and childcare studies	12	22
		Knowledgeable about learning processes in children	10	12
	Language education area	Competences in language education	12	18
		CLIL teaching skills	10	15
		Knowledgeable about advantages of bilingualism	8	10
		Knowledgeable about neurolinguistics	5	6
		Being able to deal with children with special needs	3	4
Classroom management competences needed		Being able to support children's motivation	12	21
		Being able to maintain discipline	12	19
		Creating a friendly atmosphere	10	15
		Space management skills	8	15
		Voice management skills	7	14
		Being able to adapt the lesson	7	12
		Time management skills	5	11
		Cooperative working skills	5	12
Personal qualities needed	Relationship with children	Need for empathy	11	19
		Need for emotional intelligence	9	13
		Playful attitude	9	15
		Listening attitude	8	12
		Need of flexibility	8	14
		Body language skills	7	9
		Need of creativity	5	8
	Relationships in the workplace	Team work attitude	12	19
		Positive attitude towards colleagues and school board members	8	13
		Being able to establish a good relationship with parents	8	18
		Willing to improve	9	14
		Self-organisation skills	9	12
		Being passionate about teaching	8	13

(Continued)

Table 10.2 (*Continued*)

Tree nodes	Free nodes	Sources	References
Difficulties	Lack of learning/teaching materials for bilingual pre-schools	12	27
	Adapting learning materials	12	25
	Class management	10	22
	Workload	8	11
	Understanding children's needs	8	18
	Adaptation to the intercultural context	7	12
	Adapting to children's rhythms	5	8
Inadequateness of teacher training opportunities	Lack of courses focusing on pre-school learners	12	15
	Need for self-training	10	16
	Need for online courses	5	6

Findings

Language skills and linguistic de-compartmentalisation

In the interviews, both teachers and school board members identified different competences addressing multi-disciplinary domains. One of the main areas is represented by linguistic competences: most of the teachers mentioned the need for a native-like competence in Italian language and the importance of an intermediate or high level of proficiency in the children's language. Developing a linguistic competence in Turkish is fundamental not only for teaching reasons, but in particular for the creation of a deeper relationship with the children, with the local teachers and with the parents. SB3 expressed an insightful comment regarding language requirements:

> Fluency in the 'other' language is surely important; however, language competence in Turkish cannot be limited to the formal knowledge of linguistic structures, but it should become a resourceful instrument to understand the different semiotic universes of the local community. (SB3)

Another issue in the language requirements domain refers to language allocation and the idea of complementary use of the two languages, in order to avoid compartmentalisation or a hierarchical view. This is explained by the following statement by Teacher 1:

> It is important to be able to speak Turkish. The most powerful moments in class are often related to the contemporary employment of both languages, for instance when the Turkish teacher interacts with me and I code-switch or when I repeat the key words in both languages. I do not use Turkish for mere instructions and I try to avoid translation, I just employ my linguistic resources all together, so children will understand that the most important thing is learning new things, and that they can build knowledge in both languages. (T1)

Theoretical competences: Childhood education or language education?

Regarding theoretical competences, it was possible to identify two main areas, which in turn contained other subcategories, thus this node presents a double hierarchisation. Childhood education is generally considered an essential background to teach efficiently in a pre-school, as T8 illustrated in this reflection:

> I studied applied linguistics and I used to teach to adult learners, thus I was focusing on language learning process. But working with children, I feel that my teaching method should be more child-centred. (T8)

The other main node regarding theoretical competences is the 'Language education area', which includes considerations on different topics, including CLIL and the advantages of bilingualism:

> Teachers working abroad like us are more aware of bilingualism benefits. This theme is not so spread in Italy, most of Italian teachers working in Italy don't know all the advantages ... I mean, mental flexibility and all the other things that neurolinguistics has discovered. (T6)

The competences in childcare seem to be very relevant in classroom management, since the skills required to organise lessons are very different between adults and children, in particular in kindergarten with pre-literacy learners. One of the most recurrent topics in the interviews is the equilibrium between discipline and a more relaxed atmosphere; however, it is not always easy for teachers to balance their teaching behaviour:

> It is fundamental to avoid creating fear in children, but at the same time I don't like to use 'rewards' and gifts if they behave good. Sometimes it's frustrating. (T3)

The engagement of multiple resources, such as space, voice and physical presence are all considered vital to keep the lesson enjoyable, challenging and interesting for children, as T2 explained in this reflection:

> I think it's important to be able to control the voice, and in particular the different ... how can I say ... the 'colours' of the voice, according to the needs. Classroom space is also very important, you can use it in different ways to maintain the lesson active. (T2)

Beyond theoretical competences: Personal qualities

The most articulated node is 'Personal qualities needed'. These skills are related to emotional areas and personal nature and, as SB2 affirmed, they are difficult to mature:

> Being passionate and empathic is very important, but these are rare characteristics and you cannot acquire them in books: they are not intellectual features, but emotional. (SB2)

The school environment includes multiple actors, such as parents and the other teachers, thus it is important to be able to communicate with different interlocutors. The importance of relationships is described by T1:

> It is necessary to be able to work autonomously but also in team: you cannot plan your lessons only by yourself, but it is important to ask for advice, share and compare. The syllabus has to be always re-negotiated considering not only children, but the whole environment, parents' suggestions and other teachers' experiences. (T1)

Therefore, the node 'Personal qualities needed', like 'Theoretical competences', was also organised in multiple levels, according to different relational subjects. Most of the subcategories refer to the relationship with the children, which is well summarised in the following consideration:

> Empathy is the most important instrument. It is important to listen to children to understand their needs and their different intelligences. (T3)

Attitude towards professional development is also considered crucial to enhance teachers' skills and teaching quality, as SB1 mentioned in this comment:

> School Board members are always trying to find better solutions and enact improvements, so we expect teachers to show the same willingness to continue to study and improve. (SB1)

Difficulties and teacher education

The teachers mentioned different kinds of difficulties encountered in a bilingual pre-school, but the main issues were related to class management and teaching materials. All the editors who specialise in IFL usually have a series of books dedicated to young learners, but few of them focus on pre-school children, thus teachers have to adapt them. Moreover, in a bilingual context where at least half of all the lessons are taught in Italian, teachers need a huge amount of materials and they usually produce them autonomously. These difficulties are synthetised in these statements:

> Unfortunately teaching materials for 4–5-year-old children are insufficient, not only quantitatively, but also qualitatively, so we are forced to produce constantly new materials. (T4)

> There is a lot of good books for Italian pre-school children, but we have to adapt them for foreign children in a bilingual environment. (T2)

Regarding the actual training courses and qualifications for IFL teachers, most of the teachers emphasised the general lack of a specific focus on pre-school children in a bilingual context:

> During my studies, I have rarely heard about bilingual education and bilingualism advantages. In DITALS II, even if it suggests a detailed and

very useful bibliography, there is not so much on pre-school children and on bilingualism. I mostly read by myself books and articles written by English or American scholars. (T1)

Discussion: Designing the Programme

The results that emerged from teachers and school board interviews were analysed together with the data gathered from teachers' diaries, observational protocols, and children's motivation and proficiency attainment. Rather than a direct cause–consequence relation between teachers' comments and syllabus and the teachers' framework, there has been a flexible reciprocity between the school board work and teachers' needs. As Mehisto (2012: 38) suggests, there was a reiterated cycle of teacher's interviews, school board interventions on the syllabus and on the framework, and new teachers' feedback over a time span of three years. Moreover, nodes such as 'avoiding language compartmentalisation' and 'pedagogical and childcare studies', for example, were cross-analysed with literature on early language and CLIL-oriented bilingual education. The pedagogical principles of the Italian National Indications for kindergarten (MIUR, 2012) as well as pedagogical approaches such as Reggio Emilia were also considered. This will be explored in depth in the following paragraphs.

Language use and the cognitive dimension of CLIL

Analysing the answers of the interviews, it is possible to outline a general category of teachers' educational needs which includes a variety of competences and qualities associated with different theoretical backgrounds and teaching experiences.

In the linguistic competence domain, beside the need of language proficiency in Italian and in Turkish, one of the most recurrent nodes was related to the idea that Turkish and Italian can co-exist in class, without a strict separation between the two languages. The emergence of the node 'Avoiding languages compartmentalisation' can be interpreted both as a consequence and a motivation of the implementation of a CLIL-oriented bilingual syllabus. On the one hand, as the result of a preparatory in-depth study of bilingual education models, the school board has proposed to teachers a dynamic idea of bilingualism (García, 2009: 74); on the other hand, during the trial stage of the new bilingual programme, teachers have positively evaluated this model, applying the idea of de-compartmentalisation of language and supporting it as a component of the framework for teachers' competences and skills.

García (2009: 154) identified three different bilingual education programmes that embody the concept of dynamic bilingualism: two-way (or dual language), CLIL-type and multiple multilingual. All of them consider bilingualism as a resource, they promote transcultural identities and develop the ability 'to use languages for functional interrelationships and not simply for separated functional allocations' (García, 2009: 119). In the study school case, Turkish and Italian languages are both employed in dynamic interrelated practices, according to the children's spontaneous communicative actions.

The school adopted a CLIL-type bilingual model, which can be defined as a dual-focused educational approach, in which the two dimensions of language and contents are interwoven (Coyle *et al.*, 2010). The aim of CLIL approach is not limited to the development of linguistic competences, as in the additive bilingual programs, but it is extended to the general educational growth of learners (Baetens Beardsmore, 2002: 24).

In our context, it was important to consider not only the language dimension, but also the cultural and the cognitive ones, for a fuller educational perspective. CLIL practices involve the learner being active and making meaning, and to approach content not as notions to accumulate, but in an engaging and challenging way, in order to develop creative thinking and problem-solving skills (Coyle *et al.*, 2010: 44). What differentiates CLIL from other types of language learning approaches is the importance attributed to cognitive skills (Anderson *et al.*, 2001; Bloom, 1956; Cummins, 1984).

During the compilation of the syllabus, we tried to include all the main aspects of CLIL described above, in order to allow children to obtain the linguistic and cognitive benefits of this approach. The teachers involved in the study have frequently mentioned the importance of CLIL method skills, thus they were included in the framework for teachers' competences.

Not only CLIL: Pedagogical needs

In the tree node 'Theoretical competences needed', the most frequent node is 'Pedagogical and childcare studies', which can be interpreted as a choice to set the child at the centre of the educational action, instead of Italian language learning. It is possible to affirm that the interviews reflect the debate regarding the inclusion of both pedagogical and language education components during the design of the syllabus, and this double categorisation was included also in the teachers' requirements.

The programme was developed around the pedagogical principles of the Italian National Indications for kindergarten curriculum (MIUR, 2012) and it considers also some aspects of the Reggio Emilia approach (Rinaldi, 2006). In fact, teaching young children always represents a challenge, because regardless of the target of the instruction (a foreign language, subject content, etc.), it is essential to remember that every teaching action has to be aligned with a broader mission of the child's education and growth.

The main pedagogical guidelines that we considered were derived from the 'Italian National Indications for the Kindergarten Curriculum'. The document underlines that the major purpose of kindergarten is to encourage the development of identity, autonomy, competence and citizenship, with the active involvement of children and their families. The learning environment plays a special role in the educational project: it is not only the place where different activities are conducted, but it represents the integration of moments of self-care, social relationships and daily routines. The importance of the learning environment was mentioned also by teachers in 'Space management skills' nodes. In the National Indications, five different 'fields of experience' are identified: the self and others; body and movement; images, sounds and colours; speech and words; and knowledge of the world (MIUR, 2012: 18). These areas are fundamental to organise children's discoveries and to guide their curiosity and inclinations in order to systematise the learning process, respecting children's timing needs. Some of these issues were also mentioned by teachers in the node 'Classroom management competences needed'.

During the process of compilation of the bilingual syllabus, we considered also the Reggio Emilia approach, a pedagogical philosophy developed by the teacher and educator Loris Malaguzzi during the 1960s in the city of Reggio Emilia, in Italy, which today enjoys a worldwide reputation. Reggio Emilia theories are based on several inspirations from the most relevant psychological and pedagogical thinking of the 20th century, including Piaget, Vygotsky and Dewey (Edwards *et al.*, 2010: 56). A specific innovation introduced by Malaguzzi is 'the hundred languages of children' theory, which underlines the multiplicity of children's semiotic possibilities. In order to enhance the many languages of children, every Reggio Emilia school supports children in experimenting with different materials, tools and media (Gandini, 2008). The multiplicity of children's languages fosters dialogue, interconnection and conceptualisation: 'When you draw, you can support not only your graphic language, but also your verbal language, because you make your concept deeper. And when the concept becomes deeper, the languages are enriched' (Rinaldi, 2006: 193).

Even if Reggio Children does not focus on bilingual development, when designing the syllabus we selected some aspects that could be introduced in the study school and adapted to the specific needs of a bilingual context.

The main feature adapted from Reggio Children was the idea of a spiral-based and flexible syllabus, which could allow children to revisit their experiences and focus on the learning process rather than on the outcomes. Moreover, the policy making group at the school decided that the syllabus content should be aligned with the Turkish Governmental Education Program for Preschools. This choice resulted in a more integrated and ecological educational environment and in a positive collaboration and synergy between Turkish teachers and Italian teachers. This reflects the definition of dynamic bilingualism that the school wanted to foster: disregarding the additive programmes, in the school both Turkish and Italian are a vehicle for knowledge, experience and exploration, as expressed also by teachers in the node 'Avoiding language compartmentalisation'.

Another aspect inspired by Reggio Children was the strategy of working in small groups so that several activities are managed in groups of five or six children. The Turkish educational environment is highly competitive, even from a young age. Through the working-group strategy, we wanted to counter this attitude and convey the idea that 'working together is better'. Working in a group creates a strong sense of solidarity and fosters organisational dynamics, negotiation skills, peer-learning and autonomy (Rinaldi, 2006: 127). This element emerged also in teachers' interviews in the node 'Cooperative working skills'.

The concept of 'learning by doing' too derived from Reggio Children and it overlaps with CLIL approach; the teachers' role is not limited to a mere transfer of information to children, but they have to promote occasions of active learning through concrete experiences. This concept is particularly relevant in language teaching, considering that linguistic competence can be developed and reinforced only by a meaningful use of the target language. The bilingual class is naturally a problem-solving environment, because the child has to learn to communicate with the Italian teacher to efficiently express needs and suggestions, thus they immediately learn to use language 'by doing'.

Several issues described by the Reggio Children approach, including space, voice and body involvement, cover most of the teachers' ideas expressed in the nodes 'Class management' and 'Personal qualities'.

Difficulties and teacher education

The node 'Difficulties' was significant, not only for the definition of the syllabus and of the framework, but also to design pre-service and in-service training for teachers in the school. However, the lack of materials underlined in several interviews is connected to a macro-language policy issue, namely the misleading idea that in an Italian pre-school abroad a teacher can employ the same books and class resources usually employed in Italy. Nevertheless, they are normally used in Italian kindergartens controlled by MAECI, which, as described before, recruit Italian teachers without competences in IFL or in bilingual education, ending up promoting (unknowingly) an additive, or sometimes a subtracting, bilingual view. Considering this trend, the editors specialising in IFL produce very limited materials that address 4- and 5-year-old pupils (Carbonara, 2017), forcing teachers to create their own resources.

The last main node presented in the analysis is 'Inadequateness of teacher training opportunities'. Unlike the international academic contexts, in Italy there is a not only a general shortage of class materials, but also very few training opportunities regarding bilingual pre-schools, even though there are hundreds of governmental or private Italian bilingual kindergartens in the world. As described in the background to the study, the dual-route recruitment process of Italian teachers abroad leads to two very different teacher profiles in term of competences and skills; however, none of them has specific training in bilingual education. The study school is a privileged context, since the school autonomously introduced a new language policy, which included the definition of teachers' requirements for Italian bilingual kindergartens; however, it is still not a simple matter to mature the competences described in the framework, because of the lack of courses and certifications.

The framework for teachers' competences and skills

Considering teachers' interviews, the professional requirements for Italian teachers are outlined, which are clearly crucial for the enactment of the programme from which they derive. In Table 10.3, the preferential requisites to work in the school are listed, which are aligned with the ones described in 'Target Competences in The European Framework for CLIL Teacher Education',[1] with the addition of specific traits that emerged in the interviews. The structure of the framework partially follows Table 10.2.

Implications for Teacher Education

The data show that teachers' educational needs are multifaceted, however the profile of IFL teacher in pre-school bilingual contexts is not well-defined in the European documents addressing teachers' professional development, nor in Italian qualifications and training courses. This reflects the lack of teaching materials for Italian bilingual pre-schools. Teacher education for bilingual programmes in many contexts generally does not prepare teachers well for this unique context (Cammarata & Tedick, 2012), including IFL kindergarten teachers.

In this research, a framework for early language learning teachers' competences has been designed. The framework can be a resourceful tool; it could be extended to other Italian bilingual kindergartens and employed as a self-evaluating instrument by other teachers working in an early language learning context abroad. The framework might also be a starting point to design a new profile within DITALS certification focusing on young language learners at kindergarten level. Moreover, the structure of the framework is suitable to be devolved as a content table for pre-service or in-service training courses. Analysing the framework for teachers' professional competences, three main implications can be related with teacher education for bilingual environments.

Table 10.3 Framework of teachers' competences and skills

Language proficiency	• Italian native speaker or bilingual Italian-Turkish speaker (C1 level in Italian). • At least B1 level in Turkish language, in order to understand children's needs and communicate with parents. • B1 level in English to manage relationships with school office employees and parents (in case of a Turkish language competence lower than B1).
Personal qualities	• Being cooperative and available to work in group with a cross-cultural team. • Being interested in developing her/his own skills and competences, autonomously or attending in-service training and seminars organised by the school. • Have good organisational skills and autonomy. • Being empathic and child-friendly. • Being able to identify children's learning needs and listen to their suggestions. • Being flexible and able to adapt lessons according to children's needs and suggestions. • Being able to manage relationships with parents. • Being able to manage the classroom and keep the place tidy and aesthetically pleasing.
Competences	Qualifications: • Have attained a master's degree in applied linguistics and/or in early childhood education. • Have attained a certification or a master's in teaching Italian to foreigners (CELI, Itals, DITALS). Competences regarding bilingual language education: • Being aware of the advantages of bilingual education. • Being knowledgeable about the best practices in bilingual teaching and learning. • Being knowledgeable of the main features of CLIL approaches and techniques. • Being able to design lessons within the context of the bilingual programme. • Being able to apply strategies and propose activities to promote both linguistic and cognitive development in children. • Being able to plan activities to scaffold language learning in content instructions. • Being able to manage classroom interaction. • Being able to deploy strategies for supporting the transition from monolingual to bilingual teaching and learning, without compromising L1 use and avoiding language compartmentalisation. • Being able to create an authentic and meaningful learning environment. • Being able to adapt existing teaching materials/resources and produce new ones. • Being able to compile a teacher's diary and reports for the self-assessment of the programme. • Being able to promote self-assessment and peer-assessment within children. • Being able to conduct action research, interpret the results and improve teaching practices. Competence regarding young learners' education and childcare: • Being knowledgeable about the main pedagogical theories regarding child linguistic, cognitive and emotional development. • Being knowledgeable about first and second language development in children.

(Continued)

Table 10.3 (*Continued*)

• Being knowledgeable about Italian National Indications for kindergarten and the Reggio Children approach.
• Being able to manage critical facts and develop a cooperative and non-threatening environment.
• Being able to critically observe children and interpret their behaviours.

Other competences:
- Good skills in IT and digital tools (camera, projectors, etc.).
- Good skills in visual arts and craft techniques.

The first implication is in regard to the concept of language de-compartmentalisation. This idea is grounded in García's (2009) model of dynamic bilingualism, which, in turn, is rooted in Cummins' (1979) interdependence hypothesis and in the holistic view of bilingualism of Grosjean (1982). A more recent development in bilingualism studies led to the so-called 'translanguaging turn' (García & Li Wei, 2014). Teacher education should include a deep analysis of bilingual models and of language use and their allocations in bilingual education. García (2016) suggests a Critical Language Awareness approach in teacher education, in which teacher can reflect on the speaker, rather than on single languages, and can be trained in teaching strategies involving all the languages of children linguistic repertoire. Moreover, García argues that this orientation in teacher education should not be limited to pre-service domain: 'Critical multilingual awareness must be a thread that runs throughout the entire teacher education curriculum' (García, 2016: 9).

The second implication is related to the idea of the integration of early language education (in particular CLIL-oriented bilingual teaching) with pedagogical competences. The attempts to integrate aspects and good practices from both domains can be relevant in the design of teacher education programmes. A training course for teachers willing to work in bilingual contexts with young learners should consider adopting an interdisciplinary approach, including content both from language education and from childhood education. In the Italian context, these two fields are associated with two different university departments and this separation might lead to a deficiency of competences in those 'dual' professional roles, such as early language teachers in bilingual context, which requires deep preparation in both areas.

The third implication addressing teacher education, which is included in the framework and can be also be drawn from the whole micro-policy language action conducted in the study school is the importance of agency (Biesta *et al.*, 2015; Varghese & Stritikus, 2005). In teacher training courses, this issue is rarely addressed; however, in such contexts as Italian bilingual education abroad, considering the lack of professional development opportunities and specific teaching materials caused by a weak top-down language policy, programme coordinators and teachers are called upon to engage in acts of language planning. Teacher education should not be limited to providing teachers with content related to approaches and methodologies, but it might help them to become aware of their potential role as language planners. This role can be assumed to encourage teachers to conduct research actions, to observe their daily practices and their impact on students, and to experiment with new materials and teaching strategies. Observational schemes, sociolinguistic questionnaires and teachers' journals should be introduced in teacher education as valuable tools to adopt in class alongside normal teaching activities.

In conclusion, we strongly agree with García when she says, 'bilingual education is the only way to educate children in the twenty-first century' (García, 2009: 5), regardless which language is involved in the learning process. The study school can be considered a practical and positive example for other schools, researchers and teacher educators; however, serious institutional involvement in the establishment of appropriate teacher professional development courses is necessary in order to support a proper Italian bilingual education abroad.

Note

(1) Elaborated on by Marsh *et al*. in 2010 for the European Centre for Modern Languages. See http://clil-cd.ecml.at/ (accessed October 2018).

References

Amadori, G. and Campari, D. (2012) *L'italiano in Turchia. Rilevazioni Statistiche Sull'insegnamento della Lingua Italiana (Italian Language in Turkey. Statistical Survey on Italian Language Teaching)*. Istanbul: General Italian Consulate.

Anderson, L.W., Krathwohl, D.R., Airasian, P.W., Cruikshank, K.A., Mayer, R.E., Pintrich, P.R., Raths, J. and Wittrock, M.C. (2001) *A Taxonomy for Learning, Teaching, and Assessing: A Revision of Bloom's Taxonomy of Educational Objectives*. New York: Longman.

Baetens Beardsmore, H. (2002) L'impact d'EMILE/CLIL/The Significance of CLIL/EMILE. In D. Marsh (ed.) *CLIL/EMILE – The European Dimension: Actions, Trends and Foresight Potential*. Strasbourg: Public Services Contract, DG EAC European Commission.

Baker, C. (2007) Becoming bilingual through bilingual education. In P. Auer and L. Wei (eds) *Handbook of Multilingualism and Multilingual Communication* (pp. 131–154). Berlin: Mouton de Gruyter.

Baralt, M. (2012) Coding qualitative data. In A. Mackey and S. Gass (eds) *Research Methods in Second Language Acquisition: A Practical Guide* (pp. 222–244). Malden: Wiley-Blackwell.

Bazeley, P. and Jackson, K. (eds) (2013) *Qualitative Data Analysis with NVivo*. London: Sage Publications Limited.

Biesta, G., Priestley, M. and Robinson, S. (2015) The role of beliefs in teacher agency. *Teachers and Teaching* 21 (6), 624–640.

Blommaert, J. and Dong, J. (2010) *Ethnographic Fieldwork: A Beginner's Guide*. Bristol: Multilingual Matters.

Bloom, B.S. (ed.), Engelhart, M.D., Furst, E.J., Hill, W.H. and Krathwohl, D.R. (1956) *Taxonomy of Educational Objectives: The Classification of Educational Goals. Handbook 1: Cognitive Domain.* New York: David McKay.

Cammarata, L. and Tedick, D.J. (2012) Balancing content and language in instruction: The experience of immersion teachers. *The Modern Language Journal* 96, 251–269. doi:10.1111/j.1540-4781.2012.01330.x

Carbonara, V. (2016) Bilingual education: From implementation to program evaluation. A case study of an Italian-Turkish kindergarten. In S. Grucza, M. Olpińska and P. Romanowski (eds) *Bilingual Landscape of the Contemporary World* (pp. 55–74). Frankfurt, Germany: Peter Lang International Academic Publishers.

Carbonara, V. (2017) Bilingual education: A case study of an Italian-Turkish kindergarten (doctoral dissertation). Database of the University for Foreigners of Siena.

Charmaz, K. (2006) *Constructing Grounded Theory. A Practical Guide Through Qualitative Analysis.* London: Sage.

Charmaz, K. and Belgrave, L.L. (2012) Qualitative interviewing and grounded theory analysis. In J.F. Gubrium, J.A. Holstein, A.B. Marvasti and K.D. McKinney (eds) *The SAGE Handbook of Interview Research: The Complexity of the Craft* (pp. 347–366). Thousand Oaks, California, USA: SAGE Publications Inc.

Chua, S.K.C. and Baldauf, R.B. Jr. (2011) Micro language planning. In E. Hinkel (ed.) *Handbook of Research in Second Language Learning and Teaching.* (Vol. 2) (pp. 936–951). New York: Routledge.

Coyle, D., Hood, P. and Marsh, D. (2010) *CLIL, Content and Language Integrated Learning.* Cambridge: Cambridge University Press.

Cummins, J. (1979). *Linguistic Interdependence and the Educational Development of Bilingual Children.* Review of Educational Research 49, 222–251.

Cummins, J. (1984) *Bilingualism and Special Education: Issues in Assessment and Pedagogy.* Clevedon: Multilingual Matters.

Diadori, P. (2012) Training language teacher trainers: The DITALS Project. In P. Diadori (ed.) *How to Train Language Teacher Trainers* (pp. 102–132). Newcastle Upon Tyne: Cambridge Scholars Publishing.

Diadori, P., Palermo, M. and Troncarelli, M. (2009) *Manuale di Didattica Dellitaliano L2 (Handbook of Italian as a Second Language Teaching).* Perugia: Guerra Edizioni.

Edwards, C., Gandini, L. and Forman G. (2010) *I Cento Linguaggi dei Bambini: l'approccio di Reggio Emilia All'Educazione dell'Infanzia (The One Hundred Languages of Children: Reggio Emilia Approach to Childhood Education).* Bergamo: Edizioni Junior.

Enever, J. (2017) A passion for teaching, or the brightest and the best? Notions of quality in primary EFL teacher education. In E. Wilden and R. Porsch (eds) *The Professional Development of Primary EFL Teachers* (pp. 95–108). Münster/New York: Waxmann.

Gandini, L. (2008) Introduction to the fundamental values of the education of young children in Reggio Emilia. In L. Gandini, S. Etheredge and L. Hill (eds) *Insights and Inspirations: Stories of Teachers and Children from North America* (pp. 24–27). Worchester, MA: Davis Publications, Inc.

García, O. (2009) *Bilingual Education in the 21st Century: A Global Perspective.* Malden, MA and Oxford: Basil/Blackwell.

García, O. (2016) Critical multilingual language awareness and teacher education. In J. Cenoz, D. Gorter and S. May (eds) *Language Awareness and Multilingualism* (pp. 1–17). Cham: Springer International Publishing.

García, O. and Li Wei (2014) *Translanguaging: Language, Bilingualism and Education.* Basingstoke: Palgrave Macmillan.

Goullier, F., Carré-Karlinger, C., Orlova N. and Roussi, M. (2015) *European Portfolio for Pre-primary Educators The Plurilingual and Intercultural Dimension.* Graz: European Centre for Modern Languages / Council of Europe.

Grosjean, F. (1982) *Life With Two Languages*. Cambridge, MA: Harvard University Press.

Lightbown, P. and Spada, N. (2006) *How Languages are Learned* (3rd edn). Oxford: Oxford University Press.

MAECI – Italian Minister of Foreign Affairs and International Cooperation (2016) *Libro Bianco degli Stati Generali della Lingua Italiana nel Mondo*. Florence, 17–18 October 2016. See https://www.linguaitaliana.esteri.it/novita/documenti/48/dettaglio.do?=en (accessed October 2018).

Marsh, D., Mehisto, P., Wolff, D. and Frigols Martín, M.J. (2012) European framework for CLIL teacher education. See https://www.unifg.it/sites/default/files/allegatiparagrafo/20-01-2014/european_framework_for_clil_teacher_education.pdf (accessed October 2018).

Matei, G., Bernaus, M., Heyworth, F., Pohl, U. and Wright, T. (2007) *First Steps in Teacher Training. A Practical Guide. "The TrainEd Kit"*. Graz: European Centre for Modern Languages / Council of Europe.

Mehisto, P. (2012) *Excellence in Bilingual Education: A Guide for School Principals*. Cambridge: Cambridge University Press.

MIUR (2012) *Indicazioni nazionali per il curricolo della scuola dell'infanzia e del primo ciclo di istruzione (Italian national indications for kindergarten curriculum and first cycle education)*. Rome: Minister of Education, University and Research.

Muresan, L., Heyworth, F., Mateva, G. and Rose M. (2007) *QualiTraining. A Training Guide for Quality Assurance in Language Education*. Strasbourg: Council of Europe.

Newby, D., Allan, R., Fenner, A., Jones, B., Komorowska, H. and Soghikyan K. (2007) *European Portfolio for Student Teachers of Languages. A Reflection Tool for Language Teacher Education*. Graz: European Centre for Modern Languages / Council of Europe.

Rinaldi, C. (2006) *In Dialogue with Reggio Emilia. Listening, Researching and Learning*. New York: Routledge.

Varghese, M. and Stritikus, T. (2005) Nadie me dijo (Nobody told me): Language policy negotiation and implications for teacher education. *Journal of Teacher Education* 56 (1), 73–87.

Vedovelli, M. (2016) L'italiano degli stranieri, l'italiano fuori d'Italia (dall'Unità). In S. Lubello (ed.) *Manuale di linguistica italiana* (pp. 459–483). Berlin/Boston: de Gruyter.

11 Developing and Evaluating a Syllabus for Pre-service Teacher Education for Japanese Primary English Teachers: Introducing Cross-Curricular Projects

Junko Matsuzaki Carreira and Tomoko Shigyo

Introduction

English education at primary level around the world has been introduced in response to the rapid spread of globalization. In particular, in Asia it has mainly aimed to develop communicative competence by improving 'teaching methods, which tend to be based on grammar-translation in secondary schools' (Garton, 2014: 202). Although governments have offered in- and pre-service teacher training of English education due to the compulsory introduction of English education at primary level in the reform of English education (Copland *et al.*, 2014; Garton, 2014; Husein, 2014; Zein, 2015, 2016a), it has not met what in- and pre-service teachers need and what is useful and usable for them (Garton, 2014; Inoi, 2009; Kusumoto, 2008; Zein, 2016b, 2017). In addition, requirements for elementary-school teacher's qualification depend on departments of universities that stipulate it (Enever, 2014; Zein, 2016a). Therefore, teachers in the same country or the same region have different knowledge and skills of English instruction and different levels of proficiency.

In Japan, the reform of English education has also been implemented along with globalization (Japanese Ministry of Education, Culture, Sports, Science and Technology hereinafter, MEXT, 2008a: 1). English education at elementary school in Japan started around the 1990s. Since 2011, English education, which was named foreign language activities, has generally been conducted for students in 5th and 6th grades by generalist teachers in every elementary school all over Japan. The objectives of foreign language activities are:

> To form the foundation of pupils' communication abilities through foreign languages while developing the understanding of languages and cultures through various experiences, fostering a positive attitude toward communication, and familiarizing pupils with the sounds and basic expressions of foreign languages. (MEXT, 2008a: 1)

This means that foreign language activities are not to develop children's English skills, but rather to encourage them to communicate in English actively and to enable them to enjoy English language. The school guideline suggests that for the sake of attaining the objectives, 'the instruction on the content and activities should be in line with pupils' interest' (MEXT, 2008a: 2) and 'what pupils have learned in other subjects, such as the Japanese language, music and arts and handicrafts' (MEXT, 2008a: 2) should be taken 'to increase the effectiveness of teaching' (MEXT, 2008a: 2). Furthermore, the school guideline explains that generalist teachers in elementary schools, who know their pupils well, should be regarded to conduct foreign language activities.

Pre-service teacher training of primary English education has started to be offered by universities in Japan for a decade; however, its syllabus content is different among different universities and it is not clear whether it is useful and usable for generalist teachers when they conduct foreign language activities in their class. In 2020, English education at elementary school is to be a compulsory subject in 5th and 6th grades and to be conducted as foreign language activities in 3rd and 4th grades. By then, universities should develop syllabuses and curricula for pre-service teacher education, which should be useful and usable for generalist teachers.

Thus, the present study identifies what training is necessary for elementary school teachers to conduct foreign language activities; what syllabus for pre-service teachers in a university is necessary to cover approaches of foreign language learning; and what teaching methods are useful for children to learn how to use English. Furthermore, the study also provides evidence of what the pre-service teachers in the course of the primary English teaching think about the teaching methods presented in the course of the teacher training.

The study is presented in this chapter with the following structure. First, the chapter reviews generalist teachers in English education, pre-service teacher training in universities and then cross-curricular approaches and project-based learning. Second, it shows the purpose and method of the study. Third, the results and discussion are presented subsequently. Finally, the conclusions of the study are presented.

Generalist Teachers in English Education

Generalist teachers, whose major is not English education, are employed to teach a foreign language in several countries in Europe

(Enever, 2014). Enever (2014: 234) reported that there was 'a preference for generalist teacher model, with age-appropriate language teaching skills'. Sharpe (2001) stated some advantages of generalist teachers in foreign language teaching in that they have expertise in primary pedagogy, rich relationships with pupils to underpin motivation and learning, and ability to embed and integrate the foreign language into all aspects of classroom life. In addition, Mourão (2002: 128–129) mentioned some advantages of generalist teachers such as the abilities to 'understand the children's language learning difficulties', 'encourage other learning objectives such as the affective ones', have 'a long-term view of children's learning in whole sense', and 'provide continuity in the children's learning'. Furthermore, Driscoll (1999: 40) stated that generalist teachers can expose students 'again and again to the same vocabulary and phrases, in different games and activities'.

However, according to studies around the world, generalist teachers have some limitations. Some studies show that generalist teachers worry about their limited oral proficiency in English (Copland *et al.*, 2014; Garton, 2014; Husein, 2014; Inoi, 2009; Kusumoto, 2008; Zein, 2016b, 2017). Generalist teachers also lack the knowledge of methods and approaches of language learning for children (Chou, 2008; Copland *et al.*, 2014; Husein, 2014; Kusumoto, 2008; Zein, 2016b, 2017). Furthermore, they lack skills in conducting lessons in the classroom such as making lesson plans (Husein, 2014; Inoi, 2009; Kusumoto, 2008; Zein, 2017), selecting and adapting materials (Copland *et al.*, 2014; Inoi, 2009; Zein, 2017), correcting errors and giving feedback (Zein, 2017), using information and communication technology (ICT) (Copland *et al.*, 2014; Husein, 2014), enhancing students' motivation (Copland *et al.*, 2014; Husein, 2014), integrating different skills of language (Copland *et al.*, 2014; Zein, 2017), and managing classes according to different students' levels and to different class sizes (Copland *et al.*, 2014). The above studies indicate that generalist teachers in elementary schools in English as a foreign language (EFL) environments all over the world struggle to teach English because they are not trained appropriately and are not provided with the introduction of approaches to their advantages. Thus, systems and content in teacher training should be reformed to meet teachers' needs.

Pre-Service Teacher Training in Universities

Monoi (2011) researched changes of the students' knowledge and anxiety after taking a course for elementary-school teacher training of foreign language activities in a university in Japan. The data were collected before and after the course consisting of 15 lessons. The participants were asked whether they knew 39 items learned in the lessons and felt anxious about conducting foreign language activities; they were asked to describe about what they should know and what they felt anxious about. Monoi (2011) reported that the participants did not feel anxious about most of the items in the post-questionnaire. She argued that the anxiety was wiped away when the participants recognized its knowledge. On the other hand, the participants still felt anxious about the items of how to design an annual syllabus, how to make one-lesson plans and how to compose units consisting of some lessons in the post-questionnaire, although these items were taught in the sixth and seventh lectures of the course of elementary school teacher training of foreign language activities.

Matsumiya (2010: 111) investigated 'the effect on university students (who hope[d] to become elementary-school teachers) of a syllabus of a course on how to teach English in elementary schools.' The participants were students in a university which has a faculty of elementary school teacher training in Japan. First, Matsumiya quantitatively analyzed how the participants' interest, willingness and confidence in instructing English changed before and after the course in 2007 and 2008. Matsumiya found that most of the participants' interest and willingness increased in both years and that confidence of 65% participants in 2007 and over 70% in 2008 increased.

Second, Matsumiya (2010) analyzed qualitatively the participants' descriptions of their anxiety, interest and confidence before and after the course. Matsumiya found that the participants' descriptions before the course were categorized into two groups: the participants' anxiety in Group 1 was caused by their lack of proficiency of English and in Group 2 by lack of knowledge about foreign language activities. Concerning the participants' descriptions after the course, Matsumiya reported that the increase of the participants' willingness was observed from their phrases 'decreasing anxiety', 'increasing willingness' and 'understanding foreign language activities better' in their descriptions. She insisted that the changes of their feelings were attributed to acquiring what they should do as a generalist teacher in foreign language activities and to knowing that high proficiency of English was not always required in conducting foreign language activities.

Zein (2016a: 122) investigated 'whether or not the pre-service education system in Indonesia has been adequate to prepare the teachers to teach English at primary level.' First, Zein (2016a: 124) found that 'most participants were dissatisfied with pre-service education in preparing the teachers to teach in primary schools.' The participants both with and without an English background stated that they were not ready to teach English at primary level. Second, he also found that English departments dealt with the 'theoretical aspect of teaching', not with 'the practicality of English pedagogy' (Zein, 2016a: 125) at primary level. The third issue indicated that the teacher training courses for elementary school covered teacher training for teaching all subjects, so the quantity of the input of English in the courses provided for pre-service teachers was insufficient for teaching English in elementary school. The fourth issue concerned teacher educators. The participants indicated the inadequacy of teacher educators' lectures because they could not provide practical examples which were useful for pre-service teachers. In the fifth issue, it was found that the '[p]articipants stated that reform on the pre-service teacher education is necessary to help prepare student teachers with the demands of their vocation' (Zein, 2016a: 128).

Zein (2016a: 129–130) argued that the teacher training courses for elementary school should provide pre-service teachers with 'knowledge and skills on young learner pedagogy, classroom pedagogy, and theories of teaching' and with 'particular reference of how they are useful to teach English'; that English departments should provide pre-service teachers with 'specific preparation to teachers of English at primary level'. Finally, Zein (2016a: 130) suggested that teacher educators should incorporate modern approaches and ideas into their lectures, such as 'a constructivist approach' and 'an active teaching learning process'.

The studies cited above showed that in order to encourage pre-service teachers to conduct English classes confidently and decrease their anxiety, pre-service teacher training should provide them with basic knowledge, theories, and methods of primary English education, practical skills of instruction and sufficient input to develop their English proficiency.

Cross-Curricular Approach and Project-Based Learning

In the previous section, we reviewed what in- and pre-teacher training in English education at elementary level needed. However, there has been little research suggesting approaches which is usable for generalist teachers in elementary school. In this section, two approaches are discussed: *cross-curricular approach* and *project-based learning.*

First, the government curriculum guideline of foreign language activities by MEXT (2008a: 2) includes the concept of a cross-curricular approach, in which content is learned across more than two subjects:

> The instruction on the content and activities should be in line with pupils' interest. Effort should be made to increase the effectiveness of teaching by, for example, taking advantage of what pupils have learned in other subjects, such as the Japanese language, music and arts and handicrafts.

Yamamoto (2010) indicated that elementary school generalist teachers could set up opportunities to expose children to English using content from other school subjects, including maths, social studies, and so on. She argued that by using the cross-curricular approach, students could be engaged in foreign language learning at the intellectually and developmentally appropriate levels. Smith (2010: 41) also stated that 'neuroscience supports the kind of teaching which stresses the importance of helping children to make connections within and across the areas of learning in which they are engaged.'

A cross-curricular approach can be incorporated into foreign language activities if generalist teachers design syllabi, make lesson plans and conduct foreign language activities. This is because generalist teachers can 'embed and integrate the foreign language into all aspects of classroom life' (Sharpe, 2001: 116) and can design a whole syllabus covering all subjects and activities in their students' school life, either by adopting content learned in other subjects into foreign language activities or using English language in other subjects, considering students' interest and developmental and cognitive levels (Driscoll, 1999; Mourão, 2002; Sharpe, 2001). Thus, this method of instruction (i.e. a cross-curricular approach), can be supposed to be usable for generalist teachers who teach all subjects.

Second, in order to keep up with rapid changes around the world, MEXT (2008b: 1) stated that schools should equip students with 'basic and fundamental knowledge and skills' and 'the ability to think, to make decisions, to express themselves and other abilities that are necessary to solve problems by using acquired knowledge and skills, to cultivate an attitude of proactive learning and to develop pupils' individuality'. In other words, activities and lessons in every subject conducted in elementary schools should provide students with the ability of problem-solving in order for them to live in harmony with others. The ability to solve problems is developed through project-based learning (MacDonell, 2007: 6; Stoller, 2006). Stoller (2006: 24) defined that project-based learning should include 'a process and product orientation'; students' 'ownership in the project'; extension of 'a single class session'; 'the natural integration of skills'; 'a dual commitment to language and content learning'; group working or individual working; students' 'responsibility for their own learning through the gathering, processing; reporting of information form target language resources', 'a tangible final product'; and students' 'reflections on both the process and the product.'

Stoller (2006: 24–27) suggested the benefits of project-based learning: (1) link 'positive outcome of project work' to 'the authenticity of students' experiences and the language that they are exposed to and use'; (2) increase 'the intensity of students' motivation, involvement, engagement, participation, and enjoyment'; (3) inspire 'creativity, as students move away from mechanistic learning and toward endeavors that allow for and benefit from creativity'; (4) enhance students' 'language skills'; (5) improve students' 'social, cooperative, and collaborative skills'; (6) make 'students complete their projects with increased content knowledge'; (7) improve 'self-confidence, enhanced self-esteem, positive attitudes toward learning, comfort using the language, and satisfaction with personal achievements'; and (8) improve 'decision-making abilities, analytical and critical thinking skills, and problem solving'. Thus, incorporating project-based learning into foreign language activities is expected to develop problem-solving ability, language ability and social skills simultaneously.

From the neuroscientific viewpoint, 'social collaboration and distributing intelligence between various members of a group should be more frequently modelled in educational settings' (Barnes, 2015: 139) in order for a child at the ages of 8 to 14 to develop as a person who has a mature brain. Barnes (2015: 139) also suggested that the 'social activity in learning would be an external metaphor for what is invisibly happening within the developing brain.' Thus, project-based learning should be incorporated into foreign language learning as well as other subjects to help children's brains to grow.

Accordingly, the combination of a cross-curricular approach and project-based learning seems one of the most appropriate ways for generalist teachers to conduct foreign language activities in elementary school. Thus, this study was conducted in the light of this rationale.

The Purpose of the Present Study

As seen in the above studies of Monoi (2012) and Matsumiya (2010), the syllabus for elementary school teacher training of foreign language activities in university should involve comprehension of significance of foreign language activities and recognition of role of the generalist teacher in foreign language learning. What is the role of the generalist teacher in foreign language learning? As in Yamamoto (2010), Sharpe (2001), Mourão (2002) and Driscoll (1999), by introducing a cross-curricular approach, the generalist teacher at elementary school can provide their students with enough and meaningful input of English across subjects and in their school life, considering their cognitive development. Moreover, as seen in MacDonell (2007: 5) and Barnes (2015: 139), project-based learning can enhance children's ability for living, which is to work on problems in cooperation with others and which should be acquired during the children's elementary school days. Thus, a combination of a cross-curricular approach and project-based learning is useful for foreign language learning by young learners and usable for generalist teachers at elementary school, which we can call here *cross-curricular project*. Accordingly, the syllabus for elementary school teacher training of foreign language activities in university can include the following: (1) comprehension of significance of foreign language activities; (2) recognition of role of the generalist teacher in foreign language learning and knowledge of a cross-curricular project, which is useful for children and usable for generalist teachers of elementary school; and (3) making a unit of lesson plans using a cross-curricular project and microteaching.

Based upon these considerations, the present study created a syllabus that includes an introduction of cross-curricular projects which are useful for children to learn English and usable for elementary school teachers to plan and conduct foreign language activities effectively. The study then investigated how pre-service teachers in the course of elementary school teacher training of foreign language activities felt in developing a cross-curricular project and conducting their microteaching.

Thus, the following research questions were formulated:

(1) How did the pre-service teachers who took the course of elementary school teacher training of foreign language activities feel in developing a cross-curricular project?

(2) How did the participants evaluate their microteaching?

Research Methodology

Content of the courses

This study was conducted in a university, located in the west of the Kanto Region in Japan. It was established in 1966 and has two faculties: economics and international studies, which includes the Department of Child Studies. The Department of Child Studies aims primarily to train students to be elementary school teachers.

The program of primary English education in the university consists of four courses: Primary English I (PE I), Primary English II (PE II), Primary English Teaching I (PET I) and Primary English Teaching II (PET II). PE I is a course in which students learn what foreign language activities at elementary school in Japan are and experience foreign language activities. PE II is an advanced course in which students learn second language learning theories and the present school guidelines for foreign language activities, and learn how to compose some activities for a lesson (45 minutes) of foreign language activities. The courses of PET I and PET II provide students with more knowledge of foreign language learning theories, foreign language teaching approaches and methods, and more practical skills of developing lesson plans and conducting foreign language activities than those of PE I and PE II. The students discuss roles of the generalist teacher and the assistant language teacher (ALT) and what the generalist teacher should do in a class on foreign language activities. In the course of PET I, the students are required to make detailed teaching plans including project-based learning and to perform microteaching. PET II introduces cross-curricular projects. The students are required to make detailed teaching plans including cross-curricular projects and perform microteaching.

Participants

The participants in this study were 30 junior students (21 males and 9 females) who were taking PET II taught by one of the authors during the second semester (September 2015 through January 2016). Most of the participants had already taken PE I, PE II and PET I, and aimed at becoming an elementary school teacher.

Table 11.1 shows the syllabus of the course of PET II. The students first reviewed MEXT's school guidelines of foreign language activities, foreign language learning theories, foreign language teaching approaches and methods, and assessment; the students discussed what approaches and ideas were appropriate for children's foreign language learning in a Japanese EFL environment, reflecting their experiences as volunteer teachers in elementary schools. Second, PET II provided the students with knowledge of English sounds and phonics, in developing and performing activities using picture books, songs and chants in English. They also learned how to make activities using ICT. Finally, the students learned about cross-curricular projects. They were divided into nine groups consisting of three to four students. Each group was required to make a one-year syllabus including cross-curricular projects and detailed teaching

Table 11.1 Syllabus for the course of Primary English Teaching II

Lesson	Theme	Content
1	Introduction	Course guidance on Primary English Teaching II
2	Issues in children's foreign language learning (1)	Analysis of school guidelines and how to design activities for children's language learning
3	Issues in children's foreign language learning (2)	History of methods/approaches to foreign language teaching and introduction of cross-curricular projects
4	Issues in children's foreign language learning (3)	Study of teaching materials (phonics)
5	Issues in children's foreign language learning (4)	Study of teaching materials (songs, chants and picture books)
6	Issues in children's foreign language learning (5)	Study of teaching materials (using ICT)
7	Issues in children's foreign language learning (6)	Syllabus design using a cross-curricular project
8	Lesson planning (1)	Creating a syllabus (teaching plans)
9	Lesson planning (2)	Creating a syllabus (teaching plans)
10	Lesson planning (3)	Creating a syllabus (teaching plans)
11	Microteaching (1)	Demonstration/observation, review and discussion (1)
12	Microteaching (2)	Demonstration/observation, review and discussion (2)
13	Microteaching (3)	Demonstration/observation, review and discussion (3)
14	Microteaching (4)	Demonstration/observation, review and discussion (4)
15	Reflection and summary	Reflection and summary

plans of a unit and to perform 30-minute microteaching. They were also asked to evaluate the other groups' microteaching.

Data Collection and Procedure

The aim of the present study reveals how the pre-service teachers, in the course of an elementary school teacher training of foreign language activities, feel in developing a cross-curricular project and conducting their microteaching. Open-ended questions can provide the possibility for respondents to reveal their true feelings and ideas, which multiple choice or yes–no questions cannot identify (Carreira, 2016: 25–26). Therefore, the data were collected using open-ended questions.

First, in order to answer the first research question, a questionnaire was conducted in the last class of the course in January 2016. The questionnaire asked the students ($n = 30$) to answer the following questions:

(1) What made developing a cross-curricular project easy?
(2) What was interesting for you in developing a cross-curricular project?
(3) What do you think is easy when the generalist teacher uses a cross-curricular project?

The answers of each question were categorized and counted.

Second, in order to answer the second research question, the students' comments on microteaching, performed by nine groups, were collected. The students were asked to write about good points and points to be improved after they had observed the other groups' microteaching. The students' comments on good points and points to be improved were categorized and counted, respectively.

Results

The answers to the questionnaire

This section analyzes the answers to the questionnaire. The numbers of frequency in Tables 11.2 through 11.4, respectively, indicate the total numbers of answers for each categorized item. The answers to the first question of the questionnaire, 'What made developing a cross-curricular project easy?' were categorized into nine items: (1) through (9) (see Table 11.2).

The results show that from answers (1), (2), (3) and (7), 28 participants felt that cross-curricular projects would help them develop their planning of foreign language activities. From answers (4) and (8), three participants felt that cross-curricular projects would motivate children's learning (MacDonell, 2007: 5; Stoller, 2006). From answer (6), two felt that cross-curricular projects would make use of the ability of the generalist teacher

Table 11.2 The answers for the question, 'What made developing a cross-curricular project easy?'

	Answers	Frequency
(1)	Incorporating other subjects into foreign language activities.	14
(2)	That topics are not limited.	8
(3)	Having a lot of resources for plans.	5
(4)	Using what children already know.	2
(5)	That the cross-curricular project has a more positive image of learning than the traditional learning of language.	2
(6)	Using what they are interested in or what the teacher studied.	2
(7)	Having an explicit aim.	1
(8)	Being able to choose topics which interest children.	1
(9)	That there are some subjects which are easily related to English.	1

in various ways (MEXT, 2008a: 16) and from the answer (5), two felt that cross-curricular projects would improve a stereotyped image of foreign language learning. One participant, in addition, felt that content in some subjects would be easily combined with foreign language activities [see answer (9)].

The answers to the second question, 'What is interesting for you in developing a cross-curricular project?' were categorized into nine items: (10) through (18) (see Table 11.3).

The results show that from answers (11), (12), (13) and (15), 22 participants felt that cross-curricular projects would help children learn various topics and content attracting children in addition to English

Table 11.3 The answers to the question, 'What was interesting for you in developing a cross-curricular project?'

	Answers	Frequency
(10)	It is interesting to relate some topics to foreign language activities.	8
(11)	It is interesting to use knowledge of other subjects in foreign language activities.	7
(12)	It is interesting to choose topics and content that attract children.	5
(13)	It is interesting to make children aware of something else in addition to English language.	5
(14)	It is interesting to make lesson plans as the generalist teacher wants.	5
(15)	It is interesting to provide children with knowledge of other subjects besides English.	5
(16)	It is interesting to choose topics and content that are associated with children's everyday life and learning.	3
(17)	It is interesting to make learning-centered classes.	1
(18)	It is interesting to provide every child with opportunities that allow them to learn and investigate actively on their own.	1

Table 11.4 The answers to the question, 'What do you think is easy when the generalist teacher uses a cross-curricular project?'

	Answers	Frequency
(19)	It is easy to incorporate what children have already learned in other subjects into foreign language activities.	9
(20)	It is easy to link foreign language activities to other subjects.	9
(21)	It is easy to consider the developmental level of children.	8
(22)	It is easy to arouse children's interest and deepen their understanding.	5
(23)	It is easy to design activities.	4
(24)	It is easy to enrich the content.	3
(25)	It is easy to utilize knowledge and experience of their major.	1
(26)	It is easy to get reference material.	1
(27)	It is easy to utilize what is learned in foreign language activities in classes of other subjects.	1

language using their learned knowledge of other subjects. From answers (10) and (14), 13 participants felt that cross-curricular projects would be advantageous to the teacher (MEXT, 2008a: 14). Moreover, three participants felt that the teacher could choose topics that were familiar to children (16) and one participant felt that children's learning would be fostered by cooperation between the teacher and children (18).

The answers to the third question, 'What do you think is easy when the generalist teacher uses a cross-curricular project?' were categorized into nine items: (19) through (27) (see Table 11.4).

There were 31 responses indicating that using cross-curricular projects would make it easy for the generalist teacher to relate children's learning to their own knowledge, interests and perceptions (Barnes, 2015: 146; MacDonell, 2007: 6) based on answers (19), (20), (21) and (22). From answers (24), (25) and (27), five participants felt that it would be easy for the generalist teacher to expand cross-curricular projects in various ways: deepening the content, applying what is learnt in foreign language activities to classes of other subjects and utilizing a generalist teacher's specialist field. From answers (23) and (26), five felt that it would be easy for the generalist teacher to make cross-curricular projects because they would have sufficient teaching resources (MEXT, 2008a: 14).

The comments on microteaching

This section analyzes the comments on microteaching performed by nine groups. The numbers of frequency in Tables 11.5 and 11.6, respectively, indicate the total numbers of comments in each categorized item. The comments on good points were categorized into 15 items: (28) through (42) (see Table 11.5).

Table 11.5 Positive comments on microteaching

	Comments	Frequency
(28)	The teachers could carefully prepare a detailed plan and teaching materials for microteaching.	58
(29)	The activity of microteaching has originality and was enjoyable.	55
(30)	The teacher had a lot of chances to communicate with children.	48
(31)	The topics and materials were very familiar to children.	39
(32)	The microteaching plan was not only aimed at language learning.	34
(33)	The microteaching went smoothly.	20
(34)	The microteaching was child-centered.	20
(35)	The microteaching was creatively and ingeniously designed.	19
(36)	Various kinds of vocabulary were used.	12
(37)	The activity was planned to include communication between children.	12
(38)	The content/topics were explicitly related to those of other subjects.	12
(39)	The student who played a role of teacher had a crucial role in class.	7
(40)	Knowledge that had been learned was used as topics/content.	7
(41)	The activity was planned to make children become aware of differences between English and Japanese.	4
(42)	English and Japanese were alternatively and effectively used.	4

The comments in (28), (29), (30), (31) and (32) were described by a lot of participants. This means that most of the participants carefully observed the microteaching from the perspective of preparation and teaching materials, originality and enjoyment, communication with children, children's familiarity with topics and the expansion of content. The comments in (33) were related to managing a class and those in (35) were associated with designing a class. The comments in (34), (36), (37) and (38) were described by over 10 participants. They paid attention to such points as child-centered learning, usage of various kinds of vocabulary, communication and relation to other subjects, which are characteristics of cross-curricular projects. Although the comments in (39), (40), (41) and (42) were described by less than 10 participants, they are related to the role of the generalist teacher, cross-curricular projects, awareness of language and code-switching.

The comments on points to be improved were categorized into 14 items: (43) through (56) (see Table 11.6).

The comment in (43) was described by a great number of participants. The comments in (44), (45), (46), (47), (48), (49) and (50) were described by over 15 participants. Most of these items concerned content and conduct of activities, teacher talk in English and preparation. This means that the participants focused on the appropriateness of the activity and the importance of input. In addition, the number of the other comments on (51) to (56) was not so large, but some of the participants noticed that

Table 11.6 The comments on microteaching for points to be improved

	Comments	Frequency
(43)	The activity did not go smoothly.	99
(44)	The materials that were used in the activity were not appropriate enough.	34
(45)	The teacher hardly used English/the quantity of English input was not enough.	29
(46)	The activity was not creatively and ingeniously designed.	22
(47)	The teacher did not prepare for microteaching carefully.	20
(48)	English words and phrases that were used in microteaching were wrong.	19
(49)	The explanation by the teacher was not understandable.	16
(50)	The teacher did not choose appropriate activities for attaining the aim.	15
(51)	The content was difficult for children.	11
(52)	The teacher did not interact with children in English much.	11
(53)	The microteaching was not child-centered.	9
(54)	English words and phrases used in microteaching were difficult for the children.	8
(55)	The teacher did not use appropriate vocabulary.	3
(56)	The microteaching seemed not to be a class of foreign language activities, but to be that of another subject.	3

those activities should be designed in an appropriate way for children's developmental, linguistic and cognitive levels in order to attain the aims of foreign language activities by MEXT (2008a: 18).

Discussion

RQ1. How did the participants feel in developing a cross-curricular project?

In order to answer the research question 1, three questions were created: (1) what made developing a cross-curricular project easy?; (2) what was interesting for you in developing a cross-curricular project?; and (3) what do you think is easy when the generalist teacher uses a cross-curricular project? All the answers to the questions (see Tables 11.2 to 11.4) can be divided into four groups: the participants felt that developing a cross-curricular project was easy and interesting, and that a cross-curricular project would be easy to use for generalist teachers because (A) the cross-curricular project enriches the content of foreign language activities in (2), (3), (9), (10), (15), (24) and (26); (B) the cross-curricular project encourages students to reuse their knowledge in another context through language activities in (1), (4), (11), (19) and (20); (C) the cross-curricular project enables generalist teachers to design foreign language activities in their own way in (6), (14), (16), (21), (23) and (25); and (D) the cross-curricular project arouses students' interest and deepens their understanding in (8), (12), (13), (18) and (22).

Groups (A) and (D) are regarding benefits of project-based learning (MacDonell, 2007: 6; Stoller, 2006). Group (B) concerns effective learning for children. The more often children are exposed to target learning items, the better they can understand them (Smith, 2010: 40). Group (C) indicates usability for generalist teachers. Groups (A), (B), (C) and (D) all mean that the teacher training course introducing a cross-curricular project was helpful to generalist teachers in making lesson plans and conducting lessons because the participants felt that cross-curricular projects would expand their resources for making foreign language activities and give them more clues for arousing their children's interest and commitment to learning.

In sum, the participants felt that developing a cross-curricular project was easy and interesting; that a cross-curricular project would be easy for generalist teachers to use; and that cross-curricular projects would increase children's commitment to learning in class. This suggests that through cross-curricular projects, generalist teachers can provide children with first-hand experience in English, rather than an exercise such as a typical drill used in foreign language learning at school (Barnes, 2015: 145; MacDonell, 2007: 6; Stoller, 2006).

Furthermore, the present study revealed that cross-curricular projects would be useful for children and their language learning because cross-curricular projects encourage children to use all their knowledge and skills (Barnes, 2015: 148; MacDonell, 2007: 6). This is evidenced by participants' understanding of the crucial points of English education for young learners through making a cross-curricular project: richness/authenticity of content, children's motivation, meaningful repetition, language learning in context, consideration of the cognitive and developmental level of children, and so on.

RQ2. How did the participants assess their microteaching?

All of the comments on microteaching were coded for qualitative analysis in order to answer research question 2. All the comments on microteaching for good points (see Table 11.5) and points to be improved (Table 11.6) can be divided into eight groups: preparation in (28) and (47), progress of the lesson in (33) and (43), communication in (37) and (52), richness of content in (32) and (56), language materials in (36), (54) and (55), developmental levels of content in (31) and (51), child-centered learning in (34) and (53) and creativity in instruction in (35) and (46).

Some of them correspond to what in-service teachers worried about in the previous studies discussed in Generalist Teachers in English

Education: preparation in (28) and (47) means making lesson plans and developing teaching materials (Copland *et al.*, 2014; Husein, 2014; Inoi, 2009; Kusumoto, 2008; Zein, 2017); language materials in (36), (54) and (55) means using appropriate classroom English proficiently (Copland *et al.*, 2014; Garton, 2014; Husein, 2014; Inoi, 2009; Kusumoto, 2008; Zein, 2016b, 2017); and creativity in instruction in (35) and (46) means using differentiated instruction in English in the classroom (Copland *et al.*, 2014). Although the participants were not in-service teachers but pre-service teachers, they evaluated their microteaching in a manner quite similar to in-service teachers.

Furthermore, developmental levels of content in (31) and (52) and child-centered learning in (34) and (53) are included in knowledge of methods and approaches to language learning for children (Chou, 2008; Copland *et al.*, 2014; Husein, 2014; Zein, 2016, b2017). The items of communication in (37) and (52), richness of content in (32) and (56), developmental levels of content in (31) and (51) and child-centered learning in (34) and (53) are features included in cross-curricular approaches and project-based learning. Thus, it can be said that the participants understood assessment from the perspective of the cross-curricular approach and project-based learning while making a cross-curricular project. They assessed the microteaching from various points of view including management of class, content of cross-curricular projects, expansion of content, the role of the teacher and language awareness. They did not learn temporary skills of instruction of foreign language activities, but comprehensive and extensive skills for conducting foreign language activities in the syllabus including cross-curricular projects.

Conclusions

The present study was the first step for developing the pre-service teacher training course of elementary school English education, which would suggest some important pedagogical implications for elementary school English education in Japan. In particular, the present study showed that the syllabus in the course of elementary school teacher training including cross-curricular projects were useful for children to learn how to use English and were usable for generalist teachers. There are, however, some limitations to the present study. First, this study adopted only three questions and the participants' comments on microteaching as data collection instruments. Although qualitative analysis including open-ended questions can provide varied and detailed information about what respondents think and feel (Carreira, 2016: 107), qualitative analysis is dependent on the interpretative activity of the person who does the analysis (Janasik *et al.*, 2009: 440). Thus, more rigorous studies such as pre- and post-measurements with a control group should be conducted in the future. Morever, the three questions only asked about students' positive experiences, which leads to a positive bias. Therefore, they are not truly open-ended questions.

Second, the data were collected from only 30 pre-service teachers in the course of the elementary school teacher training of English. In order to suggest the usefulness of cross-curricular projects, more data should be collected. Finally, the present study explored the pre-service teacher training course of elementary school English education, but not in-service generalist teachers in elementary school. We should pay more attention to in-service generalist teachers at elementary school and investigate whether or not cross-curricular projects would be effective for them in the future. Further research in this area is necessary.

References

Barnes, J. (2015) *Cross-Curricular Learning 3–14* (pp. 137–148). California: Sage Publications.

Carreira, J.M. (2016) *Motivational Model of English Learning among Elementary School Students in Japan.* Hiroshima: Keisuisha.

Chou, C.-H. (2008) Exploring elementary English teachers' practical knowledge: A case study of EFL teachers in Taiwan. *Asia Pacific Education Review* 9 (4), 529–541.

Copland, F., Garton, S. and Burns, A. (2014) Challenges in teaching English to young learners: Global perspectives and local realities. *TESOL Quarterly* 48 (4), 738–762.

Driscoll, P. (1999) Teacher expertise in the primary modern foreign languages classroom. In P. Driscoll and D. Frost (eds) *The Teaching of Modern Foreign Language in the Primary School* (pp. 27–49). London: Routledge.

Enever, J. (2014) Primary English teacher education in Europe. *ELT Journal* 68 (3), 231–242.

Garton, S. (2014) Unresolved issues and new challenges in teaching English to young learners: The case of South Korea. *Current Issues in Language Planning* 15 (2), 201–219. doi:10.1080/14664208.2014.858657

Husein, R. (2014) A profile of exemplary teachers of English for young learners at the primary school. *Jurnal Pendidikan Humaniora* 2 (4), 311–321.

Inoi, S. (2009) A survey of primary school teachers' attitudes toward implementation of English activities. *Ibaraki Daigaku Kyouiku Jissen Kenkyuu* 28, 49–63.

Janasik, N., Honkela, T. and Bruun, H. (2009) Text mining in qualitative research: Application of an unsupervised learning method. *Organizational Research Methods* 12, 436–460.

Kusumoto, Y. (2008) Needs analysis: Developing a teacher training program for elementary school homeroom teachers in Japan. *University of Hawai'I, Second Language Studies* 26 (2), 1–44.

MacDonell, C. (2007) *Project-based Inquiry Units for Young Children: First Steps to Research for Grades Pre-K-2.* Ohio: Linworth Pub Co., pp. 2–8.

MEXT (2008a) *Course of Study Commentary of Elementary School: Foreign Language (Shogakko gakushu shido yoryo kaisetsu gaikokogo-hen).* Tokyo: Toyokan Publishing, pp. 1–25.

MEXT (2008b) *Course of Study Commentary of Elementary School: General Provisions.* See http://www.mext.go.jp/component/a_menu/education/micro_detail/__icsFiles/afieldfile/2011/04/11/1261037_1.pdf (Retrieved 24 January 2017).

Matsumiya, N. (2010) Changes in attitudes toward teaching English on the part of university students studying to be elementary school teachers: The effect of a relevant teaching methods course. *Journal of Quality Education* 3, 111–134.

Mourão, S.J. (2002) Specialist or generalist? *Educação & Comunicação* 7, 126–133.

Monoi, N. (2011) A trial to develop a syllabus for prospective elementary school teachers to try their ability to teach foreign language activities. *Chiba Daigaku Kyouiku Gakubu Kenkyuu Kiyou* 59, 21–27.

Monoi, N. (2012) A trial to develop a course for developing prospective elementary school teachers' ability to teach foreign language activities: Based on a questionnaire survey. *Chiba Daigaku Kyouiku Gakubu Kenkyuu Kiyou* 60, 97–103.

Sharpe, K. (2001) *Modern Foreign Languages in the Primary School: The What, Why & How of Early MFL Teaching.* London: Kogan Page.

Smith, J. (2010) *Talk, Thinking and Philosophy in the Primary Classroom* (pp. 37–42). Exeter: Learning Matters.

Stoller, F. (2006) Establishing a theoretical foundation for project-based learning in second and foreign language contexts. In G.H. Beckette and P.C. Miller (eds) *Project-Based Second and Foreign Language Education: Past, Present, and Future* (pp. 19–40). Information Age Publishing: Connecticut.

Yamamoto, R. (2010) English instruction to junior high school students based on cross curriculum at elementary school. *Kyoto Kyouiku Daigaku Kyouiku Jissen Kenkyuu Kiyou* 10, 153–161.

Zein, M.S. (2015) Preparing elementary English teachers: Innovations at pre-service level. *Australian Journal of Teacher Education* 40 (6), 104–120. doi:10.14221/ ajte.2015v40n6.6

Zein, M.S. (2016a) Pre-service education for primary school English teachers in Indonesia: Policy implications. *Asia Pacific Journal of Education* 36 (S1), 119–134. doi:10.1080/ 02188791.2014.961899

Zein, M.S. (2016b) Government-based training agencies and the professional development of Indonesian English for Young Learners teachers: Perspectives from complexity theory. *Journal of Education for Teaching: International Research and Pedagogy* 42 (2), 205–223. doi:10.1080/02607476.2016.1143145

Zein, M.S. (2017) Professional development needs of primary EFL teachers: Perspectives of teachers and teacher educators. *Professional Development in Education* 43 (2), 293–313. doi:10.1080/19415257.2016.1156013

Part 4

Perceptions, Knowledge and Assessment

12 Perceptions and Knowledge of Bilingualism and Bilingual Children among Early Childhood Educators in Australia: Implications for Teacher Education

Larissa Jenkins, Elisabeth Duursma and
Catherine Neilsen-Hewett

Introduction

The increasing number of bilingual children attending early childhood services across Australia has motivated the need for greater awareness around how to best support the unique needs of culturally and linguistically diverse children (Espinosa, 2015; Hu *et al.*, 2014). Despite the extensive research documenting the benefits of bilingualism, many Australian children do not receive the necessary support to foster their home language (Byers-Heinlein & Lew-Williams, 2013; Genesee, 2015; Sandhofer & Uchikoshi, 2013). Currently, little is known about how educators perceive and support bilingual children's language development in early childhood care and education (ECEC) settings. ECEC refers to any service providing education and care on a regular basis to children under the age of six.

This chapter focuses on a study we conducted to examine the perceptions and knowledge of mono- and bilingual early childhood educators in Australia. As most of the research on bilingualism has focused on school-aged children, this chapter attempts to heighten the importance of providing early childhood educators with education and training on bilingualism and how best to support bilingual children in early childhood settings.

Research has demonstrated that dual language acquisition offers significant developmental benefits. Bilingualism is associated with advancements in abstract reasoning, phonological awareness, numeracy and reading ability (Han, 2012; Sandhofer & Uchikoshi, 2013; Turnbull *et al.*, 2003). When children are able to maintain their home language, this promotes a strong sense of identity and provides a foundation for second language learning and enhances executive function (Adescope *et al.*, 2010; Rich & Davis, 2007; Shin, 2010).

Many of the benefits of bilingualism are dependent in part on the use of effective strategies designed to support bilingual children's language acquisition (Byers-Heinlein & Lew-Williams, 2013; Cazebas & Rouse, 2014; Genesee, 2015). Strategies to support bilingualism include incorporating literacy experiences in the home such as shared book reading, teaching all children in the classroom phrases in other languages, using non-verbal communication and engaging in authentic cultural experiences (Cazebas & Rouse, 2014; Giambo & Szecsi, 2015; Rutledge, 2010). Bilingual educators can play a crucial role in enriching the learning of linguistically diverse children through providing access to the child's home language, facilitating partnerships with families and assisting monolingual staff in their support of bilingual children (Gerrity, 2003; Harvey & Myint, 2014).

Most of the research on bilingualism has focused on school-aged children and across international contexts, while few studies have looked at examining educators' understanding and support of bilingual children in the Australian ECEC context.

It is important educators support the home language of bilingual children through the provision of quality learning experiences in both languages (Baker, 2011; Espinosa, 2015). When children receive little support for their home language, this can lead to subtractive bilingualism or language loss (Cabezas & Rouse, 2014; Conboy, 2013; Verdon *et al.*, 2014). This highlights the need to support the language development of bilingual children in order to reduce the risk of becoming disconnected from their cultural and linguistic heritage. This study contributes to the existing literature by exploring the role of educators' perceptions in fostering the learning and development of bilingual children in ECEC settings.

Bronfenbrenner's (1979) ecological systems theory provides a framework for examining the influence of educators' perceptions and knowledge on bilingualism, and their support for bilingual children's learning and development within ECEC settings. The ecological approach emphasizes the importance to develop a sense of connection and consensus across different contexts related to children's lives in order to promote positive outcomes for bilingual children. Fostering positive partnerships with families within the early childhood educational context provides an important platform from which to promote positive outcomes for bilingual children. The theory, though, also highlights the potential for negative effect when connections are fragile or disjointed. This can occur when the educational cultural context is incongruent with the home cultural context.

Multiple studies have demonstrated the impact of educators' perceptions on their approaches to pedagogy and practice in ECEC settings (e.g. Braun, 2011; Cazebas & Rouse, 2014). The beliefs educators hold regarding culture and language background play a crucial role in the level of support they provide to foster the learning and development of bilingual children (Ball, 2012; Barcelos & Kalaja, 2012). In this chapter, we report on a study that was interested in whether an educator's language background has an impact on their perceptions of bilingual children in ECEC settings. The specific questions addressed were:

(1) Do monolingual and bilingual educators differ in their understanding of bilingualism?
(2) Do monolingual and bilingual educators differ in their perceptions of how to support bilingual children in an (ECEC) setting?
(3) Do monolingual and bilingual educators differ in their perceptions of their relationships with bilingual children in an ECEC setting?

Bilingual children's ability to communicate with educators can have an impact on their relationship with educators either positively or negatively (Burchinal *et al.*, 2002; Pianta & Stuhlman, 2004). Teachers and children who share the same ethnic backgrounds, tend to have a more positive teacher–child relationships, as reported by the educator (Graves & Howes, 2011; Howes & Shivers, 2006). We expected educators to have a more positive relationship with monolingual children compared to bilingual children, as reported by educators themselves. We also predicted that bilingual educators who shared their language with a child would have a more positive perception of their relationship. We expected educators with higher qualifications and greater experience working with bilingual children to have more positive perceptions of their relationships with these children.

Methodology

We used a mixed method approach, within a multiple case study design to provide a detailed description and analysis of the phenomenon across two ECECs (O'Leary, 2014). Mixed method research involves a combination of qualitative and quantitative research to provide a comprehensive analysis of the issue. This is effective in addressing the problem statement as it provides deeper insight into educators' perceptions of their relationships with bilingual children. In this study it allowed comparisons between monolingual and bilingual educators in relation to their perceptions of bilingualism (Baxter & Jack, 2008).

Participants

Two monolingual and two bilingual educators from two early childhood centres participated in the study. Bilingual educators were defined as those that speak two or more languages on a regular basis (Purcell *et al.*, 2007). Monolingual educators spoke only one language. Educators self-identified as either monolingual or bilingual. All four participants were female and had been working in their current services between three months and two and a half years. Table 12.1 provides an overview of the key demographics for the participants.

Table 12.1 Educator demographics

	Monolingual educator 1 (M1)	Bilingual educator 2 (B1)	Monolingual educator 1 (M2)	Bilingual educator 2 (B2)
Centre	Centre 1	Centre 1	Centre 2	Centre 2
Language background	English	Bengali & English	English	Bengali & English
Gender	Female	Female	Female	Female
Age	20	39	38	52
Qualification	Traineeship	Early childhood diploma	BEd: Early childhood	Early childhood diploma
Years of experience	1 year	7 years	14 years	7 years
Time at current centre	1 year	2 years	3 months	2.5 years

The participants were recruited by sending information about the study and criteria for inclusion to a local government-run children's service in South West Sydney. This geographical area was selected based on the diversity present in the local community with 34% of the total population born overseas and 25% speaking a language other than English at home (ABS, 2016). The organization nominated two early childhood settings based on the presences of bilingual children as well as monolingual and bilingual educators. Once consent was obtained, the director of each service provided information on the study to the educators and two were selected based on their interest in the project. A demographic profile of both classrooms is outlined in Table 12.2.

Measures

Educator Perception Questionnaire

The Educator Perception Questionnaire (EPQ) was adapted from the Teacher Perception Questionnaire (Christopoulou *et al.*, 2012), which was originally designed to examine the attitudes of primary school teachers towards bilingual children in Cyprus. Adjustments were made to the

Table 12.2 The demographic profile of the early childhood centres

	Centre 1	Centre 2
Number of staff	10 staff	13 staff
Total number of rooms	2 rooms	2 rooms
Total number of children enrolled at the centre	50 children	62 children
Number of bilingual children	4 bilingual children	22 bilingual children
Number of children who shared a mutual home language with bilingual educator	0 children	6 children
Mean age of children	44 months	49 months
Gender of children in classroom	10 male	14 male
	8 female	12 female

questionnaire to focus on children aged three to five years in an Australian early childhood context. The original questionnaire included a dichotomous true or false response scale. We changed the response scale to a 5-point Likert rating scale: (5) strongly agree, (4) agree, (3) neutral, (2) disagree, (1) strongly agree.

The items from the EPQ were grouped into six main thematic groups to allow for comparisons of key trends. Four items were used to assess the nature of bilingualism. Five items were related to children's ECEC experience, academic achievement and development in relation to bilingualism. The third thematic group referred to children's ECEC experience and language development in relation to bilingualism and consisted of four items. Twelve items were used to assess teaching related perceptions. Familial connection and the home learning environment were assessed using four items. The final thematic group consisted of two items assessing the early childhood centre in relation to bilingualism. The mean for each statement was calculated across all educators, as well as for monolingual and bilingual educators. This allowed for comparison of the perceptions of monolingual and bilingual educators in relation to supporting and understanding the needs of bilingual children. A difference in the means of 1-point or more was considered to be meaningfully significant.

Semi-structured interviews

Semi-structured interviews were conducted with all four participating educators. The interview was largely informed by the information that emerged from the EPQ. Educators were invited to discuss their views on bilingualism, the support provided to bilingual children in the ECEC and reflect on their social interactions with the children. The interviews lasted from 45–60 minutes and were recorded using an audio device. Questions included 'How do you define bilingualism?', 'What strategies do you use to support bilingual children within the service?' and 'What are some of the challenges you have experienced when supporting bilingual children?' The interviews were transcribed and then coded to determine the key themes within the data. A combination of inductive and deductive approaches were used to determine the themes. Inductive analysis is a bottom-up approach whereby the themes are strongly linked to the data, while deductive analysis is a top-down approach to determine themes that rely on theoretical or existing concepts (Braun & Clarke, 2006). In this way, the themes emerged from examination of the research literature on bilingualism as well as the analysis of the data collected in the study. Key themes included bilingualism, advantages, challenges, etc. Each theme had specific codes associated with it. Coding involved searching through the data to determine themes, categories and ideas. The researcher read through the transcribed interviews and added written comments along-side relevant responses to determine particular trends or themes. The transcripts were then systematically analysed for repeating concepts and clustered into themes. The relevant data was transferred to a table that compared the responses of monolingual and bilingual educators in rela-tion to the themes. This allowed the researcher to explore the differences between monolingual and bilingual educators' perceptions of bilingual children, but also to determine the frequency of certain codes or themes. This case study is a cross-case which means that themes are analyzed across the cases to determine similarities and differences.

The Student–Teacher Relationship Scale

Educators' perceptions of their relationships with monolingual and bilin-gual children were assessed using the Student–Teacher Relationship Scale (STRS) (Pianta, 2001). The STRS is designed to measure teachers' percep-tions of their relationships with a particular child. The short form version consists of 15 items Likert-type format ranging from 1 (definitely does not apply) to 5 (definitely applies) and consists of two subscales; *closeness* and *conflict*. *Conflict* items explore 'perceived negativity within the relationship', and *closeness* items examine the 'extent to which the relationship is character-ized as warm, affectionate and involving open communication' (Jerome *et al.*, 2009: 922). All four educators filled out the STRS for each of the children who attended the same day as the focus educators. The STRS was completed on a total of 44 children (27 of which were bilingual) across the two ECEC ser-vices. The STRS takes approximately five minutes to complete per child.

The STRS has good internal consistency. Cronbach's alpha for *con-flict* was 0.92, *closeness* was 0.86 and *dependency* was 0.64. Dependency was not included in this study.

The STRS was analyzed by grouping the individual items under the *close-ness* and *conflict* scores. The mean and standard deviations on the *closeness* and *conflict* scores were calculated across the six main variables: educational context (Centre 1 and Centre 2), individual educators (M1, M2, B1, B2), edu-cator language (monolingual or bilingual), child language (monolingual and bilingual), mutual home language (same and different), and child gender (male and female). A chi-square analysis was then conducted to determine whether educators' perceptions of their relationships differed depending on educator characteristics, child characteristics or the centre.

Results

The analyses of the questionnaire and the interview revealed more similarities than differences among the monolingual and bilingual educators. Differences were primarily due to educators' level of experience and context at their centre. Bilingual educators were more likely than monolingual educators to agree that a child must have attained a high level of proficiency in at least two languages to be considered bilingual and that a bilingual child can be exposed to two languages yet not speak both languages fluently. All educators appeared to have a limited understanding of the stages of language acquisition, regardless of whether they were monolingual or bilingual.

Descriptive statistics from the EPQ revealed that both groups of educators believed that there was no difference between monolingual and bilingual children with respect to academic achievement or the level of support required in the early childhood environment. Bilingual educators were more likely to agree that bilingualism improved cognitive development ($M = 3.5$ and $M = 4.5$, for monolingual and bilingual educators respectively), and that bilingual children were more talented than monolingual children ($M = 2$ versus 3 for monolingual versus bilingual educators). Bilingual educators were more likely to disagree with statements that suggest a negative impact of bilingualism on the child.

The interviews revealed that overall, educators reported more challenges around bilingualism than advantages. Comparisons across educational contexts showed that educators at Centre 1 were more likely to cite challenges associated with bilingualism than educators from Centre 2.

The next sections highlight some of the key themes from the interviews and the questionnaire.

Stages of language acquisition

Educators' knowledge of the stages of language acquisition varied. One of the monolingual educators described sequential and simultaneous bilingualism without using the terminology;

> From when they are a baby they're spoken to in either just one language and then as they grow older and go to daycare they learn their second language or sometimes the parents might speak to them in both languages. (M2)

The other monolingual educator (M1) was unaware of the stages of language acquisitions but did identify that children were often withdrawn at first: 'I would say they are withdrawn [when they first arrive]' (M1). Both bilingual educators explained that children learn their home language from their families and then learnt the second language through other sources such as television or educational settings; 'When you're a child you listen to your parents and you learn automatically your [home] language ... and then English you learn from ... school' (B2). These findings suggest that all educators appeared to have a limited understanding of the stages of language acquisition, regardless of whether they were monolingual or bilingual. However, the monolingual educator focused on sequential and simultaneous bilingualism while bilingual educators focused on sequential bilingualism.

Perceptions of developmental advantages and challenges of bilingualism

The EPQ investigated educators' perceptions with regard to bilingual children's ECEC experience, academic achievement and development. The means presented in Table 12.3 revealed that both groups of educators believed that there was no differences between monolingual and bilingual children with respect to academic achievement or the level of support required in the early childhood environment. Bilingual educators, however, were more likely to agree that bilingualism improved cognitive development ($M = 3.5$ and $M = 4.5$, for monolingual and bilingual educators respectively) and that bilingual children were more talented than monolingual children ($M = 2$ and $M = 3$, for monolingual and bilingual educators respectively). Bilingual educators were also more likely to disagree with statements that suggest a negative impact of bilingualism on the

Table 12.3 Summary of Educator's agreement with statements about children's early childhood education and care experience, academic achievement and development in relation to bilingualism

Statements about children's early childhood education and care experience, academic achievement and development in relation to bilingualism	Mean	Mean for Monolingual	Mean for Bilingual
Bilingualism improves children's cognitive development	4	3.5	4.5
Bilingual children experience academic disadvantages by speaking more than one language	1.5	2	1
Bilingual children are more likely to experience language difficulties, disorders or delays	1.75	2	1.5
Bilingual children are more talented than monolingual children	2.5	2	3
Bilingual children require additional support in the early childhood environment	2.75	3	2.5
Bilingual children are no different to the other children in the educational setting	3.75	3.5	4
Bilingual children often appear more withdrawn than their peers	2	2	2

child. In particular, bilingual educators ($M = 1$) strongly disagreed with the view that bilingual children experience academic disadvantages by speaking more than one language.

All four educators addressed the advantages and challenges of bilingualism throughout their interviews. Overall, the educators reported more challenges around bilingualism than advantages. Comparisons across educational contexts also shows educators at Centre 1 were more likely to cite challenges associated with bilingualism than educators from Centre 2.

Advantages of bilingualism

Monolingual and bilingual educators had similar understandings of the advantages associated with bilingualism. Educator responses around advantages of bilingualism focused on the linguistic, cognitive and social benefits. Three of the four educators identified the linguistic advantages of bilingualism. Monolingual Educator 2 (M2) believed that acquiring multiple languages ensured children could communicate with extended family members and maintain their cultural identity: 'They can understand their home language so with their Aunt, Uncles when they are together for occasions ... they understand what's going on, whereas if they only speak one language they wouldn't understand what's happening' (M2). Both bilingual educators felt that children's ability to speak two or more languages was a major advantage of bilingualism: 'It is definitely a big advantage that if you use that two languages and more like two, three languages ... you can use that if needed' (B2).

Two of the educators shared an example of how a bilingual child helped educators overcome a language barrier with a new child who spoke limited English;

> We had a child that was new and could hardly speak English but the other child could speak the same language as him and he was saying 'oh he wants this' ... They wouldn't talk to each other but he could just understand. (M1).

Two of the participants (M2 and B2) recognized that bilingual children experience cognitive benefits, as their brains need to process more than one language. 'It's good cognitively. They're thinking about words ... and how to say them ... in two different ways' (M2). Another educator commented, 'They have to work out the two languages. They have to find the way how we can use that two languages ... Their brains work that way' (B2).

Challenges of bilingualism

Challenges around bilingualism raised by educators included communication difficulties with children and families, lower academic achievement, challenging behaviours and confusion. Table 12.3 suggests that monolingual educators were more likely to mention challenges than bilingual educators. However, the greater differences appear to be centre-based, with Centre 1 citing more challenges than Centre 2. Within this centre, the educator completing her traineeship (M1) reported the greatest number of challenges. Monolingual Educator 1 (M1) identified communication difficulties as a significant challenge to effectively supporting bilingual children. While she did not feel that bilingualism prevented bilingual children from engaging and playing with other children, it did present difficulties when attempting to communicate and build connections with the child. She recalled an experience where she asked the child if he had prayed before his meal and her feeling of alarm when he nodded and continued to eat (thinking he did not understand what she had said); 'I remember looking at the teacher going "oh no" and she goes "that's all we can do"' (M1). The educator also felt a sense of helplessness at being unable to comfort the child using verbal reassurance; 'I couldn't communicate with them when they were upset. I could only really try to physically comfort them because the things I was saying wasn't helping' (M1).

Educators from Centre 1 shared examples of how communication difficulties had caused a bilingual child to become distressed;

> We had a bilingual child first start off he was just upset ... we just couldn't do anything for him. We just had to set up a bed near the gate because that's where he wanted to be, close to the gate ... He was just that upset and used to being spoken to in that other language. (M1)

She explained that the staff had to seek assistance from the family in order to reassure and calm the child. Bilingual Educator 1 recalled an experience where the educators could not understand what a young child wanted and as a result the child became distraught; 'In the baby's rooms ... we had to call parents because ... he was just crying and crying ... but we are not understanding' (B1). Three of the four educators reported having difficulty communicating with parents and the extended family; when asked how the centre overcame this challenge, the educator described how the teacher would use visual aids to ensure the family understood the message. Another monolingual educator shared an example of being unable to pass important messages about a child onto the grandparents due to a lack of spoken English: 'When the grandparents come in they know "hello", "how are you" but they sort of don't know much more ... So you have to ring the parent if you have a message to pass onto them' (M2). Bilingual Educator 1 recalled how a child's mother had brought a friend along to the centre who spoke English to help her communicate with the staff.

One bilingual educator believed that bilingual children can experience academic disadvantages. She was able to speak from a parent's perspective on how her own child often felt reluctant to share ideas in the classroom; 'They can catch up a little bit late than the monolingual student ... He knows the answer but he doesn't want to express' (B1). This, however, appeared to be an isolated view, with none of the other educators identifying specific issues with respect to academic achievement.

Perceptions around language development of bilingual children

Analyses of the questionnaire responses show that both monolingual and bilingual educators shared common perceptions around bilingual children's ECEC experience and language development. Interestingly, both monolingual and bilingual educators had a limited understanding of the stages of language development among bilingual children. The bilingual educators did stress the importance of children learning their home language through their families. The educators believed that bilingual children can experience confusion when exposed to different languages at home and at the early childhood setting. They also felt that a bilingual child is demonstrating confusion when they mix words together in the same sentence. Switching between languages when speaking, called code-mixing, however, reflects knowledge of both languages (Gutiérrez-Clellen *et al.*, 2009) and does not imply children are confused.

Both groups of educators strongly disagreed that it is best for a child to be exposed to one language to ensure they can speak it fluently and that a family should speak the language spoken at the early childhood service at home. Studies do show that when parents maintain the home language, instead of switching to the dominant language, this assists children in acquiring the dominant language, as well as maintaining the home language (Drury, 2013; Espinosa, 2012).

Code-mixing

The interviews reflected differences in monolingual and bilingual educators' understanding of code-mixing. Monolingual educators focused on the concept of code-mixing to a greater extent than bilingual educators. Both M1 and M2 felt that children were demonstrating confusion when they mixed words from two languages in the same sentence. 'They go through a stage of confusion ... They sort of mix two languages together' (M2). The educator also acknowledged that it probably appeared to demonstrate confusion more to the adult than to the child. Another educator recounted how parents frequently mixed their languages when communicating with their child; 'They are raised like that and so it's like they are trying to do the same thing [as their parent] but it's just confusing them a bit' (M1).

Educators' perceptions of how to support bilingual children in ECEC settings

The interview and questionnaire data explored educators' understanding of effective strategies to support bilingual children in ECEC settings. The EPQ revealed that educators appeared to have positive attitudes towards teaching related perceptions of bilingualism. Monolingual and bilingual educators differed on five of the 12 items. Both monolingual and bilingual educators agreed that they considered a child's linguistic and educational needs, incorporated a child's first language and practised cultural sensitivity in their classroom. All four educators felt confident in their knowledge of bilingualism and their ability to deal effectively with bilingual children when issues arose at the ECEC service. Bilingual educators ($M = 5$ and $M = 3$, for monolingual and bilingual educators respectively) were more likely to agree that they held high expectations of all children in their class, whereas monolingual educators ($M = 4.5$) were more likely than the bilingual educators ($M = 2.5$) to agree that they knew where to find resources or access support services around bilingual children. Bilingual educators strongly agreed with the view that bilingual educators were more knowledgeable and capable of supporting bilingual children. They also were more likely than monolingual educators to agree that educators should receive training in relation to bilingual children and that they adopted specific strategies to support bilingual children attending the ECEC setting. This suggests that early childhood educators receive little to no training in how to best support bilingual children and their families.

The role of bilingual educators

Both bilingual and monolingual educators recognized the valuable role that bilingual educators play in ECEC settings. The roles identified by educators included the inclusion of the home language, facilitating partnership with families, assisting monolingual staff and building secure attachments. One of the key roles mentioned by the educators was the inclusion of home language and culture. One monolingual educator was particularly passionate about utilizing bilingual educators during literacy experiences: 'You can read it in English and then they'll read it in the other language' (M2). Bilingual Educator 1 (B1) commented on how she included her home language during group times through singing nursery rhymes. Another monolingual educator (M1) stated, 'I think they have, not a responsibility, but they're the ones who are bringing more cultural things into the centre' (M1). The educator also noted, however, that the bilingual educators in her centre rarely incorporated their home language.

Both educators from Centre 2 recognized the important role bilingual educators had in building partnerships with families. The monolingual educator from this centre mentioned on a number of occasions, throughout the interview, about her bilingual colleague's ability to effectively communicate with families; 'Bilingual educators would obviously find it easier to speak to parents ... if they speak the same second language other than English' (M2). She also explained how she had accessed support from bilingual educators to communicate with families with limited English about their child's development. Bilingual Educator 2 reflected on how her presence had helped families feel comfortable in the ECEC service;

> When they walk in they feel ... my English ... is really poor. So when you welcome them and ... find someone who speaks their language they feel really comfortable. It's nice to hear that parents go to the community and they explain to other parents that [I] help. (B2)

There were similarities and differences in monolingual and bilingual educators' understanding of the role of bilingual educators. All educators agreed that bilingual educators foster the inclusion of the home language, facilitate partnerships with families and assist monolingual staff. However, they differed with respect to bilingual educators' role in promoting smooth transitions (M2) and building relationships (B2).

Strategies to support bilingual children

All four educators interview identified strategies to support bilingual children within early educational contexts. These included incorporating the home language, learning key phrases, using communication techniques, adopting a relational pedagogy, building partnerships with families, integrating home languages within literacy experiences, promoting cultural awareness and supporting the acquisition of the second language.

Monolingual and bilingual educators had different perceptions around the best way to support a child who had limited English;

> Firstly communicate with the parents, get the information on key words that they might use at home. If you have multicultural staff that speak their first language, use them to assist that child with the settling process. Talk to the child using ... non-verbal as well as verbal gestures. (M2)

The other monolingual educator (M1) felt that educators needed to build a secure relationship with the child, as well as use facial expressions and hand gestures to support communication: 'I think trying to connect with them as much as you can straight away' (M1). Bilingual Educator 1 believed that it was important for educators to support the bilingual child in forming friendships through encouraging them to communicate and play with other children. According to Bilingual Educator 2, the first step is to build relationships with the child and their parents and then support the acquisition of English;

> First thing is ensuring parents ... feel secure and then their child feels secure. First make the parents comfortable, 'It's ok to not know English'. [With] the children I use body gestures and pick up from cues what they need and try to fulfil their needs. After that build the relationships and slowly, slowly educate the English. But first thing is make attachment and build a relationships with the parents and the child. (B2)

Both Monolingual Educator 2 and Bilingual Educator 1 believed that bilingual children require additional support in the early childhood environment;

> Obviously they need extra support because ... they're learning the second language. We sort of assist them, spend more time communicating with them. Teaching the routines and rules and even ... through songs I guess they are learning to speak another language. They need a lot of help in the early childhood setting just to feel comfortable and to be able to communicate with them. (M2)

The majority of educators reported programming and planning in the same way for all children regardless of whether the child was bilingual or monolingual.

Building partnerships with families

Perceptions around familial involvement were assessed both through the interview data and the EPQ. Results showed educators in this study emphasized the importance of building partnerships between the home and ECEC setting in order to effectively support bilingual children. The EPQ revealed that both groups of educators held common perceptions around familial connection and the home learning environment. Bilingual and monolingual educators were interested in learning about the child's cultural background and home language, encouraged the parents to use their first language at home and actively sought to build partnership with families. The only difference was that monolingual educators were more likely to agree that they found it difficult to communicate with bilingual parents, particularly when their English was limited.

While forming partnerships with families was mentioned by all educators as an effective way of supporting bilingual children, the extent to which educators built partnerships with bilingual families varied. The educators from Centre 2 were proactive in encouraging families to contribute to the curriculum by sharing aspects of their culture and language; '[For] Chinese New Year one of the mums came and she made dumplings so the children understand ... the process. Another one ... the lady brought ... the Indian costume. Another child brought the Ektara [a musical instrument from Bangladesh]' (B2). Monolingual Educator 2 also provided an example of when a Spanish speaking parent taught the children to count to 10 in Spanish and read books to the children in Spanish.

The educators from Centre 1 discussed trying to build partnership with bilingual families. 'We talk with families and if they are interested to incorporate something then they can' (B1). The bilingual educator (B1) recalled how a mother did dragon drawings with the children and gave them a traditional gift with a coin inside for Chinese New Year. While Bilingual Educator 1 acknowledged that they rarely invited parents in to share their language with the children, the monolingual educator (M1) indicated that there were plans to incorporate more languages in the future: 'The other week we were talking [to a] Chinese parent and we asked her if she would like to come in and sing some songs because her child will walk around singing songs in their language' (M1). She also reported communicating with bilingual families in order to identify any concerns that they might have about their child so the centre could then provide support to the families. She reflected on some of the concerns held by the parents: 'We did have parents coming in, asking if they are connecting with other children and playing ... then we tell them they are even though they aren't speaking the same language, they are still connecting'.

Monolingual Educator 1 reflected a lack of awareness of the cultural and language backgrounds of children when she mentioned that a parent was planning on visiting the centre to read books in their language but she was unsure what language they spoke: 'Another child he said his dad is coming in to read some books to us ... . I don't know what language they are' (M1).

The impact of qualifications and experience

While there were no clear patterns across monolingual and bilingual educators, the impact of qualifications and experience on the educators' ability to support bilingual children was evident in a number of their responses. The participants had varied opinions on extent to which their prior education had prepared them to educate bilingual children. The two bilingual educators had completed a diploma in early childhood and felt that the course had placed greater emphasis on cultural awareness than bilingualism: 'We had cultural things. How you can support the language' (B1). One of the monolingual educators was undertaking her traineeship and had not yet covered anything on bilingualism in her course. She mentioned that the final two units focused on promoting Aboriginal and Torres Strait Islander cultural safety and developing cultural competence. One of the monolingual educators reflected on her bachelor degree: '[It] prepared me to a certain extent ... to be more understanding, more patient, more supportive of children who are learning a second language' (M2).

While none of the educators had participated in any professional development or training around supporting bilingual children, all educators believed it would be beneficial. The bilingual educator also agreed that training would be useful in assisting all educators in understanding the needs of bilingual children:

> If you have training ... it would really improve your knowledge. It is benefi-cial to have that training. Not only bilingual educator but other educator also understanding different language and they can provide that because it's all about gaining knowledge and providing that in the centre. (B2)

Monolingual Educator 1 acknowledged that she previously did not feel that training was necessary in order to effectively support bilingual children. However, on further reflection she now believed that it would raise educators' awareness of the different ways to incorporate a child's language and culture into the program: 'After this I would think yes but before this I probably would've thought ... they would probably be able to bring in things [without training], but our educators might not be aware of how to incorporate things into the centre' (M1).

Three of the four educators lacked knowledge on the theories that related to bilingualism and language development. Only one educator was able to identify a specific theory. 'Vygotsky, Piaget. I know the basic ones. Not sure I can think of relating to bilingualism. Unless you can go ... Vygotsky, scaffolding the child's learning with language' (M2). Both monolingual educators indicated that it was difficult to truly feel knowledgeable about bilingualism as they only spoke one language. '[I don't feel knowledgeable about bilingualism] only because I'm not bilingual, I'm monolingual. So I don't feel confident about it' (M2).

Educational context

Both the questionnaire and interviews revealed educators' perception of the ECEC context in relation to bilingual children. According to educators' responses to statements included in the EPQ, both groups appear to have positive perceptions towards the early childhood centres' support and inclusion of bilingual children. Both monolingual and bilingual educators agreed that the centre adopted specific policies and practices in relation to bilingual children. However, bilingual educators were more likely to agree that the centre was inclusive of all children and offered equal opportunities regardless of their language background.

Educators' perceptions of their relationships with bilingual children

The Student–Teacher Relationship Scale (STRS), complemented by the semi-structured interviews, provided insight into educators' perceptions of their relationship with bilingual children. In order to analyze the results for the STRS, the scores for the individual items on the *closeness* scale were combined to create a total composite closeness score. The same procedure was conducted for the *conflict* subscale. A high score means the relationship was characterized by high levels of *closeness* or high levels of *conflict*. The range for the *closeness* score was 19–35 and 8–31 for *conflict*. The range of scores shows more variation for *conflict* than for *closeness* as evident from the wider range.

Descriptive statistics were calculated for all of the variables. Tables 12.4 and 12.5 shows the means of the total combined scores and standard

Table 12.4 Mean, standard deviation and chi-square for scores on closeness

Closeness	Mean (SD)	Chi-square (df)
Educational context		12.54 (15)
Centre 1	30 (5.6)	
Centre 2	30 (4.3)	
Educators		50.26 (45)
M1	31.6 (4.1)	
B1	28.6 (4.7)	
M2	28.42 (4.62)	
B2	32 (3)	
Child language		15.58 (15)
Monolingual	31.6 (3)	
Bilingual	29.1 (4.74)	
Educator language		15 (15)
Monolingual	29.7 (4.64)	
Bilingual	30 (4)	
Mutual Home language		5.16 (22)
Same	32 (2)	
Different	30 (4.5)	
Child gender		19.53 (15)
Female	31 (3.7)	
Male	29.4 (4.8)	

$*p < 0.05; **p < 0.01; ***p < 0.001.$

deviation on the *closeness* and *conflict* subscales for the variables educational context (Centre 1 or Centre 2), individual educators (M1, M2, B1, B2), educator language (monolingual or bilingual), child language (monolingual and bilingual), mutual home language (same or different), and child gender (male or female).

A series of chi-square analyses were conducted between the scores on *closeness* and *conflict* and the educational context, educator (i.e. language) and child (i.e. language, gender) characteristics. No significant differences were found on the *closeness* scores for any of the variables. However, for the *conflict* subscale, significant differences emerged for educational context, educators (M1, M2, B1, B2) and whether the educator was bilingual or monolingual. Comparisons across educational contexts revealed Centre 1 scored higher on perceived *conflict* than Centre 2. For individual educator effects, M2 and B2 perceived their relationships to be characterized by lower levels of *conflict* than did B1 and M1. Analyses showed bilingual educators reported significantly higher *conflict*

Table 12.5 Mean, standard deviation and chi-square for scores on conflict

Conflict	Mean (SD)	Chi-Square (df)
Educational context		32.34* (22)
Centre 1	17 (6.26)	
Centre 2	12 (4.2)	
Educators		112.65*** (66)
M1	17 (8)	
B1	17 (5)	
M2	11 (5)	
B2	12 (2)	
Child language		24.38 (22)
Monolingual	15.29 (5.87)	
Bilingual	13.17 (5.49)	
Educator language		44.68** (22)
Monolingual	13.64 (7)	
Bilingual	14.37 (4)	
Mutual Home language		16.92 (15)
Same	12 (2.28)	
Different	14.15 (5.86)	
Child gender		20.96 (22)
Female	12.9 (5.53)	
Male	15 (5.72)	

$*p < 0.05; **p < 0.01; ***p < 0.001.$

scores with children, regardless of the language background of the child, than monolingual educators did.

Relational pedagogy

Within the interviews, two educators mentioned the importance of building relationships with bilingual children to ensure they feel safe, secure and supported. Bilingual Educator 2 stated that while supporting the acquisition of the second language was important, the first priority should be to build a relationship with that child: 'Slowly, slowly educate the English. But first thing is make attachment and build a relationship with the parents and the child' (B2). She also explained that using her home language when comforting a bilingual child helped the child to feel a second of belonging: 'Babies kind of comforting them, making … strong attachments with them too. If I use my language they feel … somebody is from my [culture]' (B2).

One of the monolingual educators recalled how forming a connection with a bilingual child helped him to transition smoothly into the centre.

She explained that as time progressed the child was more comfortable arriving at the centre and was more settled when his mother left;

> Trying to connect with them as much as you can straight away. I found with the child, the Arabic child, trying to connect with him when he could come in straight away. As time went on, he would come in and smile and say hello. (M1)

Overall, the interview data revealed few differences between the monolingual and bilingual educators in relation to their understanding of relational pedagogy in supporting bilingual children. The results from the STRS highlighted the differences in educators' perceptions of their relationships with children depending on the educational context, individual educator and language background of the educator (monolingual or bilingual).

Discussion

An aim of the study was to examine whether monolingual and bilingual educators differ in their understanding of bilingualism. Overall, educators held similar beliefs around the education of monolingual and bilingual children. Where differences did exist, however, bilingual educators tended to hold more positive attitudes towards bilingualism than did monolingual educators. This was evident as bilingual educators were more likely than monolingual educators to agree with positive statements about bilingualism and disagree with statements that suggest that bilingualism negatively impacts children's development. This is not surprising as bilingual speakers tend to have better metalinguistic awareness or the abilities to think about the nature, meaning, types and functions of the language and to reflect upon them (Pratt & Grieve, 1984).

The findings also pointed to differences in attitudes and perceptions as a function of context, with educators from the two different centres differing from one another in terms of their understanding of the nature of bilingualism. Both monolingual and bilingual educators had differing levels of understanding about the stages of language acquisition in the early years. Although she did not use the terms, only one educator (M2) was able to describe the notion of sequential and simultaneous bilingualism. Simultaneous bilingualism refers to children who obtain two languages at the same time, whereas sequential bilingualism involves children learning a second language once their first language is partly mastered (Clarke, 2009). This may be explained, in part, by the educator being the only participant who had completed a degree in early childhood education. Research conducted in other domains suggests that higher qualifications improve educators' knowledge of child development and their ability to provide appropriate pedagogy (Goldenberg et al., 2013; Rockel, 2009; Sylva et al., 2004). Findings such as these underscore the need for professional development that better prepares educators for working with children from cultural and linguistically diverse backgrounds, providing educators with specific information on bilingualism and language acquisition.

While the educators described categories of bilingualism, they were unable to identify the stages children progress through as they acquire a second language. One educator (M1) did mention that bilingual children were often withdrawn when they first arrived at the centre.

The four educators in this study identified a series of challenges they had encountered when dealing with bilingual children in ECEC settings. These included: communication difficulties with children and families, confusion when learning two languages, academic disadvantages and challenging behaviours, and educators' beliefs and attitudes. Research conducted in other domains has revealed that educators with higher qualifications are more capable of dealing with challenges and meeting the needs of children (Rockel, 2009; Sylva et al., 2004). These findings highlight the need for researchers to develop a deeper understanding of how characteristics of the educational context interact with educator characteristics and experience to influence quality educational practice. The limited knowledge educators had on language development in general, an in particular on bilingualism, stresses the need to teach early childhood educators about these important aspects in order to better support bilingual children. This is an important issue as the number of linguistically and culturally diverse children enrolled in early childhood is increasing worldwide.

The main disadvantage reported by educators was difficulty communicating with the bilingual child and their family; this was particularly pronounced for monolingual educators. This is consistent with previous research, which highlighted the importance of having bilingual educators in ECEC services that share a mutual home language with the child (Gerrity, 2003; Tabors, 2008). The ecological perspective highlights the importance of building partnerships with families as they are the first educators of their child and have invaluable information to share about their language and cultural background (Bronfenbrenner, 1979). In this way, it is important for educators to adopt strategies to overcome the communication barriers to ensure a sense of connection and consensus across both contexts. Again, this stresses the need for better preparing early childhood educators during their training or through professional development how to establish respectful and supportive relationships with the families of their children.

The educators in this study, in particular those in Centre 1, were more likely to focus on the challenges rather than the benefits of bilingualism. This reflects a deficit approach whereby educators focused on the negatives of bilingualism, rather than focusing on the strengths and advantages. This is consistent with findings in the overarching literature that suggests that there is a tendency for society and even researchers to adopt a deficit model of bilingualism (De Angelis & Dewaele, 2009; Paradis et al., 2010). Research by Lee and Oxelson (2006) in the school settings found that teachers with negative attitudes towards home languages were more likely to provide limited support for children's home language. Given the influence of educators' attitudes on practice, it is important to overcome this deficit view to ensure bilingual children receive effective support.

The findings of this study reveal that while there were similarities between monolingual and bilingual educators' in their understanding of bilingualism, there were also key differences. These included differences in terms of their understanding of the advantages of bilingualism, the role of code-mixing in language development, second language acquisition and the challenges of bilingualism within the ECEC setting. The main differences that emerged were often due to centre context or level of experience, with educators in Centre 2 reporting fewer challenges than Centre 1. The influence of educator qualifications and educator experience were also evident within the findings as the degree qualified educator had the greatest level of understanding of the stages of language acquisition, while the trainee reported the most number of challenges. In addition, bilingual educators' personal experience influenced their understanding of language acquisition. All early childhood educators should receive training in the basic aspects of language development and bilingualism in order to better support the development of children's language, either bilingual or monolingual. Children from bilingual families offer a wealth of opportunities for the early childhood centre and other children. However, educators need to know how to communicate and establish relationships with families in order to benefit from the cultural and linguistic knowledge families can offer the centre.

The findings from the Student–Teacher Relationships Scale (STRS) revealed that differences emerged as a result of the educational context, individual educators and whether or not the educator was monolingual or bilingual. Results from the interview reinforced the crucial role of relationships in providing effective support to bilingual children. While it was expected that educators would express more positive relationships with monolingual children, the data in this study revealed that the language background of the child had no impact on educators' perceptions of their relationships. This was a positive finding as it highlights that there were no biases against children from different cultural and linguistic backgrounds.

A myriad of research underscores the significance of high quality relationships for improved academic achievement, development of social-emotional skills, reading competence, language abilities as well as a smoother transition to school (Burchinal *et al.*, 2002; Crosnoe *et al.*, 2004; Pianta *et al.*, 2009). Moreover, relational pedagogy supports bilingual children in developing competencies in both languages (Ewing & Taylor, 2009). Despite this, only two educators (M1 and B2) mentioned in the interviews the importance of building relationships with bilingual children. These findings reinforce the importance of relationships in ensuring bilingual children feel safe, secure and supported.

Research Limitations and Directions for Future Research

The findings of the current study, while important, should be examined within the context of the research design and limited generalizability. This study was largely qualitative in its approach and included a small sample size with only four educators participating in the research. While this limits the generalization of findings, the results of the study still contribute to our emerging understanding of the impact of both educator characteristics and the educational context on educators' perceptions of bilingual children.

The present study utilized a range of self-report measures to explore educators' perceptions of bilingualism. While self-report measures are useful in gaining insight into educators' beliefs, they provide little information on actual practice. These measures are also open to exaggeration or overestimation by the participants (Quick & Hall, 2015). Future research would benefit from a deeper analysis of the links between approaches to relational or intentional pedagogy and the educational and developmental outcomes of bilingual children. A range of other techniques need to be used to explore the differences between monolingual and bilingual educators' understanding and support of bilingual children, such as observations of classroom practice.

Educators play a crucial role in shaping the short- and long-term outcomes of bilingual children. In order to adequately support children from culturally and linguistically diverse backgrounds, educators need to have a stronger understanding of the unique need of bilingual children in the early education context. This study has explored the factors that influence educator perceptions in relation to bilingual children. While there were differences between monolingual and bilingual educators' perceptions, the primary influencing factors on educators' attitudes towards bilingualism appeared to be the educational context and level of experience working with bilingual children. These findings suggest that educator perceptions' are not only influenced by their language background, but also the educational context in which they teach. The increasing number of linguistically diverse children in early childhood educational and care contexts highlights the need for further research that explores the different factors that can either positively or negatively impact educators' perception of bilingual children.

This study also stresses the need for better early childhood education around language development bilingualism. Educators would also benefit from more training on how to interact and support the families of the children they are caring for. Families offer a wealth of knowledge and expertise and children and their families should be seen as assets, in particular when they bring culturally and linguistically diversity with them. However, as the educators expressed, it is not always easy to communicate with them and training educators could assist with this.

Acknowledgement

This chapter is based on the honour's thesis, part of the fulfillment for the Bachelor of Education: Early Years awarded to the first author.

References

ABS (Australian Bureau of Statistics) (2012) *Reflecting on a Nation: Stories from the 2011 Census: 2012–2013.* See http://www.abs.gov.au/ausstats/abs@.nsf/lookup/2071.0main+features902012-2013.

ABS (Australian Bureau of Statistics) (2016) Campbelltown (NSW). Retrieved from http://quickstats.censusdata.abs.gov.au/census_services/getproduct/census/2016/quickstat/LGA11500?opendocument

Adescope, O.O., Lavin, T., Thompson, T. and Ungerleider, C. (2010) A systematic review and meta-analysis of the cognitive correlates of bilingualism. *Review of Educational Research* 80 (2), 207–245.

Baker, C. (2011) *Foundations of Bilingual Education and Bilingualism* (5th edn). Bristol: Multilingual Matters.

Ball, C.E. (2012) *The Richness Diversity Brings: Diverse Languages and Literacies in Early Childhood Education.* Master of Education Thesis, Auckland University of Technology, Auckland, New Zealand. See http://aut.researchgateway.ac.nz/bitstream/handle/10292/4752/BallCE.pdf?sequence=3%20%%20target=. (Retrieved 29 October 2018).

Barcelos, A.M.F. and Kalaja, P. (2012) Beliefs in second language acquisition. In C.A. Chapelle and M.A. Malden (Eds) *The Encyclopedia of Applied Linguistics* (pp. 1–6). Malden, MA: Wiley-Blackwell.

Baxter, P. and Jack, S. (2008) Qualitative case study methodology: Study design and implementation for novice researchers. *The Qualitative Report* 13 (4), 544–559.

Braun, S. (2011) *Unseen Threads: Weaving the Stories between Teacher Beliefs and Classroom Practice.* Masters of Education, University of Manitoba, Manitoba, Canada.

Braun, V. and Clarke, V. (2006) Using thematic analysis in psychology. *Qualitative Research in Psychology* 3 (2), 77–101.

Bronfenbrenner, U. (1979) *The Ecology of Human Development: Experiments in Nature and Design.* Cambridge, MA: Harvard University Press.

Burchinal, M., Peisner-Feinberg, E.S., Pianta, R.C. and Howes, C. (2002) Development of academic skills from preschool through second grade: Family and classroom predictors of developmental trajectories. *Journal of School Psychology* 40 (5), 415–436.

Byers-Heinlein, K. and Lew-Williams, C. (2013) Bilingualism in the early years: What the science says. *Learning Landscapes* 7 (1), 95–112.

Cazebas, C. and Rouse, E. (2014) How do early childhood teachers understand and support the needs of young English language learners. *Asia-Pacific Journal of Research in Early Childhood Education* 8 (1), 57–78.

Christopoulou, M., Pampaka, M. and Vlassopoulo, M. (2012) Cypriot teachers' attitudes on bilingualism. *International Journal of Business and Social Science* 3 (11), 46–58.

Clarke, P. (2009) Supporting children learning English as a second language in the early years (birth to six years). See http://www.fletchermontessori.com.au/uploads/supporting_children_english_2nd_language.pdf (Retrieved 29 October 2018).

Conboy, B. (2013) Neuroscience research: How experience with one or multiple languages affects the developing brain. In F. Ong and J. McLean (eds) *California's Best Practices for Young Dual Language Learners: Research Overview Papers* (pp. 1–50). Sacramento, CA: California Department of Education (CDE). See http://www.cde.ca.gov/sp/cd/ce/documents/dllresearchpapers.pdf (Retrieved 29 October 2018).

Crosnoe, R., Johnson, M.K. and Elder, G.H. (2004) Intergenerational bonding in school: The behavioral and contextual correlates of student-teacher relationship. *Sociology of Education* 77 (1), 60–80.

De Angelis, G. and Dewaele, J.M. (2009) The development of psycholinguistic research on crosslinguistic influence. In L. Aronin and B. Hufeisen (eds) *The Exploration of Multilingualism* (pp. 63–77). Amsterdam, Netherlands: John Benjamin.

Drury, R. (2013) How silent is the 'Silent Period' for young bilinguals in early years settings in England? *European Early Childhood Education Research Journal* 21 (3), 380–391.

Espinosa, L. (2012) Promoting early language and literacy development of English language learners: A research-based agenda? *Concept Paper*, United States. See http://earlysuccess.org/sites/default/files/Espinosa%20research%20Based%20Agenda.pdf (Retrieved 29 October 2018).

Espinosa, L.M. (2015) Challenges and benefits of early bilingualism in the United States' context. *Global Education Review* 2 (1), 14–31.

Ewing, A.R. and Taylor, A.R. (2009) The role of child gender and ethnicity in teacher-child relationship quality and children's behavioral adjustment in preschool. *Early Childhood Research Quarterly* 24 (1), 92–105.

Genesee, F. (2015) Myths about early childhood bilingualism. *Canadian Psychology/Psychologie Canadienne* 56 (1), 6–15.

Gerrity, R. (2003) Responding to cultural and linguistic diversity of refugee babies, toddlers and their families. *The First Years: Nga Tau Tautahi, New Zealand Journal of Infants and Toddler Education* 5 (2), 33–37.

Giambo, D.A. and Szecsi, T. (2015) Promoting and maintaining bilingualism and biliteracy: Cognitive and biliteracy benefits and strategies for monolingual teachers. *The Open Communication Journal* 9 (1), 56–60.

Goldenberg, C., Hick, J. and Lit, I. (2013) Dual language learners: Effective instruction in early childhood. *American Educator* 3 (2), 26–29.

Graves, S.L. and Howes, C. (2011) Ethnic differences in social-emotional development in preschool: The impact of teacher child relationships and classroom quality. *School Psychology Quarterly* 26 (3), 202–214.

Gutiérrez-Clellen, Cereijido, G.S. and Leone, A.E. (2009) Codeswitching in bilingual children with specific language impairment. *International Journal of bilingualism*, 13 (1), 91–109.

Han, W.J. (2012) Bilingualism and academic achievement. *Child Development* 83 (1), 300–321.

Harvey, N. and Myint, H.H. (2014) Our language is food: Can children feed on home languages to thrive, belong and achieve in early childhood education and care? *Australasian Journal of Early Childhood* 39 (2), 42–50.

Howes, C. and Shivers, E. (2006) New child-caregiver attachment relationships: Entering child-care when the caregiver is not an ethnic match. *Social Development* 15 (4), 547–590.

Hu, J., Torr, J. and Whiteman, P. (2014) 'Parents don't want their children to speak their home language': How do educators negotiate partnerships with Chinese parents regarding their children's use of home language and English in early childhood settings? *Early Years: An International Research Journal* 34 (4), 255–270.

Jerome, E.M., Hamre, B.K. and Pianta, R.C. (2009) Teacher-child relationships from kindergarten to sixth grade: Early childhood predictors of teacher-perceived conflict and closeness. *Social Development* 18 (4), 915–945.

Lee, J.S. and Oxelson, E. (2006) 'It's not my job': K-12 teacher attitudes toward students' heritage language maintenance. *Bilingual Research Journal* 30 (2), 453–477.

O'Leary, Z. (2014) *The Essential Guide to Doing Your Research Project* (2nd edn). London: SAGE Publications.

Pratt, C. and Grieve, R. (1984) The development of metalinguistic awareness: An introduction. Metalinguistic awareness in children: Theory, research, and implications. In W.E. Tunmer, C. Pratt and M.L. Herriman (eds) *Metalinguistic Awareness in Children* (pp. 2–11). Berlin, Germany: Springer-Velag.

Paradis, J., Genesee, F. and Crago, M.B. (2010) *Dual Language Development and Disorders*. Baltimore, MD: Paul H. Brookes Publishing Company.

Pianta, R.C. (2001) *Student-Teacher Relationship Scale: Professional Manual*. Lutz, FL: Psychological Assessments Resources Inc.

Pianta, R.C. and Stuhlman, M.W. (2004) Teacher-child relationships and children's success in the first years of school. *School Psychology Review* 33 (3), 444–458.

Pianta, R.C., Steinberg, M.S. and Rollins, K.B. (2009) The first two years of school: Teacher child relationships and deflections in children's classroom adjustment. *Development and Psychopathology* 7, 295–312.

Rich, S. and Davis, L. (2007) Insights into the strategic ways in which two bilingual children in the early years seek to negotiate the competing demands on their identity in their home and school worlds. *International Journal of Early Years Education* 15 (1), 35–47.

Purcell, J., Lee, M. and Biffin, J. (2007) Supporting bilingual children in early childhood. *Learning Link News* 1 (2), 1–5.

Quick, J. and Hall, S. (2015) Part two: Qualitative research. *Journal of Perioperative Practice* 25 (7), 129–133.

Rockel, J. (2009) A pedagogy of care: Moving beyond the margins of managing work and minding babies. *Australian Journal of Early Childhood* 34 (3), 1–8.

Rutledge, S. (2010) Teachers' perspectives on literacy assessment and instruction with language-minority students. *Elementary School Journal* 96 (3), 311.

Sandhofer, C. and Uchikoshi, Y. (2013) Cognitive consequences of Dual Language Learning: Cognitive function, language and literacy, science and mathematics, and social-emotional development. In F. Ong and J. McLean (eds) *California's Best Practices for Young Dual Language Learners: Research Overview Papers* (pp. 51–89). Sacramento, CA: California Department of Education (CDE). See http://www.cde.ca.gov/sp/cd/ce/documents/dllresearchpapers.pdf (accessed 14 April 2016).

Shin, S.J. (2010) Teaching English language learners: Recommendations for early childhood educators. *Dimensions of Early Childhood* 38 (2), 13–21.

Sylva, K., Melhuish, E., Sammons, P., Siraj, I. and Taggart, B., with Smees, R., Tóth, K., Welcomme, W., and Hollingworth, K. (2014) Students' educational and developmental outcomes at age 16: Effective Pre-school, Primary and Secondary Education (EPPSE 3-16) Project Research Report. University of Oxford, Birkbeck, University of London, Institute of Education, University of London. London: Department for Education.

Tabors, P. (2008) *One Child, Two Languages: A Guide for Early Childhood Educators of Children Learning English as a Second Language* (2nd edn). Baltimore, MD: Paul H. Brookes.

Turnbull, M., Hart, D. and Lapkin, S. (2003) Grade 6 French immersion students' performance on large-scale reading, writing and mathematics tests: Building explanations. *Alberta Journal of Educational Research* 49 (1), 6–23.

Verdon, S., McLeod, S. and Winsler, A. (2014) Language maintenance and loss in a population study of young Australian children. *Early Childhood Research Quarterly* 29 (2), 168–181.

13 What Educators of Young Dual Language Immersion Students Learn from a Bilingual Approach to Assessment

Katherine M. Griffin, Alison L. Bailey and Rashmita S. Mistry

Introduction

Unprecedented immigration growth as well as increasingly global economic conditions that demand multilingualism and multiculturalism have fuelled recent interest in dual language immersion (DLI) programmes in the USA (Bailey & Osipova, 2016). DLI is a form of bilingual education that typically involves the dominant societal language (e.g. English) and a partner language (e.g. Spanish, Mandarin) with roughly equal numbers of proficient speakers in each language serving as linguistic models for one another. Academic content (e.g. mathematics) is taught using the two languages to varying degrees (Hopewell & Escamilla, 2014; Li *et al.*, 2016; Lindholm-Leary & Genesee, 2014). The increased demand for and availability of this programming, most commonly offered from preschool through the primary school years (ages 4 to 11), signals a shift from viewing linguistic and cultural diversity as a challenge to be overcome to appreciating more than one language and multicultural exposure as assets to be encouraged and fostered in young students (Bailey & Osipova, 2016).

For US teachers, this means developing pedagogical practices that can support linguistic minority students learning English as an additional language, as well as proficient English and initial English-only students learning a programme partner language as their additional language. Teachers must be able to foster broad multicultural understanding that is also frequently a goal of DLI programming. Furthermore, students are expected to stay on par with their peers in English medium instruction (EMI) in terms of academic achievement.

Despite the rapid increase of such programmes in the US, there is little consensus regarding curriculum specifications (e.g. proportion of time spent learning academic content in the two languages; Mehisto & Genesee, 2015). Further, few comprehensive, longitudinal studies assessing growth in young students' development across a range of linguistic, academic, cognitive cultural and socioemotional domains are available to inform teachers' professional development in ways that may maximize the positive impact of dual language learning. Recently, the Migration Policy Institute concluded 'Together, the lack of longitudinal research and dearth of multilingual assessments complicate efforts to ensure that early childhood education programs are adequately preparing students' (McNamara, 2016).

The classroom research described in this chapter addresses these limitations and can inform continuing education of in-service teachers and those designing professional learning experiences. Specifically, we focus on how teachers in a DLI programme engaged in a professional learning community (PLC) model of professional development, and how they use bilingual assessment data collected as part of a longitudinal evaluation of the programme to inform their classroom practice. In doing so, we share examples of classroom practice that can benefit professionals in a variety of DLI settings as well as discuss how these data can inform professional development more broadly.

The Dual Language Immersion Context

Research suggests that in terms of academic achievement, students in DLI programmes usually perform as well as or better than peers in monolingual classrooms (Cobb *et al.*, 2009; for a review see Lindholm-Leary & Genesee, 2014). Bilingual students generally demonstrate greater levels of cognitive control (i.e. inhibiting distractions, holding information in working memory and adjusting to changes in the environment) (e.g. Adesope *et al.*, 2010) as well as metalinguistic awareness (i.e. can reflect on and manipulate different features of language) (e.g. Bialystok & Barac, 2012). However, the education field has paid less attention to a broader set of outcomes such as students' own perceptions of their language and academic competencies, and their multicultural understanding including identity, language attitudes, and intergroup relations. Yet we know from prior research that these factors are important personal and prosocial developments in young students (e.g. Eccles, 1999; Genesee, 2008; Imbens-Bailey, 1996; Quintana, 2008; Ruble *et al.*, 2004).

Furthermore, DLI students' language arts and other academic achievements have traditionally only been assessed in English (Bailey *et al.*, 2008). This vastly limits our understanding of students' linguistic and academic development. Escamilla and colleagues note from their perspectives as writing researchers:

> Much can be lost and misunderstood when English-only assessment practices are applied to the writing development of emerging bilingual students.... Biliteracy writing assessment for those children who are fortunate enough to attend schools that are actively developing their bilingual advantage illustrates that much can be gained. (Escamilla *et al.*, 2017: 14)

More broadly, an expanded definition of success in a DLI environment – one that includes assessments of children's English and Spanish language arts, their performances in academic content areas in both languages, and cognitive cultural and socioemotional developments – provides a more contextualized understanding of the impact of such programmes on young students.

The larger project from which the data discussed in this chapter are drawn, used this broader definition of programme progress in its assessment of a DLI (English–Spanish) programme. Specifically, we conducted longitudinal assessments of students' academic, linguistic, cognitive, and social emotional development across a four-year period (i.e. kindergarten to third grade) for a cohort of students in the DLI programme and their peers at matched grades in EMI classrooms at the same school. The project used a researcher–practitioner collaboration model to inform all stages of research from design and data collection to interpretation of results. Specifically, we used a professional learning community (PLC) model of professional development to focus on teacher practices in assessment and instruction. While models vary, the basic structure of a PLC is that educators gather to reflect on daily practice in order to improve student outcomes (Vescio *et al.*, 2008). PLCs emphasize educators having a shared vision of learning (Blankenship & Ruona, 2007), as well as the need for educator collaboration and discussion of student learning (DuFour, 2004; Vescio *et al.*, 2008). For the current project, the research team met with members of the DLI teaching team and administrators to initially observe their classrooms, on a monthly basis in the first year, to develop new measures of social and cognitive development, and thereafter in a semi-annual PLC conference to discuss student progress based on the empirical evidence gathered from annual student assessments, as described below. The purpose of these meetings was two-fold: they served as both a space for teachers and administrators to reflect on and use evaluation data of their programme and for the research team to better understand DLI student development and teacher practice through collaboration and discussion with teachers.

Specifically, this chapter elaborates on four key insights for in-service teachers derived from PLC meetings and teacher interviews: (1) ways that standardized assessments of language arts and other academic achievement can complement teacher classroom assessment practices; (2) the importance of comprehensively monitoring DLI student development; (3) how data generated by bilingual assessments can be used by teachers for instructional discussion making; and (4) the merits of assessing students bilingually for DLI accountability. These insights are illustrated using teacher reactions to data of student progress presented and discussed as part of regularly organized cross-grade PLC meetings, and individual teacher surveys and interviews.

Overview of School Setting and PLC Research Partnership

The research-school collaboration for this project was conducted with a university-affiliated elementary school (students 4 to 12 years) in southern California. The school has an explicit commitment to diversity across race, ethnicity, gender, language, socioeconomic status (SES), and family structure. The DLI programme has existed as an educational strand within the school for more than 25 years, with about a third of students at each grade (approximately 25 students) participating in DLI and the remainder in EMI classrooms. The DLI programme currently reflects a model that teaches predominantly in Spanish (i.e. 90% Spanish–10% English instructional focus) in the early grades (pre-kindergarten–kindergarten) to provide sufficient language exposure in an otherwise English dominant society, with gradual increase of English to 50% by the fifth grade.

Participants

Teachers

In this chapter, we draw on teacher discussion during the PLC meetings, supplemented by follow-up surveys and interviews conducted with five DLI teachers during the spring of the cohort's third-grade year. All five were female and chosen because they had taught the students at one of each of the grades the cohort had completed or were currently the cohort's teachers (see Table 13.1).

Students

Student-level data comprise the longitudinal subsample ($n = 48$) of the larger project cohort ($n = 64$) in the Spanish–English DLI programme and peers in EMI classrooms kindergarten to third grade. The longitudinal subsample includes all students for whom we have complete data. Remaining students either left or joined the cohort at different time points. Several students were emergent bilinguals at school entry in English and another language (most often Spanish). Remaining students were monolingual English speakers (see Table 13.2).

Table 13.1 Teacher background information

Teacher	Grade of cohort when taught	Years in DLI education	Teaching philosophy
Elizabella	Kindergarten	11	Elizabella guides learning towards self-discovery so that students are able to construct their own understanding through meaningful experiences. She strives to create a warm and stimulating learning environment that engages students and motivates them to become excited about learning.
Sofia	1st & 2nd	12	Sofia takes time to understand each student's background, strengths and areas that need targeted support for further growth. Teaching the student as a whole, for who they are and what they bring into the classroom including language, is what attracted Sofia to the school.
Victoria	3rd*	4	Victoria is able to integrate her love of languages, her bicultural heritage, her arts-integration background, and her belief in learning through doing and exploring.
Marisol	3rd*	6	Marisol is a strong believer in the power of dual language education to empower, ignite, and inspire future leaders and believes that all children are writers, engineers, artists, scientists, and so much more.
Kelly	3rd*	9	Kelly believes that all children have the ability to learn and deserve teachers who have high expectations for them. She says her students trust themselves as learners because they know they are working in a risk-free environment where differences are celebrated.

*Teacher teaches in a third/fourth grade combination classroom but the cohort has only completed third grade to date.

Table 13.2 Student demographic information: Longitudinal subsample at third grade

		DLI	EMI
Number		16	32
Gender		50% Female	59% Female
Race			
	European American	25%	46.9%
	Latinx*	37.5%	3.1%
	Multiracial Latinx	18.8%	12.5%
	Asian American	6.3%	15.6%
	Multiracial non-Latinx	12.5%	15.6%
	African American	0	3.1%
	Missing	0	3.1%
Household income	Median income	US $100,000–$199,999	US $200,000–$349,999
Language	English dominant	37.5%	87.5%
	Balanced Spanish–English Bilingual	62.5%	12.5%

*The term Latinx is a gender-neutral reference to students of Latino/a (Hispanic) origin.

Methods

Bilingual approach to assessment

For this project, we adopted a bilingual approach to assessment in two ways: (1) we included direct assessment at kindergarten to third grade of DLI and EMI students' academic achievement in reading, writing and mathematics, conducted in English, using the Woodcock Johnson-III (WJ-III; Woodcock *et al.*, 2008), a widely used norm-referenced standardized test of achievement and for DLI students, also using the Spanish version of this assessment, the Batería-III (Woodcock *et al.*, 2007); and (2) for all additional measures, Spanish trans-adaptations (i.e. translated and culturally adapted) were developed and DLI students were given the option to complete tasks in either English or Spanish with a bilingual research assistant, and permitted to codeswitch between English and Spanish, although few students opted to be assessed in Spanish on these measures. Table 13.3 shows the schedule of assessments. Assessments were selected because they measure bilingual language arts and mathematics achievement as well as student perceptions and attitude towards their language acquisition and academic competencies. At kindergarten and first grade, students' perceptions of academic and cognitive competencies, attitudes towards school, teacher–child relations, peer acceptance, and perceived English and Spanish language abilities of hypothetical target children of different races and ethnicities were assessed. The assessment was carried out using author-approved modifications of the Pictorial Scale of Perceived Competence and Social Acceptance for Young Children measure (Harter & Pike, 1984), and supplemented by the Feelings About School measure (Valeski & Stipek, 2001). While not the primary focus of this chapter owing to space constraints, we also assessed students' racial/ethnic intergroup attitudes, using an adapted version of the Attitudes Toward Immigrants measure (Brown, 2011), and language attitudes based on story stem completions (Bailey & Zwass, 2015). Where relevant to the teachers' discussions of bilingual assessment and instructional practices, we also report these data.

Table 13.3 Schedule of assessments reported in this chapter

	Kinder	1st Grade	2nd Grade	3rd Grade
Perceived competence & social acceptance	✓	✓		
Feelings about school	✓	✓		
Attitudes towards immigrants	✓	✓		✓
Language attitudes	✓	✓		✓
Woodcock Johnson-III (English)	✓	✓	✓	✓
Batería-III (Spanish)*	✓	✓	✓	✓

*The Batería-III collected with DLI students only.

Teacher follow-up questionnaire and interviews

At the conclusion of the PLC meeting during which researchers presented data on the kindergarten to third grade academic trajectories based on the WJ-III and the Batería-III, teachers were asked to complete a brief, follow-up online questionnaire regarding their interpretation and reflections of how the findings did or might inform their teaching practices. Questions were mostly open-ended and focused on teacher practice and assessment (e.g. 'In what ways can the information presented help you with your classroom practice?', 'What might you do differently after learning about these findings?', 'In what ways do the results reinforce what you already do?'). Guided by the selected DLI teachers' responses to the questionnaire, interviews were semi-structured and covered teachers' reactions to linguistic and academic achievement, and student perceived competence data, as well as their current assessment and data use practices. Reviewing notes and transcriptions of these data, we identified themes related to bilingual assessment practices.

Findings

Four key insights emerged from the teacher questionnaires and interviews regarding the evidence-based assessment data and how teachers envisioned utilizing the data in their bilingual classroom environments: (1) ways that standardized assessments of academic achievement complement teacher classroom assessment practices; (2) importance of comprehensively monitoring student development; (3) how data generated by bilingual assessments can be used in instruction; and (4) merits of assessing students bilingually for accountability. We review each from the teachers' perspectives as well as make connections to the student data.

Standardized assessments complement classroom assessment practices

One major strength teachers identified was the project's use of norm-referenced, standardized assessments (i.e. WJ-III and Batería-III) administered longitudinally from kindergarten onwards, independent of the school's own annual achievement assessments that are only administered from third grade onwards. One benefit of computing longitudinal brief achievement test scores based on the specific subtests from the WJ-III and the Batería-III (i.e. letter word identification, word attack, spelling, editing, applied problems and quantitative concepts), is that we could compare student performance across years and to the published performances of native English and Spanish speakers with whom the tests are normed (Woodcock *et al.*, 2007, 2008). In this section, we discuss the day-to-day classroom assessment approaches taken by teachers and how individual student performance on annual administration of the WJ-III and Batería-III complement these practices.

Writing

DLI teachers across all grade levels used formative assessment techniques as a means of monitoring students' writing development in both languages, including one-on-one conferencing and quick writing assessments. Teachers also emphasized balancing critical feedback with encouragement. Sofia described balancing a focus on writing conventions with developing the content of students' stories and their love of writing in both English and Spanish.

> We do cover conventions ... It's just how we go about in assessing it. So what we pay a lot of attention to [first] is the content – what students are writing – because that's really where we see: Can they sequence? Is there a flow to their stories? ... Once we start going into the phases where they're revising, or when they're editing and revising, that's more where we sit with them and we do begin [to] look at conventions. We want to make sure that we continue to encourage and that we continue to build on this love for writing. Which can sometimes be challenging ... especially when students are being asked to write in a language that they may not feel as successful [in].

While teachers reported often relying on formative writing assessment, it was formal, summative classroom assessment that proved important to guiding the approach to spelling pedagogy by the teachers of the third/fourth grade combination classroom. Teachers had been concerned to see student writing on the WJ-III and Batería-III as amongst their students' weaker achievement results and felt this stemmed from them typically paying less attention to writing conventions (Table 13.4). Similarly, after noticing students' struggling on a spelling assessment in *Palabras a Su Paso [Words their Way]* (Bear *et al.*, 2013), Marisol explained,

> We reassessed, and then we actually decided just to be a little bit more strategic ... . [In small groups] we spent about 20 minutes talking about the words, talking about the spelling patterns, and even doing some whiteboard mini-assessments on the spot talking about the spelling pattern that we were focusing on ... to really see that the spelling patterns that they're learning about, that they're actually using it.

In these ways, summative assessment was critical for teachers' practice in the classroom and worked to complement their formative approaches to assessing writing.

While Marisol worried about children's writing in Spanish, the Batería-III results suggest that students' writing scores were close to being on par with their native Spanish-speaking peers, with whom the test is normed. DLI students' Spanish writing scores were within one standard deviation of the test average across grade levels although not as high as their English writing skills at Kindergarten (see Table 13.4).

Table 13.4 DLI students' Woodcock Johnson-III and Batería-III scores

	Grade	Woodcock Johnson-III mean (SD)	Batería-III mean (SD)	t-test of significance
Brief achievement	Kinder	116.31 (14.80)	102.25 (13.95)	$t = 2.61$ (15), $p = 0.020$*
	1st	117.00 (15.08)	108.73 (16.68)	$t = 1.36$ (14), $p = 0.197$
	2nd	111.44 (16.68)	107.75 (10.51)	$t = 1.17$ (15), $p = 0.261$
	3rd	108.00 (12.63)	112.94 (8.89)	$t = -2.00$ (15), $p = 0.064$
Reading	Kinder	114.38 (11.96)	99.94 (10.76)	$t = 4.65$ (15), $p < 0.001$*
	1st	119.07 (10.84)	107.47(12.42)	$t = 3.03$ (14), $p = 0.009$*
	2nd	113.38 (9.19)	108.69 (11.53)	$t = 2.25$ (15), $p = 0.040$*
	3rd	111.44 (7.87)	114.50 (11.59)	$t = -1.49$ (15), $p = 0.158$
Writing	Kinder	112.25 (13.98)	100.44 (11.36)	$t = 3.09$ (15), $p = 0.008$*
	1st	102.67 (17.23)	99.93 (17.58)	$t = 0.46$ (14), $p = 0.654$
	2nd	105.13 (14.22)	95.88 (9.46)	$t = 2.11$ (15), $p = 0.053$
	3rd	99.88 (18.13)	96.00 (11.36)	$t = 0.93$ (15), $p = 0.370$
Mathematics	Kinder	116.88 (13.46)	85.44(21.38)	$t = 4.09$ (15), $p = 0.001$*
	1st	112.20 (12.73)	91.60 (17.14)	$t = 4.06$ (14), $p = 0.001$*
	2nd	110.94 (14.77)	99.44 (11.75)	$t = 2.88$ (15), $p = 0.011$*
	3rd	105.06 (10.45)	99.44 (10.42)	$t = 3.55$ (15), $p = 0.003$*

Note: Test mean = 100 (SD = 15).
*Statistically significant difference between Woodcock Johnson-III & Batería-III scores,
  $p < 0.05$.

Reading

Our results also indicated that DLI students' reading abilities were on par with monolingual Spanish speakers, as they performed at or above the Batería-III average (Table 13.4). In the classroom, teachers once again reported using formative and summative approaches. In kindergarten, Elizabella indicated that she monitors her students' reading abilities by helping them identify their 'just right books' – which Elizabella describes as 'books that are at the child's independent reading level, [that] they can read with ease to improve fluency, practice reading strategies, and build their confidence as readers'. In her classroom library, Elizabella has different book collections sorted into colour-coded baskets, from which students select their own books to read daily. Elizabella and the teaching assistants read these 'just right books' with children one-on-one periodically throughout the year. In these informal assessments, Elizabella and the team take notes to monitor individual progress and to inform lesson plans. Based on monitoring children's reading in informal settings, Elizabella has a clear sense of how her students are progressing before summative classroom assessments are given towards the middle and end of the year.

Kelly and Marisol described their use of Teachers College Reader's Workshop model for teaching and assessment (Reading and Writing Project, n.d.). The teachers diligently translated and prepared Reader's Workshop lessons in Spanish, and also developed an assessment tool that mirrored their pedagogical approach. Kelly explained how the third/fourth grade teachers worked to develop a much-needed measure of Spanish reading ability that did not rely on student's writing abilities as the existing commercial measures have done. 'And if you're assessing a language learner and then all of a sudden you add the layer of writing, you don't get a true statement of what they really know.' All three third grade teachers expressed the desire for more teaching and assessment materials in both English and Spanish aligned to their pedagogical approach (e.g. Reader's and Writer's Workshop) – a perennial problem with DLI programming in the USA as students move into the higher grades (Bailey & Osipova, 2016).

Mathematics

Teachers were particularly interested in assessing student performance in mathematics, as the programme had recently switched from teaching mathematics in English four out of five days to teaching it in Spanish four out of five days instead. The results indicated that although students' mathematics performance in Spanish was lower than in English, overall performance in both languages was within one standard deviation of the test norms (Table 13.4).

In the classroom, teachers monitored student's mathematics progress through both formative and summative assessment, as Marisol describes in her lesson:

> A typical math block would ... [start] with a warm up. Usually it's a lot of mental math but sharing what went on in our heads ... . We try to ... make their thinking visible through our warm ups. And then we will present a problem. It might have like a teaching point or a focus, so like 'We're focusing today on being precise or checking your answers' ... And then they go off to problem solve, usually it's with partners, and then at the end of class we have about 15 minutes where we come together and we share some of their strategies ... we compare each other's strategies. Then we try to come up with like these big ideas ... or conjectures as we're solving problems.

During these periods, Marisol takes notes on student progress and shares them with the teaching team on a shared document website. She supplemented this formative practice with pre-and post-assessments, which the teachers developed to match student needs.

Importance of comprehensive monitoring of student progress

A second key insight from the teacher data was the importance of assessing student progress across a wide array of domains. In this section, we discuss teachers' strategic use of bilingual partnerships and the cultivation of a bilingual identity to support children's academic and linguistic confidence.

Fostering bilingual partners, friendships, and collaborations

Teachers in the DLI programme valued peer collaboration as an important component of their classroom practice and supported larger linguistic and academic goals. Specifically, teachers at every grade reported using bilingual partnerships (e.g. children at different Spanish or English proficiency levels working together) to foster language development and provide support across academic and social domains.

For example, Sofia, a first/second combination grade teacher, reported that bilingual partnerships were critical for students' understanding of materials. In first/second grade, partnerships were formally arranged, with students being surveyed several times throughout the year to determine Spanish or English dominance. Beyond the linguistic and academic benefits, Sofia explained how bilingual partnerships allowed students to learn more about peers' cultural backgrounds and heritage languages.

> They will change and they do change even the way they say certain words. So they would say 'Oh, la palabra es ellos' … But then they would say, 'Oh but Jesse because your family is from Argentina, you would say 'aye-jos'.

Through partnerships, the teachers brought together linguistic, academic, and social development to promote and support children's holistic growth within the DLI context. These practices align with our research findings. Results with the larger cohort showed by first grade, DLI students reported greater levels of peer acceptance (e.g. I have friends to play with; I am invited to sit with others at snack; rated 1–5) ($M = 3.45$, SD $= 0.47$) than did EMI students ($M = 3.0$, SD $= 0.72$), $t = -2.72$, $p < 0.05$; Bryne et al., 2013). Furthermore, students' attitudes towards the Spanish and English languages and speakers as revealed by completion of story stems (e.g. giving the resolution to a story about a language barrier between two students) begin as neutral in kindergarten and first grade but become more positive by third grade. Results with the larger cohort also suggest that by first grade proportionally more DLI students (77%) rationalized story characters' language use with integrative motivations (e.g. to belong to a group), whereas the majority of EMI students (54%) provided instrumental motivations (e.g. to complete a task), $\chi^2(2, n = 52) = 6.35, p < 0.04$ (Bailey et al., 2015).

Bilingual identity development in the DLI classroom

A consistent theme across the years was an emphasis on celebrating and discussing the multiple identities that students brought to and developed within their DLI classrooms. Teachers discussed the importance of children's bilingual, racial/ethnic, *and* academic identities (i.e. as writers and readers) for students' academic success. They regularly used a variety of practices to promote their students' bilingual identity development. For example, Elizabella purposely used the 11 different languages that students knew in her kindergarten class in the daily 'good morning' song. In her first/second grade combination class, Sofia engaged in read-alouds early in the school year with multilingual and language learner characters from culturally diverse backgrounds. In third/fourth grade, Victoria described reading Alma Flor Ada's poem, *Bilingüe*, a poem in Spanish and English about being bilingual, and discussing it with students early in the year to help them think about their own bilingual identities.

All three of the third/fourth grade DLI teachers emphasized the importance of promoting a bilingual identity among their students as a means of enhancing their academic confidence and in turn, their achievement. Victoria and Kelly believed that not all their students started the year identifying as bilingual but that this motivated teachers, as Victoria explains, to focus on bilingual identity development.

> If your parents speak English at home and you're in this programme you don't really think of yourself as bilingual. You think of yourself as 'I speak English. I'm American. I just happen to be in this school where I study in Spanish.' And I think what we really want to foster is this … . It's the shift. 'Well actually you're bilingual. You don't just happen to be in a school where you're being taught in Spanish. That's true but a result of that … you are no longer monolingual. You are bilingual.'

Teachers' efforts to expand their students' notions of who can be considered bilingual do appear to be warranted. Student bias towards equating language abilities with race or ethnicity was reflected in the measures of student social development. Indeed, both the DLI and EMI students' ratings (on a scale of 1–5) of various language proficiencies of racially and ethnically diverse hypothetical target children (TC) indicated that they associated language with particular races and ethnicities. Specifically, by first grade we found that students in both programmes rated the Chinese American TC as significantly less proficient in English ($M = 3.35$, $SD = 1.06$) than either the African American ($M = 4.30$, $SD = 1.09$) or European American TC ($M = 4.61$, $SD = 0.75$), and rated the Mexican American TC as significantly less proficient in English ($M = 3.82$, $SD = 1.13$) than the European American TC ($p < 0.05$) (overall Wilks's lambda $= 14.200$ (3.41), $p < 0.001$, using mixed factorial ANOVA). These distinctions continued into third grade with students similarly rating the Chinese American and Mexican American TC as less proficient in English than either the African American ($p < 0.05$) or European American TC ($p < 0.05$) (overall Wilks's lambda = 18.440 (3.43), $p < 0.001$). Even more pronounced were the associations between language proficiency and race/ethnicity for the Spanish and Chinese languages: students rated the Mexican American TC as significantly more proficient in Spanish and the Chinese American TC as more proficient in Chinese than any other TC ($p < 0.05$). This tendency to believe that language ability was related to race/ethnicity began as soon as kindergarten (overall Wilks's lambda = 8.708 (3.43), $p < 0.001$ and Wilks's lambda = 20.034 (3.43) $p < 0.001$ for Spanish and Chinese proficiency, respectively) and continued at every grade for students regardless of programme (overall Wilks's lambda = 19.464 (3.42), $p < 0.001$ and Wilks's lambda = 46.769 (3.42), $p < 0.001$ for Spanish and Chinese proficiency, respectively at first grade, and overall Wilks's lambda = 101.45 (3.43), $p < 0.001$ and Wilks's lambda = 172.620 (3.43), $p < 0.001$ for Spanish and Chinese proficiency, respectively at third grade).

Building linguistic confidence

Results from our measure of perceived competence further suggested that students were confident in their own linguistic abilities, with DLI students rating themselves as more competent in Spanish than their EMI peers in kindergarten (DLI: $M = 3.30$, SD = 0.61); EMI: $M = 2.51$, SD = 0.81), $t = -4.75$, $p < 0.001$) and first grade (DLI: $M = 3.68$, SD = 0.31); EMI: $M = 2.68$, SD = 0.73), $t = -7.42$, $p < 0.001$). These findings were supported by teachers' accounts. Sofia, for example, reflected on how she sees this shift taking place over the two years students spend in her first/second grade classroom.

> I do see [a shift in confidence] especially with our second years … what I notice with my second years is that they feel very comfortable going between both languages. That they feel comfortable answering in Spanish but also feel just as comfortable to answer in English.

The increase in linguistic confidence that Sofia reports was reiterated by all teachers and attributed both to students' developing relationships with peers who have greater proficiency in Spanish, and with their own developing bilingual identities, emphasizing the importance of paying attention to such social aspects of development within DLI classrooms.

How bilingual academic assessment informed instruction

We asked teachers to consider how they do or might use the bilingual academic achievement test data (i.e. the WJ-III and Batería-III) presented at the PLC meetings to inform their own practices. In a third key insight, teachers focused on issues of interpretation for their instructional decision making.

As shown in Table 13.4, in kindergarten, DLI students' brief achievement test scores were higher in English than in Spanish. By first grade, DLI students' English and Spanish brief achievement test scores were at or above the test norms, suggesting good mastery of both languages. Teachers identified these results as important when considering what practices they could adopt in the future, as outlined below.

Language of instruction

There is debate in the education community about the appropriate amount of time to spend in each of the partner languages of a DLI programme (Mehisto & Genesee, 2015). Teachers spoke about this tension and how the bilingual student achievement data reinforced their belief that a 90% Spanish–10% English model did not limit students' English language abilities in the early grades and used the data as a justification for increasing Spanish instruction time in the upper grades where it has traditionally been pared back to 50%. Kelly reported using the bilingual students' third grade performance data on the brief achievement tests of the WJ-III and Batería-III to advocate for increased Spanish instruction during a fifth/sixth grade teacher team meeting.

> 'Okay you're asking us to really bring this programme all the way to [the 5th/6th grade], and reduce the instructional minutes in English and do them more in Spanish, why should we do that?' And 'Where is your proof?' So showing this [the academic achievement data in both languages] was … like 'Look, it's not that we're telling you this has worked somewhere else. This has actually been done at your school and it actually proves that whatever we're doing – and there's a lot to do still – but it proves a lot of what we're doing – it's working'.

Domain-specific achievement

Teachers also took away domain-specific lessons about where their students were excelling and where they needed more support. As Marisol explains, 'This information will definitely inform us. We need to continue to foster their skills in reading since this is a strength. Also, we need to further focus on writing.' Sofia thought about the data in terms of how it soothed her own worry, especially about mathematics.

> I often wonder how much language impacts their ability to demonstrate conceptual understanding [in mathematics], especially when given an assessment where [neither] scaffolding nor front loading is available. The results were helpful in seeing that.

Bilingual academic assessment therefore played an important role in supporting teacher practice and giving them confidence in the practices that they were implementing in the classroom. As DLI educators, teachers were constantly looking to adapt their pedagogical approaches to best serve children in both languages, and bilingual assessment data helped teachers in this regard.

The merits of assessing students bilingually for DLI accountability

A final key insight addresses the common concern expressed by teachers that stakeholders worry students in DLI programming do not perform on par academically with EMI peers. As shown in Table 13.5, our project findings suggest that DLI students' language arts and mathematics performances in English across time were comparable to their peers in EMI. One DLI teacher reacted to this saying, 'I feel this information not only verifies the work that we are doing [at the school] but also helps dissipate the misconceptions that dual programmes keep students behind in reading, writing, and math.' We review how the bilingual assessment data helped teachers' address the concerns of two key stakeholders – parents and the larger school community.

Parents

Many teachers reflected on how the bilingual assessment data speak to concerns that parents have about the DLI programme. Marisol explained that as their children get older parents tend to worry more.

> There's a feeling from parents once they get to [the 5th/6th grades] that … it's all going to change. They're getting ready for middle school. So at the end of 4th grade, … parents [ask] 'Are they where they need to be or do we need to exit them out? Do they need more English?'

Table 13.5 DLI compared with EMI students' Woodcock Johnson-III scores

	Grade	DLI mean (SD)	EMI mean (SD)	t-test of significance
Brief achievement	Kinder	116.31 (14.80)	114.88 (11.09)	$t = -0.38\ (46), p = 0.707$
	1st	117.00 (15.08)	115.44 (12.95)	$t = -0.37\ (45), p = 0.716$
	2nd	111.44 (16.68)	109.75 (13.00)	$t = -0.39\ (46), p = 0.698$
	3rd	108.00 (12.63)	109.07 (11.74)	$t = 0.28\ (45), p = 0.775$
Reading	Kinder	114.38 (11.96)	113.72 (9.52)	$t = -0.21\ (46), p = 0.837$
	1st	119.07 (10.84)	116.94 (11.74)	$t = -0.59\ (45), p = 0.556$
	2nd	113.38 (9.19)	108.81 (10.45)	$t = -1.48\ (46), p = 0.145$
	3rd	111.44 (7.87)	108.94 (9.36)	$t = -0.91\ (45), p = 0.366$
Writing	Kinder	112.25 (13.98)	110.63 (9.26)	$t = -0.48\ (46), p = 0.633$
	1st	102.67 (17.23)	106.22 (13.19)	$t = 0.78\ (45), p = 0.440$
	2nd	105.13 (14.22)	105.22 (9.66)	$t = 0.03\ (46), p = 0.979$
	3rd	99.88 (18.13)	107.23 (14.97)	$t = 1.48\ (45), p = 0.145$
Mathematics	Kinder	116.88 (13.46)	113.84 (13.51)	$t = -0.73\ (46), p = 0.467$
	1st	112.20 (12.73)	113.28 (11.02)	$t = 0.30\ (45), p = 0.767$
	2nd	110.94 (14.77)	110.28 (15.40)	$t = -0.14\ (46), p = 0.888$
	3rd	105.06 (10.45)	108.26 (11.36)	$t = 0.94\ (45), p = 0.353$

Specifically, Marisol thinks the bilingual assessment data are important because it helps parents trust the often protracted *process* of becoming bilingual.

> To think about a child being completely bilingual and biliterate, ...
> takes many years. So one of the hardest things is to tell parents, like
> wait it out ... and trust us in the process. So that's kind of what I
> was thinking in using this data, could really back up that notion ...
> Although they might be getting a lot or the majority of their instruction
> in Spanish they're doing fine in English so I think it's about putting par-
> ents at ease.

The larger school community

Beyond parental concerns, teachers spoke about the importance of the data for demonstrating success to their colleagues throughout the school. Victoria believed other teachers often thought of the DLI programme as experimental and not academically rigorous.

> There needs to be 100% buy-in from the teachers as a whole school ... .
> And I think there have been, a lot of varying views on the programme
> because it's been through ups and downs and so to have solid hard core
> data, it's for teachers here at the school.

Similarly, Marisol believed some of her EMI colleagues may be unfamiliar with the benefits of bilingualism and these type of data could be important in showing them such benefits.

> It proves to our colleagues that what we are doing works ... I went
> through a [bilingual teacher education] programme and I've been in bilin-
> gual classrooms since my freshman year in college – it's just who I am,
> what I breathe, right, is bilingual education. But to my colleagues this is
> something new and maybe something crazy ... I think there's so much
> value in this data for transference, for bilingualism and that really proves
> that we're doing the right thing.

Overall, demonstrating student success in both languages gave teachers a valuable resource to demonstrate that their classroom practices aided, rather than hindered, student achievement.

Conclusions and Implications

In terms of student development across the early school years, we found that DLI students are well on their way to becoming bilingual. On average, the performance in English and Spanish was on par with that of native speakers at their grade level; they were performing academically as well as their EMI peers, and perhaps not surprisingly rated themselves as more competent in Spanish than EMI peers. DLI students also understood that people use language for integrative reasons, centred on feelings of wanting to belong to a language group. Regardless of programme, these elementary-age students were already beginning to associate language use with racial and ethnic backgrounds.

For students learning English as an additional language, DLI programmes offer the opportunity to learn language from English proficient peers and forestall the social isolation often experienced in transitional bilingual education or sheltered English instructional programmes (Block, 2011). For English proficient students, the experience can foster enrichment in an additional language and broader cultural understanding. While the bilingual education field has repeatedly called for the bilingual assessment of students (e.g. Escamilla *et al.*, 2017), research has been lacking in how teachers can use such data. This study reveals how teachers make practical use of bilingual information generated by bilingual assessment. The findings have implications for dual-language educators and researchers.

For educators

Our findings highlight the importance of discussing and cultivating bilingual identity development early on with DLI students, as we know this is a critical developmental period for children's identity development (Hazelbaker *et al.*, 2017). Although children felt confident in their own English and Spanish language skills, they also associated linguistic proficiency in majority and minority languages with racial/ethnic heritage. That children are reflecting on their own and others' linguistic capabilities as a marker of racial/ethnic heritage highlights the importance of the bilingual identity development that teachers reported engaging in to help children see themselves and others as potentially proficient in many languages.

The larger project findings also showcase the impact of researchers and educators working in collaboration and partnership. In the PLCs and interviews, teachers shared the importance of reflecting on bilingual assessment data in terms of their classroom practice and programme goals. Research suggests that PLCs can improve teacher instruction and student achievement (Vescio *et al.*, 2008) and our findings suggest that use of bilingual assessment data enrich those discussions for DLI educators. The teachers found the use of a PLC model of teacher professional development to be useful and important to their practice with the caveat that the process requires time and planning. For instance, Marisol reflected on PLCs saying, 'The PLC model at the [school] was the most effective professional development for our school because of the amount of experience and expertise of the community of educators and the shared philosophies. However, proper time and leadership needs to be allocated to do this work!' The school principal reiterated this, saying, 'The dual language programme benefits tremendously from having a Professional Learning Community where teachers share their best practices and where they discuss challenges and ways of addressing them for the benefit of all dual language students.' Given the challenges that teachers in this chapter faced finding materials and assessments that fit the DLI environment, the principal's statement highlights the particular benefit that PLCs may provide in bilingual settings.

For researchers

Given the increasing linguistic and ethnic diversity of US schools, it is important that we increase understanding of educational practices that can serve the greatest number of students and our society at large. In this study, we document student development over time within one DLI context. While the sample is not large and limited in its generalizability to other DLI programmes, the findings demonstrate the utility of collecting comprehensive and longitudinal bilingual assessment data for improving understanding of the efficacy of DLI programmes and students' bilingual developmental trajectories (e.g. Escamilla *et al.*, 2017). The collaboration with DLI educators also benefited the research from inception to interpretation. We hope that researchers will use and expand PLCs and other collaborative models to produce research that can best serve the needs of teachers and students.

Significance

The significance of findings from this longitudinal study are worth noting. While seemingly requisite, yet rarely implemented, bilingual assessment appears key to understanding the impact of DLI programmes both for educators and researchers. Bilingual assessment was key to demonstrating that students in a DLI programme were performing, on average, on a par with peers in EMI. Students' dual-language experiences also suggested unique and positive social outcomes for these students. Bilingual assessment helps guide teacher practice and can reassure educators, parents and other key stakeholders of the linguistic, academic and personal benefits of learning in two languages.

Acknowledgements

First and foremost, we thank the students, teachers, and administrators who are participants in the school-research partnership. We owe a debt of gratitude to Norma Silva and Gabby Cárdenas for their continued feedback and support. We also thank the many graduate and undergraduate student researchers who helped with data collection, in particular, Cathy Coddington, Rachel Zwass, Crystal Bryne, Victoria Rodriguez-Operana, Karla Rivera-Torres and Taylor Hazelbaker for their project management and data analysis assistance. Finally, for research support, Alison Bailey and Rashmita Mistry acknowledge the Council on Research of the UCLA Academic Senate, the Graduate School of Education and

Information Studies (GSE&IS) Dean's Diversity Student Support Initiative and the CONNECT Research Office of GSE&IS. Alison Bailey thanks the Haynes Foundation for support from a Faculty Fellowship Year.

References

Adesope, O.O., Lavin, T., Thompson, T. and Ungerleider, C. (2010) A systematic review and meta-analysis of the cognitive correlates of bilingualism. *Review of Educational Research* 80 (2), 207–245.

Bailey, A.L. and Osipova, A.V. (2016) *Children's Multilingual Development and Education: Fostering Linguistic Resources in Home and School Contexts.* Cambridge: Cambridge University Press.

Bailey, A.L. and Zwass, R.H. (2015) Language attitudes story prompts. In D. Castro (ed.) *Report of Researcher-Developed Measures of Dual Language Learners* (pp. 1–6). Texas: University of North Texas.

Bailey, A.L., Moughamian, A.C. and Dingle, M. (2008) The contribution of Spanish language narration to the assessment of early academic performance of Latino students. In A.K. McCabe, A.L. Bailey and G. Melzi (eds) *Spanish-Language Narration and Literacy: Culture, Cognition, and Emotion* (pp. 296–331). New York: Cambridge University Press.

Bailey, A.L. Zwass, R. Rivera-Torres, K. and Mistry, R. (2015) Young children's development of 'Sociolinguistic Cognition' about different languages and their speakers. Poster presented at the Biennial Conference of the Society for Research in Child Development, April, Philadelphia, PA.

Bear, D.R., Invernizzi, M., Johnston, F. and Templeton, S. (2013) *Palabras a su Paso: El Estudio de Palabras en Accion.* Essex: Pearson Education, Inc.

Bialystok, E. and Barac, R. (2012) Emerging bilingualism: Dissociating advantages for metalinguistic awareness and executive control. *Cognition* 122 (1), 67–73.

Blankenship, S.S. and Ruona, W.E. (2007) Professional learning communities and communities of practice: A comparison of models, literature review. Paper presented at the Academy of Human Resource Development International Research Conference in The Americas, March, Indianapolis, IN.

Block, N. (2011) The impact of two-way dual-immersion programs on initially English-dominant Latino students' attitudes. *Bilingual Research Journal* 34 (2), 125–141.

Brown, C.S. (2011) American elementary school children's attitudes about immigrants, immigration, and being an American. *Journal of Applied Developmental Psychology* 32 (3), 109–117.

Bryne, C., Coddington, C., Mistry, R. and Bailey, A.L. (2013) Preschool children's awareness of race/ethnicity: Links to perceived competence and intergroup attitudes in dual-language school. Poster presented at the Biennial Conference of the Society for Research in Child Development, April, Seattle, WA.

Cobb, B., Vega, D. and Kronauge, C. (2009) Effects of an elementary dual language immersion school program on junior high school achievement. In D.L. Hough (ed.) *Middle Grades Research: Exemplary Studies Linking Theory to Practice* (pp. 1–20). Charlotte, NC: Information Age Publishing.

DuFour, R. (2004) What is a 'professional learning community'? *Educational leadership* 61 (8), 6–11.

Eccles, J.S. (1999) The development of children ages 6 to 14. *The Future of Children* 9 (2), 30–44. doi:10.2307/1602703

Escamilla, K., Butvilofsky, S. and Hopewell, S. (2017) What gets lost when English-only writing assessment is used to assess writing proficiency in Spanish-English emerging bilingual learners? *International Multilingual Research Journal*, 1–16. doi:10.1080/19313152.2016.1273740

Genesee, F. (2008) Early dual language learning. *Zero to Three* 29 (1), 17–23.

Harter, S. and Pike, R. (1984) The pictorial scale of perceived competence and social acceptance for young children. *Child Development* 55 (6), 1969–1982.

Hazelbaker, T., Mistry, R.S. and Bailey, A. (2017) Let's talk about race: Children's racial and ethnic identification across the early elementary school years. Poster presented at the Biennial Meeting of the Society for Research in Child Development, April, Austin, Texas.

Hopewell, S. and Escamilla, K. (2014) Biliteracy development in immersion contexts. *Immersion and Context-Based Language Education* 2 (2), 181–195.

Imbens-Bailey, A.L. (1996) Ancestral language acquisition: Implications for aspects of ethnic identity among Armenian-American children and adolescents. *Journal of Language and Social Psychology* 15, 422–443.

Li, J., Steele, J., Slater, R., Bacon, M. and Miller, T. (2016) Teaching practices and language use in two-way dual language immersion programs in a large public school district. *International Multilingual Research Journal* 10 (1), 31–43.

Lindholm-Leary, K. and Genesee, F. (2014) Student outcomes in one-way, two-way, and indigenous language immersion education. *Journal of Immersion and Content-Based Language Education* 2 (2), 165–180.

McNamara, K. (2016) *Dual Language Learners in Head Start: The Promises and Pitfalls of New Reforms.* Migration Policy Institute. See https://www.migrationpolicy.org/article/dual-language-learners-head-start-promises-and-pitfalls-new-reforms (accessed 26 October 2018).

Mehisto, P. and Genesee, F. (2015) *Building Bilingual Education Systems: Forces, Mechanisms, and Counterweights.* Cambridge: Cambridge University Press.

Quintana, S.M. (2008) Racial perspective taking ability: Developmental, theoretical, and empirical trends. In S. Quintana and C. McKown (eds) *Handbook of Race, Racism, and the Developing Child* (pp. 16–36). Hoboken, NJ: Wiley.

Reading and Writing Project. (n.d.) See http://readingandwritingproject.org (accessed 14 July 2017).

Ruble, D.N., Alvarez, J., Bachman, M., Cameron, J., Fuligni, A., Garcia Coll, C. and Rhee, E. (2004) The development of a sense of 'we': The emergence and implications of children's collective identity. In M. Bennett and F. Sani (eds) *The Development of the Social Self* (pp. 29–76). East Sussex: Psychology Press.

Valeski, T.N. and Stipek, D.J. (2001) Young children's feelings about school. *Child Development* 72 (4), 1198–1213.

Vescio, V., Ross, D. and Adams, A. (2008) A review of research on the impact of professional learning communities on teaching practice and student learning. *Teaching and Teacher Education* 24 (1), 80–91.

Woodcock, R.W., Muñoz-Sandoval, A.F., McGrew, K.S. and Mather, N. (2007) *Batería III Woodcock-Muñoz Normative Update.* Boston, MA: Houghton Mifflin Harcourt.

Woodcock, R.W., Shrank, F.A., McGrew, K.S. and Mather, N. (2008) *The Woodcock-Johnson III Tests of Achievement Normative Update.* Boston, MA: Houghton Mifflin Harcourt.

Conclusion

14 Early Language Learning Teacher Education: Present and Future

Sue Garton

Introduction

Once considered a neglected area of research, teaching English to young learners is now enjoying far more attention, with a number of recent book length publications (e.g. Bland, 2015; Copland & Garton, 2018a; López-Gopar, 2016; Rich, 2014; Spolsky & Moon, 2012), an *ELT Journal* special issue in 2014 (Copland & Garton, 2014) and a state-of-the art paper (Butler, 2015). However, research on primary languages other than English, and especially on teacher education for primary language teachers is still noticeably a poor relation compared to other areas of the field. This might seem surprising, given that Garton *et al.* (2011: 14) found that 'training in new language teaching methodologies' was the biggest single factor that primary English teachers globally felt would improve their teaching situation, while Emery (2012) found that 79% of the teachers in her survey felt they needed more support. These results indicate that, for teachers at least, whether they are pre- or in-service, their professional development remains problematic. Moreover, studies such as Kabilan and Veratharaju (2013), Le and Do (2012) and Zein (2015, 2017a) have found that YL English language teacher education is often inadequate in preparing teachers for the realities of the primary classroom. Therefore, in spite of the fact that languages were introduced into the primary curriculum over 25 years ago in some cases (Enever, 2014; Garton, 2014), some long-standing issues around primary language teacher education persist. In this final chapter, I will briefly revisit some of these issues before considering in more detail how the chapters in this volume address the challenges and/or take us beyond them and finally considering where we go from here.

Before moving to the discussion, it is necessary to note some issues around terminology. For the purposes of this chapter, I use *trainees* to refer all the teachers taking part in the research reported in the volume, whether they are in-service or pre-service teachers. I also use *teacher training, teacher education* and *teacher development* synonymously, although I am well aware of the debates around their use and the different meanings that have been given to the terms (see, e.g. Barkhuizen & Borg, 2010; Richards, 2009). I also use the term *Modern Languages (ML)* to refer to languages other than English.

Long-Standing Issues

It is now a given that policies have been implemented to introduce languages into primary schools around the world at an ever-earlier age, with an overwhelming majority focusing on English (see, e.g. the chapters in Enever *et al.*, 2009; Rixon, 2013). Such policies have often been introduced without careful thought given to who will actually teach the language with a consequent shortage of primary school teachers with an English specialism. Two solutions have generally been proposed: homeroom teachers are often required to take English lessons even with limited English proficiency, or specialised English teachers, often taken from higher levels such as secondary school are employed (see, e.g. Butler, Chapter 2; Hu, 2007; Zein, 2015). The result is that many teachers are not trained to teach English at primary level, and in many cases, teacher education programmes do not address these issues. Enever (2014), for example, highlights the current weaknesses in teacher education in Europe in this regard, but also points out that such weaknesses are likely to be more widespread (see Kabilan & Veratharaju, 2013 for the case of Malaysia and Zein, 2015, 2017a for Indonesia). As Butler (Chapter 2) notes, each approach brings its own advantages and challenges.

English in the primary curriculum often entails other policy initiatives such as government-mandated changes to teaching methodologies, usually with a focus on communicative approaches such as communicative language teaching (CLT) or task-based learning and teaching (TBLT). Issues arising from such innovations include, for example, the incompatibility of such meaning-based approaches, developed in Western classrooms for adults, with local educational traditions. While some training has usually been given in the new approaches, this may be very introductory, leaving teachers feeling confused as to how to implement them in their classrooms (Butler, 2005; Littlewood, 2007). Training may also be very theoretical with little input on how to put it into practice (see Zein, 2015 for the case of pre-service education in Indonesia and Zein, 2017a for in-service education). Moreover, trainers themselves may not have a deep understanding of the approach and especially how it can be used in a YL context (Butler, Chapter 2; Le & Do, 2012; Zein, 2016a).

The experiences of Loan, the teacher described by Canh (Chapter 3), resonate strongly with the issues outlined so far. Canh shows how Loan's initial teacher training left her ill-prepared for the specific needs of young learners and vividly presents her frustration at her attempts to implement the techniques she had been taught. Canh also draws out the professional isolation that Loan suffered, noting her lack of opportunities for furthering her professional development. Inequalities of access to teacher development have been noted (Butler, Chapter 2) with bureaucracy often hindering the process (Zein, 2016c). Opportunities for teachers to further their expertise in teaching English to young learners beyond initial teacher education or short (and often theoretical) in-service courses are rare (Emery, 2012; Zein, 2015, 2017a). In many ways, Canh (Chapter 3) sets out the agenda for YL language teacher education that is addressed by other chapters in the book.

There are some signs of improvement, however. Rich (2018) notes that the provision of teacher education for primary English teachers follows the trajectory identified by Kaplan and Baldauf (1997) for educational reforms more generally:

> to initially prioritise in-service support and to move to establish pre-service support at a later date. Thus in most countries the development of add-on short training programmes to help in-service teachers acquire basic competence in TEYL instruction is seen as a priority area. However, an observable trend in countries where TEYL has now been established for some time, such as in much of western Europe, Turkey and parts of East Asia, is the growth of pre-service TEd to ensure that teachers are better prepared and trained for work with young learners from the outset. (Rich, 2018: 47–48)

It is against the backdrop of long-standing challenges and a new optimism that the chapters in this volume are set. The chapters here represent a step forward in our understanding of teacher education for primary language teachers in a number of ways. First of all, they generally reflect Rich's (2018) more optimistic view of the field, with many presenting the reader with possibilities and affordances, rather than obstacles. Secondly, they bring fresh perspectives to some of the long-standing issues, such as shifting from teacher-centred to learner-centred pedagogies in contextually appropriate ways. Thirdly, they address new areas of the field, which teachers working on the ground have long been aware of, but which have generally been neglected in research. These include the links between teacher education and L1 literacy as well as the role of bilingualism in the YL classroom. Finally, there has traditionally been little overlap between teaching English to speakers of other languages (TESOL) and modern foreign languages, but a number of chapters in this volume focus on languages other than English (see Chapters 6, 9, 10, 12 and 13). Taken together, all the chapters show that research in one area can clearly inform the other. I discuss each of these key themes from the chapters below.

Shifting Pedagogies

As mentioned above, 'transmissive and prescriptive' teaching methods (Butler, Chapter 2) still seem to be very common in YL language teacher education (see also Boivin, Chapter 9), leaving teachers ill-equipped for the realities of the 21st century learner-centred and communicative primary classroom. Even where more learner-centred pedagogies are introduced, Enever (2014) reports that teachers still faced difficulties in changing their traditional roles during some phases of their lessons.

A number of authors in this volume have researched a variety of ways in which the gap between theory and practice can be successfully overcome. One way has been to shift from purely theoretical courses by introducing a more applied approach, in particular in the form of actual teaching practice. Zhang (Chapter 5), Chou (Chapter 7) and Boivin (Chapter 9) all show how the practicum, during which trainee teachers were given the opportunity to teach in actual classrooms, enabled a much deeper understanding of learner-centred pedagogies. Even a short practicum experience, such as that reported by Chou (Chapter 7) had a notable effect on the pedagogical knowledge development of trainee teachers. In Chou's case, the practicum was also supported by microteaching and by classroom observations, while Carreira and Shigyo (Chapter 11) also used microteaching, showing that even where lengthy practicums are not feasible, it is possible to use a combination of classroom and teaching experiences and still bring about a shift in pedagogical approaches. Moreover, Boivin (Chapter 9) also evidences the positive impact on the pedagogy of the experienced teachers who were supporting the trainees in her study, showing that such an approach to language teacher education can have an effect beyond the immediate beneficiaries.

However, all the authors show the importance of careful structuring and planning of the teaching practice, and therefore the learning opportunities, in such a way that the experience promotes and develops reflective practitioners who are able to develop their own practice. Chou (Chapter 7) emphasises the important role of the supervisor in developing trainees' pedagogical knowledge while Zhang (Chapter 5) does this through a learning study approach. Zein (Chapter 4) demonstrates how reflective practices based on teachers' own classroom language can lead to transformative scaffolding that fosters learning. Boivin (Chapter 9) uses a three-stage framework based on collaboration, construction and reflection (CCR). All of these chapters present frameworks for embedding new and contextually appropriate pedagogies in the practices of trainee language teachers that have clear applications beyond the immediate context of the studies.

Classroom-based experiences are not the only ways in which changes in pedagogy can be achieved. Carreira and Shigyo (Chapter 11) introduced a completely new approach to their generalist teachers who had to teach foreign language activities in Japan. Their successful introduction of a cross-curricular approach using project-based learning for pre-service teachers is a timely example, as some governments are starting to move away from CLT and on to content and language integrated learning

(CLIL) as an approach to primary language teaching (see, e.g. Hüttner *et al.*, 2013). As the introduction of CLIL repeats similar issues to the introduction of CLT, with inadequate teacher training, this chapter has relevance well beyond the immediate Japanese context and is a reminder of the capacity of local research findings to resonate globally (Garton *et al.*, 2011).

Practitioner research is also shown to be successful in bringing about change in teaching practices. Chou (Chapter 7) with her learning studies approach and Kirkgöz (Chapter 8) through collaborative action research were both able to develop the pedagogic practices of their participants. However, both show the need for careful planning, structuring and above all support for teachers involved in such projects and Chou shows how, for pre-service teachers at least, the load may be too much.

The final way in which changes in teaching practices can be brought through data-based learning (Borg, 1998). Borg (1998: 281) advocated the analysis of classroom data because,

> By allowing teachers to function as data analysts in the study of other teachers' – and ultimately of their own – behaviours and beliefs, such activities can promote a more holistic form of self-reflection than those based solely on the behavioural analysis of teaching.

Although Borg was primarily talking about using classroom extracts from third party sources, Zein (Chapter 4) shows how, by analysing video extracts from their own and their colleagues' classrooms, the teachers in his study were able to develop greater awareness of their own and their peers' language use. They were able to identify effective language use, and one successful example drawn from the study is the ability of a teacher to imagine herself as a young learner, leading to reflections that potentially change the way teachers interact with their learners. The use of actual classroom data in teacher education has potential applications beyond language use and would seem to be an underused and under-researched tool.

So far, we have focused on how the research reported in this volume has addressed the significant and long-standing issue of bringing about changes in YL language pedagogy. However, there are other areas that have so far been relatively neglected in the YL language teaching research literature.

Joining the Dots

Copland and Garton (2018b) note that foreign language teaching and bilingualism are often treated as separate disciplines, and to this we may also add literacy as a third area. However, there is clearly much that these disciplines can learn from each other and from cooperation, as some of the chapters in this volume show.

Macrory's (Chapter 6) focus on foreign language literacy in language teacher education, and specifically the use of phonics, borrows much from the area of L1 literacy studies. Like the chapters in the previous section, she also focuses on opportunities to put training into practice. However, she found a lack of opportunities to either observe or practice phonics because of a lack of languages in the curriculum. Macrory's study focuses on orthography and the use of phonics, but her work also points to the potential for more research into the usefulness of a range L1 literacy practices to improve YL's L2 (see, e.g. Majthoob, 2014 on how English as a foreign language (EFL) materials were adapted to meet the literacy needs of young Bahraini learners).

While many children in the world are bilingual or multilingual in their everyday lives (Blackledge & Creese, 2010), bilingualism has often been ignored in the foreign language teaching literature and in language teacher education. It is therefore refreshing to see chapters that address this. Two chapters report on studies that give us a better understanding of how language teacher education can support teachers working in bilingual classrooms. Jenkins, Duursma and Neilsen-Hewett (Chapter 12), through their examination of the attitudes of bilingual and monolingual teacher educators show the need to support both in-service and pre-service teachers in developing pedagogies that are appropriate for bilingual children and encourage, rather than discourage, bilingual language education. Griffin, Bailey and Mistry (Chapter 13) compare assessment practices in dual language immersion (DLI) and English medium instruction classrooms. Their study shows how data from DLI assessment can be used to inform teacher decision-making and suggest classroom practices that can support young bilingual learners, with obvious implications for teacher education. Carbonara (Chapter 10) on the other hand, focuses on bilingual kindergarten education for Turkish children learning Italian and develops a CLIL-type bilingual model to prepare teachers to teach in bilingual contexts, while Boivin's (Chapter 9) study is situated in a mainstream school but with special lessons based on multiliteracy principles using Cummins's (2009) transformative multiliteracies pedagogy to support teachers in developing trilingual lessons in Russian, Kazakh and English. All of these chapters represent steps not only in moving the field towards the integration of bilingualism and modern languages, but away from the deficit model of bilingualism that has persisted in modern language teaching.

While English dominates the language teaching landscape, the chapters above make it clear that it is by no means the only language taught (see, e.g. Eurydice, 2017 for the situation in Europe). Research in TESOL and research in modern languages have traditionally seen little overlap and tend to be treated as separate fields, whereas this volume brings together research from across languages. The chapters already cited in this section are indicative of the range of languages addressed in the volume, to which we can add Macrory's (Chapter 6) focus on modern languages (French, German and Spanish) in the UK, with her study on the use of phonics and the opportunities afforded (or not) by teaching practice to implement teacher learning, which has implications for all language teaching.

A number of chapters also offer insights into the ways in which bilingual education may be organised. In Griffin *et al.*'s (Chapter 13) US-based study, early grades focus on Spanish with 90% of the instructional focus on this language in the early grades (pre-kindergarten–kindergarten) before moving to 50:50 by fifth grade. Carbonara's (Chapter 10) Turkish–Italian bilingual school offers one third of the lessons in Italian in the primary school level, switching to a CLIL model at middle school level. However, the 8 hours per week on the timetable is in stark contrast to the 2–3 hours that are usually the maximum available (Butler, Chapter 2; Garton *et al.*, 2011).

Taken together, these chapters demonstrate the common ground that research into languages has and clearly show that the implications for primary language teacher education are similar whatever the language focus. More research cooperation across languages in the future can only add to our knowledge base and strengthen the field.

Collaboration

One very strong message that emerges from virtually all the chapters in this volume is the importance of collaboration in YL language teacher education research. The projects reported here have been so successful because the collaboration amongst those taking part was successful. This may be through peer collaboration (e.g. Chou, Chapter 7; Kirkgöz, Chapter 8), collaboration between trainees and teacher educators (e.g. Canh, Chapter 3; Macrory, Chapter 6; Carreira & Shigyo, Chapter 11) or between trainees, teacher educators and experienced teachers (e.g. Zhang, Chapter 5; Boivin, Chapter 9). A combination of these is one that implements collaboration between trainees themselves, and then between trainees and teacher educators (Zein, Chapter 4).

The chapters also give examples of a wide range of ways in which collaboration can take place. For example, in Zein (Chapter 4) trainees and teacher educators discuss video clips of the classroom language, while in Zhang (Chapter 5) we see teachers discussing their learning study together. In Kirkgöz (Chapter 8), teachers and teacher educators work together in the design and implementation of collaborative action research projects, while the trainees in Boivin (Chapter 9) collaborated with the classroom teachers in lesson design and in reflecting on the outcomes of the project.

What these chapters show are the range of participants who can take part in language teacher education research, the variety of roles they can take and how they can work effectively together. They also show the rich outcomes that constructivist approaches to teacher education can achieve across a variety of contexts.

Looking Forward

While the current state of the field gives some room for optimism, there is still much work to be done. So where do we go from here? The chapters in this volume have presented a number of solutions to key challenges in primary language teacher education, but, like all good research, they have also raised a number of new questions.

First of all, a major challenge lies in the lack of space on general primary teacher education programmes for languages, which is the norm in many countries such as Bangladesh (Hamid, 2010), China (Hu, 2007), Indonesia (Zein, 2017b) and Vietnam (Nguyen, 2011) and other contexts in East Asia (Zhou & Ng, 2016). Butler (Chapter 2) and Macrory (Chapter 6) both raise this issue in this volume. While changing government curricula is likely to be beyond the remit of most teacher education research, investigating the most effective, creative and successful ways of exploiting limited spaces would seem to be important for the future.

Second, the chapters in this volume represent an important step in integrating research from related areas such as literacy and bilingualism (see, e.g. Chapters 9, 12 and 13). However, much work still remains in these areas. This includes, for example, the ways in which teacher education responds to the implications of Jenkins *et al.*'s work (Chapter 12) and can support teachers in promoting bilingualism in language teaching (Chapter 9). Support for the bilingual classroom is also connected to critical approaches to primary language teaching (see, e.g. López-Gopar, 2016) and these two areas should be high on the teacher education research agenda.

Third, perhaps the biggest challenge that teacher education of other languages and English in particular face is equality of access. Zein (2016b) highlights that accesses to government-based training programmes are very limited, primarily with a major focus in urban areas. Nonetheless, many training programmes are constrained by debilitating bureaucracy (Zein, 2016c). The situation is underlined dramatically by Loan (Canh, Chapter 3) whose voice is representative of perhaps the majority of language teachers around the world today. The research reported in the chapters in this volume gives cause for optimism, but it can touch only a very small number of teachers, often living in relatively privileged situations (i.e. in towns and cities where access to teacher education may be relatively easy). Research into how and in what forms teacher education can reach a much wider audience of language teachers so that learners are also given more equal opportunities to learn, remains on the research agenda for the future (Zein, 2016c).

Fourth, we need more longitudinal studies and we need more large-scale quantitative studies. Griffin *et al.* (Chapter 13) is an excellent example of a longitudinal study, but these are generally lacking in the field. In particular, studies on the long-term effects of teacher education on teaching practices would be especially welcome. Bailey *et al.* (1996) found that when faced with the difficulties of the classrooms, teachers would often revert to traditional ways of teaching even during their teaching practice. Farrell (2015) notes that teachers often find the reality of life after teacher education difficult to cope with and calls for more post-training support. More research is needed to see whether the theories and pedagogies that are taught during teacher education programmes have a lasting effect on classroom practices; however, none of these studies is large-scale. If we are to obtain a more comprehensive and global understanding of early language teacher education, then we need to add to the undoubtedly valuable but generally relatively small-scale qualitative studies with much larger-scale quantitative studies.

Finally, while many voices have been heard in this volume, one voice that is notably absent is that of the young language learner. Young learners have been involved as research informants in other areas. Butler (2007), for example, looked at the attitudes of young learners towards their teachers' accents. Researchers in the ELLiE project (Enever, 2011) found that young learners were able to articulate relatively sophisticated reasoning around their language, while Kuchah (2013) found that primary school children had clear ideas about what constituted good teachers and good teaching.

Some work has also been done on involving young learners as researchers (e.g. Pinter & Zandian, 2014; Pinter *et al.*, 2013), and it would seem to be logical that in the future, learners should also have an active role in research determining the direction of primary language teacher education. Given that multiparticipatory research on YL teacher education is on the rise (e.g. Kabilan & Veratharaju, 2013; Zein, 2015, 2016a, 2016b), future research could include young learners, adding to the already established participation of teachers and teacher educators.

Conclusion

It is fair to say that research into primary language teaching was relatively slow in catching up with the reality of the spread of languages to young learners, although the speed and the extent of the phenomenon was difficult to predict. However, this is now a flourishing field with an ever-growing body of high quality research from around the world. The chapters in this volume have a major contribution to make to the field in that they show successful solutions to a number of long-standing challenges. At the same time, while they are firmly rooted in their local context, they also show once again the power of the local to resonate globally in a field such as ours.

References

Bailey, K.C., Bergthold, B., Braunstein, B., Jagodzinski, N., Fleischman, M.P., Holbrook, Tuman, J., Waissbluth, X. and Zambo, L.J. (1996) The language learner's autobiography: Examining the 'apprenticeship of observation'. In D. Freeman and J.C. Richards (eds) *Teacher Learning in Language Teaching* (pp. 11–29). Cambridge: Cambridge University Press.

Bland, J. (ed.) (2015) *Teaching English to Young Learners: Critical Issues in Language Teaching with 3–12 Year Olds*. London: Bloomsbury.

Blackledge, A. and Creese, A. (2010) *Multilingualism: A Critical Perspective*. London: Continuum.

Borg, S. (1998) Data-based teacher development. *ELT Journal* 52 (4), 273–281.

Barkhuizen, G. and Borg, S. (2010). Editorial: Researching language teacher education. *Language Teaching Research* 14 (3), 237–240.

Butler, Y.G. (2005) Comparative perspectives towards communicative activities among elementary school teachers in South Korea, Japan and Taiwan. *Language Teaching Research* 9 (4), 423 – 446.

Butler, Y.G. (2007) How are nonnative-English-speaking teachers perceived by young learners? *TESOL Quarterly* 41 (4), 731–755.

Butler, Y.G. (2015) English language education among young learners in East Asia: A review of current research (2004–2014). *Language Teaching* 48, 303–342. doi:10.1017/S0261444815000105

Copland, F. and Garton, S. (2014) Key themes and future directions in teaching English to young learners: Introduction to the special issue. *ELT Journal* 68 (3), 223–230.

Copland, F. and Garton, S. (eds) (2018a) *TESOL Voices: Insider Accounts of Classroom Life – Young Learner Education*. Alexandria, VA: TESOL Press.

Copland, F. and Garton, S. (2018b). Moving forward with young learner research in English language teaching. In F. Copland and S. Garton (eds) *TESOL Voices: Insider Accounts of Classroom Life – Young Learner Education* (pp. 141–145) Alexandria, VA: TESOL Press.

Cummins, J. (2009) Transformative multiliteracies pedagogy: School-based strategies for closing the achievement gap. *Multiple Voices for Ethnically Diverse Exceptional Learners* 11 (2), 38–56.

Education, Audiovisual and Culture Executive Agency (2017) *Eurydice Brief: Key Data on Teaching Languages at School in Europe*. https://publications.europa.eu/en/publication-detail/-/publication/ff10cc21-aef9-11e7-837e-01aa75ed71a1/language-en/format-PDF (accessed 24 October 2018).

Emery, H. (2012) *A Global Study of Primary English Teachers' Qualifications, Training and Career Development*. ELT Research Papers 12-08. London: British Council.

Enever, J. (ed.) (2011) *ELLiE. Early Language Learning in Europe*. London: British Council.

Enever, J. (2014) Primary English teacher education in Europe. *ELT Journal* 68 (3), 231–242.

Enever, J., Moon, J. and Raman, U. (eds) (2009) *Young Learner English Language Policy and Implementation: International Perspectives*. Reading: Garnet.

Farrell, T.S.C. (2015) Second language teacher education: A reality check. In T.S.C. Farrell (ed.) *International Perspectives on Language Teacher Education* (pp. 1–15). Basingstoke: Palgrave Macmillan.

Garton, S. (2014) Unresolved issues and new challenges in teaching English to young learners: The case of South Korea. *Current Issues in Language Planning* 15 (2), 201–219. doi:10.1080/14664208.2014.858657

Garton, S., Copland, F. and Burns, A. (2011) *Investigating Global Practices in Teaching English to Young Learners*. ELT Research Papers 11-01. London: The British Council.

Hamid, M.O. (2010) Globalisation, English for everyone and English teacher capacity: Language policy discourses and realities in Bangladesh. *Current Issues in Language Planning* 11 (4), 289–310. doi:10.1080/14664208.2011.532621

Hu, Y. (2007) China's foreign language policy on primary English education: What's behind it? *Language Policy* 6, 359–376.

Hüttner, J., Dalton-Puffer, C. and Smit, U. (2013) The power of beliefs: Lay theories and their influence on the implementation of CLIL programmes. *International Journal of Bilingual Education and Bilingualism* 16 (3), 267–284.

Kabilan, M.K. and Veratharaju, K. (2013) Professional development needs of primary school English language teachers in Malaysia. *Professional Development in Education* 39 (3), 330–351.

Kaplan, R.B. and Baldauf, R.B. (1997) *Language Planning: From Practice to Theory.* Clevedon: Multilingual Matters.

Kuchah, H. (2013) Context-appropriate ELT pedagogy: An investigation in Cameroonian primary schools. Unpublished PhD thesis, University of Warwick.

Le, V.C. and Do, C.T.M. (2012) Teacher preparation for primary school English education: A case of Vietnam. In B. Spolsky and Y.-I. Moon (eds) *Primary School English-Language Education in Asia: From Policy to Practice* (pp. 106–121). New York: Routledge.

Littlewood, W. (2007) Communicative and task-based language teaching in East Asian classrooms. *Language Teaching* 40 (3), 243–249.

López-Gopar, M.E. (2016) *Decolonizing Primary English Language Teaching (Linguistic Diversity and Language Rights).* Bristol: Multilingual Matters.

Majthoob, S. (2014) Adapting materials to meet the literacy needs of young Bahraini learners. In S. Garton and K. Graves (eds) *International Perspectives on Materials in ELT* (pp. 53–68). Basingstoke: Palgrave Macmillan.

Nguyen, H.T.M. (2011) Primary English language education policy in Vietnam: Insights from implementation. *Current Issues in Language Planning,* 12 (2), 225–249. doi:10.1080/14664208.2011.597048

Pinter, A. and Zandian, S. (2014) 'I don't ever want to leave this room': Benefits of researching 'with' children. *ELT Journal,* 68 (1), 64–74.

Pinter, A., Kuchah, K. and Smith, R. (2013) Researching with children. *ELT Journal,* 67 (4), 484–487.

Rich, S. (ed.) (2014) *International Perspectives on Teaching English to Young Learners.* Basingstoke: Palgrave Macmillan.

Rich, S. (2018) Early language learning teacher education. In S. Garton and F. Copland (eds) *The Routledge Handbook of Teaching English to Young Learners* (pp. 44–59). London: Routledge.

Richards, J.C. (2009) Second language teacher education today. *RELC Journal* 39 (2), 158–176.

Rixon, S. (2013) *British Council Survey of Policy and Practice in Primary English Language Teaching Worldwide.* London: British Council.

Spolsky, B. and Moon, T. (eds) (2012) *Primary School English-Language Education in Asia: From Policy to Practice.* New York: Routledge.

Zein, M.S. (2015) Preparing elementary English teachers: Innovations at pre-service level. *Australian Journal of Teacher Education* 40 (6), 104 – 120. doi:10.14221/ajte.2015v40n6.6

Zein, M.S. (2016a) Pre-service education for primary school English teachers in Indonesia: Policy implications. *Asia Pacific Journal of Education* 36 (S1), 119–134. doi:10.1080/02188791.2014.961899

Zein, M.S. (2016b) Government-based training agencies and the professional development of Indonesian English for Young Learners teachers: Perspectives from complexity theory. *Journal of Education for Teaching: International Research and Pedagogy,* 42 (2), 205–223. doi:10.1080/02607476.2016.1143145

Zein, M.S. (2016c) Factors affecting the professional development of elementary English teachers. *Professional Development in Education* 42 (3), 423–440. doi:10.1080/19415257.2015.1005243

Zein, M.S. (2017a) Professional development needs of primary EFL teachers: Perspectives of teachers and teacher educators. *Professional Development in Education* 43 (2), 293–313. doi:10.1080/19415257.2016.1156013

Zein, M.S. (2017b) Language-in-education policy on primary EFL: The case of Indonesia. *International Journal of Pedagogies and Learning* 12 (2), 133–146.

Zhou, Y. and Ng, M.L. (2016) English as a foreign language (EFL) and English medium instruction (EMI) for three- to seven-year-old children in East Asian contexts. In V.A. Murphy and M. Evangelou (eds) *Early Childhood Education in English for Speakers of Other Languages* (pp. 137–156). London: British Council.

Index